Rhetoric
and Writing

Composition at UWF

Third Edition

Edited by:

Bre Garrett, Director of Composition

Editorial Team:

Jasara Norton

Hannah Trevino

Kyndall Turner

University of West Florida
First-Year Composition Program

Custom Edition with

PRAXIS

A Brief Rhetoric
Third Edition
by Carol Lea Clark

FOUNTAINHEAD
PRESS

Fountainhead Press's green initiatives include:

Electronic Products and Samples. Products are delivered in non-paper form whenever possible via Xample, an electronic sampling system. Instructor samples are sent via a personalized web page that links to PDF downloads.

FSC-Certified Printers and Recycled Paper. All of our printers are certified by the Forest Service Council, which promotes environmentally and socially responsible management of the world's forests. This program allows consumer groups, individual consumers, and businesses to work together hand in hand to promote responsible use of the world's forests as a renewable and sustainable resource. Most of our products are printed on a minimum of 30 percent post-consumer waste recycled paper.

Design: Ellie Moore
Praxis Developmental Editor: Amy Salisbury-Werhane

Some photos provided by Shutterstock.

Books may be purchased for educational purposes.

For more information, please visit our website at www.fountainheadpress.com.

ISBN: 978-1-68036-604-4

Printed in the United States of America

Contents

Chapter 2: Responding Rhetorically   65

Chapter 3: Analyzing Rhetorically   113

Chapter 4: Inventing Rhetorically   171

Chapter 5: Researching Rhetorically   211

Chapter 6: Writing Rhetorically   265

Chapter 7: Revising Rhetorically   409

Introduction

Composition at UWF: Situating Yourself as a Writer

Bre Garrett

"You will travel new paths. You will write new genres."

Figure I.1 • Map of UWF Campus

Welcome to Composition at the University of West Florida. If you are using this textbook in your class, you are enrolled in ENC 1101 or ENC 1102, the six-hour first-year Composition sequence at UWF. This book provides a foundational knowledge for both courses, introducing a vocabulary for which you can talk about and name parts of the writing process. As the title of the book suggests, rhetoric and writing are connected subjects of study and comprise the content of your first-year Composition courses. In ENC 1101 and ENC 1102, you will learn how rhetoric, or the art of effective communication, can improve your writing by making you a more informed and more reflective writer and reader. ENC 1101 and 1102 will introduce you to writing, reading, and researching for academic and public contexts by teaching you how to identify and analyze rhetorical situations. As a college student and emerging professional, you will write a number of different genres. Having a knowledge of rhetorical analysis will help you enter different writing situations with more authority.

On your semester or year-long journey through Composition at UWF, you will experience a process of re-mapping, locating new places, thoughts, habits, and people that influence your writing. You will learn new ideas and concepts; you will use new words and read new texts. You will travel new paths. You will write new genres. You will face new challenges and milestones. Your identity as a writer will evolve, and your writing and rhetorical knowledge will expand. Of course, you arrive to class with a repertoire of experience that will help you succeed.

By this point in your life, you are an experienced writer and communicator. You might not self-identify as an "author," but you engage in writing all the time. You generate and select topics for discussion, discover and develop ideas, engage in conversation, draw from evidence, and participate in debates. You have a depth of experience from which to pull when you encounter an *exigence*, or a motivation, that prompts you to write or speak. You have *commonplaces* from where you turn when you face writing challenges or constraints: outlines, free-writing, peer conversation, research, and memory. You are a prolific writer and reader if you consider the numerous interactions in your day that involve the deliberate exchange of sending and receiving messages. You communicate via language, images, gestures, music and sound effects. You respond to the world through body language, email, Facebook and Twitter posts, Instagram shares and follows, instant messages, and even silence—or those intentional acts of non-response. You go through the motions of writing, of researching. When you question, when you inquire, you seek to know more, and you may search for answers by conducting online searches, or having conversations with others, or reading credible sources.

Writing for university and public audiences means that you must consider your work as published and peer-reviewed—ready for audience reception. For high school writing projects, you might recall writing with the aim of conveying information, demonstrating your comprehension of a text or your familiarity with a research topic. This type of writing may not have required you to take a stance and argue your point. When given opportunities to make an argument in your high school papers, you likely did so for a persuasive paper in which you expressed your opinion and then incorporated examples from your personal experience as support. Such writing projects are certainly important in your trajectory as a writer and thinker, as they likely help you acquire foundational experience with writing and rhetorical knowledges.

Writing in college makes use of this past experience but goes beyond it by synthesizing research and opinion. In "academic" writing assignments, you will often be prompted to express your opinion by making an argument and supporting your claims with credible research. Argument and analysis are the distinguishing features of college-level writing. Whether you are composing written, visual, or digital texts, you are either explicitly or implicitly pitching an argument to an audience. The strength and potential success of your argument depends on your research plan and evidence: the expert opinions, data, facts, and sometimes anecdotal examples that support your reasons for why you hold a particular stance on a topic.

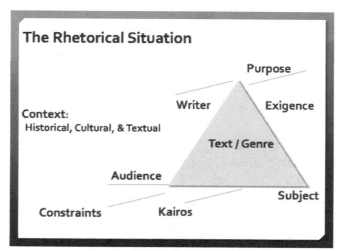

Figure I.2 • Diagram of the Rhetorical Situation

In Composition at UWF, you will participate in a high-quality program of study that emphasizes critical writing, reading, and thinking. You will study writing and reading as rhetorical acts. The diagram above shows the inter-related parts of a rhetorical situation. You might also understand this as a communication exchange. Notice, "text" or "genre" centers the triangle. By examining genre, writers can learn important criteria in terms of conventions, or expected norms and rules, about a particular writing situation. Genre describes the point-to-able parts of a text's frame and structure—the recognizable features that identify a type of writing as *that* type of text. Genre also informs sentence style, tone, and voice (e.g., whether a writer uses formal tone and when passive voice is preferable over present). A particular genre—such as an email—performs certain actions, aims, and purposes. For example, in writing an email to a faculty member to request a letter of recommendation, your tone remains professional, clear, and polite. You include a formal salutation and a subject header. Ideally, you would send the email with ample time for the faculty member to grant your request, showing respect for your audience. In other situations, you may quickly send an email response to a friend in which you abbreviate your language and include exclamation points about plans for the night. Email emerged as an electronic version of a letter. Over the last twenty years, the email has become one of the most common means of professional and interpersonal communication. Depending on where, on what device you compose an email, on a computer or phone, also influences how and what you write: considerations of technology, mode, and delivery fall under textual context.

ENC 1101 and 1102 will prepare you to enter and engage in diverse writing contexts. You will read many different texts, analyzing writing as situated within historical, cultural, and social contexts. Students are challenged to engage deeply with ideas, texts, and media through reading, research, discussion, and writing.

Understanding and Using *Rhetoric and Writing*

Rhetoric and Writing is a required textbook used in both ENC 1101 and 1102. You use the book for two semesters, and we identify this two-semester use as a benefit not only because it reduces financial cost, but more so because the text builds a foundational knowledge across the two different yet inter-related courses. In ENC 1101, the text introduces writing as a rhetorical situation and presents argument structures that provide a basis for writing and communicating in academic contexts. Students read about and engage in writing processes, learning about recursive stages such as invention, or how to create and discover new ideas for project topics and how to enter conversations by conducting primary and secondary research. In ENC 1102, rhetorical knowledge advances to include a study of genre and audience; students write a rhetorical analysis essay that examines a rhetorical situation and the interaction among writer, audience, and subject or message. In ENC 1102, students may focus more on historical and cultural context and kairos, or the opportune moment for communication, whereas 1101 may emphasize first-person exigence, writer's purpose, and audience as concepts that help students understand and develop arguments.

This edition of the book consists of seven chapters that range from rhetorical definitions, theories, and application to different stages of the writing process. The members of the First-Year Composition Program offer this book as a collection of voices, theories, and practices. Throughout the book, readers will find recurring references to *Case Studies*. These sections are particular parts of the book written by UWF Composition faculty. Proudly, *Rhetoric and Writing* also publishes several UWF student essays written in ENC 1101 and ENC 1102. Chapter Three includes two ENC 1102 award winning rhetorical analysis essays: "The Bridge Builder" by Mary Oglesby and "The Reality of Modern Day Slavery" by Caitlyn Waters. Chapter 6 "Writing Rhetorically" showcases several argumentative, research essay award winners from ENC 1101, including "To Test or Not to Test—That Is the Question" by Catherine Lambert, "Should the UK Accept More Refugees?" by Tabitha Read-Cayton, "Buying Bisexuality" by Mollie Nichole Lynch, "The Abusive Effects Left on a Child" by Elexus Toque, "Elite Adjustments: A Nation's Inadvertent Pitfall" by Taylor Anliker. Chapter 6 also includes a rhetorical analysis essay, "Using Aristotle's Appeals with Attitude" written by James Austin Benfell Williams and a memoir essay, "Live Life for You" written by Malik Ware.

Image credit: Photographer Christopher Mills, "Tracks to Florida." Wheatpasting Installation by Rachael Pongetti and Art Beyond Walls, Words by Lewis Warsh from his poem "When You Wore A Tulip" first published in his book *Alien Abduction* (Ugly Duckling Presse, 2015).

Defining Rhetoric

Why Rhetoric Is Important in My Writing

Meaghan Elliott
Ph.D. student in
Composition & Rhetoric
University of New Hampshire

Here is a partial list of the things I needed to write today:

- An email to someone in my field asking her questions for a seminar paper I'm writing
- A lesson plan I intend to use for my students in this week's class
- An email to a family member
- Text messages to a friend in the hospital
- A reading response for a doctoral course I'm taking
- A grocery list for my boyfriend
- This short essay about rhetoric

All of these are rhetoric. Rhetoric is inescapable because we use it every time we use words to address an audience. Rhetoric gives us tools for deciding how to be successful in any given situation, and it acknowledges that words and languages were designed for people to communicate with each other. People think, we feel, we judge others. In each of these actions, we have *logos*, *pathos*, and *ethos*. Rhetoric is what makes us human.

In the list I provided, I have seven different scenarios with seven different audiences. In each one, I judge (sometimes consciously, sometimes unconsciously) how effectively to present myself and my message. This means no two pieces of writing will look or sound the same. We make rhetorical judgments based on to whom we are speaking and what we know about our audience, and these judgments affect the way we write each document.

Rhetoric is important because it helps us get work done in the world, and it helps us organize how we interact with the places and people around us. This is a field older than Aristotle but still as relevant as it has ever been. Without my careful use of rhetoric, my lesson plans would fall flat, my family member may be insulted, and my boyfriend might bring home Brussels sprouts instead of broccoli. I hate Brussels sprouts. We use rhetoric all the time, whether we know it or not. But knowing about rhetoric and knowing how to use it effectively and creatively makes us better at it. I couldn't get through my day without it.

"Stop! In the Name of Rhetoric"

By C.S. Satterwhite

Rhetoric is everywhere. If we take Aristotle's definition of rhetoric to task—the ability to identify and use persuasion in a multitude of areas—we observe that the public is constantly being asked to do one thing or another. Humans consume texts and messages on a daily basis. This is especially true in our hyper-consumer and political culture. Whether walking down the street, watching television, reading a magazine, or researching on the internet, we are all constantly subject to some form of persuasion. As a culture, we are consumed by images, messages, and texts that persuade us to *do things* and *act in particular ways*. Advertisements are the most common, but there are so many other instances. We call these **rhetorical situations**.

A **rhetorical situation** is a textual moment or instance in which someone or some entity attempts to persuade an audience to do something. Does this sound like a broad definition? The definition sounds broad because, as rhetoric is everywhere, rhetorical situations are also nearly everywhere.

To demonstrate just how ubiquitous rhetorical situations are, let's look at one of the most common rhetorical situations in our daily life: the stop sign.

Stop signs have been around nearly as long as the automobile. Although the signs themselves vary to some extent, the stop sign itself is fairly universal and is a great place to analyze a rhetorical situation.

First, let's unpack our rhetorical tool kit for the basics: *Ethos, Pathos, Logos*, and *Kairos*. Now, let's use these rhetorical tools to do a quick analysis of a stop sign.

Your first question may be, how could a stop sign hold *ethos*? If we define *ethos* as demonstrating credibility, then we easily find a symbol we trust and to which we assign authority. When you see a stop sign, you're seeing an act of government policy. For the most part, wherever a stop sign is placed, some government entity acted to place that sign there. In the United States, the signs are mostly uniform—bright red octagons with large white letters urging motorists to stop driving and pay attention to traffic at a particular intersection. Getting the government to do anything is no small task, even for something as seemingly minor as a stop sign. Why? The credibility of the government is at stake with the safety of the public, even at your neighborhood intersection. Whatever an individual's feelings about the government, most people pay attention to the government's stop signs. In this regard, the stop sign also represents an *ethos* derived from community compliance. If individuals abide by the declaration to "Stop," driving conditions remain safer for all on the street. Stop signs provide an ordinance.

Consider other signs that we see placed on smaller streets by non-governmental bodies, such as a "cat crossing" sign erected by your neighbor to protect the feral cats he feeds. While you may love cats, and pay a little more attention if you see a cat crossing sign, the *ethos* of the "cat man" is less persuasive (generally speaking) than the *ethos* of the government's stop sign.

Stop sign taken in East Hill neighborhood in Pensacola, FL. Sign has a red and white sticker that reads Meow below the word "stop."

The next question is obvious: How could a stop sign have any ***pathos***? While the stop sign itself is devoid of emotions, if you have ever been in an accident you can certainly understand the emotions involved with traffic safety. Even if you've personally never been in an accident, seeing the ambulance on the side of the road with someone being wheeled away in a stretcher is always a sad sight.

Often, the sight of auto accidents often triggers an emotional response—and it should. According to the Fatality Analysis Reporting System, not heeding stop signs kills thousands of people each year. The sight of a collision is enough for many drivers to put their phones down, turn off the radio, double-check the seatbelt, and pay attention to the road. This is an emotional response caused by an accident. Without thinking about our own mortality, we usually stop at stop signs because we fear pain and death. The color red triggers its own emotions, as well as large block letters persuading us to listen to this singular appeal: STOP!

For the most part, stop signs aren't randomly placed on the road. Usually placed at intersections and cross roads, stop signs often follow a logical pattern. Of course there are exceptions, but there is a certain **logos** involved with the placement of stop signs. Furthermore, the logic behind the sign's request is evident: stop here, make sure someone isn't going to hit you, and you might not die at this intersection. This doesn't guarantee someone will stop, but the *logos* involved with a stop sign is one of the most important aspects of this rhetorical situation. The government places a sign at a specific intersection for public safety, which usually follows a logic related to traffic patterns. Stop here or you might die. A pretty logical idea, really.

Lastly, we have **kairos**, or timing. In general, for your actions to be most effective they need to happen at a certain time and place. Of course, timing is important for a stop sign to be functional. As one could imagine, stopping in the middle of an intersection is probably the worst place to stop. Stop signs do not creep up on us, though. If we're paying attention while driving, we can see most stop signs from a distance. The more driving experience we have, the more we realize that we need to prepare to stop at a certain point if we are to survive. As with many things in life, timing is important. The *kairos* related to a stop sign, again for obvious reasons, is important if we want to "arrive alive," as the saying goes.

Let's review. What has taken place in this instance is a quick assessment of a rhetorical situation: in this case, of a stop sign. When you see a stop sign, you acknowledge the credibility of the organization that placed the sign there (*ethos*), at least in this one instance. You know you should stop, either from personal or secondary experience, to avoid the physical and emotional pain of an accident (*pathos*). You understand the logic behind stopping at intersections (*logos*) for your safety and that of others, and specifically stopping at a certain point is clearly important (*kairos*).

Your analysis of this rhetorical situation probably came with little thought, maybe even subconsciously.

From there, all of the information for a quick analysis of a rhetorical situation is available for your use (*logos, pathos, ethos,* and *kairos*). Now it's up to you to decide for yourself whether or not you will do as the stop sign demands, or do something else. As with most rhetorical situations, the rhetor can only do his or her best to persuade you to make an ethical choice with all the faculties at your disposal (to paraphrase Aristotle). Ultimately, the decision is yours to make. To stop or not to stop: that is the question (to misquote Shakespeare). You've assessed the rhetorical situation and made your decision based off of the analysis. Good job!

As rhetoric is everywhere, our recognition of rhetorical situations is an important step as we become critical thinkers. Understanding how to decode rhetoric, using the tools given to us (*ethos, pathos, logos,* and *kairos*) helps to make sense of the rhetorical situation, and thus helps us to better understand the complex world around us.

While this might sound challenging, take comfort in your own intellect. If you can analyze a rhetorical situation like a stop sign (or a cat crossing sign), you can certainly do the same for an advertisement, news story, political speech, or a book.

What Is Rhetoric?

You have probably heard someone say of a politician's speech, "Oh, that's just rhetoric," meaning the politician's words are empty verbiage or hot air. The politician is attempting to sound impressive while saying nothing that has real meaning. Or perhaps the politician is making promises listeners believe he or she has no intention of keeping. The use of rhetoric in speeches—both bad speeches and good ones—is only the most visible use of rhetoric.

Rhetoric happens all around us, every day. Rhetoric is a persuasive language act—whether accomplished by speech, written texts, or images. It is the video footage of a demonstration on YouTube. It is the headlines on blog articles. It is the *Declaration of Independence*. Sam Leith explains,

> Rhetoric is language at play—language plus. It is what persuades and cajoles, inspires and bamboozles, thrills and misdirects. It causes criminals to be convicted, and then frees those criminals on appeal. It causes governments to rise and fall, best men to be ever after shunned by their friends' brides, and perfectly sensible adults to march with steady purpose toward machine guns [. . .]
>
> It is made of ringing truths and vital declarations. It is a way in which our shared assumptions and understandings are applied to new situations, and the language of history is channeled, revitalized, and given fresh power in each successive age.[1]

Your parents and teachers have used rhetoric on you since you first understood the words "yes" and "no." And you've been using it right back to them, whenever you want to persuade them to let you do something that is contrary to their stance on a topic.

The word *praxis* can be translated as "process" or "practice." Aristotle, the great Greek rhetorician, employed the term in a special way to mean practical reasoning for which the goal was action. To be practical in the Aristotelian sense is a little different from what being practical means today. It indicates the ability to apply abstract theory to concrete situations and, thus, to move from theory to action. Moreover, praxis embodies a creative element that raises it above the mundane or merely pragmatic. Therefore, "practicing rhetoric" is not practice in the sense of rehearsal. Rather, it is performing, or applying, or acting out rhetoric—taking theory and turning it into action.

Rhetoric has been studied in an organized manner since the days of the ancient Greeks and Romans. The elites of both countries studied persuasive argument out of necessity. Their democratic systems of government required that citizens

---

1. Leith, Sam. *Words Like Loaded Pistols: Rhetoric from Aristotle to Obama*. Basic, 2012, p. 6.

be able to argue persuasively in public, since there were no attorneys or professional politicians.

Today, rhetoric is still used in courts of law and political forums, but it is also studied in academia because it causes us to examine critically our own as well as others' ideas. Persuasive argument compels us to consider conflicting claims, to evaluate evidence, and to clarify our thoughts. We know that even wise, well-intentioned people don't always agree, so we consider others' ideas respectfully. After one person presents a persuasive argument, either orally or in writing, others respond to that argument with support, modification, or contradiction. Then, in turn, more individuals counter with their own versions, and thus, the interchange becomes a conversation.

"What's Rhetoric Got To Do With It?"

By N. Fox Edele

> *Language exerts a hidden power, like the moon on the tides.*
> —Rita Mae Brown

"I'm majoring in Environmental Science. Why do I need to take a writing course?" students will often ask. Substitute your own field of study—Criminal Justice; Engineering; Exercise Science; and the ever-popular "Undeclared"—and maybe you wonder the same thing: "What am I doing in a college writing class?"

"Students in Class."
Licensed by Creative Commons.

And it's true that you won't spend your life writing academic essays, especially the kinds of English papers and research projects you wrote in high school. Courses in your major subjects will train you to write the kinds of **genres** that are specific to your profession: field reports in archeology, programs of treatment in physical therapy, case studies in psychology, analytical essays in literature.

But when you graduate to the university classroom—enter Building 51 on this campus, for example, with your laptop or tablet, or notebook and mechanical pencil, you also move to another way of thinking and talking about **composition**. Your class work isn't limited to grammar worksheets, five-paragraph essays, and writing papers only the teacher reads. The class asks you to identify as a writer, as a researcher, as a reader—as someone with something to say. In fact, your early writing probably taught you more than you suspect about how to focus your mind and express yourself clearly. You enter the classroom with critical thinking skills that will serve you well no matter what classes you take in college or which profession you pursue in your life beyond this campus. We need to be honest about that: you probably know more than you think.

Composition teaches you to think like a writer, to theorize writing practice, to make informed choices about topic selection and research options, to work with peers to develop critical reading and reflection skills, to make design choices about organization and format, to name and identify audiences for your work. Here, you will learn that we actually use and understand language in ways that are older, deeper, more complex and meaningful than the kind of composition that American poet Langston Hughes once called his "Theme for English B."

In this poem he rebels against the typical bland and standardized composition; he writes the "theme" and critiques it at the same time:

> The instructor said,
> Go home and write
> a page tonight.
> And let that page come out of you—
> Then, it will be true.
> I wonder if it's that simple? ...
>
> So will my page be colored that I write?
> Being me, it will not be white.
> But it will be

a part of you, instructor.
You are white—
yet a part of me, as I am a part of you.
That's American.
Sometimes perhaps you don't want to be a part of me.
Nor do I often want to be a part of you.
But we are, that's true!
As I learn from you,
I guess you learn from me— ...

This is my theme for English B.

The work he does with words—analyzing the effect of the composition on him as a writer and on his teacher as his reader—is called **rhetoric**. By adding the term **rhetoric** to the more familiar word, composition, you are invited to enter a conversation and custom, or **discourse**, that began over 2,500 years ago.

"Once you open the door of rhetoric, you can't ever close it again," a young Latina student in San Diego wrote, a decade ago, as she spoke to her classmates about her own important issue, immigration. Rhetoric teaches you to become aware of the ways we invent, design, and deliver our messages to one another. With rhetoric you learn to understand that our languages work in powerful and strategic ways—to celebrate and teach; to deliberate and preach; to discover, express, entertain, manipulate, console, and warn.

And you learn, finally, to view the word **language** as more colorful, complicated, and diverse than words alone can illustrate. Think of your Facebook wall, your class site on eLearning, the YouTube video whose link you text to a friend, or the podcast you may some day compose for an international marketing conference. This understanding is crucial in the digital culture that we are building, and that is, at the same time, building and shaping us. As we communicate with one another, we shift and adapt language depending on **medium** and **purpose**: songs, performances, videos, tweets, as well as the family dinner at Thanksgiving, the campaign for voting rights, scripture on the Sabbath, the team meeting at Starbucks. Rhetoric shows us how to identify and select genre based on audience and purpose. Rhetoric opens "the door" to understanding how our multiform language works. Rhetoric shows you how to add your own distinctive voice to a conversation that has been ongoing since we as human beings first learned to speak, to argue, draw our maps and faces and geographies, and tell our stories.

Why Does Rhetoric Matter?

You are surrounded by rhetoric—images, signs, movements, and words that we combine and weave together in compositions we call **texts**. You encounter and read texts all the time—your cell phone screens, your News Feed, the books you study and movies you view, as well as the faces, customs, and fashions you find on Campus Avenue, or the streets of New York City, or a country far from your hometown.

The messages you've received have taught you how to invent and deliver your own texts—like the young artist pictured here on Gallery Night in Seville Square downtown, analyzing the composition of a work of graffiti art. What you see her doing is practicing rhetoric—asking how the image-text is put together, what its message or

Practicing rhetoric on Gallery Night in downtown Pensacola. Photo by N. Fox Edele

argument might be, and demonstrating at the same time her membership in the community of art students and American citizens with the right to speak freely. Her posture, clothing, action, and, no doubt, the content of her conversation all deliver to us a **message** of independence, urban savvy, confidence, and community engagement.

And by "reading the text" of this photo, you are practicing rhetoric, too.

We use rhetoric with a **purpose**: it is a mark of our intelligence. Rhetoric is not careless, or random, or "whatever goes"; rhetoric does not cut off a conversation with a curt and meaningless phrase such as, "It is what it is." Rather, rhetoric is about starting and furthering conversation. However, we could analyze **rhetorically** the reasons why people use this phrase, and ask about their intended message—who they think they are; who they think WE are; what they're saying about the possibility of pursuing the topic; whether they are being a kind of "anti-detective," shutting down curiosity. These questions help us understand the **rhetoricity** of that common little seemingly harmless phrase, "It is what it is."

Think about it: as you enter your classrooms, campus, dorm or apartment complex, neighborhood in Perdido or Pace, or beach at Gulf Breeze, your steepled church, or streets downtown that lead to Al Fresco, Saenger film series—as you experience your daily life—you are experiencing and participating in rhetoric—in the making of meaning around your community. Maybe you see a Crimson Tide logo on a young man's shirt, or an owl tattoo on a young woman's wrist, maybe you wear a Navy sweatshirt, drive a fuel-efficient car, take a "screen-free" day, recycle your Smart Water bottles.

Each of these common everyday places and sights is telling us a story, making an argument for the ways we create and value community.

Like Devin, your colleague here at UWF, you might marshal your facts and graphics and create a sign (pictured below) to **communicate** your message of materialism to your peers—to change how they think, or act. Like Cassie, you could teach the class about veterans who need attention and care when their service has ended. You might, like Nick, insist that children need a healthy diet—or you could speak passionately with Brian, Nelson, and Tameka of your generation whose future seems submerged in fear of tuition debt.

Devin's mash-up, "The Root of All Evil."

Remember—we are using rhetoric whenever we tell a story, make a statement, make a point, express a part of our identities, discover what we're thinking, try to persuade one another that we're right, or at least have a valid point to be heard, acknowledged, understood.

Editing Workshop, Pace Library, UWF. Photo by N. Fox Edele

And remember, whether we're talking about a page of cursive written with mechanical pencils, or a dance, or an IM typed on a keyboard or screen, or a YouTube video or owl tattoo on our forearm, we are entering a **rhetorical tradition** that is as old—and as global—as the human use of language itself.

Quickshots to think about:

1. Create a glossary of the terms in bold in this section: **genre; composition; rhetoric; discourse; language; text; argument; communicate; rhetorical tradition.**

2. How has this brief introduction to rhetoric expanded your idea beyond writing a composition for English class?

3. How can you apply the terms defined in this section to a text you've invented or designed or delivered to communicate a statement or story important to you?

Next up in Part 2: Rhetorical DNA

A "world tour" of rhetoric in ancient Africa, China, Greece, India, Native America, and how these cultures are still alive in our communication now.

Rhetoric and Power

Aristotle defined rhetoric as "the faculty of discovering, in a given instance, the available means of persuasion," which we might paraphrase as the power to see the means of persuasion available in any given situation. Each part of this definition is important. Rhetoric is power. The person who is able to speak eloquently, choosing the most suitable arguments about a topic for a specific audience in a particular situation, is the person most likely to persuade. In both Greece and Rome, the primary use of rhetoric was oratory—persuasion through public speaking. However, the texts of many famous speeches were studied as models by students, and prominent rhetoricians wrote treatises and handbooks for teaching rhetoric. To Greeks and Romans, a person who could use rhetoric effectively was a person of influence and power because he could persuade his audience to action. The effective orator could win court cases; the effective orator could influence the passage or failure of laws; the effective orator could send a nation to war or negotiate peace.

Skill with rhetoric has conveyed power through the ages, though in our contemporary world, rhetoric is often displayed in written text such as a book, newspaper or magazine article, or scientific report, rather than presented as a speech. Persuasive communication also can be expressed visually, as an illustration that accompanies a text or a cartoon that conveys its own message. Indeed, in our highly visual society, with television, movies, video games, and the internet, images can often persuade more powerfully than words alone.

Using rhetoric effectively means being able to interpret the rhetoric we are presented with in our everyday lives. Knowledge of persuasive communication or rhetoric empowers us to present our views and persuade others to modify their ideas. By changing ideas, rhetoric leads to action. By influencing actions, rhetoric affects society.

Selected Definitions of Rhetoric

Aristotle, 350 BCE—Rhetoric is "the faculty of discovering, in a given instance, the available means of persuasion."

Cicero, 90 BCE—Rhetoric is "speech designed to persuade" and "eloquence based on the rules of art."

Quintilian, 95 CE—Rhetoric is "the science of speaking well."

Augustine of Hippo, ca. 426 CE—Rhetoric is "the art of persuading people to accept something, whether it is true or false."

Anonymous, ca. 1490–1495—Rhetoric is "the science which refreshes the hungry, renders the mute articulate, makes the blind see, and teaches one to avoid every lingual ineptitude."

Heinrich Cornelius Agrippa, 1531—Rhetoric is "nothing other than an art of flatter, adulation, and, as some say more audaciously, lying, in that, if it cannot persuade others through the truth of the case, it does so by means of deceitful speech."

Hoyt Hudson, 1923—Rhetoric is effective persuasion. "In this sense, plainly, the man who speaks most persuasively uses the most, or certainly the best, rhetoric; and the man whom we censure for inflation of style and strained effects is suffering not from too much rhetoric, but from a lack of it."

I. A. Richards, 1936—Rhetoric is "a study of misunderstanding and its remedies."

Sister Miriam Joseph, 1937—Rhetoric is "the art of communicating thought from one mind to another, the adaptation of language to circumstance."

Kenneth Burke, 1950—Rhetoric is, "the use of words by human agents to form attitudes or to induce actions in other human agents."

Gerard A. Hauser, 2002—"Rhetoric, as an area of study, is concerned with how humans use symbols, especially language, to reach agreement that permits coordinated effort of some sort."

Explore

Activity 1.1 • **Historical Usage of the Word "Rhetoric"**

Read through the list of historical definitions of the word "rhetoric," and choose one that you find interesting. In a discussion, compare your chosen definition with those of your classmates.

Are We All Greeks?

As Americans, we owe an immense debt to ancient Greek civilization. Our laws, our democratic form of government, our literature, and our art have their roots in ancient Athens. Earlier generations of Americans and Western Europeans who often studied Latin and Greek may have had a clearer understanding of the direct connections between our culture and Athens of the fourth and fifth centuries BCE. Indeed, the English poet Percy Bysshe Shelley famously said, "We are all Greeks" because of the essential influence of ancient Greek culture upon Western civilization. However, even translated into twenty-first-century American English, the linkage is still there.

Something quite amazing happened in Athens, around 500 BCE. Instead of being invaded by a foreign country who appointed a puppet ruler or experiencing a coup in which a strong man seized power, the people peaceably chose to put in place a direct democracy. Attica (with its capital Athens) was not the only city-state to have a democracy, but it was the most successful. During the golden age of Greece, from roughly 500 BCE to 300 BCE, art, architecture, and literature thrived.

Direct or radical democracy meant all male citizens of Attica over the age of 20 could vote in the Assembly, the policy-making body of the city-state. They did not elect senators or representatives as we do today. Each of these men *voted directly*. Moreover, they could settle differences with fellow citizens by suing in the law courts. Out of 250,000 to 300,000 residents in Attica, some 30,000 were citizens. Amazingly, it was not unusual for 10,000 of these eligible men to vote in the Assembly. The law courts had juries of 500 or more. Imagine trying to speak to an audience of 10,000 people without modern loudspeakers. Even with the wonderful acoustics in Greek theatres, it would have been a challenge.

Ordinary citizens were required to speak in the Assembly or the courts to promote laws or defend themselves from lawsuits, since there were no attorneys or professional politicians. Certainly, speaking before such large audiences necessitated special skills acquired only through extensive training and practice. Many sought out teachers to help them learn how to speak persuasively, and, indeed, training in rhetoric became the primary method of education for the elite young men (and even a few women).

The earliest teachers of the verbal persuasive skills we now call rhetoric were Sophists who migrated to Athens from Sicily and other Greek states. Some of their viewpoints were curiously modern—for example, some argued that knowledge is relative and that pure truth does not exist. However, they became known for teaching their pupils to persuade an audience to think whatever they wanted them to think. Sophists such as Gorgias often presented entertainment speeches during which they would argue, on the spur of the moment, any topic raised by the audience, just to show they were able to construct effective arguments for any subject.

Claiming the Sophists' rhetoric could be employed to manipulate the masses for good or ill, and that rhetoricians used it irresponsibly, Plato coined the term, *rhetorike*—from which we take the term, "rhetoric"—as a criticism of the Sophists. Ironically, Plato demonstrates excellent rhetorical techniques himself when he condemns rhetoric by arguing that only the elite who are educated in philosophy are suited to rule, not the rhetoricians. Aristotle, Plato's student, took a more moderate viewpoint toward rhetoric. Indeed, he was the first philosopher to classify rhetoric as a tool for practical debate with general audiences. His book *On Rhetoric* (though it was probably lecture notes possibly combined with student responses rather than a manuscript intended for publication) is the single most important text that establishes rhetoric as a system of persuasive communication.

Athens, even in its glory days, seethed with controversy and bickering over the many inefficiencies of democracy. Men trained in rhetoric executed two coups, the Tyranny of the Four Hundred in 411 BCE and the Tyranny of the Thirty in 404 BCE, neither of which was an improvement; after each coup, democracy returned. Moreover, Athenians fought wars with Persia (the Battle of Marathon in 490 BCE and the Battle of Thermopylae in 480 BCE) and Sparta (the Peloponnesian War in 431–404 BCE and the Corinthian War of 395–387 BCE). Finally, the armies of Philip II of Macedonia defeated Athens at the Battle of Chaeronea in 338 BCE, ending Athenian independence. Despite coups and wars, democracy remained in place in Athens for nearly 200 years.

If Americans might be called Greeks because our country is based on Greek traditions, this does not mean that rhetoric does not appear in all cultures. True, one might say that all civilizations have some sort of persuasive negotiation process; but profound differences exist between cultures in terms of what verbal strategies are considered persuasive. Indeed, disparity in expectations and the actions of individuals and groups from different traditions can be a cause of strife in any culture.

Explore

Activity 1.2 • Contemporary Usage of the Word "Rhetoric"

Find at least two recent but different examples involving uses of the word "rhetoric." For example, search your local newspaper for an example of how the word "rhetoric" is being used. A search of the *Dallas Morning News* for the word "rhetoric" led to a story about citizen efforts to clean up a neglected area of town: "He now hopes for help to finally fill the gap between rhetoric and reality." Or ask a friend, fellow employee, or a family member to tell you what the word "rhetoric" means, and write down what they say. Discuss your examples in your small group, and present the best ones to the class.

Visual Map of Meanings for the Word "Rhetoric"

The word map for the word "rhetoric" shown in Figure 1.1 on the next page has branches for different meanings of the word, with some branches splitting again to display subtle subsets of connotation. It was created by a website, *Visual Thesaurus* (www.visualthesaurus.com), which computes visual word maps for any word inputted in its search box. The idea is that words lead to branches that lead to more words, inspiring users to think of language in new ways.

If you recreate the rhetoric word map at the *Visual Thesaurus* site and place your cursor over any of the circles connecting the branches, a small box will pop up that defines that connection. One of these connection boxes is visible in Figure 1.1. Notice it says, "using language effectively to please or persuade." This is the branch of the visual map that is closest to the meaning of "rhetoric" as used in this book. The other branches illustrate other contemporary uses of the word.

Activity 1.3 • Explore the Visual Map of the Word "Rhetoric"

Explore

In your small group, choose one of the five branches of words in the visual map of the word "rhetoric." Go to one or more good dictionaries and explore the meanings of the words in that branch. A good place to start would be the *Oxford English Dictionary (OED)*, which your college library may offer online. The *OED* offers intricate analyses of the histories of word meanings. Report to the class what you find out about the words on your particular branch.

Figure 1.1 • Word Map for "Rhetoric"

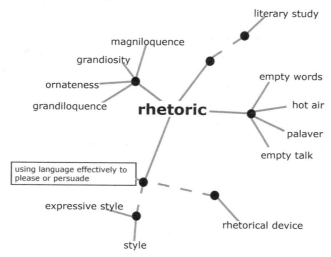

Have you bought hummus or coconut water at the grocery store? Worn a henna tattoo? Then you may have participated in Columbusing, the art of "discovering" something, usually from another culture, that is not new. The term echoes Columbus's "discovery" of the New World, which had long been inhabited by non-Europeans.

Brenda Salinas writes about Columbusing in this article published on NPR.com.

There isn't anything inherently wrong about eating hummus or getting a henna tattoo, argues Salinas. She attempts to persuade you that the problem is the stripping of cultural context from the item, in effect, engaging in cultural appropriation. To the Latinos who grew up eating empanadas, for example, it can feel like theft when Buzzfeed raves about "a hand pie, a little foldover pie that you can fit in your hand. They have flaky crusts and can be sweet or savory."

As you read Salinas's article, think about occasions when you may have engaged in Columbusing.

"Columbusing": The Art of Discovering Something that is Not New
by Brenda Salinas

If you've danced to an Afrobeat-heavy pop song, dipped hummus, sipped coconut water, participated in a Desi-inspired color run or sported a henna tattoo, then you've Columbused something.

Columbusing is when you "discover" something that's existed forever. Just that it's existed outside your own culture, nationality, race or even, say, your neighborhood. Bonus points if you tell all your friends about it.

Why not? In our immigrant-rich cities, the whole world is at our doorsteps.

Sometimes, though, Columbusing can feel icky. When is cultural appropriation a healthy byproduct of globalization and when is it a problem?

All the Rage

Buzzfeed Food published an article asking, "Have you heard about the new kind of pie that's *all the rage* lately?" It's a hand pie, a little foldover pie that you can fit in your hand. They have flaky crusts and can be sweet or savory. You know, exactly like an empanada, a Latin American culinary staple.

On face value, it seems stupid to get worked up over an empanada. I mean, it's just a pastry, right? But "discovering" empanadas on Pinterest and calling them "hand pies" strips empanadas of their cultural context. To all the people who grew up eating empanadas, it can feel like theft.

Feeling Overlooked

When it comes to our culinary traditions, Latinos are used to feeling robbed.

Latino activists spoke out in May when Chipotle announced plans to print original stories by famous writers on its paper goods and failed to include any Mexican-Americans or Latinos on the roster. The American-owned chain can profit from Mexican culture while overlooking the harsh reality of how Latinos have been treated in this country.

On Cinco de Mayo, chef Anthony Bourdain asked why Americans love Mexican food, drugs, alcohol and cheap labor but ignore the violence that happens across the border. "Despite our ridiculously hypocritical attitudes towards immigration," writes Bourdain, "we demand that Mexicans cook a large percentage of the food we eat, grow the ingredients we need to make that food, clean our houses, mow our lawns, wash our dishes, look after our children."

In this promotional photo shot, TV star Jennie Garth sprays the crowd with orange at the Shout Color Throw at Dodger Stadium in Los Angeles. Events like this one are being held in Europe and the United States, but most organizers don't mention that these events are inspired by the Hindu festival of Holi—but stripped of religious meaning.

Photo Credit: Jeff Lewis/AP Images for SC Johnson

It's frustrating when even the staunchest anti-immigration activists regularly eat Mexican food. It seems like a paradox to relish your fajitas while believing the line cook should get deported.

Admittedly, cultural appropriation is an integral and vital part of American history. And one day, empanadas might become as

A man sprays colored dye on people dancing during Holi celebrations in India. Holi, the Hindu festival of colors, also heralds the coming of spring—a detail that partiers at the Shout Color Throw might miss.

Photo Credit: Rajesh Kumar Singh/AP

American as pizza (yes, I appreciate the irony of that statement). But the day when Latinos are considered as American as Italian-Americans, well, that feels further away.

Why It Hurts

The condolence prize for being an outsider is that you can take solace in the cultural traditions that make you unique. When outsiders use tweezers to pick out the discrete parts of your culture that are worthy of their attention, it feels like a violation. Empanadas are trendy, cumbia is trendy, but Latinas are still not trendy.

Code Switch blogger Gene Demby writes, "It's much harder now to patrol the ramparts of our cultures, to distinguish between the appreciators and appropriators. Just who gets to play in which cultural sandboxes? Who gets to be the bouncer at the velvet rope?"

Playing Explorer

Of course, there is no bouncer, but we can be careful not to Columbus other culture's traditions. Before you make reservations at the hottest fusion restaurant or book an alternative healing therapy, ask yourself a few questions:

> Who is providing this good or service for me?
>
> Am I engaging with them in a thoughtful manner?
>
> Am I learning about this culture?
>
> Are people from this culture benefiting from my spending money here?
>
> Are they being hurt by my spending money here?

It is best to enter a new, ethnic experience with consideration, curiosity and respect. That doesn't mean you have to act or look the part of a dour-faced anthropologist or an ultra-earnest tourist. You can go outside your comfort zone and learn about the completely different worlds that coexist within your city. If you're adventurous, you can explore the entire world without leaving the country and without needing a passport.

Just remember, it's great to love a different culture and its artifacts, as long as you love the people too.

Activity 1.4 • Analyzing Columbusing as an Argument

" 'Columbusing': The Art of Discovering Something that Is Not New" is a rhetorical document because the author is attempting to persuade her audience to believe something. In a group, use these review questions to discuss what Salinas is arguing.

1. What does Salinas want her audience to do differently? How does she define Columbusing? What does it have to do with Columbus?

2. Make a list of the examples Salinas gives of Columbusing. Then, make a list of other Columbusing items or activities you have bought or engaged in. Share your group's list with the class.

3. What does Salinas say we can do to avoid Columbusing other cultures' traditions? Do you agree that these are good suggestions? Why or why not? Discuss these questions in your group, and share your thoughts with the class.

Rhetorical Argument

Often, in our culture, the word *argument* is taken to mean a disagreement or even a fight, with raised voices, rash words, and hurt feelings. We have the perception of an argument as something that leads to victory or defeat, winners or losers. A *rhetorical argument,* however, is the carefully crafted presentation of a viewpoint or position on a topic and the giving of thoughts, ideas, and opinions along with reasons for their support. The persuasive strength of an argument rests upon the rhetorical skills of the rhetor (the speaker or the writer) in utilizing the tools of language to persuade a particular audience.

Types of Argument

Academic arguments can be divided into several different categories, depending upon the extent of the writer's desire to persuade and the scope of the conversational exchange.

1. **Makes a point.** One type of argument simply makes a point about a topic. The article in this chapter, " 'Columbusing': The Art of Discovering Something that Is Not New," argues, for example, that buying hummus or getting a henna tattoo is Columbusing, which labels as new something ancient from another culture. To do so strips the cultural context from things or

activities. The subtext of the article suggests Columbusing is a bad thing and should be avoided. If the author of this type of argument offers sufficient evidence to back up the thesis, no one is likely to disagree, except to say, perhaps, the author is overreacting or the point the author makes is not important.

2. **Aims to persuade.** A second type of argument involves a controversial issue, and the writer's aim is to persuade the audience to change its stance on the matter. For the writer, the ideal result would be that members of the audience alter their positions to coincide with the writer's viewpoint. In this second type of argument, it is essential that the writer offer the complete structure of thesis, evidence, possible opposing viewpoints which are discussed and countered, and a conclusion. "The Sleepover Question," another reading in this chapter, presents this kind of argument. The author, who has conducted research in both America and Holland, argues the controversial position that if American parents would adopt more liberal attitudes toward their children's sexuality, like the parents in Holland, "the transition into adulthood need not be so painful for parents or children." A reading in Chapter 3, "Executions Should Be Televised," offers a more extreme version of this type of argument. Either executions are televised or they aren't, and the writer advocates that they should be.

3. **Tries to find common ground.** A third type of argument emphasizes multiple perspectives and viewpoints and tries to find common ground participants can agree upon.

    In Chapter 6, Rogerian (or common ground) argument, named after psychologist Carl Rogers, is discussed and outlined. Rogerian argument has four elements: introduction, common ground and common arguments, a position or argument, and a positive statement of how the position could, at least in some instances, benefit the opposition.

These three types of arguments represent points in a spectrum, and all persuasive texts may not neatly fit into one of the three categories. A crucial thing to remember, though, is that all arguments involve the presentation of a line of reasoning about a topic or an issue—a thesis, hypothesis, or claim—and the support of that reasoning with evidence.

Aristotle's Three Appeals

Aristotle identified three appeals (see Figure 1.2) or three ways to persuade an audience, and we are still using these today, though often without using the Greek terms to identify the means of persuasion.

Ethos—The rhetor persuades by means of his or her character or credibility. In oratory, the speaker projects an air of confidence and authority. In writing, *ethos* is conveyed by the writer's qualifications or the authorities cited and also by the quality of the writing.

Pathos—The rhetor persuades by playing upon the listener's (or reader's) emotions. He or she may refer to children, death, disaster, injustice, or other topics that arouse pity, fear, or other emotions.

Logos—The rhetor persuades by using reasoning and evidence. Arguments based on *logos* employ deductive or inductive reasoning.

Figure 1.2 • Aristotle's Three Appeals

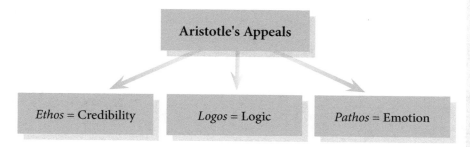

Although a good argument will contain at least traces of all three appeals, skilled rhetors analyze their audiences to determine which of the three will be most persuasive for that particular audience. Then, they construct arguments that emphasize that particular appeal.

In addition, a knowledgeable rhetor considers the time, place, audience, topic, and other aspects of the occasion for writing or speaking to determine the **kairos**, or opportune moment for the argument (see Figure 1.3). This factor or critical moment both provides and limits opportunities for appeals suitable to that moment. For example, someone giving a commencement address has certain opportunities and constraints. Likewise, an attorney writing a last-minute appeal for someone on death row has a very different set of options.

Figure 1.3 • *Kairos*

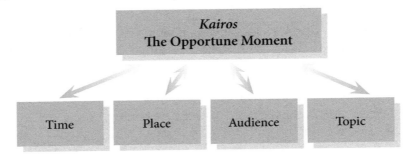

Microsoft Just Laid Off Thousands of Employees With a Hilariously Bad Memo

by Kevin Roose

Kevin Roose's essay, "Microsoft Just Laid Off Thousands of Employees With a Hilariously Bad Memo" illustrates the dangers of not considering kairos. When Stephen Elop needed to lay off more than 10 percent of Microsoft workers under his supervision, Elop did not say anything one might expect—like "sorry," or "I regret," or "thank you for your service." In a memo to the affected employees, he did not even get around to the news of layoff until the eleventh paragraph.

If Elop had considered the kairos of the situation, then he would have realized his audience would not be interested in all the planning information he crowded into the memo. They would want to know the bad news, if it had to be told, near the beginning of the memo. Elop, as Roose reveals in his analysis of the memo, was more interested in his corporate strategy than in what his audience at that time and place needed or wanted to hear.

The essay was published in New York Magazine.

Typically, when you're a top executive at a major corporation that is laying off more than 10 percent of your workforce, you say a few things to the newly jobless. Like "sorry." Or "thank you for your many years of service." Or even "we hate doing this, but it's necessary to help the company survive."

What you don't do is bury the news of the layoffs in the 11th paragraph of a long, rambling corporate strategy memo.

And yet, this was Microsoft honcho Stephen Elop's preferred method for announcing to his employees today that 12,500 of them were being laid off. (18,000 are being laid off companywide; Elop, the former head of Nokia, oversees the company's devices unit, which was hardest hit by the layoffs.)

How bad was Elop's job-axing memo? Really, really bad. It's so bad that I can't even really convey its badness. I just have to show you.

Here's how it starts:

Hello there,

Hello there? *Hello there?* Out of all the possible "you're losing your job" greetings, you chose the one that sounds like the start to a bad OKCupid message? "Hello there" isn't how you announce layoffs; it's what you

Stephen Elop, lead-burier.
Photo Credit: Josh Edelson/AFP/Getty Images

say right before you ask, "What's a girl like you doing on a site like this? ;)" It's the fedora of greetings.

Anyway, carry on. Let's hear the bad news:

> **Microsoft's strategy is focused on productivity and our desire to help people "do more." As the Microsoft Devices Group, our role is to light up this strategy for people. We are the team creating the hardware that showcases the finest of Microsoft's digital work and digital life experiences, and we will be the confluence of the best of Microsoft's applications, operating systems and cloud services.**

Wait, what does this have to do with layoffs?

> **To align with Microsoft's strategy, we plan to focus our efforts. Given the wide range of device experiences, we must concentrate on the areas where we can add the most value. The roots of this company and our future are in productivity and helping people get things done. Our fundamental focus—for phones, Surface, for meetings with devices like PPI, Xbox hardware and new areas of innovation— is to build on that strength. While our direction in the majority of our teams is largely unchanging, we have had an opportunity to plan carefully about the alignment of phones within Microsoft as the transferring Nokia team continues with its integration process.**

Oh, I get it. This is the warm-up. You're giving me a few minutes to sit down, compose myself, grab the Kleenex. Now you're going to drop the hammer.

> **It is particularly important to recognize that the role of phones within Microsoft is different than it was within Nokia. Whereas the hardware business of phones within Nokia was an end unto itself, within Microsoft all our devices are intended to embody the finest of Microsoft's digital work and digital life experiences, while accruing value to Microsoft's overall strategy. Our device strategy must reflect Microsoft's strategy and must be accomplished within an appropriate financial envelope. Therefore, we plan to make some changes.**

"Financial envelope"? You don't literally keep all of Microsoft's cash in a big envelope, do you? Anyway, "changes." I know what that's supposed to mean. Now, please, give it to me straight: tell me I'm fired.

We will be particularly focused on making the market for Windows Phone. In the near term, we plan to drive Windows Phone volume by targeting the more affordable smartphone segments, which are the fastest growing segments of the market, with Lumia. In addition to the portfolio already planned, we plan to deliver additional lower-cost Lumia devices by shifting select future Nokia X designs and products to Windows Phone devices. We expect to make this shift immediately while continuing to sell and support existing Nokia X products.

To win in the higher price segments, we will focus on delivering great breakthrough products in alignment with major milestones ahead from both the Windows team and the Applications and Services Group. We will ensure that the very best experiences and scenarios from across the company will be showcased on our products. We plan to take advantage of innovation from the Windows team, like Universal Windows Apps, to continue to enrich the Windows application ecosystem. And in the very lowest price ranges, we plan to run our first phones business for maximum efficiency with a smaller team.

WTF. Is this some kind of joke? DO I HAVE A JOB OR NOT?

We expect these changes to have an impact to our team structure. With our focus, we plan to consolidate the former Smart Devices and Mobile Phones business units into one phone business unit that is responsible for all of our phone efforts. Under the plan, the phone business unit will be led by Jo Harlow with key members from both the Smart Devices and Mobile Phones teams in the management team. This team will be responsible for the success of our Lumia products, the transition of select future Nokia X products to Lumia and for the ongoing operation of the first phone business.

I AM GNAWING ON MY MOUSE PAD IN ANGER. ALL I WANT TO KNOW IS WHETHER I NEED TO START SELLING MY PLASMA TO MAKE RENT NEXT MONTH. PLEASE TELL ME THIS BIT OF INFORMATION.

As part of the effort, we plan to select the appropriate business model approach for our sales markets while continuing to offer our products in all markets with a strong focus on maintaining business continuity. We will determine each market approach based on local market dynamics, our ability to profitably deliver local variants, current Lumia momentum and the strategic importance of the market to Microsoft. This will all be balanced with our overall capability to invest.

Our phone engineering efforts are expected to be concentrated in Salo, Finland (for future, high-end Lumia products) and Tampere, Finland (for more affordable devices). We plan to develop the supporting technologies in both locations. We plan to ramp down engineering work in Oulu. While we plan to reduce the engineering in Beijing and San Diego, both sites will continue to have supporting roles, including affordable devices in Beijing and supporting specific US requirements in San Diego. Espoo and Lund are planned to continue to be focused on application software development.

Blah blah blah I don't even care anymore. You have numbed me to the afflictions of mankind with phrases like "business continuity" and "market dynamics." And now you're probably going to use some crazy euphemism, like "streamline," to tell me I'm fired. Go ahead.

We plan to right-size our manufacturing operations to align to the new strategy and take advantage of integration opportunities. We expect to focus phone production mainly in Hanoi, with some production to continue in Beijing and Dongguan. We plan to shift other Microsoft manufacturing and repair operations to Manaus and Reynosa respectively, and start a phased exit from Komaron, Hungary.

"Right-size"! "Phased exit"! Oh, you are so killing this. You get an extra snack ration at CEO summer camp.

In short, we will focus on driving Lumia volume in the areas where we are already successful today in order to make the market for Windows Phone. With more speed, we will build on our success in the affordable smartphone space with new products offering more differentiation. We'll focus on acquiring new customers in the markets where Microsoft's services and products are most concentrated. And, we'll continue building momentum around applications.

Life is empty. All that remains is dust.

We plan that this would result in an estimated reduction of 12,500 factory direct and professional employees over the next year.

> **These decisions are difficult for the team, and we plan to support departing team members' with severance benefits.**

There it is, finally. In paragraph 11. I would react more strongly to the news that I'm laid off, but my synapses are no longer firing properly. The badness of this email has rewired my brain's circuitry. All I understand now is business-school jargon. And death. Sweet death.

> **More broadly across the Devices team, we will continue our efforts to bring iconic tablets to market in ways that complement our OEM partners, power the next generation of meetings & collaboration devices and thoughtfully expand Windows with new interaction models. With a set of changes already implemented earlier this year in these teams, this means there will be limited change for the Surface, Xbox hardware, PPI/meetings or next generation teams.**

> **We recognize these planned changes are broad and have very difficult implications for many of our team members. We will work to provide as much clarity and information as possible. Today and over the coming weeks leaders across the organization will hold town halls, host information sharing sessions and provide more details on the intranet.**

Oh, good. Because if it's one thing I need right now, it's more details.

> **The team transferring from Nokia and the teams that have been part of Microsoft have each experienced a number of remarkable changes these last few years. We operate in a competitive industry that moves rapidly, and change is necessary. As difficult as some of our changes are today, this direction deliberately aligns our work with the cross company efforts that Satya has described in his recent emails. Collectively, the clarity, focus and alignment across the company, and the opportunity to deliver the results of that work into the hands of people, will allow us to increase our success in the future.**

> **Regards,**

"Regards?" Really? We started at OKCupid stalker, and you're ending at "over-eager candidate for summer internship?" Well, okay. Sure. Whatever. Not like it matters.

> **Stephen**

Collaborate

Activity 1.5 • Discuss Microsoft's Memo Laying Off Employees

In a small group, discuss Stephen Elop's memo to employees who were being laid off and Roose's colorful commentary.

1.   What would you think if you received such a memo? How is Elop ignoring *kairos* in his memo? Reread the section earlier in the chapter in which *kairos* is discussed, and then decide with your group how Elop fails to take *kairos* into consideration in writing his memo. Report to the class.

2.   Discuss what employees would have preferred to hear from Elop, assuming they must be laid off. Share your conclusions with the class.

Reading 1.3

This selection by Amy Schalet was first published in The New York Times. *"The Sleepover Question" hazards an argument that many Americans—or at least American parents—may find controversial. Backed by her credentials as a professor of sociology, Schalet cites research from 130 interviews, both in the United States and the Netherlands, and tackles the issue of whether or not American parents should allow their adolescent children to have sex in the family home. Pay particular attention, for she shows how to argue a subject that is not only controversial but often ignored.*

The Sleepover Question
by Amy Schalet

NOT under my roof. That's the attitude most American parents have toward teenagers and their sex lives. Squeamishness and concern describe most parents' approach to their offspring's carnality. We don't want them doing it—whatever "it" is!—in our homes. Not surprisingly, teenage sex is a source of conflict in many American families.

Would Americans increase peace in family life and strengthen family bonds if they adopted more accepting attitudes about sex and what's allowable under the family roof? I've interviewed 130 people, all white, middle class and not particularly religious, as part of a study of teenage sex and family life here and in the Netherlands. My look into cultural differences suggests family life might be much improved, for all, if Americans had more open ideas about teenage sex. The question of who sleeps where when a teenager brings a boyfriend or girlfriend home for the night fits within the larger world of culturally divergent ideas about teenage sex, lust and capacity for love.

Kimberly and Natalie dramatize the cultural differences in the way young women experience their sexuality. (I have changed their names to protect confidentiality.) Kimberly, a 16-year-old American, never received sex education at home. "God, no! No, no! That's not going to happen," she told me. She'd like to tell her parents that she and her boyfriend are having sex, but she believes it is easier for her parents not to know because the truth would "shatter" their image of her as their "little princess."

Natalie, who is also 16 but Dutch, didn't tell her parents immediately when she first had intercourse with her boyfriend of three months. But, soon after, she says, she was so happy, she wanted to share the good news. Initially her father was upset and worried about his daughter and his honor. "Talk to him," his wife advised Natalie; after she did, her father made peace with the change. Essentially Natalie and her family negotiated a life change together and figured out, as a family, how to adjust to changed circumstance.

Respecting what she understood as her family's "don't ask, don't tell" policy, Kimberly only slept with her boyfriend at his house, when no one was home. She enjoyed being close to her boyfriend but did not like having to keep an important part of her life secret from her parents. In contrast, Natalie and her boyfriend enjoyed time and a new closeness with her family; the fact that her parents knew and approved of her boyfriend seemed a source of pleasure.

The difference in their experiences stems from divergent cultural ideas about sex and what responsible parents ought to do about it. Here, we see teenagers as helpless victims beset by raging hormones and believe parents should protect them from urges they cannot control. Matters aren't helped by the stereotype that all boys want the same thing, and all girls want love and cuddling. This compounds the burden on parents to steer teenage children away from relationships that will do more harm than good.

The Dutch parents I interviewed regard teenagers, girls and boys, as capable of falling in love, and of reasonably assessing their own readiness for sex. Dutch parents like Natalie's talk to their children about sex and its unintended consequences and urge them to use contraceptives and practice safe sex.

Cultural differences about teenage sex are more complicated than clichéd images of puritanical Americans and permissive Europeans. Normalizing ideas about teenage sex in fact allows the Dutch to exert *more* control over their children. Most of the parents I interviewed actively discouraged promiscuous behavior. And Dutch teenagers often reinforced what we see as 1950s-style mores: eager to win approval, they bring up their partners in conversation, introduce them to their parents and help them make favorable impressions.

Some Dutch teenagers went so far as to express their ideas about sex and love in self-consciously traditional terms; one Dutch boy said the advantage of spending the night with a partner was that it was "Like Mom and Dad, like when you're married, you also wake up next to the person you love."

Normalizing teenage sex under the family roof opens the way for more responsible sex education. In a national survey, 7 of 10 Dutch girls reported that by the time they were 16, their parents had talked to them about pregnancy and contraception. It seems these conversations helped teenagers prepare, responsibly, for active sex lives: 6 of 10 Dutch girls said they were on the pill when they first had intercourse. Widespread use of oral contraceptives contributes to low teenage pregnancy rates—more than 4 times lower in the Netherlands than in the United States.

Obviously sleepovers aren't a direct route to family happiness. But even the most traditional parents can appreciate the virtue of having their children be comfortable bringing a girlfriend or boyfriend home, rather than have them sneak around.

Unlike the American teenagers I interviewed, who said they felt they had to split their burgeoning sexual selves from their family roles, the Dutch teens had a chance to integrate different parts of themselves into their family life. When children feel safe enough to tell parents what they are doing and feeling, presumably it's that much easier for them to ask for help. This allows parents to have more influence, to control through connection.

Sexual maturation is awkward and difficult. The Dutch experience suggests that it is possible for families to stay connected when teenagers start having sex, and that if they do, the transition into adulthood need not be so painful for parents or children.

Activity 1.6 • Analyze "The Sleepover Question"

Collaborate

In a group, discuss these review questions about the emphasis of *logos* in "The Sleepover Question."

1. Can you paraphrase the logic of the argument? How does emotion (*pathos*) play a role in resistance to this argument?

2. What do you think about the "not under my roof" approach to a parent controlling a teen's sexuality versus the Dutch approach of allowing a teen's partner to sleep over?

3. How do stereotypes play against the argument for a more open approach to teen sex in America? How much of parents' discomfort with their teen potentially having sex is guided by how their parents treated the subject when they were teens?

4. In the article, the writer discusses the link between the use of oral contraceptives and lower teen pregnancy rates but does not mention the risk of STDs or condom use. Is it irresponsible of the author not to discuss the risk of STDs and sex, especially when she is willing to discuss teen pregnancy? Does it feel like an incomplete argument without discussing STDs?

After you've discussed these questions as a group, individually reflect on what you would say in a letter to the editor about this article.

Become Part of the Academic Conversation

As a student, you are asked to comment on or analyze texts others have written. In effect, you are expected to join academic conversations that are already in progress. How do you do that? How do you know what kind of response is appropriate? Have you ever entered a party where everyone is talking excitedly? Most likely, you paused near the doorway to get a sense of who was there and what they were discussing before you decided who to talk to and what to say. Or, have you become part of a Facebook group or a listserv discussion group? If so, you know it is a good idea to "lurk" for a while before asking questions or contributing a remark. Writing an academic paper involves a similar process. You read about a subject until you have a good grasp of the points authorities are debating. Then you find a way to integrate your own ideas about that subject with the ideas of others and create an informed contribution to the conversation.

For example, the following students' introductions to movie reviews demonstrate they not only understand the films and have interesting things to say about them;

their writing also displays knowledge of what others have written about the films, whether the students agree with those evaluations or not.

▮   Roger Ebert claims that audience members who haven't seen the first two *Lord of the Rings* films (Peter Jackson, 2001, 2002) will likely "be adrift during the early passages of [the third] film's 200 minutes." But then again, Ebert continues, "to be adrift occasionally during this nine-hour saga comes with the territory" (par. 3). Ebert, though, misses one crucial fact regarding *Lord of the Rings: The Return of the King* (2003). This third installment opens with a flashback intended to familiarize new spectators about what happened in the previous two films. Within these five minutes, the audience discovers how Gollum (Andy Serkis) came to be corrupt through the destructive power of the Ring. The viewer, therefore, will not necessarily be "adrift," as Ebert claims, since the lighting, setting, and sound in the opening of *The Return of the King* show the lighter, more peaceful world before Gollum finds the ring, compared to the darker, more sinister world thereafter.

▮   "It's hard to resist a satire, even when it wobbles, that insists the most unbelievable parts are the most true" (*Rolling Stone* par. 1). This is Peter Travers's overarching view of Grant Heslov's satire, *The Men Who Stare at Goats* (2009). Travers is correct here; after all, Goats's opening title card, which reads, "More of this is real than you would believe," humorously teases the viewer that some of the film's most "unbelievable parts" will, in fact, offer the most truth. We experience this via Bill Wilson's (Ewan McGregor) interview of an ex "psy-ops" soldier, when Wilson's life spirals out of control, and all the other far-fetched actions presenting "reality." But again, it is the film's opening—specifically, its setting, camera movements and angles, dialogue, effects, and ambient noise—that sets the foundation for an unbelievably realistic satire.[2]

In both of these introductions, the students quote reviews by professional film critics and respond to the critics' opinions. Moreover, the students continue their arguments by using the critics' ideas as springboards for their own arguments. These two short examples indicate these students have learned how to counter positions advocated by authorities without losing their own voices. If the rest of their essays continue as they have begun, the students will have written essays

---

2. Marshall, Kelli. "Entering a Conversation, Teaching the Academic Essay." *Unmuzzled Thoughts about Teaching and Pop Culture*, Tumblr, 23 Oct. 2010, kellirmarshall.tumblr.com/post/1391060136/entering-a-conversation-teaching-the-academic.

to which others can reply, thus continuing the conversation. Later in this text-book, you will have your own chance to enter the conversation of film reviews by reviewing a favorite movie of your own.

The Burkean Parlor

Kenneth Burke, philosopher and rhetorician, described the "unending conversation" that surrounds each of us. To do academic research, we must enter the conversation of people who already know the topic and have discussed part or all of it before we are even aware the topic exists. Burke wrote,

> Imagine that you enter a parlor. You come late. When you arrive, others have long preceded you, and they are engaged in a heated discussion, a discussion too heated for them to pause and tell you exactly what it is about. In fact, the discussion had already begun long before any of them got there, so that no one present is qualified to retrace for you all the steps that had gone before. You listen for a while, until you decide that you have caught the tenor of the argument; then you put in your oar. Someone answers; you answer him; another comes to your defense; another aligns himself against you, to either the embarrassment or gratification of your opponent, depending upon the quality of your ally's assistance. However, the discussion is interminable. The hour grows late, you must depart. And you do depart, with the discussion still vigorously in progress.[3]

Activity 1.7 • Joining the Conversation

Collaborate

Divide into groups of five or six members. Have one member of each group leave the room for five to ten minutes. Meanwhile, each group selects a topic and begins conversing about it. When the excluded member of the group returns, the group simply continues their conversation. When the excluded member figures out what the conversation is, he or she can join it by making a comment or asking a question.

After a few minutes, have each of the excluded group members tell the class what it was like to enter a conversation after it had already started. As a class, discuss how this is similar to what you experience when you research an academic topic and write about it.

---

3. Burke, Kenneth. *The Philosophy of Literary Form: Studies in Symbolic Action.* U of California, 1967, pp. 110-11.

Collaborative Groups Help Students Enter the Academic Conversation

Likely, your writing class will include collaborative group work as part of the mix of activities, along with lecture, class discussion, and in-class writing. You may wonder why there is so much talk in a writing class, which is a good question. Use of collaborative groups is based on extensive research, which shows that students who work in small groups as part of their courses tend to learn more and retain the knowledge longer than students who are not asked to work in groups. Also, research shows students who participate in collaborative group work generally are more satisfied with the course. Groups give students a chance to apply knowledge they have learned and provide a change of pace from lectures or other class activities. There are several types of groups, and your class may include one or all of them.

- **Informal, one-time pairs or groups.** After presenting some material, your instructor may ask you to turn to the person next to you and discuss the topic or answer a question.

- **Ongoing small classroom groups.** Usually, these groups work together for a significant part of the semester, and your instructor may assign roles to members of the group such as recorder, facilitator, editor, and spokesperson. Often, the roles will rotate, so everyone has a chance to try out each job. Your instructor may give you a job description for each role or train the class in the tasks for each role.

- **Task groups.** These groups are formed to write a report, complete a project, or do some other task together. These groups meet several times, often outside of class. The products of these groups are usually graded, and your instructor will often require members to rate each other on their performance.

- **Peer editing groups.** When you have completed a draft of an essay or other text, your instructor may ask you to exchange papers in pairs or within small groups. You will be asked to read your classmate's paper carefully and make comments, either on a peer editing form or on the paper itself. Likewise, your classmate will read and make comments on your paper. Then, when your paper is returned, you can make revisions based on your classmate's comments.

An added benefit to the use of collaborative groups in writing classes is that students can help each other figure out what the ongoing conversation is for a particular topic or issue before writing about it. Also, groups provide a forum where students can practice making comments that are part of that conversation.

Case-Study: Team Work Success

By Justin McCoy

Self-Knowledge Strategies for Project Team Success

Context: *This section begins by explaining how the strategy of self-knowledge optimizes project team success. Then what follows is a description of how Gretchen Rubin's 4 Tendencies Framework, a practical self-knowledge strategy linked to expectations and habit development, functions as a precursor to project team assignments. Included in this content is a 4 Tendencies personal engagement activity to help you better understand yourself and others prior to launching your team project.*

The Value of Self-Knowledge

Beyond mastering the logistics of tackling shared work, you may feel most ill-equipped for one unwelcome hurdle of working on a project team in particular: navigating diverse personalities. You'll likely work with people who are very different from you in both your education and professional careers. How you react to these differences could make or break your team's—and therefore your—success.

Below are scenarios you might've experienced during a team project that stem from personality differences. If you've never worked on a project team before, then you can anticipate that such issues might arise.

- You're frustrated by others' inability to follow rules or fulfill deliverables they've committed to in a timely manner.

- You find it challenging to empathize with your project team members and their varied approaches to the assignment at hand.

- Unique communication styles and email etiquette, in addition to different preferred mediums for group communication, cause miscommunication and confusion within the team network.

- You struggle to manage your own behavior and stay organized because of a difficult member of your group who you feel consistently impedes progress.

These differences can be serious sources of conflict that risk thwarting project team success. Up to this point, your kneejerk response to engaging with diverse personalities you don't understand may have been a negative one.

But inadvertently fueling the conflict will only exacerbate team discord and put your project in peril.

So what are you to do if you find someone's personality contrary or frustrating? Since you can't change other people, it's worthwhile instead to focus on how you can manage your own responses to other people, even those you find challenging. In her book *Better Than Before*, a compilation of concrete strategies for habit development, Gretchen Rubin prescribes self-knowledge strategies to help understand yourself and others better. For Rubin, self-knowledge doesn't require you to change what you're doing, but to learn to see yourself accurately. By understanding what works for you (because what works for you doesn't work for others), you strengthen good habits and break bad ones. The potential to act on understandings of who you are and gain insights on how others might be different can be a powerful force for shaping behaviors linked to mitigating conflict on a team.

Self-Knowledge Strategies

Two accessible key strategies that offer a lot of potential for project team development include taking personality quizzes and journaling. A lot of literature has been produced on these topics, including not only original theories and books on personality frameworks and journaling but also research studies assessing the utility and benefits linked to each.

Disclaimer alert: the first strategy—taking personality quizzes—might seem counterintuitive because it relies on categorization, a potentially confining process. Although the way you understand the world is through some level of mediated categorization (e.g., the process of capturing demographics as well as the way you choose to represent yourself to the outside world), history warns that categorization can be detrimental to identity. For instance, at one time, it was the prevailing cultural belief that marginalized categories such as enslaved people were inherently inferior to those in power. This belief was used to justify inequality. The self-knowledge strategies prescribed in this section, however, function as a framework for navigating social activity: to see your behaviors more clearly and to engage with whether or not various personality frameworks accurately confirm aspects of your personality.

The landscape of personality quizzes is vast. Self-knowledge through personality assessments such as Myers-Briggs and Strengths Finders is a mainstay in the professional world. Many organizations facilitate these personal engagement activities as part of their corporate culture, or the ethos of a company, through both formal and informal professional development workshops. These sessions might focus on a wide range of topics: personality assessments, generation studies, multi-cultural and diversity training, and other team-building exercises. The office where you'll work will likely have some form of professional development because it contributes not only to the success of the company but also to employee's sense of value and purpose within the company.

Regarding journaling, it's almost too good to be true that something so easy can be so beneficial. And, to be clear, there's no right way to journal; for instance, you can type your thoughts on a computer in lieu of handwriting. And don't worry about the pressure to maintain a fancy journal with nice penmanship and artistic doodles. Although the possibilities are endless when it comes to journaling, you can just keep it simple. Scribbling down your thoughts on a legal pad or old notebook will do. Studies show that journaling can even be beneficial for managing anxiety; many therapists and counselors make use of this simple yet effective strategy.

Here are some sample journal entries to help know yourself better:

1. Recount a personal memory that prompted greater understanding about yourself or the world.

2. What did you enjoy doing when you were a kid? How might this activity translate to a career that interests you in adulthood?

3. What is your philosophy on food and exercise? How does this philosophy align with or depart from your weekly routine?

4. Write about something that's bothering you in your work or personal psyche today (e.g., intrusive thoughts or memories, a toxic friend, a missed deadline, anxiety over an upcoming event or assignment, a nagging task, a dormant goal or friendship, etc.). After engaging with your negative thoughts, self-soothe by correcting assumptions, posing questions, cutting yourself some slack, being kind to yourself, and/or acknowledging progress.

While you're at it, you might consider extending your self-knowledge practices to include taking the quiz on *Pottermore.com* to determine your Hogwarts house and to research your zodiac and horoscope. While these examples may seem less efficacious and evidence based, they can still provide us with attributes that we can weigh against how we see ourselves. And you could even engage others in a discussion of confirming or denying attributes of your quiz results. Either way, reflection is still happening, and bringing others into that reflection process promotes further reflection and builds community. I, for example, definitely identify with being a Capricorn and, after a lengthy period of delusion, a Slytherin. Now I embrace those aspects of my personality—the good parts, at least.

Harnessing the power of self-knowledge is immensely beneficial to project team harmony. In practice, self-knowledge strategies not only prompt reflection and observation about who you are and how you respond to the world but also enhance your self-command when engaging with others.

Writer Snapshots

What's the value of exploring a self-identification strategy such as taking a personality quiz, reflecting in a journal, or even researching a horoscope?

Judy Young

"Self-identification can help us to learn more about ourselves—to see the motivations behind our behaviors so that we can try to modify them when it seems helpful.

Written reflections, such as in a journal, are also a way to learn more about ourselves, as they can shed light on motivations generally and give us clues to what influences our personal vicissitudes. Journaling, in my experience, can even highlight specific or current issues that require our attention but that might otherwise evade identification in the press of day-to-day activities.

Probably the best way to use these tools is all together, to create a full picture of the individual and maybe clues to the need for change or to promote cultivation of effective habits or behaviors. I have my doubts about the effectiveness of horoscope research, but if it helps, it helps. I can't argue—nor would I wish to—with success."

•••

"People claim to know themselves based on the connection with others and with themselves, but taking a
personality quiz can help people become more well-
rounded. These personality quizzes do not define
who people are, but open the doors to personal improvement. When someone realizes how they meet
outer and inner expectations, for example, it is easier
to set and accomplish goals.

Sarah Hamilton

There is also an external benefit. There are multiple
tests giving various perspectives of personalities, and by taking these quizzes,
people can learn how to interact with other people. Collaboration is necessary
for occupations, and it is a great tool to have among friends and family. Knowing oneself and knowing how to interact with others is a valuable skill, so it is
worthwhile for people to open their minds to personality assessments."

• • •

Breya Marolt

"I dive into personality quizzes on occasion, but I
mostly enjoy looking at my horoscope. Self-identification strategies allow me to know myself and
those around me better. I look at horoscopes of
those close to me on an almost regular basis and
the first time I meet a new person. I like to see if the
people around me really do fit their sign, and in my
experience, they usually do. It can be insightful to see yourself written down
on paper. Whether it be the good or bad, it's important to know who you are as
a person and how you affect those around you. You can take that information
and decide from there on how you want to live your life or change yourself for
the better."

• • •

"I think taking an identity quiz can really help you
characterize what type of person you are. Such
activities help you learn so much more about
yourself and may give you some insight into why
you act and think the way you do.

You may value some of the things that are being said because they may make your life less

Abbie Huff

difficult. They may show you things about yourself that you didn't even know, and you may end up trying or doing new things that you love—or feeling empowered for embracing the things you love now."

•••

Gretchen Rubin's 4 Tendencies Framework: Are You an Upholder, an Obliger, a Questioner, or a Rebel?

Have you ever wondered why some people have little trouble fulfilling both personal resolutions and professional goals? Or why others struggle to fulfill inner commitments they aspire for themselves, yet these folks have no trouble meeting work deadlines from a boss? Or perhaps you or someone else you know questions expectations as arbitrary until it makes logical sense to do them. You may have even observed those who resist all expectations, doing only what they want to do. These varied responses make up the distinct Tendencies in Gretchen Rubin's 4 Tendencies Framework, which Rubin developed a quiz for and discusses at length on her podcast *Happier with Gretchen Rubin* and in her most recent *New York Times* bestselling book, *The Four Tendencies Framework*.

Instead of attempting to account for broad aspects of personality, Rubin's personality framework focuses on how you respond to expectations: inner expectations such as a New Year's resolution and outer expectations such as a work deadline from a boss. For Rubin, understanding your tendency not only helps you strengthen habits through self-knowledge but also makes you more empathetic to tendencies different from your own. For instance, if you know you are sending an email to a Questioner, then you can optimize your chances of getting what you need from the Questioner by helping him or her understand why the request is important. Questioners, as you'll learn in this section, will resist an outer expectation until the "why" they crave makes logical sense.

Here are Rubin's defining features for each of the 4 Tendencies, along with mantras from her post-quiz detailed reports illustrating each Tendency's meaning.

- Upholder—meets outer and inner expectations

  "I do what others expect of me—and what I expect from myself."

- Obliger—meets outer expectations and resists inner expectations

"I do what I have to do. I don't want to let others down, but I may let myself down."

■ Questioner—resists outer expectations and meets inner expectations

"I do what I think is best, according to my judgment. If it doesn't make sense, I don't do it."

■ Rebel—resists outer and inner expectations

"I do what I want, in my own way. If you try to make me do something— even if I try to make myself do something—I'm less likely to do it."

What follows in this section is a look at the traits and striking patterns of each Tendency, all of which are highlights gleaned from Rubin's work. Keep in mind that there is no hierarchy of the Tendencies, meaning that Rubin doesn't consider one Tendency any better than another. Each Tendency has its own strengths and weaknesses. Do you identify with any of these Tendencies? Take the quiz linked at the end of this section to discover your Tendency.

Upholder

According to Rubin, Upholders readily meet both outer and inner expectations alike with little trouble. These people are the Hermione Grangers of the world. They are self-directed rule followers who strive not to let down others or themselves. In the absence of rules, they look for the rules beyond the rules to apply structure where there is none. Working well in environments where expectations and protocols are clearly defined, Upholders embrace discipline, as Rubin often points out in her work, as their freedom.

When trying to strengthen a habit linked to a personal or professional goal, Upholders are responsive to the strategies of clarity, scheduling, and monitoring, three habit strategies Rubin discusses in her book *Better Than Before*. This means that if an Upholder can articulate and clarify a goal, put it on the calendar, and measure and monitor progress, then he or she will successfully fulfill that task.

Sounds good to be an Upholder, right? Well, this Tendency, like the others, is not without its weaknesses. For instance, Upholders may be impatient and judgmental toward the other Tendencies because of their inability to "just do things" readily. Because Upholders don't require outer accountability in their response to expectations, they aren't inclined to create accountability for others, so it makes sense that Upholders are reluctant to delegate work—

even when they probably should. Upholders may also blindly follow rules to a fault simply because they are established rules or have become a mainstay in an Upholder's routine. In addition, Upholders are terrified of failure and are very hard on themselves when they perceive they've failed or fallen short of perfection.

What's more is that others may perceive Upholders as not agreeable and a killjoy because of Upholders' obligation to expectations. Upholders may struggle to omit seemingly pointless expectations from their to-do list, exhausting not only others but also themselves. Rubin warns that this Upholder behavior can lead to "tightening," a striking pattern that hits Upholders when they're anxious over inner and outer expectations being off balance.

Obliger

If you identify with being a "people-pleaser" yet lack the self-motivation to keep a New Year's resolution or sustain personal goals you set for yourself, then you probably fall into the Obliger category. Additionally, you might be in the Obliger camp if you often talk about your need for self-care because you're mournful over attending to others and neglecting yourself. Obligers, Rubin explains, may mistake themselves for Upholders since both Tendencies share a commitment to fulfilling outer expectations. But, unlike Upholders, Obligers struggle to meet inner expectations because Obligers wrestle with the self-preservation required to attend to their personal goals. For instance, if you're an Obliger who aspires to launch and sustain a workout routine, you may be setting yourself up for failure if you exercise alone because, characteristic of your Tendency, you respond readily to outer accountability, not inner commitment alone. Similarly, if you're an Obliger who used to be in an athletics program in high school, such as soccer, football, volleyball, tennis, baseball, etc., you may have sustained physical activity more easily than you do now if you currently don't have a team structure in which others rely on you and a coach holds you accountable.

If this sounds like you, never fear: Rubin prescribes an easy solution. Since Obligers prioritize outer expectations over inner expectations, Obligers should simply attribute outer accountability to their inner commitments. Through this process, Obligers' inner expectations become outer expectations. In the example of the fitness goal above, instead of attempting to sustain a solo workout routine, it could be more worthwhile for an Obliger to join a running group, hire a trainer, take a class, or employ another outer accountability measure that he or she will be receptive to.

But let's not overlook Obligers' strengths, which are numerous: they make good leaders on a team when others depend on them; they are cooperative team players all around; they are friendly, accommodating, and likeable; and they are reliable and accountable to others.

Plot twist: sometimes Obligers rebel against the outer expectations they typically so readily respond to. No, this doesn't put them in the Rebel category, which comes later in this section. Rubin calls this striking pattern the dreaded Obliger Rebellion. This phenomenon occurs when the weight of outer expectations becomes too burdensome for Obligers. Essentially, this striking pattern is akin to burnout, something Obligers are vulnerable to because of anxiety over saying "no" to others and imposing boundaries.

Questioner

Do you love data and information? Would you make a good verbal interrogator? Do you research a product extensively to ensure you make an informed decision before purchasing? Does your incline to question and dive deep into topics impede your progress or suspend decision-making? Has a boss or teacher ever mistaken your questions as challenging authority, even though you simply want to understand why you're being asked to complete a school or work task? Do you question the legitimacy and usefulness of the 4 Tendencies quiz? Did you take the quiz multiple times and get different results? If so, then you're likely a Questioner. If you're not a Questioner, then maybe you've been frustrated by one before: they need to know the "why" about everything, yet don't like to be questioned themselves.

But Questioners wouldn't have it any other way. They resist outer expectations but readily meet inner expectations. Through the process of questioning and researching, doing only the things that make sense for them to do, outer expectations become inner expectations for a Questioner.

This Tendency has some useful strengths that the other Tendencies might consider emulating. Having a Questioner on your team, for instance, can help you reconsider the validity of accepted norms. More specifically, Rubin proposes that Upholders and Questioners make good partners because the Questioner may help the Upholder see that certain rules are arbitrary and that some items on the Upholder's to-do list are not priority and could be scratched out.

However, according to Rubin, the strengths of a Tendency are also the weaknesses. If something doesn't make logical sense to a Questioner, then he or she won't do it. Likewise, if a Questioner doesn't respect the authority of others—a doctor or teacher, for example—then the Questioner isn't going to listen to these folks. Although ensuring credibility of those around you can be a good thing, Questioners risk appearing contrarian at times, as if they are challenging authority. Additionally, the rabbit hole of research pursued by a Questioner could result in "analysis paralysis," a striking pattern Rubin diagnoses in Questioners. If you're a Questioner, then you may be no stranger to this phenomenon, which could leave you feeling like your researched ideas are more aplenty than your actual decisions.

Rebel

Dun, dun, dun: make way for the Rebel, the resister of both outer and inner expectations. If you consider yourself spontaneous, unconventional, creative, and restless and resistant to "settling down," then you're squarely in the Rebel category. Rubin discerns from her surveyed results and research that the Rebel Tendency is the smallest category, meaning that the fewest people fall into this camp. Interestingly though, Rubin also observes that Rebels make up the bulk of the military and police force, environments that provide structure for the Rebel to push back against as well as opportunities to take risks.

Identity-driven independent thinkers, Rebels usually know they're Rebels and can do anything they want to do. But Rubin is clear that the choice must be theirs. For this reason, they may appear uncooperative and inconsiderate in both their career and relationships. For example, an Upholder would perceive a Rebel who thinks he or she is immune to the rules everyone else must follow as quite unsavory, to say the least. Rebels struggle with routine and planning, and many of the habit-strengthening strategies Rubin prescribes for the other Tendencies, such as scheduling and monitoring, do not work for the Rebel.

So what are you to do if you find yourself stuck on a team project with a Rebel? Because Rebels can do anything they want to do but do the opposite of what they're told, they can be easily manipulated. That is, you can say to a Rebel, "you're not going to do that long run tomorrow," then the Rebel will likely show up motivated to prove you wrong. Perhaps a more ethical and professional strategy Rubin recommends, though, is to present consequences as options to the Rebel. This means that instead of telling a Rebel who is chronically late that he or she must be present tomorrow at 9 a.m. for the team meeting, you could present encouraging options: 1) "if you attend the meeting tomorrow, our coworkers and I will be really energized by your creative ideas and unique perspective; 2) "if you aren't at the meeting tomorrow, the boss will have to talk to you about company policy and ruin your day, and the team will miss out on your stellar ideas."

Although one of Rubin's popular mantras includes the sentiment "you can manage yourself, but not others," the Rebel Tendency seems to be an exception: communicating with a Rebel might demand that the other Tendencies attempt to manage the Rebel. Rubin may not agree with this last point though, so you be the judge.

FYIs

Below are two quick FYIs you might be wondering:

1. I, the author of this section's content, am an Upholder. Therefore, you may have interpreted some subtle or not-so-subtle biases in my descriptions of the Tendencies. Although I'd make the case that these descriptions align with Rubin's characterizations of the Tendencies, I'll admit that Upholders have a challenging time relating to the other Tendencies, especially the Rebels. If you take issue with the way that your Tendency was represented, then this could make good fodder for discussion in your composition class. Either way, I can attest that since I've learned about the Four Tendencies, I've become more empathetic to people who respond to expectations differently than I. My hope is that the Four Tendencies Framework will help you, as Rubin intends, to know yourself better and understand others better, skills that will serve you well as you navigate working with others throughout your educational and professional career.

2. Many people presume that you can change your Tendency or that you're a combination of a couple of Tendencies. However, Rubin theorizes that your Tendency is "hardwired," an idea that sounds more controversial than it is. For Rubin, your Tendency characterizes your natural inclines and behavior patterns, so why spend all your time trying to change your kneejerk reaction to expectations when you can simply accept it as a reality of your behavior so that you can rewire your environment to fulfill inner and outer expectations? For example, Obligers often lament that they want to be Upholders, but if you're an Obliger—just like any of the other Tendencies—you can achieve both inner and outer expectations by knowing yourself better. In the case of the Obliger, specifically, an

Obliger must attribute outer accountability to his or her expectations to achiever personal and professional goals.

Resources

Below are resources for Rubin's work you might consider exploring if you'd like to know more about the 4 Tendencies Framework and the content mentioned in this section:

- The book *The Four Tendencies*
- The book *Better Than Before*
- The podcast *Happier with Gretchen Rubin*
- Post-Quiz Detailed Reports
- *gretchenrubin.com*

Self-Knowledge Activity

1. Take Gretchen Rubin's 4 Tendencies Quiz at this URL: https://www.surveygizmo.com/s3/3706759/Gretchen-Rubin-s-Quiz-The-Four-Tendencies.

2. Review the post-quiz detailed report you'll gain access to following the quiz.

3. Summarize your Tendency, including strengths and weaknesses, in a written reflection. Explain whether or not you identify with your results and in what ways. Include real-life examples.

4. Get in same-Tendency groups (e.g., an Upholder group, an Obliger group, a Questioner group, and a Rebel group) and discuss how you confirm or depart from your Tendency result.

5. Get in mixed-Tendency groups (e.g., groups made up of three to four different Tendencies) and compare real-life examples of how you respond to inner and outer expectations.

Writer Snapshots
What is your Tendency? Do you identify with this result?

Rustian Phelps

"I'm a Questioner. According to the results of my Tendencies test, I try to meet my own expectations, but not necessarily the expectations of others. When asked to do something, I usually want justification for doing it and assurance of the efficacy of such a project.

I do identify strongly with my Tendency, but only after spending several weeks comparing my behaviors to the qualities outlined in my report. I like being a Questioner because my having questioned and researched everything gives me confidence in my day-to-day decision-making.

On the other hand, the tendency to question can be a burden. I often find I have what Rubin calls "analysis paralysis," an inability to make decisions without copious amounts of data. I often feel that I don't have enough information to make an informed decision, a personal quirk that sometimes leaves me feeling profoundly unprepared even when I might actually be over-prepared. I often fall into a trap of thinking I have to know everything there is to know about a topic—an impossible prospect—before I can feel I know enough. When I went in to orally defend my comprehensive exams, I had so much to say that I couldn't get my thoughts out coherently. Then I questioned whether my committee passed me because my work was good or because they were obliging me.

The good news is that others know I am the way I am, and they come to me for advice or brainstorming sessions. I'm proud and honored by their confidence in me. When I first read my report, I thought calling someone a Questioner was perhaps just another way of saying that person is a pain in the neck, and maybe that assessment is correct to some extent, but I think being a Questioner also makes me intellectually curious and ethically thoughtful. If I could change my Tendency, I wouldn't; being a Questioner is a good thing."

● ● ●

"I am classified as an Upholder, which means I meet inner and outer expectations alike. I confirm my result primarily in that I try to avoid letting people down and fear making mistakes.

I'm also self-directed and have little trouble meeting commitments to myself such as my inner expectation to work out and be healthy.

Eric Vinke

Additionally, I identify with this Tendency because I hate saying 'no' to people and that can be good and bad because I need to be able to adjust my schedule for more people and not just myself!"

• • •

"I am an Obliger, meaning I thrive on meeting outer expectations while neglecting to meet inner expectations. Deadlines, daily goals, helping others, a schedule: all of these contribute to my outer expectations. My ability to readily meet outer expectations makes me a dependable person to others, a trait which stimulates my Obliger Tendency. However, such a dependence on meeting outer expectations results in my neglecting my personal goals. Forming habits such as eating healthy, exercising daily, or perfecting a skincare routine is extremely difficult for me. And, since Obligers have a difficult time saying 'no'

Kara Griffith

to people, we are prone to Obliger Rebellions. These rebellions may result in our unfriending people who have abused our Obliger privileges, or we may rebel in symbolic ways, such as getting a drastically new haircut.

I identify with all aspects of my Tendency, especially the need to set daily goals for myself. I also find forming habits to be extremely difficult, and in time I have realized that I need to make inner expectations, such as working out, an outer expectation in order to meet a goal."

• • •

"The Tendency I received was Rebel. Basically, a Rebel does not like to be told what to do or even be expected to do something. Rebels want to do whatever they want to do whenever they want to do it. In fact, we Rebels will often do the opposite of what others expect of us because we resist expectations.

De'Asia Lewis

I do identify with being a Rebel in many ways. For instance, if I intend to clean my room when I get home from class, I won't do it if my mom tells me to. I feel that I can do anything that I want to do, but it has to be my choice.

However, as a Rebel, I am creative, unconventional, and an independent thinker."

• • •

"According to Gretchen Rubin's quiz, I am a Questioner. This means I basically question all expectations, and respond to an expectation only if I conclude that it makes sense. Gretchen Rubin says Questioners tend to take direction only from people they respect. Basically they ask 'why?' and won't accept the answers until they get all the facts.

Amber Hubbard

I agree with basically every aspect of the Questioner Tendency. I have always asked questions since I was a baby, a trait I inherited from my mom. My grandmother, my mom's mom, has said we will basically argue with a stop sign until we understand why. I have learned over the years not to question as much as I'm inclined to, mainly so that I don't annoy people too much with my incessant questioning. I love to learn and strategize plans just like a Questioner."

• • •

Ryan McCourt

"My dominant tendency is Obliger. The Obliger is the one who meets outside expectations but has trouble meeting inner expectations. In order for Obligers to meet inner expectations, they must connect inner aspirations to outer accountability.

While I certainly do identify with nearly every aspect of the Obliger tendency, it is almost frustrating for me to admit it. Many of the common problems that Obligers face are problems that I have been struggling with for my entire life, and it is frustrating to see them explained so simply. Going forward, I will use what I have learned when tackling new goals."

• • •

"I am an Obliger. Obligers are selfless people-pleasers, thinking of others before themselves. They have problems keeping habits, and they have to be pushed and encouraged to do something for themselves. There are some strengths in being an Obliger; for instance, people go to you for advice because you care. Obligers are also pretty funny if I say so myself, and it feels great to be selfless. But there are weaknesses such as people taking advantage of you. It's difficult for Obligers to say 'no,' and we can be pretty emotional and possibly resentful because of that trait.

Leilanie Monrouzeau

In a way, being an Obliger describes me, but not fully. Although I am selfless and think of others before myself, I keep habits pretty easily. I don't need someone to encourage me every time I feel down, and I usually cut people off when I feel that I'm being taken advantage of. I would say I've learned to adopt the useful traits of other Tendencies: I question a lot when it comes to finding proof, and I like to have detailed information; sometimes, I like to bend the rules and not always do what people want me to do."

• • •

"My result from the quiz labeled me as a Questioner. I absolutely identify with this. I'm able to cope with changing situations by questioning the cause and effect of my expectations. By coming to a conclusion that makes sense to me, I'm able to follow new goals I set for myself.

Faith Green

At times, though, my constant questions may annoy people and are exhausting even to myself. I have trouble writing papers sometimes because there is so much information to analyze that I can't come to a solid conclusion. I feel like I abandon an argument more than I actually propose one. There's always a "but" or "what if" that remains in my mind long after the paper is turned in, making me feel like I've failed no matter what grade I get back."

• • •

Project Team Development

Context: *This section includes content on the nature of shared work, including the benefits and pitfalls of working on project teams. The purpose of this content is to help you mitigate conflict when tackling your next group project in not only your college courses but also in the workforce beyond the classroom.*

The Potential Pitfalls of Working on a Project Team

Let's cut to the chase: shared work, variously called group work or team projects, can be very controversial. You've likely had to complete a team project as a requirement for a course at some point in your education. This past experience no doubt informs your current feelings toward these types of assignments. A team project can test your patience, invoke feelings of peril over your grade, and make you question the value of teamwork altogether. Perhaps you can even relate to one or more of the following pitfalls when tackling shared work:

- You and your teammates struggled to define and delegate various roles on your team.

- One or more of your teammates were consistently unavailable to meet outside of class.

- You had to pull up the slack of your unmotivated team members to complete the project.

- One or more of your teammates wouldn't be cooperative when communicating with teammates either face to face or electronically.

- You found a teammate's personality to be insufferable, either because of his or her rebellious disposition, negativity, or peculiar need to shine the brightest among the group members.

- When generating ideas, you and your teammates can't seem to agree or come to a consensus.

- The project was not successful, and the blame was pinned on you.

And the list of project team woes could go on. Although some of us may enjoy a team-oriented atmosphere, others may be distrusting of teammates' abilities as well as their commitment to follow through. Perhaps working alone has served you well up till this point because you're a firm believer in the well-known mantra "if you want something done right, you have to do it yourself." Although this outlook may be useful when mustering up the will to persevere through an arduous task, the unfortunate truth is that not being a team player could create more unnecessary work for you and negatively impact your employment potential in your career.

By discussing the drawbacks of working on a project team, you can begin to anticipate conflict before it arises and equip yourself with strategies for resolving team discord and dysfunction. In addition, brainstorming all the potential ways a team project could be unsuccessful will help you come to terms with the realities of shared work and shift your perspective in a way that creates opportunities for practicing real-world, professional skills.

The Benefits of Working on a Project Team

So, if we can all conjure up a horror story of working with others, how could anyone defend shared work? Well, in fact, working with others is the reality of the world. You'll be hard pressed to find a job where working with others never happens. After you graduate, you'll most likely work in an office where you encounter people every day, whether or not you enjoy their company. You may even have to complete important work tasks with others on an official project team. Either directly or indirectly, you'll most likely be participating in shared work to some extent. Reframing shared work as preparation for employment in "the real world" can help us begin to see the value in working on a project team—and in practicing teamwork skills in college prior to launching a career.

Now let's consider additional reasons why project teams might be beneficial. For instance, working with others can provide you with a support group, a potential source of encouragement when presented with a big project. Beyond sharing the burden of the workload, project teams provide opportunities to practice various skills useful for curating our identities as professionals. Below are just a few of these skills, along with an action-driven description of each.

- **Connection:** Express empathy for other team members, reserving judgment and not putting too much stock in first impressions.

- **Inclusion:** Give your team members' opportunities to articulate their ideas. Listening to diverse input may shift your perspective or ignite your own new ideas.

- **Identification of Strengths and Weaknesses:** Identify all team members' individual strengths and weaknesses in addition to gaging their interests regarding what team roles they'd like to explore. Understanding how you and your team members can best contribute to the team effort will have a positive impact on your team's performance and ultimate success.

- **Role Delegation:** Once you've identified individual strengths and weaknesses, define and assign various roles on your team. If one or more roles require contributions from multiple team members, then assign a "team lead" who takes ownership of the role by being responsible for coordinating with other team members to complete the action items linked to the role.

- **Collaboration:** Collaborate to transform knowledge and develop an informative and engaging product. Keep an open mind when working with others so that you don't overlook potential strengths or ideas that could be harnessed for the benefit of the team project.

- **Time Management:** Exchange contact information, set expectations for how you'll communicate throughout the production process, and develop a timeline that reflects the team's meeting schedule as well as project milestones such as draft deadlines, deliverables, and project stages. A project timeline will help your team streamline efficiency by keeping everyone on the pathway to success.

■   **Effective Communication:** Communicate to optimize the likelihood that you'll receive a positive response from others. For example, when persuading others of your ideas and scheduling times to meet outside of class, express your requests in a logical, kind, and fair way. In addition, make an effort to express understanding when conflict arises.

■   **Professionalism:** Hone your professional prowess by maintaining a demeanor that is cooperative, enthusiastic, and helpful, in addition to modeling behavior that is in the best interest of the team. This disposition will help ensure you are fulfilling commitments and expectations set by your team.

Executing these skills will not only optimize success for your team but also prepare you for the professional world. Pursuing and embracing teamwork opportunities as valuable learning experiences will soften the jolt of shared work and collaboration when you launch your career.

Writer Snapshots

What are the benefits and potential pitfalls of working with others on a project team?

Daylin Beauchamp

"Team projects can be very fun and successful; however, they can also be a disaster. Working on a team project can be challenging because you have to be mindful of others' opinions and beliefs while also presenting and clarifying your own. Scheduling time for meetings is also a difficult task because everyone has their own busy life with too many things to do, but the assignment still needs to get done. The major upside of working on a team is that you can divvy up the work, and if a task is difficult and you're unsure how to proceed, you have more brains than one to solve the problem. Depending on the project and your team members' willingness to communicate and be professional, the team project could go smoothly or spiral into chaos."

● ● ●

"There are many good and bad things to be considered when approaching a team project. One good thing about working on a team is that you do not have to do everything by yourself. Instead, you can expect to share the workload with others. Additionally, team members can exchange ideas to enhance creativity and progress. Another major benefit is that you'll learn from other people's points of view. The potential dark side of working on a project team is that a team member may not be putting forth enough effort; also, working through scheduling conflicts can be grueling. But these issues can be remedied if team members are willing to invest in their shared goal."

Dianni Minelli

• • •

Jamar Gaskins

"Working with others can be very beneficial at times, and at other times, it can be a bit stressful. The benefits include more diverse input and creativity, more eyes to recognize an error, and more people to split the workload with. However, the dreaded conflict that might arise could be that team members get lazy and don't follow through on their commitments, differing opinions could lead to incessant arguing or bickering, or you may constantly having to step in and manage the quality of a team member's contribution."

• • •

Why Study Rhetoric?

Rhetoric, or persuasive communication, happens all around us every day, in conversation at the grocery store, in blogs, on television, and in the classroom. We Americans constantly air our opinions about almost everything. Sometimes it is to convince others to share our opinions, and sometimes the reason is to engage in a dialogue that will help us understand the world around us, and sometimes it is to persuade others to action.

Argument is essential to human interaction and to society, for it is through the interplay of ideas in argument that we discover answers to problems, try out new ideas, shape scientific experiments, communicate with family members, recruit others to join a team, and work out any of the multitude of human interactions essential for society to function. When issues are complex, arguments do not result in immediate persuasion of the audience; rather, argument is part of an ongoing conversation between concerned parties who seek resolution, rather than speedy answers.

Rhetoric provides a useful framework for looking at the world, as well as for evaluating and initiating communications. In the modern world, writing and communicating persuasively is a necessary skill. Those who can present effective arguments in writing are, in the business world, often the ones who are promoted. In addition, those who are able to evaluate the arguments presented to them, whether by politicians, advertisers, or even family members, are less likely to be swayed by logical fallacies or ill-supported research.

Also, writing rhetorically is a tool with sometimes surprising uses. Research shows that we are more likely to remember material we have written about rather than simply memorized. Also, through the process of writing, writers often find that they initiate ideas and connections between ideas that they might not otherwise have found. Thus, writing may lead to new discoveries.

Rhetoric is a part of our everyday lives. When we're in a conversation with someone, we use rhetoric on a conscious or subconscious level. If you go to class wearing the T-shirt of your favorite musician or band, you're ultimately sending a rhetorical message identifying yourself as a fan of that artist or group.

If you've ever written a profile on a dating site, you've used rhetorical principles to convince an audience of potential partners to contact you or to write you back if you have chosen to make the first contact. You build *ethos* by talking about yourself in order to build credibility among potential partners, and you establish *pathos* when you talk about an interest that is shared by a potential mate.

Being able to use the tools of rhetoric effectively gives you the power to control your communication—both incoming and outgoing—and to affect your environment in a positive way.

Collaborate

Activity 1.8 • How Do You Use Rhetoric?

In your small group, make a list of five ways that you use rhetoric in your everyday lives. Then, create a list of five ways studying rhetoric could make a difference in your lives. As a class, compare the lists.

Rhetorical Arguments Stand the Test of Time

Abraham Lincoln's Gettysburg Address is the short speech that the president delivered at the site of the Battle of Gettysburg where, four months previously, the Union Army defeated Confederate forces. His was not the only talk that day at the dedication of the Soldiers' National Cemetery, but it is the only one remembered. In just over two minutes, he was able to reframe the Civil War not just as a victory for the North but as a "new birth of freedom" for all Americans. Now, following the 150th anniversary of the Civil War, is a good time to remember Lincoln's rhetoric—in terms of both the content and the style of his speech.

Reading 1.4

Text of the Gettysburg Address

by Abraham Lincoln

Four score and seven years ago, our fathers brought forth on this continent, a new nation, conceived in Liberty and dedicated to the proposition that all men are created equal.

Though no actual recording exists of Abraham Lincoln giving the speech, you can listen to others reading it aloud if you search on the internet for "recording of Gettysburg Address." Listen to the speech, noting the phrase "Four score and seven years ago," which is so famous that Americans know instantly, when it is quoted by orators or writers, that it is a reference to Lincoln. Consider what arguments the president makes in his speech. Think about their relevance today.

Now we are engaged in a great civil war, testing whether that nation, or any nation so conceived and so dedicated, can long endure. We are met on a great battlefield of that war. We have come to dedicate a portion of that field, as a final resting place for those who here gave their lives that that nation might live. It is altogether fitting and proper that we should do this.

But, in a larger sense, we cannot dedicate—we cannot consecrate—we cannot hallow—this ground. The brave men, living and dead, who struggled here, have consecrated it, far above our poor power to add or detract. The world will little note, nor long remember what we say here, but it can never forget what they did here. It is for us the living, rather, to be dedicated here to the unfinished work which they who fought here have thus far so nobly advanced. It is rather for us to be here dedicated to the great task remaining before us—that from these honored dead we take increased devotion to that cause for which they gave the last full measure of devotion—that we here highly resolve that these dead shall not have died in vain—that this nation, under God, shall have a new birth of freedom—and that government of the people, by the people, for the people, shall not perish from the earth.

Activity 1.9 • Paraphrase the Gettysburg Address

Rephrase each sentence of the Gettysburg Address in your own words, putting it in twenty-first century wording rather than Lincoln's ceremonial, nineteenth-century phrasing. In a paraphrase, the text does not become shorter; it is recreated in different words. This is a useful technique in helping you understand a text. It is also helpful when you are writing an analysis of a text because you can use your paraphrase rather than long, block quotes. Remember, though, when you are writing an essay, you must cite a paraphrase in the text and also include it in your list of references.

Activity 1.10 • Comment on Your Classmate's Paraphrase of the Gettysburg Address

In your small group, trade your paraphrase of the Gettysburg Address with the paraphrase of the person next to you. Read through the document carefully, looking for how well your partner paraphrased, rather than commented on, Lincoln's words. Mark each place where a comment or analysis appears. Give the paper back to the author for revision, if needed.

Why might it be useful to paraphrase a document rather than analyze or comment on it?

Respond to Visual Rhetoric

To the ancient Greeks and Romans, rhetoric largely involved verbal skills—the use of words to persuade an audience. But rhetoricians were also aware that how something was said was sometimes as important as what was said, so they also studied the use of visual cues such as gestures and tone of voice to deliver oral arguments. Today, concern with gestures and other visual cues used to persuade an audience is encompassed in visual rhetoric, which could be defined as the use of images or other visual elements as argument.

Supreme Court Justice Ruth Bader Ginsburg, for example, wears different jabots, or collars, with her black robe to visually communicate her opinion of different court decisions. In this, she differs from the other justices who tend to wear similar collars, no matter their stance on a court ruling.

In an interview with Katie Couric, Justice Ginsburg decoded her jabots. She wears a studded black velvet collar when she issues a dissenting opinion about a court ruling. She wears her favorite, a white beaded jabot from South Africa, when she is not trying to send a message. When she wants to signal her agreement with the majority court opinion, she wears a beaded gold lace jabot.

As a student, you can train yourself to be aware of visual clues expressed in clothing choices such as messages on T-shirts, colors of men's ties, or women's preferences of jeans or dresses.

Ruth Bader Ginsburg's dissent jabot.

The favorite jabot from Cape Town, South Africa.

The majority opinion collar.

ollaborate

Activity 1.11 • Decoding Clothing Choices as Visual Rhetoric

In a small group, review these discussion questions in consideration of Supreme Court Justice Ruth Bader Ginsburg's choice of jabots or collars.

1. Search the internet using the keywords "Ruth Bader Ginsburg jabot." What other jabots do you find? What do you think of her choices to indicate her agreement or dissent with the court decision on a case?

2. Discuss your own clothing choices in your small group. Are you making a rhetorical statement when you choose your clothes for work, class, or leisure time? How so?

3. Find an example of a rhetorical clothing choice on the internet or in a magazine or newspaper. Bring it to class and explain to your group what the person is conveying with his or her clothing. Choose your group's most interesting example and present it to the class.

Chapter Exercises

Compose

Activity 1.12 • Keep a Commonplace Book

Ancient rhetoricians performed speeches with little warning, often to advertise their services as teachers of rhetoric. Thus, they frequently memorized arguments about specific topics that could be adapted to the audience and situation on a moment's notice. They called these memorized arguments "commonplaces." Commonplace books are an outgrowth of the Greek concept of commonplaces, but they are a little different. They became popular in the Middle Ages as notebooks in which individuals would write down quotes or ideas about a particular topic. These notations might later be used to generate an idea for a composition. In more modern times, people have created commonplace books in the form of scrapbooks in which they collect quotes as well as drawings and clippings. Thus, they become a record of a person's intellectual life and can be saved for later reference.

For this class, take a notebook, perhaps one with a colorful or interesting cover, and keep notes, quotes, vocabulary words, and clippings related to the topics discussed in class. As your instructor directs, this commonplace book may be graded as evidence of class participation, or it may be a private journal. Take a look at the commonplace books shown here for ideas. Be creative and enjoy adapting this ancient journal form to record ideas that interest you.

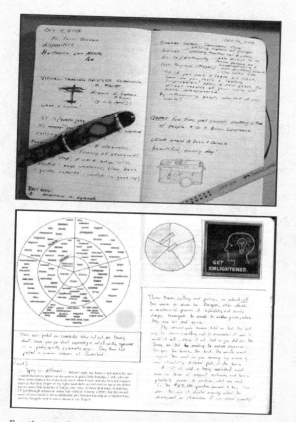

For thousands of years, people have been keeping commonplace books, a kind of journal or diary in which the author includes quotes, drawings, and images.

Image credit: "Pensacola Women's March, January 21, 2017" by Melanie La Gassé.

chapter 2

Responding Rhetorically

Why I Annotate Readings

Isidro Zepeda
M.A. in English Composition and
Applied Linguistics & TESL
California State University, San
Bernardino

Annotations are maps that detail our journeys through texts. My annotations are not random; instead, they show my responses to a text. As I engage the words of a text with my own words, complex ideas become more accessible to me. My words leave my footprints on the text.

When I annotate, I converse with voices that have traveled similar paths before me, and this activity allows my own ideas to flourish. These ideas are possessed with more than pleasure; they have a purpose that completes a specific task I have set forth to accomplish. For me, annotations are not simply notes on a text—they are marks demonstrating how my ideas interact with other authors' ideas to produce something new, even if it is just another idea. Our annotations also describe our uniqueness, since they represent how we view and interpret the world.

To annotate means to experience, at a more intimate level, the relationship between text and reader. The annotation process allows the reader to merge with the text—to become an active voice within the margins. In its most simplistic function, annotations help us keep track of all the ideas, connections, and realizations we have during our conversations with texts.

Later, when I am composing my own essay or article, and I wish to utilize quotes or paraphrases from a text I have annotated, the footprints of my words immediately draw me to the portions of the other text I previously found important. Then my annotations can lead to more than a voice in the margins. The words of my new text can engage the annotated text in a conversation of ideas.

Thinking Critically, Reading Rhetorically

Today we study texts to encourage students to develop the critical thinking skills essential for understanding the scientific method and for making effective judgments in the workplace and in civil life. This student-centered emphasis would have seemed strange to ancient Greek and Roman rhetoricians and their students. They believed that a rhetor's skill was best developed by honoring the skills of those who excelled in the past. Therefore, a large part of the educational process involved having students study the texts of well-regarded speeches, memorize and recite them, and model new compositions based on those speeches' approaches to topics and language style. As Isocrates explained,

> Since language is of such a nature that it is possible to discourse on the same subject matter in many different ways—to represent the great as lowly or invest the little with grandeur, to recount the things of old in a new manner or set forth events of recent date in an old fashion—it follows that one must not shun the subjects upon which others have composed before, but must try to compose better than they. ("Panegyricus")

Thus, students in ancient Greece or Rome would have been presented with a text, often read aloud by a teacher, and they would be asked to transcribe or copy it down with the idea that they would internalize the skills of the master rhetor who had originally given the speech. Then, they would be asked to write about the same subject in a way that built upon what they had learned from the master text but incorporated their own personal attitudes or perspectives.

Today, rather than being asked to model new compositions based upon the techniques of classic texts, students are asked to read texts carefully and then to engage in critical thinking and discussion about those texts.

Critical thinking involves considering issues thoughtfully and independently. Critical thinkers do not believe facts or opinions just because they are published—whether in newspapers, textbooks, on television, or on the internet. Nor do they focus upon just understanding or memorizing information, as in facts and figures. Critical thinkers examine the reasoning behind the information in front of them, looking for premises and considering the inferences drawn from those premises. They are able to think for themselves, making logical connections between ideas, seeing cause and effect relationships, and using information to solve problems.

Habits of Critical Thinkers

By Laura Herbek

- Strive to hold informed stances (based on fact and logical reasoning that can be proven right or wrong) versus unsubstantiated opinions (based on emotions and personal preferences that cannot be proven right or wrong)

- Reflect carefully on things you read, watch, and listen to

- Conduct thorough research and make judgments based on your findings as opposed to gathering evidence to support a predetermined opinion

- Be willing to engage with multiple perspectives, especially those you don't understand or agree with

- Work to solve problems rather than simply identify them

Activity 2.1 • Think about Critical Reading

Compose

Freewrite for five minutes about a controversial issue about which you have a strong opinion. Consider why you believe what you do about this issue. What outside influences or sources have influenced your position? In what ways has the opposing side also influenced what you believe about the issue?

After you finish freewriting, look back at what you have written and consider the social (other people, articles, videos, etc.) nature of the sources that have influenced you. In your group or as a class, discuss the influences—not the particular issues themselves—that have affected your opinion. How have you decided what to believe?

Reading rhetorically makes use of critical thinking skills, but it also involves looking at texts as arguments and evaluating them for validity, adequacy of evidence, and presence of bias. Moreover, reading rhetorically involves having a knowledge of rhetoric and specialized Greek terms such as *logos, pathos, ethos,* and *kairos*—words that were defined briefly in Chapter 1 and will be discussed more extensively in Chapter 3. Practice reading rhetorically as you read the following article.

Reading 2.1

Worldwide, activists protest the use of laboratory animals to test cosmetics, according to "Do You Know How Your Mascara is Made?" The article has a tag line that reads, "Across the globe, countless animals continue to suffer in painful tests simply to bring new skin creams, hair dyes, and other nonessential cosmetics to market. But the cruelty-free campaign is leading the charge to ban cosmetic animal testing worldwide by engaging consumers and companies, rewriting laws, and advancing the science of safety testing."

The article was printed in All Animals, *a publication of the Humane Society. The magazine aims to bring to the public stories about the Humane Society and the humane movement.*

Arna Cohen, the author, is online editor and producer for the Companion Animals Division, Humane Society of the U.S.

Do You Know How Your Mascara is Made?
by Arna Cohen

Customers grabbing a late-morning cup of coffee in downtown Brussels caught a strange sight two years ago. Suddenly, across the street, on the grounds of the European Commission, there were rabbits everywhere.

Some seemed to emerge from nearby bushes. Others slipped out from behind city walls as pedestrians stopped to watch and curious faces peered down from office windows. And then, right there on an open stretch of sidewalk, on a Wednesday in June, those rabbits began to dance.

As a happy burst of music piped out over a nearby sound system—"Saturday night, I feel the air is getting hot"—27 advocates in white rabbit costumes stepped, hopped, clapped, and spun in unison. Reporters snapped photos. A few onlookers began to move with the song. And atop a stone wall, two women unfurled a large white banner: "350,000 Petition for EU Cosmetics to be Cruelty-Free in 2013."

The flash mob gathered to shine a spotlight on the issue of cosmetics animal testing in the European Union—one white rabbit representing each member country. "It attracted quite a lot of attention, as you might imagine," says Wendy Higgins, remembering a round of applause as the dancing concluded. The local media even asked for an encore, to capture more footage.

Immediately afterward, Humane Society International and Lush cosmetics company delivered stack upon stack of signatures to the European health commissioner, calling on him to support a March 2013 ban on the sale of animal-tested cosmetics.

"It was quite an emotional event, I have to say. I had a tear in my eye," says Higgins, HSI European communications director." This had a real sense of meaning, and it was such a joyful event. But all of us knew, for animals in laboratories being tested on for cosmetics, there is no joy. There is no happy moment. And we were there, speaking up for them."

The eventually successful petition was one in a series of rapid-fire victories achieved recently by HSI and The HSUS's Be Cruelty-Free Campaign. Last year alone, Israel banned the sale of all newly animal-tested cosmetics, India prohibited animal tests of cosmetics within its borders, and China announced that it will no longer require animal testing for domestically manufactured nonmedicated cosmetics. In South Korea, the government invested more than $150 million to establish the country's first nonanimal testing center, further committing to accept alternative methods for safety assurance of medicated cosmetics such as sunscreens and anti-wrinkle creams.

Progress has been most striking in the European Union: Five months after those white rabbits danced their jig in Belgium, the health commissioner stated he would fully implement the March 2013 ban on the import and sale of cosmetics newly tested on animals or containing ingredients tested on animals, regardless of where such tests are conducted. With an EU testing ban already in place since 2009, the 2013 sales ban marked the final piece in a 20-year struggle by advocates to remove cruelty from the beauty equation there, and the domino that is knocking down barriers worldwide, says Troy Seidle, HSI director of research and toxicology.

"With the EU closing its doors to animal-tested cosmetics, the beginning of the end of global cosmetics cruelty is within our grasp. It is a major moral milestone in the history of ending cosmetics animal testing."

Pascaline Clerc, HSUS senior director of animal research issues, adds that the EU decision has wider implications for animal testing of noncosmetic products such as paint, coffee sweeteners, and household cleaners. "This is the first step in replacing animals used for toxicity testing in general. People can see that it can be done."

An animated bunny is taken from the wild and imprisoned in a research laboratory. He is locked in a full-body restraint system and a chemical is applied to his eyes, which blister and turn red.

A rabbit-costumed flash mob marches toward EU headquarters in Brussels in June 2012, bearing 350,000 signatures against cosmetics animal testing. Exposing the cruelty behind the beauty industry has been the focus of intense efforts by the animal protection movement for decades, marked by boycotts, protests, petitions, and extraordinary levels of consumer participation.

Photo Credit: Virginia Mayo/Associated Press

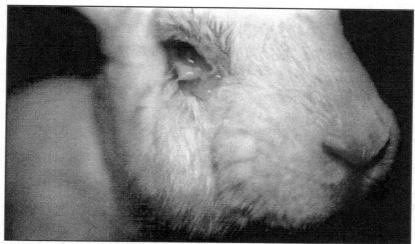

Pain-filled lives and deaths are the fate of rabbits and other animals used for cosmetics testing. Alternative methods are gaining traction thanks to a growing recognition that animal tests are poor predictors of how substances will affect people.

Photo Credit: PETA

Bright Eyes, a video created by HSI partner Choose Cruelty Free Australia, is based on a true story (with creative license: Unlike the animated specimen, laboratory rabbits are not obtained from the wild; they're purpose-bred for research). For 70 years, rabbits have been the go-to animal for the Draize eye irritation test the video depicts. They spend their short lives undergoing the procedure without anesthetic before being killed when no longer "useful."

The Draize test is only one in a litany of toxicity tests performed on animals, each more horrifying than the last. In the acute oral toxicity test, the needle of a syringe is forced down the throat of a rat and a massive dose of the test substance injected into her stomach to determine the amount that causes death. The animal can experience diarrhea, convulsions, bleeding from the mouth, seizures, and paralysis. The same procedure is used to assess smaller amounts in repeated dose toxicity tests, which last daily for one to three months or longer.

In carcinogenicity tests, rats and mice are exposed to substances daily for up to two years to see if they develop tumors; reproductive toxicity tests involve daily exposure of pregnant rats and up to two generation of pups, often by force-feeding (a method that seems doubly unnecessary given that most personal care products are applied to the skin). Even tests that aren't measuring fatal doses ultimately end in death, notes Catherine Willett, HSUS director of regulatory toxicology, risk assessment, and alternatives:

"Oftentimes you need to kill the animal to see what has actually happened at the microscopic level." Typical killing methods include asphyxiation, neck-breaking, and decapitation.

A dubious science underpins the physical and psychological suffering endured by animals in laboratories, as results of tests done on rodents and rabbits are poor predictors of a substance's effect on humans. Spurred by widening acknowledgment of these limitations, scientists are increasingly focused on developing state-of-the-art, human-relevant, animal-free alternatives.

The days of the Draize test, for one, look to be numbered. Many governments approve the use of cow or chicken corneas left over from the meat industry for certain types of eye irritancy tests. The next generation of tests will use human cells, such as a new artificial cornea under development by Japanese researchers that could ultimately replace rabbits entirely. Preliminary evaluations of the tissue have obtained results that more closely predict effects on human eyes than animal tests have.

Meanwhile, the number of rabbits used in skin irritation and corrosion tests is being reduced thanks to computer modeling analyses and other techniques. Skin cells can be grown in petri dishes, says Willett: "You add two or three different kinds of cells to an artificial scaffold, and they start to form tissues that look and behave just like living tissues"—imitating skin on body parts as varied as the nose, trachea, and lungs. And Procter & Gamble scientists recently developed the first nonanimal method for skin allergy testing; chemicals are assessed in test tubes for their allergic reactivity according to the amount of depletion they cause in proteins known as peptides.

As critical as these developments are, an emerging body of research is seeking to transcend such one-on-one test replacements with a more exhaustive approach that focuses on predicting chemical pathways in the human body. "Where does the chemical enter the body? How does it enter the body?" says Willett: "Does it bind to a receptor and cause a cascade of things to happen in the cell? Does it chemically modify a protein?

"And you can actually map this out from many different kinds of chemicals that cause different kinds of reactions," she continues. "You can actually get a pretty decent idea of what a chemical is going to do based on the biological pathway it affects. It's a completely different way of thinking about testing than has ever been done before. People who know about this are very excited about it."

Governments have embraced the changes, with agencies such as the FDA, EPA, and Department of Defense investing in complex computer models, "organs on a chip," and other technologies, says Willett. "Similar investment is being made around the world, in the European Union, Japan, Brazil, Korea, and elsewhere."

Where alternative testing methods are not available, companies can create new cosmetics by choosing among thousands of ingredients that have been tested in the past and proven to be safe.

Taken together, these options provide a counter argument to industry claims that animal testing is the only possible way to assess safety. "Now that we've had the technical progress, the politicians have become—well, they've lost sympathy," says Seidle.

The EU import and sales ban was the initial focus of the Be Cruelty-Free Campaign, a global push to rewrite laws, train technicians in alternative testing methods, and engage consumers and corporations. Stalled for years, an EU testing ban was originally passed in 1993, with a five-year phase-in period, but the cosmetics industry managed to secure delay after delay, claiming that it needed more time to replace animals in testing. Finally, in 2009, all animal testing of finished cosmetics and their ingredients was prohibited within EU borders; a ban on sales of products animal-tested elsewhere was slated to go into effect in 2013.

But in 2012, it again appeared that the cosmetics industry might impede progress. So HSI delivered the European health commissioner a large Valentine's Day card from singer Leona Lewis, asking him to have a heart for animals. They held meetings with policymakers. They asked European citizens to send postcards in support. And then, immediately following the purposely upbeat, positive white rabbit event, they brought 350,000 signatures to that pivotal June meeting, including ones from celebrities such as Ricky Gervais, Kesha, Sir Roger Moore, and Chrissie Hynde.

"Even though only two HSI lobbyists were allowed into the meeting, they weren't in that room alone," Higgins says. "They said that when they stepped into that room, they felt the hands of those 350,000 people on their shoulders, spurring them on. And that's what it's all about. That's what all of the petition-collecting was all about, was that moment where we could say: We're watching. Europe is waiting for you to do this."

Nine months later, they had their ban. "We probably would have been looking at more delays if our campaign hadn't been there to really hold the EU's feet to the flame," says Seidle.

With the mission accomplished in Europe, the Be Cruelty-Free Campaign is working to achieve similar progress in other lucrative sales markets: Brazil, South Korea, Russia. In India, dedicated personnel hired with funds from a Lush grant recruited Bollywood stars and thousands of consumers to help HSI pressure officials to replace animal tests with alternative methods in the country's regulations of cosmetics manufacturing. "We went as far as we could with the Bureau of Indian Standards," says Seidle, "and from there we engaged some lead members of parliament and really just ratcheted up the heat with a very high-impact public campaign, which got the drug controller's attention, and he personally went in with our letter in hand and said, 'Yes, we're just going to do this; get it done.'"

In June, HSI launched Be Cruelty-Free China, turning its focus to a critical battleground where the government has required all cosmetics for sale, both domestically produced and imported, to be safety-tested on animals in government laboratories, and where in recent years the lure of huge profits—$24 billion spent on cosmetics and personal care items in 2012—has proven irresistible to Mary Kay and other companies that had been cruelty-free for decades.

Decisions by these companies to surrender their principles have outraged their customers. When Urban Decay, a popular cruelty-free company, announced that it would sell in China, thousands expressed anger through email, social media, and online petitions, prompting company executives to reverse course.

Seeking to bring this element of popular pressure to bear on the government, HSI partnered with three Chinese organizations, "one that's very connected politically, one that's very media-wise, and one that's a youth social media organization," says Seidle. Advocates began spreading the cruelty-free message on the Chinese social media platform Weibo, with more than 500 million users, while press releases began naming companies that refuse to sell in China because of the testing policy.

"We've been actively disseminating information to the Chinese consumers for the first time ever," says Seidle. "No one has ever done that before, to explain this is how your cosmetics are being tested; this is what's involved;

this is what the idea of cruelty-free means." The European Union health commissioner applied additional leverage, meeting with Chinese officials to discuss animal testing as a barrier to trade.

A significant breakthrough came in November, when the China Food and Drug Administration announced that it would allow domestic cosmetics manufacturers to opt out of mandatory animal testing in favor of using previously collected ingredient safety data and possibly alternative test methods accepted by EU regulators—allowing Chinese goods to be sold in the world's largest cosmetics market. The Institute for In Vitro Sciences is now training Chinese scientists in alternative methods, thanks to an $80,000 grant from HSI, The HSUS, and the Human Toxicology Project Consortium.

The change comes into force in June and doesn't yet apply to imported cosmetics or to "special-use" products like hair dyes, sunscreens, and antiperspirants. But in meetings with HSI, the CFDA has indicated that, after the change has been implemented and assessed, it may be extended to the other categories. Companies are still free to continue animal testing if they so choose, so HSI's next focus will be to persuade regulators to ban the tests altogether.

In small ways, consumers have shown their approval of the government's change of heart. In Dalian, a port city in northeast China, animal advocates adorned with rabbit ears held several events that attracted 2,700 people, hundreds of whom signed HSI's Be Cruelty-Free China pledge and a petition supporting the government's plans. A tiny percentage of a huge populace, but notable in a nation not known for freedom of expression.

In the U.S., the state of cosmetics testing is somewhat of a different story. Even with the availability of cutting-edge technology, even with years of safety data on thousands of chemicals, even with no legal requirements that cosmetics be tested on animals, many American companies continue the practice in part because it's what they've always done.

Fear of lawsuits is a factor in their conservatism, says The HSUS's Willett. In our litigious society," people will sue the company and they will sue the FDA. Not only do you have to convince the regulators that the method you used to evaluate your chemical was sound, but you have to make it legally defensible. Because animal tests are the historical measure that we've used, people feel that they're on safer ground."

And profit sings its siren song. The bulk of animal testing these days is done in the lucrative field of anti-aging products that claim to reduce wrinkles, lighten brown spots, or lift sagging skin. The chemical ingredients in these treatments affect the body's structure, thus pushing them into the category of over-the-counter drugs and, if an ingredient has never been used before, making it subject to mandatory animal testing (see "What's in a Name," humanesociety.org).

"It's so sad that these animals are dying for . . . the myth that we can hold back the march of time," says Lush ethics director Hilary Jones." Companies sell that myth and sell us these miracle ingredients that disappear two or three months later, to be replaced by a new miracle ingredient, all of them tested on animals."

With a strong industry lobby keeping a legislative ban on animal testing a nonstarter, the Be Cruelty-Free Campaign's focus in the U.S. has been on public education. According to a 2013 poll, a majority of Americans oppose animal testing of cosmetics, and they actually feel safer if alternatives are used instead. But even so, consumers here simply aren't as engaged, or informed, as they have been in the EU, says The HSUS's Clerc. "When we started this campaign, people were surprised that animal testing was still around. They thought we had moved beyond that."

Reaching out especially to a new generation concerned about what they put in and on their bodies, the campaign engages music, television, and film stars to spread the message through Twitter and public service announcements. It recently teamed with Miss DC 2013 Bindhu Pamarthi, who announced she was willing to compete barefaced in the Miss America 2014 pageant if it would draw attention to her platform of ending cosmetics animal testing. Although Pamarthi didn't ultimately compete barefaced and didn't ultimately win the crown, she did get a Facebook shout-out from R.E.I.G.N., the pageant's makeup partner, which honored her "thought provoking platform" and called her "a beyond beauty inspiration to us all."

The campaign also partners with bloggers who search out cruelty-free cosmetics and personal care products, doing intensive detective work on manufacturers before making recommendations. On Jen Mathews's My Beauty Bunny blog, every item is tested on staff members before being recommended to readers. Today, the blog receives 100,000 views a month, while 140,000 people follow along on Facebook. But Mathews's reach extends beyond the known numbers, with the blog winning multiple awards and featured in magazines and on television, radio, and websites.

Mathews began supporting animal welfare in college. "I was one of those college students who was posting things on billboards all over campus and the faculty were constantly taking them down." She would put animal rights fliers in her bill payment envelopes, "doing everything I could, grass roots, to get the message out. [. . .] Now I'm able to take that to the Web."

While Mathews's mission is to show consumers that cruelty-free beauty products are high quality, affordable, and widely available, Clerc focuses within the industry, seeking examples to share with companies that want to adopt humane business models. The strategy, she says, "is to find those companies that have done the right thing from the beginning and prove they can still be profitable; they can innovate without animal testing."

One such company is Biao, whose laboratory evaluates skin care compounds for safety using technology such as gene chips that allow mass in vitro cell testing. Founder Nicole Baldwin's entrepreneurial journey began as a little girl, when she suffered serious burns on her face, neck, and chest after upsetting a pot of boiling water on herself. Her grandmother, who was a nurse at the time, created a treatment from botanicals and other natural products, using formulas that had been passed down to her from her own mother.

Years later, when Baldwin was stationed with the U.S. Army in Afghanistan, her skin suffered again, this time from stress, dust, and the extreme temperatures of the arid desert climate. When none of the commercial products she tried provided relief, Baldwin decided to develop her own skincare line. Returning home to Houston after her tour, she became a licensed aesthetician.

A second tour of duty took Baldwin back to Afghanistan, where, using her grandmother's remedies and her own experience as inspiration, she began to create face and body treatments formulated with sustainable organic plant oils and extracts. She named the line Biao—an acronym for "beautiful inside and out"—as a tribute to her grandmother, whose care healed not just Baldwin's skin but her self-esteem and confidence. "I am following in her footsteps," Baldwin said in an interview with ABC News, "and I'm very glad that at 81 years old she's able to see me do this."

Baldwin attributes her cruelty-free philosophy to her relationship with her childhood pet, a German shepherd abandoned by his previous owners. After she saved Spicy from choking on a chicken bone, Baldwin says he "followed behind me everywhere. When I would awake for school, he would be in . . . my bedroom door. . . . When I would ask him to get me a newspaper, he would go get it. . . . I discovered that animals were so similar to humans. Spicy knew that I had saved his life." Experiencing this kind of bond, Baldwin couldn't fathom subjecting an animal to the cruelty of testing.

Prai Beauty, a skincare company founded in 1999 by HSUS board member Cathy Kangas, shares its cruelty-free status as a key component of its sales pitch on the home shopping networks where it sells in the U.S. and six countries. Kangas says a survey following the product launch found that "the most overwhelming thing that excited [customers] . . . was it being cruelty-free. It really mattered to 72 percent of all of our customers."

The financial success of Prai, with $30 million in annual sales, and other companies founded on humane principles, such as Paul Mitchell, Aubrey Organics, and Burt's Bees, clearly demonstrates that cruelty-free can be good business—business that the cosmetics industry can no longer profitably ignore. "Companies that are still testing on animals will soon lose money and market shares," notes Clerc. And now, the stakes are even higher for those selling in countries that have taken a stand against animal testing. "Those companies will see those markets slipping away from them if they don't move away from animal testing rapidly."

Collaborate

Activity 2.2 • Analyze "Do You Know How Your Mascara is Made?"

In your small group, discuss the following questions, and then report your group's opinion(s) to the class.

1. After reading "Do You Know How Your Mascara is Made?" identify the problem the author is concerned with.

2. What is the author arguing in the article?

3. What evidence of animal testing does the author offer? Is it sufficient to support the argument?

4. What laws or changed laws does the author mention that lend credibility to the argument?

5. Does the argument appeal primarily to *ethos, pathos,* or *logos*? How so?

6. Who published the article? Does the organization have a particular bias?

Activity 2.3 • Why Is Activity 2.2 Critical Reading?

After your group completes Activity 2.2, freewrite for five minutes about the questions you answered in your group in response to Activity 2.2. What do those questions ask you to do that is reading critically?

Ways of Reading Rhetorically

Reading theorist Louise Rosenblatt suggests a technique for analyzing written texts—particularly those with few visual cues other than words on paper or a computer screen. She says that we take the pattern of verbal signs left by the author and use them to recreate the text, not in the exact way the author perceived the text, but guided by it.

So, as we read, there is a constant stream of response to the text. However, Rosenblatt says that even as the reader is recreating the text, he or she is also reacting to it. Thus, there are two interacting streams of response involved as the person moves through the text. The reader, rather than being a passive receptor for the author's text, actually participates in the creative process during reading.

However, we read differently depending on the text and the occasion. For example, if you take a paperback novel on an airplane trip, you probably read simply for entertainment and to pass the time in the air. If you read *King Lear* for a literature class, you read for the plot, characterization, and other elements that you know will be discussed in class. If you read a chapter in your chemistry textbook before an exam, you are focusing on remembering concepts and details that might be on the test. Reading as a writer is another type of reading. You examine the text with an eye for the choices the writer made when crafting the text, such as whether the writer begins with a narrative introduction, a quote from a noted authority, or a startling statement. You notice, for example, what people are mentioned in the text, either as authorities or participants in activities.

Rosenblatt also makes a useful distinction between two main kinds of reading—aesthetic reading and efferent reading.[1] In **aesthetic reading**, the reader is most interested in what happens "during the reading event, as he fixes his attention on the actual experience he is living through," according to Rosen-

---

1. Rosenblatt, Louise Michelle. "Efferent and Aesthetic Reading." *The Reader, the Text, the Poem: The Transactional Theory of the Literary Work,* Southern Illinois UP, 1994, pp. 22-47.

blatt. Readers focus upon the ideas, images, and story of the text that evoke an aesthetic experience in the moment of reading. **Efferent readers**, in contrast, read to learn from the text, and, thus, according to Rosenblatt, "concentrate on the information, the concepts, the guides to action, that will be left with him when the reading is over."

Reading rhetorically is efferent reading, focusing not on the experience of reading but on the information the text conveys and upon the way an argument is established and supported in a text. Some arguments are written in an engaging style that is a pleasure to read, while others are written in a highly emotional tone that arouses a visceral response in the reader. A text that inspires aesthetic reading must sometimes be read several times in order for the reader to focus on the structure of the argument beneath the creative language.

Some theorists say that critical thinking is "thinking about thinking" or "reasoning about reasoning," and that is exactly what reading rhetorically involves— reasoning about whether or not a text presents a reasoned argument. A good way to begin reading rhetorically is to be aware of the essential elements of an argument and identify these elements in the text you are evaluating.

The elements of an argument include a debatable issue, clearly stated, for which an audience is to be persuaded. Without an issue, a text may be simply informative, rather than persuasive. Those individuals or groups holding a position may be considered biased toward that position. For example, the reading in this chapter, "Do You Know How Your Mascara is Made?" was published by the Humane Society and expresses a clear argument against the use of animals for testing cosmetics. Because the Humane Society has a stated agenda about animal rights, the article should not, then, be the only source cited in an academic essay about the issue of animal testing in the production of cosmetics. An argument about this issue, put forward in academic writing, should be backed by additional reliable evidence from sources that are unbiased— independent articles not written by the Humane Society. The use of biased sources for support evidence can lead to a biased argument. Moreover, to be fair and complete, an argument must contain an acknowledgment of opposing argument(s). Otherwise, the reader may be left with unanswered questions about why alternatives are not considered. And finally, a well-written argument features a conclusion, which may include a call to action.

See the Checklist of Essential Elements in an Argument on the next page.

Checklist of Essential Elements in an Argument

☑ **A debatable issue.** By definition, for a text to be an argument, there must be at least two sides that can be asserted and supported.

☑ **A clearly stated position, claim statement, or thesis.** Arguments assert different kinds of claims, such as taking a position on an issue of fact, asserting a cause and effect relationship, declaring the value of some entity, or advocating for a solution to a problem; but, in each case, after you read the argument, you should be able to restate or summarize the position, claim, or thesis in one or two sentences.

☑ **An audience.** To evaluate an argument, you need to know the original intended audience or place of publication, so that you can decide if the argument takes into account the audience's attitudes, background, and other factors. Ask yourself, for example, if the writer is assuming too much or too little background knowledge on the part of the audience or if the writer is using language that assumes the reader's agreement on the issue when that assumption is not warranted.

☑ **Evidence from reliable sources.** Quotes, statistics, and other evidence should be credited to reputable sources, even if your text is not a document that offers academic-style citations. The evidence should be sufficient to support the author's position or thesis.

☑ **Acknowledgment of the opposing argument.** A good rhetorician does not ignore any potential weaknesses in the argument. It is better to acknowledge points in favor of the opposing argument and then, if possible, refute the opposition's strong points than it is to allow an audience to poke holes in an argument.

☑ **A conclusion and/or call to action.** An argument can be concluded in a variety of effective ways, but it is important to note that it does, indeed, conclude. The conclusion can be a call to action on the part of the audience, but it should not be the beginning of an additional argument that is not supported by the evidence presented.

Reading 2.2

Several years ago, Stacy Snyder was a fairly typical 25-year-old college student training to be a teacher. That all changed forever when she did something that she probably thought was harmless fun—she posted a photo of herself on a social network site. In this article published in The New York Times, *Jeffrey Rosen uses Snyder's case to illustrate how notions of privacy are changing because of the ever-growing presence and popularity of social networking sites. What is even more alarming, according to Rosen, is that photos and information, once posted on the web, are there forever. The web does not forget, and this lack of forgetting is changing society's ability to forgive and forget.*

You may enjoy posting status updates about your life on a Facebook or Twitter account; however, with employers increasingly conducting background checks on such sites, it's very important to be careful about what you choose to post. This includes status updates, photographs, and videos. If you read the following article carefully, you may never look at social networking sites quite the same again.

The Web Means the End of Forgetting

by Jeffrey Rosen

Four years ago, Stacy Snyder, then a 25-year-old teacher in training at Conestoga Valley High School in Lancaster, Pa., posted a photo on her MySpace page that showed her at a party wearing a pirate hat and drinking from a plastic cup, with the caption "Drunken Pirate." After discovering the page, her supervisor at the high school told her the photo was "unprofessional," and the dean of Millersville University School of Education, where Snyder was enrolled, said she was promoting drinking in virtual view of her underage students. As a result, days before Snyder's scheduled graduation, the university denied her a teaching degree. Snyder sued, arguing that the university had violated her First Amendment rights by penalizing her for her (perfectly legal) after-hours behavior. But in 2008, a federal district judge rejected the claim, saying that because Snyder was a public employee whose photo didn't relate to matters of public concern, her "Drunken Pirate" post was not protected speech.

When historians of the future look back on the perils of the early digital age, Stacy Snyder may well be an icon. The problem she faced is only one example of a challenge that, in big and small ways, is confronting millions of people around the globe: how best to live our lives in a world where the internet records everything and forgets nothing—where every online photo, status update, Twitter post and blog entry by and about us can be stored forever. With websites like LOL Facebook Moments, which collects and shares embarrassing personal revelations from Facebook users, ill-advised photos and online chatter are coming back to haunt people months or years after the fact.

Examples are proliferating daily: there was the 16-year-old British girl who was fired from her office job for complaining on Facebook, "I'm so totally bored!!"; there was the 66-year-old Canadian psychotherapist who tried to enter the United States but was turned away at the border—and barred permanently from visiting the country—after a border guard's internet search found that the therapist had written an article in a philosophy journal describing his experiments 30 years ago with LSD. According to a recent survey by Microsoft, 75 percent of U.S. recruiters and human-resource professionals report that their companies require them to do online research about candidates, and many use a range of sites when scrutinizing applicants—including search engines, social networking sites, photo- and video-sharing sites, personal websites and blogs, Twitter and online gaming sites. Seventy percent of U.S. recruiters report that they have rejected candidates because of information found online, like photos and discussion-board conversations and membership in controversial groups.

Technological advances, of course, have often presented new threats to privacy. In 1890, in perhaps the most famous article on privacy ever written, Samuel Warren and Louis Brandeis complained that because of new technology—like the Kodak camera and the tabloid press—"gossip is no longer the resource of the idle and of the vicious but has become a trade." But the mild society gossip of the Gilded Age pales before the volume of revelations contained in the photos, video and chatter on social media sites and elsewhere across the internet. Facebook, which surpassed MySpace in 2008 as the largest social-networking site, now has nearly 500 million members, or 22 percent of all internet users, who spend more than 500 billion minutes a month on the site. Facebook users share more than 25 billion pieces of content each month (including news stories, blog posts and photos), and the average user creates 70 pieces of content a month. There are more than 100 million registered Twitter users, and the Library of Congress recently announced that it will be acquiring—and permanently storing—the entire archive of public Twitter posts since 2006.

In Brandeis's day—and until recently, in ours—you had to be a celebrity to be gossiped about in public: today all of us are learning to expect the scrutiny that used to be reserved for the famous and the infamous. A 26-year-old Manhattan woman told *The New York Times* that she was afraid of being tagged in online photos because it might reveal that she wears only two outfits when out on the town—a Lynyrd Skynyrd T-shirt or a basic black dress. "You have movie-star issues," she said, "and you're just a person."

We've known for years that the web allows for unprecedented voyeurism, exhibitionism and inadvertent indiscretion, but we are only beginning to understand the costs of an age in which so much of what we say, and of what others say about us, goes into our permanent—and public—digital files. The fact that the internet never seems to forget is threatening, at an almost existential level, our ability to control our identities; to preserve the option of reinventing ourselves and starting anew; to overcome our checkered pasts.

In a recent book, "Delete: The Virtue of Forgetting in the Digital Age," the cyberscholar Viktor Mayer-Schönberger cites Stacy Snyder's case as a reminder of the importance of "societal forgetting." By "erasing external memories," he says in the book, "our society accepts that human beings evolve over time, that we have the capacity to learn from past experiences and adjust our behavior." In traditional societies, where missteps are observed but not necessarily recorded, the limits of human memory ensure that people's sins are eventually forgotten. By contrast, Mayer-Schönberger notes, a society in which everything is recorded "will forever tether us to all our past actions, making it impossible, in practice, to escape them." He concludes that "without some form of forgetting, forgiving becomes a difficult undertaking."

It's often said that we live in a permissive era, one with infinite second chances. But the truth is that for a great many people, the permanent memory bank of the web increasingly means there are no second chances—no opportunities to escape a scarlet letter in your digital past. Now the worst thing you've done is often the first thing everyone knows about you.

The Crisis—and the Solution?

Concern about these developments has intensified this year, as Facebook took steps to make the digital profiles of its users generally more public than private. Last December, the company announced that parts of user profiles that had previously been private—including every user's friends, relationship status and family relations—would become public and accessible to other users. Then in April, Facebook introduced an interactive system called Open Graph that can share your profile information and friends with the Facebook partner sites you visit.

What followed was an avalanche of criticism from users, privacy regulators and advocates around the world. Four Democratic senators—Charles Schumer of New York, Michael Bennet of Colorado, Mark Begich of Alaska and Al Franken of Minnesota—wrote to the chief executive of Facebook,

Mark Zuckerberg, expressing concern about the "instant personalization" feature and the new privacy settings. In May, Facebook responded to all the criticism by introducing a new set of privacy controls that the company said would make it easier for users to understand what kind of information they were sharing in various contexts.

Facebook's partial retreat has not quieted the desire to do something about an urgent problem. All around the world, political leaders, scholars and citizens are searching for responses to the challenge of preserving control of our identities in a digital world that never forgets. Are the most promising solutions going to be technological? Legislative? Judicial? Ethical? A result of shifting social norms and cultural expectations? Or some mix of the above? Alex Türk, the French data protection commissioner, has called for a "constitutional right to oblivion" that would allow citizens to maintain a greater degree of anonymity online and in public places. In Argentina, the writers Alejandro Tortolini and Enrique Quagliano have started a campaign to "reinvent forgetting on the internet," exploring a range of political and technological ways of making data disappear. In February, the European Union helped finance a campaign called "Think B4 U post!" that urges young people to consider the "potential consequences" of publishing photos of themselves or their friends without "thinking carefully" and asking permission. And in the United States, a group of technologists, legal scholars and cyberthinkers are exploring ways of recreating the possibility of digital forgetting. These approaches share the common goal of reconstructing a form of control over our identities: the ability to reinvent ourselves, to escape our pasts and to improve the selves that we present to the world. [. . .]

In the near future, internet searches for images are likely to be combined with social-network aggregator search engines, like today's Spokeo and Pipl, which combine data from online sources—including political contributions, blog posts, YouTube videos, web comments, real estate listings and photo albums. Increasingly these aggregator sites will rank people's public and private reputations. In the Web 3.0 world, Michael Fertik, a Harvard Law School graduate, predicts people will be rated, assessed and scored based not on their creditworthiness but on their trustworthiness as good parents, good dates, good employees, good baby sitters or good insurance risks.

One legal option for responding to online setbacks to your reputation is to sue under current law. There's already a sharp rise in lawsuits known as Twittergation—that is, suits to force websites to remove slanderous or false posts. Last year, Courtney Love was sued for libel by the fashion designer Boudoir Queen for supposedly slanderous comments posted on Twitter, on Love's MySpace page and on the designer's online market-place-feedback page. But even if you win a U.S. libel lawsuit, the website doesn't have to take the offending material down any more than a news-paper that has lost a libel suit has to remove the offending content from its archive.

Some scholars, therefore, have proposed creating new legal rights to force websites to remove false or slanderous statements. Cass Sunstein, the Obama administration's regulatory czar, suggests in his new book, "On Rumors," that there might be "a general right to demand retraction after a clear demonstration that a statement is both false and damaging." (If a newspaper or blogger refuses to post a retraction, they might be liable for damages.) Sunstein adds that websites might be required to take down false postings after receiving notice that they are false—an approach modeled on the Digital Millennium Copyright Act, which requires websites to remove content that supposedly infringes intellectual property rights after receiv-ing a complaint.

As Stacy Snyder's "Drunken Pirate" photo suggests, however, many people aren't worried about false information posted by others—they're worried about true information they've posted about themselves when it is taken out of context or given undue weight. And defamation law doesn't apply to true information or statements of opinion. Some legal scholars want to expand the ability to sue over true but embarrassing violations of privacy— although it appears to be a quixotic goal.

Daniel Solove, a George Washington University law professor and author of the book, *The Future of Reputation*, says that laws forbidding people to breach confidences could be expanded to allow you to sue your Facebook friends if they share your embarrassing photos or posts in violation of your privacy settings. Expanding legal rights in this way, however, would run up against the First Amendment rights of others. Invoking the right to free speech, the U.S. Supreme Court has already held that the media can't be prohibited from publishing the name of a rape victim that they obtained from public records. Generally, American judges hold that if you disclose something to a few people, you can't stop them from sharing the informa-tion with the rest of the world.

That's one reason that the most promising solutions to the problem of embarrassing but true information online may be not legal but technological ones. Instead of suing after the damage is done (or hiring a firm to clean up our messes), we need to explore ways of preemptively making the offending words or pictures disappear.

Zuckerberg said in January to the founder of the publication TechCrunch that Facebook had an obligation to reflect "current social norms" that favored exposure over privacy. "People have really gotten comfortable not only sharing more information and different kinds but more openly and with more people, and that social norm is just something that has evolved over time," he said.

However, norms are already developing to recreate off-the-record spaces in public, with no photos, Twitter posts or blogging allowed. Milk and Honey, an exclusive bar on Manhattan's Lower East Side, requires potential members to sign an agreement promising not to blog about the bar's goings on or to post photos on social-networking sites, and other bars and nightclubs are adopting similar policies. I've been at dinners recently where someone has requested, in all seriousness, "Please don't tweet this"—a custom that is likely to spread.

But what happens when people transgress those norms, using Twitter or tagging photos in ways that cause us serious embarrassment? Can we imagine a world in which new norms develop that make it easier for people to forgive and forget one another's digital sins? [. . .]

Perhaps society will become more forgiving of drunken Facebook pictures in the way Samuel Gosling, the University of Texas, Austin, psychology professor says he expects it might. And some may welcome the end of the segmented self, on the grounds that it will discourage bad behavior and hypocrisy: it's harder to have clandestine affairs when you're broadcasting your every move on Facebook, Twitter and Foursquare. But a humane society values privacy, because it allows people to cultivate different aspects of their personalities in different contexts; and at the moment, the enforced merging of identities that used to be separate is leaving many casualties in its wake. Stacy Snyder couldn't reconcile her "aspiring-teacher self" with her "having-a-few-drinks self": even the impression, correct or not, that she had a drink in a pirate hat at an off-campus party was enough to derail her teaching career.

That doesn't mean, however, that it had to derail her life. After taking down her MySpace profile, Snyder is understandably trying to maintain her privacy: her lawyer told me in a recent interview that she is now working in human resources; she did not respond to a request for comment. But her success as a human being who can change and evolve, learning from her mistakes and growing in wisdom, has nothing to do with the digital file she can never entirely escape. Our character, ultimately, can't be judged by strangers on the basis of our Facebook or Google profiles; it can be judged by only those who know us and have time to evaluate our strengths and weaknesses, face to face and in context, with insight and understanding. In the meantime, as all of us stumble over the challenges of living in a world without forgetting, we need to learn new forms of empathy, new ways of defining ourselves without reference to what others say about us and new ways of forgiving one another for the digital trails that will follow us forever.

Explore

Activity 2.4 • Discuss "The Web Means the End of Forgetting"

In your small group, discuss the following questions, and then report your group's opinion(s) to the class.

1. What is the significance of the article's title?

2. What does Rosen mean when he suggests that in the future Stacy Snyder may be an icon?

3. What is the main point in Rosen's essay? What is he arguing?

4. Does Rosen offer sufficient evidence to make you take his argument seriously? Why or why not?

5. Are you a member of any social networking sites? What can you do in order to protect your reputation?

6. A woman interviewed in the article said, in regard to being tagged in online photos, "you have movie-star issues—and you're just a person." If you are a member of any social networking sites, do you tag friends in photos? Is it important to be careful about this? Why or why not?

Activity 2.5 • Apply the Checklist of Essential Elements in an Argument

Collaborate

Apply the Checklist of Essential Elements in an Argument (discussed on p. 81) to "The Web Means the End of Forgetting" or another text that your instructor specifies. In your group or individually, check off the following elements and be prepared to explain your selections.

- A debatable issue
- A clearly stated position, claim statement or thesis
- An audience
- Evidence from reliable sources
- Acknowledgment of the opposing argument
- A conclusion and/or call to action

Activity 2.6 • What Is the Current State of Identity Protection in Social Networking Sites?

Explore

In your group, explore news, watchdog, and government sites to see if any new laws or other protections have been implemented to safeguard individuals posting personal information on the web. Report what you learn to the class.

Close Reading of a Text

Rhetorical reading involves careful and patient attention to the text, even reading the text several times. Following are several strategies for close reading rhetorically. You do not need to use all of the reading strategies suggested for each essay you read, but as you begin to read rhetorically, you should try all of the strategies at least once to see which ones supplement your natural reading and learning style.

1. **Learn about the author.** Knowing whether an author is a biologist, a professional writer, or a politician can guide your expectations of the essay. If you are reading in a magazine or journal, you can often discover information in the contributor's notes at the beginning or end of the essay or at the beginning or end of the magazine. Many books have a dust jacket or a page giving a short biography of the author. As you learn about the author, jot down any impressions you may have about the author's purpose in writing the essay. Does the author have an obvious agenda in promoting a certain viewpoint on the topic?

2. **Skim the text.** Once you've gotten to know the author a little, it is helpful to read the essay quickly and superficially by reading the introduction, the first sentence in every paragraph, and the conclusion. Read quickly. When you skim a text, you are not trying to understand it. You are preparing for the more careful read that will follow. If the essay tells a story, skimming will give you a good sense of the chronology of the story. When is the story taking place? How much time seems to pass? If the essay is argumentative, skimming will provide knowledge of the basic structure of the argument and will introduce you to the main points of support. If the essay is primarily informative, you will learn some of the important distinctions and classifications the author uses to organize the information.

    It may be interesting to note whether you can get the gist of the reading by skimming. Has the writer provided topic sentences for paragraphs or sections? If so, the writer is trying to make his or her message easily accessible.

3. **Explore your own knowledge and beliefs on the subject.** Make a list of what you already know about the topic of the text. Then, make a list of what you believe about this topic. Finally, make a note beside each entry that marks where that information or belief came from.

4. **Reflect on the topic.** The final step before reading is reflecting on what you expect from the essay before you begin a careful reading. What does the title lead you to expect from the essay? Does your quick glance at the essay seem to support the title? How do you feel about the essay so far? Does it anger you, interest you, bore you? Do you think you have any experience that relates to the essay? Will your experience and the author's experience lead you to the same conclusions? One effective way to reflect is to freewrite on the topic of the essay. Exploring what you know before you embark on a careful reading of the essay can deepen your responses.

5. **Annotate.** Read the essay slowly, thinking about what meaning the author is trying to convey. It is a good idea to annotate as you read, particularly points that seem important and/or raise questions in your mind. If you don't want to write in your text, try photocopying assigned essays so you can annotate them. You'll probably develop your own system of annotation as you begin to use this technique more often, but here are some basic guidelines to help you begin your annotations.

▌ Underline sentences, phrases, and words that seem important to the essay.

▌ Circle words you don't know but think you understand from the context. You can look them up later to see if the dictionary definition matches the definition you assumed from the context.

▌ Write questions in the margins. If the margins aren't large enough to write a complete question, a couple of words to remind you of what you were thinking and a question mark will do. You can also write brief comments in the margins, again just a few words to remind you of your thoughts.

▌ Number or put check marks in the margin by major points. Careful annotation of each point in the margin will help you later if you choose to outline.

▌ Use arrows, lines, and symbols in the margins to connect ideas in the essay that seem related or depend on each other.

▌ Note transitions, sentence structures, examples, topic sentences, and other rhetorical moves that seem particularly effective in the essay by writing a brief comment or an exclamation mark in the margin next to the underlined text.

See Figure 2.1 on page 96 for an example of an annotated article.

6. **Outline.** An excellent way to distill the meaning of a text is to create an informal outline of the argument. If, as part of annotating the essay, you jot down the main subject of each paragraph in the margin, this will allow you to see the organization of the essay and outline it easily. An outline should list the focus of the essay and track how that focus unfolds paragraph by paragraph. If you are outlining a narrative essay, the outline will probably follow the chronology of the events. Outlining an informative essay, you might find that the outline tracks the steps of a process or reveals divisions and classifications. Outlining an argumentative essay, you'll probably find your outline works to prove a thesis by making statements which support that thesis, raising objections and refuting them, or, perhaps, proposing solutions to solve a problem.

7. **Freewrite about the text.** Another way to distill the meaning of a text after you have read it carefully is to lay the essay aside and freewrite for a few minutes about the content and purpose of the essay. If you have not tried freewriting before, it is easy. You simply put your pen to

the paper, focus the topic in your mind, and write whatever comes to mind about the topic for a set period of time, perhaps five minutes. If you cannot think of anything to write, you write, "I can't think of anything to write," and then you continue writing what is in your mind. You may find it helpful to begin your freewriting by writing, "This essay is about . . ." and continue writing, explaining to yourself what you think the essay is about.

8. **Summarize the text.** Write a summary of what you consider to be the primary meaning of the text. Your summary should answer certain questions about claims, support, purpose, and audience.

   ▌ What is the author of the essay trying to show or prove (claim)?

   ▌ What does the writer use to convince me that he or she is well informed or right (support)?

   ▌ Why did the writer choose to write this essay (purpose)?

   ▌ Who is the author addressing or writing for (audience)?

   To write a clear summary, you have to understand the essay. You might test your understanding by reading the essay again and deciding whether your summary is accurate. Writing summaries helps you understand your assignments and prepares you for the numerous summaries you will complete.

Checklist for Close Reading of a Text

☑ Learn about the author.

☑ Skim the text.

☑ Explore your knowledge and beliefs on the subject.

☑ Reflect on the topic.

☑ Annotate the text.

☑ Outline the text.

☑ Freewrite about the text

☑ Summarize the text.

Reading 2.3

The Point When Science Becomes Publicity

by James Hamblin, M.D.

One of the sources of academic disdain for popular health media is its reputation for sensationalism and exaggeration. "If You've Ever Eaten Pizza, You'll Want to Read About the Toxin That Is Pretty Certainly Ravaging Us From the Bowels Outward" or "This Common Household Item Is Definitely Killing You, Says a New Study"—when the actual study only posited that a "possible association may potentially exist" between, say, exposure to antibacterial soap and liver disease in a handful of mice who were exposed to more antibacterial soap than any human could ever dream of using, even if they washed their hands literally every time they went to the bathroom.

Have you read health-scare articles like "If You've Ever Eaten Pizza, You'll Want to Read About the Toxin That Is Pretty Certainly Ravaging Us From the Bowels Outward" or "This Common Household Item Is Definitely Killing You, Says a New Study"? Can you trust the information presented by such sensationalized articles? Maybe not. According to the Atlantic *article, "The Point When Science Becomes Publicity," the actual studies that are the basis of such articles may blur the distinction between a possible association and a definite connection. Moreover, psychology professor Petroc Sumner traced the source of numerous extreme articles to press releases written by public relations departments of the researchers' own universities rather than to the news media or the researchers themselves.*

James Hamblin, M.D., the article's author, is a senior editor at the Atlantic, *where he writes a health column.*

Petroc Sumner, a professor of psychology at Cardiff University in Wales, has been trying to pinpoint exactly where exaggeration in science reporting comes from. At what level, in the ladder from lab data to news headline, are most inaccuracies introduced?

Yesterday Sumner and colleagues published some important research in the journal BMJ that found that a majority of exaggeration in health stories was traced not to the news outlet, but to the press release—the statement issued by the university's publicity department.

"The framing of health-related information in the national and international media has complex and potentially powerful impacts on healthcare utilization and other health-related behavior," Sumner and colleagues write. "Although it is common to blame media outlets and their journalists for news perceived as exaggerated, sensationalized, or alarmist, most of the inflation detected in our study did not occur de novo in the media but was already present in the text of the press releases."

The goal of a press release around a scientific study is to draw attention from the media, and that attention is supposed to be good for the university, and for the scientists who did the work. Ideally the endpoint of that press release would be the simple spread of seeds of knowledge and wisdom; but it's about attention and prestige and, thereby, money. Major universities employ publicists who work full time to make scientific studies sound engaging and amazing. Those publicists email the press releases to people like me, asking me to cover the story because "my readers" will "love it." And I want to write about health research and help people experience "love" for things. I do!

Across 668 news stories about health science, the Cardiff researchers compared the original academic papers to their news reports. They counted exaggeration and distortion as any instance of implying causation when there was only correlation, implying meaning to humans when the study was only in animals, or giving direct advice about health behavior that was not present in the study. They found evidence of exaggeration in 58 to 86 percent of stories when the press release contained similar exaggeration. When the press release was staid and made no such errors, the rates of exaggeration in the news stories dropped to between 10 and 18 percent.

Even the degree of exaggeration between press releases and news stories was broadly similar.

Sumner and colleagues say they would not shift liability to press officers, but rather to academics. "Most press releases issued by universities are drafted in dialogue between scientists and press officers and are not released without the approval of scientists," the researchers write, "and thus most of the responsibility for exaggeration must lie with the scientific authors."

In an accompanying editorial in the journal, Ben Goldacre, author of the book *Bad Science,* noted that bad news tends to generate more coverage than good and that less rigorous observational studies tend to generate more coverage than robust clinical trials, probably due to the applicability of the subject matter to lay readers.

Guidelines for best practices already exist among academic journals and institutional press officers, he notes, "but these are routinely ignored." So Goldacre corroborates Sumner's argument for accountability: that academics should be held responsible for what's said in the universities' press releases that publicize said academics' research. The press releases will often be read much more widely than the actual journal article, yet many academics take little to no interest in them. Instead, writing an accurate press release should be considered part of the scientific publication process.

"This is not a peripheral matter," writes Goldacre, citing research that has found that media coverage has important effects on people's health behaviors and healthcare utilization, and even on subsequent academic research.

He notes that Sumner was "generous" to avoid naming particular offenders in this study. But Sumner did share with me some of the less egregious examples by email. In one case, a journal article read[,] "This observational study found significant associations between use of antidepressant drugs and adverse outcomes in people aged 65 and older with depression." The press release went on to read[,] "New antidepressants increase risks for elderly." There are of course many reasons why taking antidepressants would be associated with worse outcomes. For example, people with worse symptoms to begin with are more likely to take antidepressants.

"It is very common for this type of thing to happen," said Sumner, "probably partly because the causal phrases are shorter and just sound better. There may be no intention to change the meaning."

There is also, almost always, an implied causal relationship when reporting on a correlation. Every time we note a correlation in anything we publish on this site, at least one of our fair commenters will jump to point out that correlation is not causation. That comment may as well just auto-populate on any article that involves science. Which is fine—even though we're deliberate in not mistaking the relationships for causal—because why even report on a correlation if you don't mean to imply in some way that there is a chance there could be causation?

I asked Sumner how he felt about the press release for his study, because I thought that would be kind of funny.

"We were happy with our press release," he said. "It seemed to stick closely to the article and not claim causal relationships, for example, where we had not."

Appropriately reported scientific claims are a necessary but not sufficient condition in cultivating informed health consumers, but misleading claims are sufficient to do harm. Since many such claims originate within universities, Sumner writes, the scientific community has the ability to improve this situation. But the problem is bigger than a lack of communication between publicists and scientists. The blame for all of this exaggeration is most accurately traced back, according to the researchers, to an "increasing culture of university competition and self-promotion, interacting with the increasing pressures on journalists to do more with less time."

In his ivory tower, in his ivory cap and gown, the academic removes his ivory spectacles just long enough to shake his head at the journalists who are trying to understand his research. The headlines and tweets are wretched misappropriations. Wretched! The ink-stained journalists shake their ink-stained heads in time at the detached academics, at the irrelevance of work written in jargon behind giant paywalls where it will be read by not more than five to seven people, including the nuclear families of the researchers. The families members who, when the subject of the latest journal article comes up at dinner, politely excuse themselves.

But the divide is narrowing every day.

"Our findings may seem like bad news, but we prefer to view them positively," Sumner and colleagues conclude. "If the majority of exaggeration occurs within academic establishments, then the academic community has the opportunity to make an important difference to the quality of biomedical and health-related news."

Figure 2.1 • Example of Close Reading Annotation

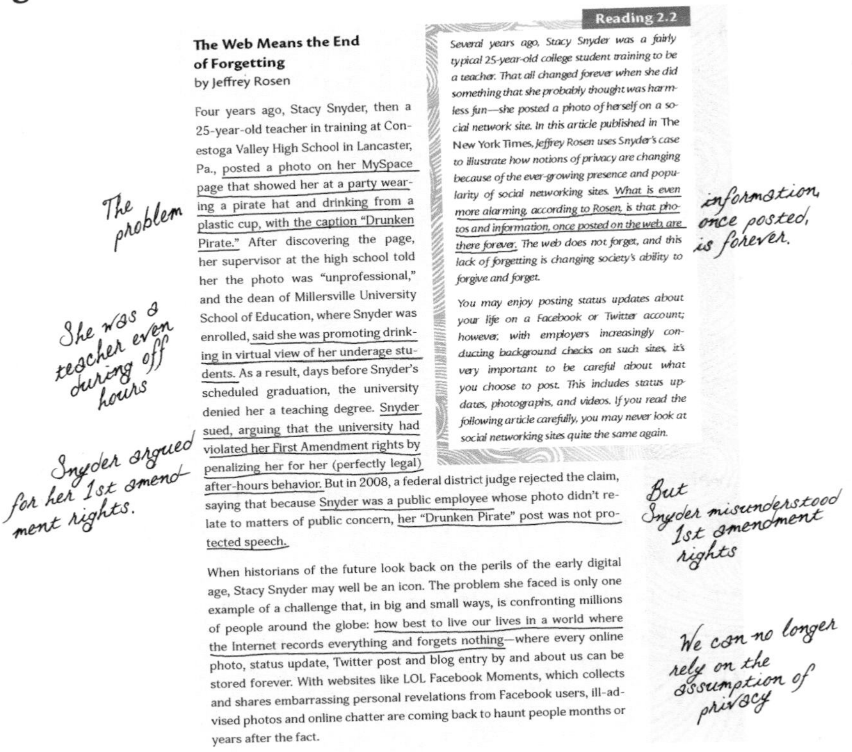

The Web Means the End of Forgetting
by Jeffrey Rosen

Four years ago, Stacy Snyder, then a 25-year-old teacher in training at Conestoga Valley High School in Lancaster, Pa., posted a photo on her MySpace page that showed her at a party wearing a pirate hat and drinking from a plastic cup, with the caption "Drunken Pirate." After discovering the page, her supervisor at the high school told her the photo was "unprofessional," and the dean of Millersville University School of Education, where Snyder was enrolled, said she was promoting drinking in virtual view of her underage students. As a result, days before Snyder's scheduled graduation, the university denied her a teaching degree. Snyder sued, arguing that the university had violated her First Amendment rights by penalizing her for her (perfectly legal) after-hours behavior. But in 2008, a federal district judge rejected the claim, saying that because Snyder was a public employee whose photo didn't relate to matters of public concern, her "Drunken Pirate" post was not protected speech.

When historians of the future look back on the perils of the early digital age, Stacy Snyder may well be an icon. The problem she faced is only one example of a challenge that, in big and small ways, is confronting millions of people around the globe: how best to live our lives in a world where the Internet records everything and forgets nothing—where every online photo, status update, Twitter post and blog entry by and about us can be stored forever. With websites like LOL Facebook Moments, which collects and shares embarrassing personal revelations from Facebook users, ill-advised photos and online chatter are coming back to haunt people months or years after the fact.

Reading 2.2

Several years ago, Stacy Snyder was a fairly typical 25-year-old college student training to be a teacher. That all changed forever when she did something that she probably thought was harmless fun—she posted a photo of herself on a social network site. In this article published in The New York Times, Jeffrey Rosen uses Snyder's case to illustrate how notions of privacy are changing because of the ever-growing presence and popularity of social networking sites. What is even more alarming, according to Rosen, is that photos and information, once posted on the web are there forever. The web does not forget, and this lack of forgetting is changing society's ability to forgive and forget.

You may enjoy posting status updates about your life on a Facebook or Twitter account; however, with employers increasingly conducting background checks on such sites, it's very important to be careful about what you choose to post. This includes status updates, photographs, and videos. If you read the following article carefully, you may never look at social networking sites quite the same again.

The problem

She was a teacher even during off hours

Snyder argued for her 1st amendment rights.

information once posted, is forever.

But Snyder misunderstood 1st amendment rights

We can no longer rely on the assumption of privacy

Activity 2.7 • Apply Close Reading to a Text

Apply the eight steps of close reading to "The Point When Science Becomes Publicity" or another reading that your instructor specifies. Review the annotation example in Figure 2.1 to begin. Next, make a copy of the text, so that you can annotate it. Then answer these questions in a small group or individually.

1. What can you learn about the author by reading a headnote or doing a search on Google or Wikipedia? Explain briefly.

2. Skim the text of the reading. What did you learn about the purpose of the text?

3. Briefly explain your own knowledge or beliefs about the subject.

4. Reflect on the topic before you read it thoroughly. What does the title lead you to expect? How do you feel about the text so far? Freewrite for five minutes, and then summarize your freewriting in a few coherent sentences.

5. Annotate then outline the essay, then freewrite for five minutes before summarizing the text. Follow the instructions on pp. 89–92 for each step.

Activity 2.8 • Discuss "The Point When Science Becomes Publicity"

According to James Hamblin, articles published in popular health media often sensationalize scientific findings. Use these questions to inform your discussion of "The Point When Science Becomes Publicity" in a small group.

1. What do you think is the source of the sensationalism in this article?

2. In effect, university publicity departments misuse rhetoric to attract reporters' attention. According to Hamblin's argument, why do they do this? Why is it a misuse of rhetoric?

3. Identify one of the examples Hamblin gives of sensationalized health news.

4. In your group, brainstorm other articles you may have read that sensationalize health news. Alternatively, find examples on the internet. Report the most interesting ones to the class.

The Rhetorical Triangle

When reading a text or listening to a speech, keep in mind the three parts of the rhetorical triangle—writer, audience, and subject (see Figure 2.2). Each of these can be framed as a question.

Figure 2.2 • The Rhetorical Triangle

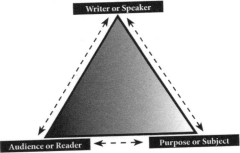

- Who is the **writer**? What is the impression the writer wants to make on the audience? What does the writer do to establish credibility (*ethos*)? How does the writer create common ground with the audience?

- Who is the **intended audience**? How would a logical appeal influence the audience? An ethical appeal? An emotional appeal? What does the audience anticipate in terms of organization and format of the presentation or paper? What is the extent of their knowledge about the subject, and do they have prejudices or preferences?

- What is the **purpose** of the communication? In the case of an argument, the purpose is to persuade. Is that the case with this reading? Is it clear what the writer wants to persuade the audience to believe or to do? Is the request phrased in a logical manner?

Explore

Activity 2.9 • Apply the Rhetorical Triangle

For each of the readings presented thus far in the textbook, identify the speaker, the audience, and the purpose. Then, analyze how each of those elements affects the content of the reading.

- "'Columbusing': The Art of Discovering Something that Is Not New," Chapter 1, p. 18.

- "Microsoft Just Laid Off Thousands of Employees with a Hilariously Bad Memo," Chapter 1, p. 25.

- "The Sleepover Question," Chapter 1, p. 30.

- "Text of the Gettysburg Address," Chapter 1, p. 59.

- "Do You Know How Your Mascara is Made?" Chapter 2, p. 68.

- "The Web Means the End of Forgetting," Chapter 2, p. 88.

- "The Point When Science Becomes Publicity," Chapter 2, p. 93.

Compos

Activity 2.10 • **Write a Summary**

Summarizing is an excellent technique to use when preparing for an exam or researching for an essay. It allows you to discern the main points of a text to see what is beneficial for you to know for the exam or paper.

With a classmate, search for an article from a newspaper or magazine that presents a strong argument. Read the article, and list the main points individually. After you've listed the main points, put them into paragraph form.

Beware of the temptation to add your own analysis of what the text is saying. For example, if you are summarizing a scientist's article on global warming, you need to be careful not to reveal your personal opinion about whether or not global warming is occurring or whether or not human actions are to blame. In this assignment, you summarize only. You do not argue or analyze.

When you're finished, compare your summary with that of your partner.

Respond to Multimedia

Increasingly, young "politically minded viewers" are plugging into YouTube, Facebook, and comedy shows like *The Daily Show* and other alternative media instead of traditional news outlets. According to a *New York Times* article, surveys and interviews during the 2008 presidential election indicate that "younger voters tend to be not just consumers of news and current events but conduits as well—sending out emailed links and videos to friends and their social networks. And in turn, they rely on friends and online connections for news to come to them." **Word of mouth** (via email) is replacing traditional media as the major news filter, at least for young viewers. Moreover, in this new process, "viewers" or "writers of email" move seamlessly back and forth between email, text-messaging, television viewing, and internet surfing, appreciating and sharing the choicest rhetorical pieces with others. "We're talking about a generation that doesn't just like seeing the video in addition to the story—they expect it," said Danny Shea, 23, the associate media editor for *The Huffington Post* (huffingtonpost.com). "And they'll find it elsewhere if you don't give it to them, and then that's the link that's going to be passed around over email and instant message." This multistream, cross-platform method of communication among younger viewers/readers is a fertile forum for rhetorical analysis.

Actually, the lines between oral, written, and visual "texts" have always been somewhat blurred. Speeches delivered orally in person or on television have a visual component, as the audience sees the speaker present the text. A written text is also, in a sense, visual because the audience's mind must process the little squiggles of ink on paper or on the computer screen into words. A visual text such as an advertisement or cartoon often includes written text, and, even if it does not, the image will inspire thoughts that are often distilled into language for expression. Reasonably, many of the same techniques used to analyze written and oral texts also can be applied to visual media (cartoons, advertisements, television, etc.).

Reading 2.4

"Flawless," the hit song from Beyoncé's fifth studio album, includes the voice of Nigerian novelist Chimamanda Ngozi Adichie delivering an excerpt from her 2012 TEDx Talk, "We Should All be Feminists." Beyoncé Giselle Knowles-Carter is a Grammy-award-winning singer, songwriter, and actress.

Adichie is the author of the acclaimed 2013 novel Americanah, *that Carolyn Kellogg of the* Los Angles Times *calls "a smart and surprisingly funny take on race and gender in contemporary society." Adichie was awarded a MacArthur "Genius" Fellowship in 2008 after the publication of her novel,* Half a Yellow Sun, *which is set during Nigeria's Biafran War. Kellogg praises the inclusion of Adichie's excerpt in the middle of Beyoncé's song.*

Excerpt from "Flawless"

by Beyoncé and Chimamanda Ngozi Adichie

We teach girls to shrink themselves

To make themselves smaller

We say to girls,

"You can have ambition

But not too much

You should aim to be successful

But not too successful

Otherwise you will threaten the man."

Because I am female

I am expected to aspire to marriage

I am expected to make my life choices

Always keeping in mind that

Marriage is the most important

Now marriage can be a source of

Joy and love and mutual support

But why do we teach girls to aspire to marriage

And we don't teach boys the same?

We raise girls to see each other as competitors

Not for jobs or for accomplishments

Which I think can be a good thing

But for the attention of men

We teach girls that they cannot be sexual beings

In the way that boys are

Feminist: the person who believes in the social

Political, and economic equality of the sexes

Activity 2.11 • **Respond to Song Lyrics**

In a small group or on your own, explore these discussion questions in response to the excerpt from "Flawless" by Beyoncé and Chimamanda Ngozi Adichie.

1. What does Chimamanda Ngozi Adichie's excerpt (from her *TEDx Talk* "We Should All be Feminists") say about what society teaches girls? What does the message in the excerpt have to do with being a feminist?

2. On the internet, locate the complete lyrics for Beyoncé's song "Flawless" and/or listen to the complete song. How do Beyonce's own lyrics compliment Adichie's excerpt?

3. What argument is Beyoncé making in her song "Flawless"?

4. What do you think of including a non-singing element such as this excerpt in the middle of a popular song? Does it add to or detract from the song's effect?

Activity 2.12 • **Consider a Song as an Argument**

In your small group, explore the internet for a song that seems to make an argument, and answer the following questions. Share your findings with the class.

1. What message is the artist/group trying to transmit with the song?

2. What are some lyrics that help to support this message?

3. How would you describe the musical style of the song? In what ways does the style of singing and instrumentation help convey the rhetorical argument?

Respond to Visual Rhetoric

Methods of analyzing visual rhetoric draw upon several theoretical traditions. In art criticism, viewers may look for symbolism in an image or consider what meaning the artist was trying to convey. Semiotics views images as having intertextuality, as similar images come to have similar meanings, and those meanings may create similar emotions in the viewer. Rhetoricians, as you might expect, consider the argument that an image may present to a viewer. They think about how the subject of the image is presented in relation to other elements in the visual, how the image is cropped, and what types of lighting and colors are present. Rhetoricians also pay particular attention to

Explore

Collaborate

the interplay between the visual image and any text that may appear with the image and how the two together construct an argument.

Courtesy BMW premium advertising

In the BMW advertisement shown above, for example, a beautiful blonde-haired young woman is presented without clothes and lying down with her hair artfully arranged in waves. *Salon* magazine reprinted a copy of the BMW advertisement, pointing out that, "in small print scrawled across her bare shoulder, it reads: 'You know you're not the first.' As your eyes drift to the bottom of the advertisement—and the top of her chest—you learn that it's an advertisement for BMW's premium selection of used cars."

Of course, sexual appeal has been used for decades to sell a whole range of products. However, what do you think is BMW's argument here? *Salon* thinks the ad is implying, "Used cars, used women" and that the ad gives a "whole new meaning" to BMW's slogan, printed in the ad: "Sheer Driving Pleasure."

The image that appears on the next page, surprisingly, isn't advertising a car. No, it is selling a community college, West Hills College, capitalizing on the idea that with all the money you would save by going to a community college, you could buy a nice car.

Courtesy West Hills College

Activity 2.13 • Interpret Advertisements

Explore

On your own, explore the rhetorical implications of the two advertisements referenced in this section using these discussion questions.

1. What is the symbolism of the beautiful young woman (presumably naked) posed as she is in the BMW advertisement?

2. What meaning do you think the tag line, "You know you're not the first," adds to the image? Then, when you realize that the image is an ad for BMW used cars, does your interpretation of this tag line's meaning change?

3. What are the creators of the West Hills College advertisement trying to say by showing the image of the student sitting on the car?

4. The use of fonts is another important element in transmitting a message in an advertisement. In the West Hills College ad, why are the words "and save" written in a different font and inserted with the caret?

5. As a college student, would you be convinced by the West Hills advertisement? Why or why not? What elements exist in the ad that would or would not convince you to attend the college mentioned?

6. Do you find the BMW advertisement amusing, objectionable, or appealing? Does it make you want to buy a used BMW?

ollaborate

Activity 2.14 • Find Advertisements with Effective Arguments

Bring to class an advertisement that you think makes an effective argument. It can be torn from a magazine or downloaded from the internet. In your small group, evaluate each advertisement for its effectiveness in selling something, and choose the one with the most successful argument. Present your choice to the class along with an explanation of why you think it is effective.

Reading 2.5

Why has Godzilla grown over the years? One possible explanation is that buildings have grown taller, and Godzilla has grown to keep up. However, Godzilla has grown at a faster rate than skyscrapers, as you can see from the graphs "Godzilla Through the Years" and "History of the World's Tallest Skyscrapers." The most recent Godzilla is three times the size of the original, while today's tallest skyscraper is much less than three times the size of the Empire State Building, the tallest building at the time of the original Godzilla.

According to an article in Sociological Images *by professor Lisa Wade, the best explanation is that the flood of advertising spawned by the internet has resulted in advertisers resorting to shock value. The article quotes media guru Sut Jhally asking, "So overwhelming has the commercial takeover of culture become, that it has now become a problem for advertisers who now worry about clutter and noise. That is, how do you make your ads stand out from the commercial impressions that people are exposed to?"*

You make Godzilla stand out by making him disproportionally large. Though the article doesn't use the term "visual rhetoric," that's what it is talking about. In today's media climate, for something, even Godzilla, to make a medial splash, it has to be bigger, weirder, more violent, or more gorgeous.

Why Has Godzilla Grown?

by Lisa Wade

Recently, the internet chuckled at the visual below. It shows that, since Godzilla made his first movie appearance in 1954, he has tripled in size.

Kris Holt, at PolicyMic, suggests that his enlargement is in response to growing skylines. She writes:

> As time has passed, buildings have grown ever taller too. If Godzilla had stayed the same height throughout its entire existence, it would be much less imposing on a modern cityscape.

This seems plausible. Buildings have gotten taller and so, to preserve the original feel, Godzilla would have to grow too.

Godzilla through the Years

50 Meters 1954-1975, 2001 | 55 Meters 1999-2000, 2002-2003 | 80 Meters 1984-1989 | 100 Meters 1991-1995, 2004 | 120-150 Meters 2014

But rising buildings can't be the only explanation. According to this graphic, the tallest building at the time of Gozilla's debut was the Empire State Building, rising to 381 meters. The tallest building in the world today is (still) the Burj Khalifa. At 828 meters, it's more than twice as tall as the Empire State Building, but it's far from three times as tall, or 1,143 meters.

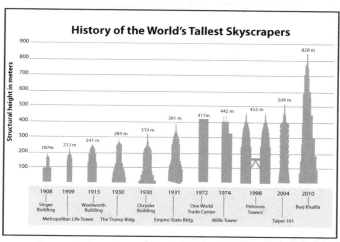

Is there an alternate explanation? Here's one hypothesis.

In 1971, the average American was exposed to about 500 advertisements per day. Today, because of the internet, they are exposed to over 5,000. Every. Day.

Media critic Sut Jhally argues that the flood of advertising has forced marketers to shift strategies. Specifically, he says

> So overwhelming has the commercial takeover of culture become, that it has now become a problem for advertisers who now worry about clutter and noise. That is, how do you make your ads stand out from the commercial impressions that people are exposed to.

One strategy has been to ratchet up shock value. "You need to get eyeballs. You need to be loud," said Kevin Kay, Spike's programming chief.

So, to increase shock value, everything is being made more extreme. Compared to the early '90s, before the internet was a fixture in most homes and businesses, advertising—and I'm guessing media in general—has gotten more extreme in lots of ways. Things are sexier, more violent, more gorgeous, more satirical, and weirder.

So, Godzilla because, eyeballs.

Activity 2.15 • Consider Shock Value in Today's Cartoon Characters

After you read Wade's article, discuss the following in your group.

1. What argument does sociology professor Lisa Wade make about the growth of Godzilla's size in advertisements over the years?

2. If you accept Wade's argument, what does it have to do with visual rhetoric?

3. What other cartoon characters in advertisements or other media also have grown or otherwise changed because of a response to the pressure to stand out from the clutter and noise of today's media world?

4. How have other cartoon characters been altered for shock value?

Interaction between Texts and Images

Many of the texts we encounter in everyday life—in newspapers, magazines, and on the internet—are not texts in isolation but texts combined with images. Indeed, when readers first glance at one of these media, likely their attention is caught first by photos, then by headlines. Only after being engaged by these attention-getting visual elements (for headlines are visual elements as well as written) are readers likely to focus on the written text. Student writers today, like professionals, have access to the use of visual elements in their compositions, and adding photos can not only catch the reader's attention but also emphasize particular points of an argument or create an overall mood.

All-Star Rockers Salute Buddy Holly
by Andy Greene

Take a look at the images in this Rolling Stone *article by Andy Greene. Greene writes about a tribute record on Buddy Holly called* Rave *that several famous musical artists contributed to. Think about how Greene's choice of text and image pairings affect the rhetorical impact of the article.*

R&R

All-Star Rockers Salute Buddy Holly

McCartney, Cee Lo, the Black Keys, Kid Rock and more cut killer covers disc

When Buddy Holly died in a plane crash in 1959, he was just 22 years old and had been writing and recording songs for only about two years. But that music—including immortal hits like "Not Fade Away" and "Peggy Sue"—has had an incalculable impact on rock history. "He was a major influence on the Beatles," Paul McCartney told Rolling Stone recently. "John and I spent hours trying to work out how to play the opening riff to "That'll Be the Day," and we were truly blessed by the heavens the day we figured it out. It was the first song John, George and I ever recorded."

A half-century later, McCartney has returned to Holly's catalog, cutting a smoking rendition of "It's So Easy." It's one of 19 newly recorded Holly covers—by an all-star lineup including the Black Keys, My Morning Jacket, Kid Rock Fiona Apple, Patti Smith, and Lou Reed—for the tribute

NOT FADE AWAY
Holly in 1950. McCartney and Cee Lo recorded new songs commemorating Holly's 75th birthday.

disc *Rave on Buddy Holly,* spearheaded by Randall Poster, music supervisor of movies such as *The Royal Tenenbaums* and *I'm Not There.* "We wanted to commemorate Buddy's 75th birthday," Poster says. "I've used a lot of his songs in movies, and they're so powerful and so ripe for interpretation."

Florence and the Machine cut a New Orleans-flavored version of "Not Fade Away" while on tour in the Big Easy last year. "My grandmother took me to the musical *Buddy: The Buddy Holly Story* when I was a kid, and it changed my life," says singer Florence Welch. "When we were in New Orleans, we decided

it would be good to use the environment around us, so we brought in local Cajun musicians." Cee Lo Green tackled the relatively obscure "You're So Square (Baby, I Don't Care)." "We wanted to keep the rockabilly intact," he says. "But we broadened it and gave it a bit of something unique to me. There's something Americana about it, something country and something African." Smith selected "Words of Love." "During the song she talks in Spanish and is sort of channeling [Holly's widow] Maria Elena Holly," says Poster. "It's so romantic and so novel. More times than not, we were just overwhelmed by the power of the renditions that we received." Despite Holly's extremely brief career, Poster thinks the set could have been even longer: "There's probably a half-dozen more songs we could have done. If I had more time and more of a budget, I would have kept on going."   ANDY GREENE

Activity 2.16 • Analyze Interaction between Texts and Images

Explore

Read the article, "All-Star Rockers Salute Buddy Holly," by Andy Greene, published in *Rolling Stone* magazine. Look at how the images and layout work together, and respond to these questions on your own.

1. What rhetorical purpose do the photos of these musicians achieve in relation to the article? Hint: think about the *ethos* (credibility, reputation, power) of these particular musicians, especially when they appear together on the page.

2. Consider the way the text is wrapped around the pictures. In particular, notice how this layout suggests a close relationship between Buddy Holly, Paul McCartney, and Cee Lo Green. What does this layout signify?

Reading 2.7

The author of the following article explains why you would want to make a Kindle cover out of an old book instead of buying a new Kindle cover. What does the article say are the drawbacks of the Kindle? Think about it. These instructions are an argument, saying in text and photos that as wonderful as the Kindle is, it does not satisfy the needs of a reader to touch and smell a book. The author attempts to rectify the Kindle's short-comings through these instructions for making a cover out of a book.

Notice also how the author uses photos to illustrate his text. If you had just the text and no photos, following the instructions would be much more difficult.

How to Make a Kindle Cover from a Hollowed Out Hardback Book

by Justin Meyers

Kindle users love reading. But let's face it—nothing compares to the feel of a book is in your hands.

Sure, Amazon's Kindle makes it possible to read more books, clears up a lot of shelf space, fits snugly in anyone's baggage and can actually be cheaper in the long run. But each reading feels the same. The only difference is the words you read and your reaction to them. You begin to miss that sometimes rough feel of a hardback book, along with the slick, almost slippery design of a paperback. Each book seems to have a smell of its own, something unique. And getting your hands dirty with ink from the finely written words was half the journey.

 The Kindle erases that part of your reading experience. It feels the same, smells the same and even looks the same. Instead of turning pages, which is different sizes, thicknesses and colors from book to book, you're pressing the same button over and over again. In some ways, reading a classic on your Kindle actually devalues its adventure. But the eBook reader is convenient, practically weightless and serves up immediate literature consumption.

So where's the compromise?

Well, you can have the best of both worlds—sort of . . .

[Twitter user] @ebonical has crafted the perfect Kindle case—out of a hardcover book. Kindle cases can be expensive, so making a homemade Kindle cover is the perfect weekend project. And chances are you already have the perfect book for your Kindle collecting dust on your bookshelf. If not, you'll need to shop the local bookstores.

"I decided to carve out the pages of a printed book and thus complete the poetic circle of digital book readers destroying the printed word.

"Getting the right book turned out to be harder than I thought as most hard-cover books are designed to be a particular size and variance is slight. Too small and the edges would be brittle. Too large and it would just become a hassle and ruin the point of having the small digital reader in the first place. With some time spent scouring thrift shops and second hand book stalls I managed, with some luck, to find what seemed to be the right book."

So, then how do you actually make the Kindle book cover?

STEP 1 Gather the Materials
- Your perfectly-sized hardcover book
- Hobby PVA glue (polyvinyl acetate) or Elmer's white glue
- Paintbrush
- Scalpel, box cutter or other sharp utility knife
- Ruler
- Pencil
- More books (for use as weights)

STEP 2 Crafting Your Kindle Case
Getting your book ready for your Kindle is an easy process, though a lengthy one.

You begin by choosing where you want your hole to start. Once you have your spot picked, you use the paintbrush to spread the glue onto the edges of the pages where the hole will be cut. Use your extra books to weigh it down during the drying process.

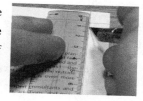

When dry, open the book back up to your chosen starting point. Use the ruler and pencil to mark your hole the size of the Kindle. Once all marked, use your utility knife to start cutting on the outline. It's probably best to use your ruler as a straight edge to help guide the blade along, for a better, straighter cut. This is the longest step, because you have a lot to cut through. The time will vary depending on how deep your book is. I wouldn't recommend *War and Peace*.

Once you've gotten all the way to the back cover, the rest is easy. Just clean up the edges of your cuts as best you can, then use your paintbrush again to spread some glue along the cut edges.

TIP: When choosing your first page to cut, it's good to actually save it for later. Don't cut with the rest of them. When you have your hole fully cut open and have applied the glue, apply another thin line on the top border of your actual first page cut (essentially, the second page). Then close the book and add the weights to the top and let dry. Saving the first page helps reduce the chance of you accidentally gluing unwanted pages to cut ones, causing you to have to cut the pages you didn't want to cut to open the hole back up. Saving your first page makes it premeditated.

After fully dried, open it up and cut the final page (first page) to open the hole up. Then, you'll need to let it dry again, with the book open. After dried, that's it. You're done!

Activity 2.17 • Write and Illustrate Instructions

Write and illustrate your own set of instructions for an activity that includes an argument.

For example, during a lawn party at the White House, First Lady Michelle Obama served Carrot Lemonade to children who gave the drink rave reviews. Such a recipe could include an introduction explaining that creating healthy adaptations of popular foods and drinks for children only works if they taste good. Or, you might write instructions for how to remove geotags from photos before posting them on Facebook or other social networking sites.

In your instructions, you could explain that this process prevents people you don't know from learning where you took the picture—and possibly learning where you live if you took it at home. Your argument would be that it is important to protect your privacy when you post photos on the internet.

Try out your instructions on a friend, so you are sure you have included all the necessary steps and illustrated them adequately. Don't forget to include a brief statement of your argument, as does the writer of the Kindle cover article.

Activity 2.18 • Summarize the Argument in Your Illustrations

Write one or more sentences summarizing your argument in the illustrations you wrote for Activity 2.17. For example, the author of "How to Make a Kindle Cover from a Hollowed Out Hardback Book" is arguing in his instructions that the Kindle is wonderful but does not completely satisfy the desire of a reader to touch and smell a book.

Image credit: "Walt Whitman" by Panhandle Slim.

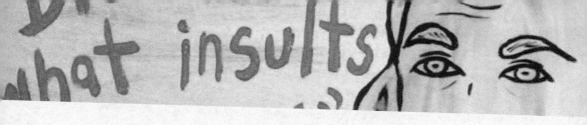

chapter 3
Analyzing Rhetorically

If You Want to Write Well, Then Read

Amber Lea Clark, M.L.S. Student in Liberal Studies, Southern Methodist University

"Readers make the best writers." I can't tell you how many times my instructors have said those words. As I have become a reader, I have learned that this is true. Reading teaches me about the construction of stories and arguments. In a movie or TV show, I almost instantly know who did it or who not to trust based on previous movies or TV shows I've watched. The same goes for analyzing arguments. Through reading critically, I have learned to see when an author is trying to convince me by manipulating my feelings versus persuading me by providing all of the facts. I can distinguish between fair representation of an issue, embellishment of truth, and bitter sarcasm. Every text needs to be taken with a grain of salt, slowly simmered, and thought about before the final evaluation can be made.

This chapter provides sample essays that illustrate different types of rhetorical arguments or appeals—arguments from *ethos* (credibility), *pathos* (emotion), or *logos* (logic). I encourage you to read them carefully. What do you see? How has each writer used his or her credibility, your emotions, or logic to reach you—the audience? How would each essay be different if the author had chosen to emphasize a different appeal, or would that even be possible?

Sentence structure, word use, and argument construction—the ability to perform each of these writing tasks effectively comes from more than just the practice we get from completing an assignment. It comes from analyzing others' arguments—my classmates' and published authors'. It comes from thinking critically as I read. Does this convince me? What is the author using for sources? Is this logical or a logical fallacy? Had I not read how other writers construct their arguments, I would never have become a better writer. Start now; become a reader.

Discover the *Kairos*–The Opening for Argument

Kairos is a Greek word often translated as the right or opportune moment to do something, though it has no exact English translation. The first recorded use of the word *kairos* is in Homer's *Iliad*, where it appears as an adjective referring to an arrow striking the "deadliest spot" on the human body. When the word appears again later in Greek writing as a noun—a *kairos*—it retains this essential meaning as an opening or aperture. Twelve bronze axes with ring openings for wooden shanks are positioned in a line, so archers can practice by aiming at the *kairos* or ring opening, with the arrow passing down the line, through each ax. Clearly,

Ancient Greek archer

launching an arrow through the *kairos* of twelve axes placed a yard apart required strength, training, practice, and a precise visual and muscle awareness of place. When people today say, "I saw my opening, and I took it," they are conveying this meaning of *kairos* as an opening, combined with the idea of *kairos* as an opportunity.[1]

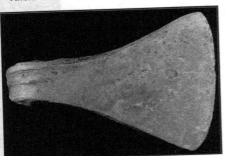

Ancient bronze ax with a ring hole for a wooden shank

Each time a rhetor (a speaker or writer) constructs an argument, he or she is working within the context of a certain moment, a particular time and place, that come together in a unique opportunity or opening for action—a *kairos*. A *kairos* both constrains and enables what a rhetor can say or write effectively in a particular situation. So, to compose the most effective text, a rhetor must do more than develop a thesis or statement of the main idea that takes a position about the subject—he or she must discover the *kairos* of the argument and its ramifications. What opportunities does the *kairos* present for making a persuasive argument, and what restrictions may be wise in consideration of the audience or occasion?

Use **Kairos** *to Make Your Own Argument*

Consider the following suggestions for determining the kairotic moment for your argument—the opening of sensitivity where you can shoot your metaphoric arrow.

▌ **Consider timeliness.** What is going on right now with the issue, and how can you emphasize that in an argument? For example, if you are writing

---

1. Rickert, Thomas. "Invention in the Wild: On Locating *Kairos* in Space-Time." *The Locations of Composition*, edited by Christopher J. Keller and Christian R. Weisser, SUNY, 2007, pp. 72-73.

about the death penalty, choose to write about the current cases on death row or the most recent person to be executed. Or, if your topic is about the unemployed exhausting their government benefits and you have, yourself, recently become unemployed, you can use your own experience as an illustration of the problem.

■ **Know your audience.** What are the characteristics of the audience? Do they agree with your position on the issue or not? What is their educational level and the extent of their knowledge about the subject? For example, if you are writing about immigration policy reform, does your audience believe there is a need for reform? Do they have personal experience with illegal or legal immigrants? You can judge the amount of background information you need to provide based upon the characteristics of your audience. Also, the most important members of the audience, so far as an argument is concerned, are not those who already agree with you but those who are neutral or even slightly opposed to your position but willing to listen. Be careful not to phrase your argument in ways that are insulting to people who do not agree with you, for if you do so, they will stop listening to you.

■ **Find a place to stand.** In the reading that follows, Dr. Martin Luther King, Jr. stood in front of the Lincoln Memorial as he gave his famous speech, "I Have a Dream." This location greatly impacts the speech and increases King's *ethos*, which we discuss in more detail below. You can make a similar rhetorical move, for example, if you live in a border community because you stand, metaphorically and physically, at an important juncture for issues such as immigration, free trade, and national security.

When Dr. Martin Luther King, Jr., gave his "I Have a Dream" speech, his words were carefully crafted to take into consideration the setting in front of the Lincoln Memorial. He said, "Five score years ago, a great American, in whose symbolic shadow we stand today, signed the Emancipation Proclamation." The words "five score" recall the "four score and seven years ago" of President Abraham Lincoln's words in the Gettysburg Address. And King also pointed out that he and his audience that day stood in the "symbolic shadow" of the president who signed the Emancipation Proclamation. In these ways, he made use of Lincoln's shadow to legitimize what he was saying about civil rights.

In other ways, however, the *kairos* of the moment limited what he could say. His audience included both the thousands of people in front of him who were dedicated to the cause of racial equality and also the audience of those millions watching on television who may or may not have agreed with his message.

Thus, the tone of his message needed to be subtly measured not to antagonize those among his audience, particularly the television audience, who may have opposed aspects of the civil rights movement such as school integration. However, he spoke to let both his supporters and his opponents know, "The whirlwinds of revolt will continue to shake the foundations of our nation until the bright day of justice emerges." Yes, King advocated nonviolent demonstrations, but they were demonstrations nonetheless; he was putting opponents on notice that the disruptions caused by demonstrations would continue "until justice emerges." King consistently took the high road while maintaining the power of the kairotic moment when he spoke. This is one reason why his words continue to be studied decades after his death.

Reading 3.1

Dr. Martin Luther King, Jr. delivered this speech on August 28, 1963, at the Lincoln Memorial in Washington, D.C., as part of the March on Washington for Jobs and Freedom. A Baptist minister, King received the Nobel Peace Prize in 1964 for his efforts to end racial discrimination through nonviolent means. He was assassinated in 1968.

I Have a Dream

by Dr. Martin Luther King, Jr.

I am happy to join with you today in what will go down in history as the greatest demonstration for freedom in the history of our nation.

Five score years ago, a great American, in whose symbolic shadow we stand today, signed the Emancipation Proclamation. This momentous decree came as a great beacon light of hope to millions of Negro slaves who had been seared in the flames of withering injustice. It came as a joyous daybreak to end the long night of their captivity.

But one hundred years later, the Negro still is not free. One hundred years later, the life of the Negro is still sadly crippled by the manacles of segregation and the chains of discrimination. One hundred years later, the Negro lives on a lonely island of poverty in the midst of a vast ocean of material prosperity. One hundred years later, the Negro is still languished in the corners of American society  and finds himself an exile in his own land. And so we've come here today to dramatize a shameful condition.

In a sense we've come to our nation's capital to cash a check. When the architects of our republic wrote the magnificent words of the Constitution and the Declaration of Independence, they were signing a promissory note to which every American was to fall heir. This note was a promise that all men, yes, black men as well as white men, would be guaranteed the "unalienable Rights" of "Life, Liberty and the pursuit of Happiness." It is obvious today that America has defaulted on this promissory note, insofar as her citizens of color are concerned. Instead of honoring this sacred obligation, America has given the Negro people a bad check, a check which has come back marked "insufficient funds."

But we refuse to believe that the bank of justice is bankrupt. We refuse to believe that there are insufficient funds in the great vaults of opportunity of this nation. And so, we've come to cash this check, a check that will give us upon demand the riches of freedom and the security of justice.

We have also come to this hallowed spot to remind America of the fierce urgency of Now. This is no time to engage in the luxury of cooling off or to take the tranquilizing drug of gradualism. Now is the time to make real the promises of democracy. Now is the time to rise from the dark and desolate valley of segregation to the sunlit path of racial justice. Now is the time to lift our nation from the quicksands of racial injustice to the solid rock of brotherhood. Now is the time to make justice a reality for all of God's children.

It would be fatal for the nation to overlook the urgency of the moment. This sweltering summer of the Negro's legitimate discontent will not pass until there is an invigorating autumn of freedom and equality. Nineteen sixtythree is not an end, but a beginning. And those who hope that the Negro needed to blow off steam and will now be content will have a rude awakening if the nation returns to business as usual. And there will be neither rest nor tranquility in America until the Negro is granted his citizenship rights. The whirlwinds of revolt will continue to shake the foundations of our nation until the bright day of justice emerges.

But there is something that I must say to my people, who stand on the warm threshold which leads into the palace of justice: In the process of gaining our rightful place, we must not be guilty of wrongful deeds. Let us not seek to satisfy our thirst for freedom by drinking from the cup of bitterness and hatred. We must forever conduct our struggle on the high plane of dignity and discipline. We must not allow our creative protest to degenerate into physical violence. Again and again, we must rise to the majestic heights of meeting physical force with soul force.

The marvelous new militancy which has engulfed the Negro community must not lead us to a distrust of all white people, for many of our white brothers, as evidenced by their presence here today, have come to realize that their destiny is tied up with our destiny. And they have come to realize that their freedom is inextricably bound to our freedom.

> We cannot walk alone.
> And as we walk, we must make the pledge that we shall always
> march ahead.
> We cannot turn back.

There are those who are asking the devotees of civil rights, "When will you be satisfied?" We can never be satisfied as long as the Negro is the victim of the unspeakable horrors of police brutality. We can never be satisfied as long as our bodies, heavy with the fatigue of travel, cannot gain lodging in the motels of the highways and the hotels of the cities. We cannot be satisfied as long as the Negro's basic mobility is from a smaller ghetto to a larger one. We can never be satisfied as long as our children are stripped of their selfhood and robbed of their dignity by a sign stating: "For Whites Only." We cannot be satisfied as long as a Negro in Mississippi cannot vote and a Negro in New York believes he has nothing for which to vote. No, no, we are not satisfied, and we will not be satisfied until "justice rolls down like waters, and righteousness like a mighty stream."[1]

I am not unmindful that some of you have come here out of great trials and tribulations. Some of you have come fresh from narrow jail cells. And some of you have come from areas where your quest—quest for freedom left you battered by the storms of persecution and staggered by the winds of police brutality. You have been the veterans of creative suffering. Continue to work with the faith that unearned suffering is redemptive. Go back to Mississippi, go back to Alabama, go back to South Carolina, go back to Georgia, go back to Louisiana, go back to the slums and ghettos of our northern cities, knowing that somehow this situation can and will be changed.

Let us not wallow in the valley of despair, I say to you today, my friends.

And so even though we face the difficulties of today and tomorrow, I still have a dream. It is a dream deeply rooted in the American dream.

I have a dream that one day this nation will rise up and live out the true meaning of its creed: "We hold these truths to be self-evident, that all men are created equal."

I have a dream that one day on the red hills of Georgia, the sons of former slaves and the sons of former slave owners will be able to sit down together at the table of brotherhood.

I have a dream that one day even the state of Mississippi, a state sweltering with the heat of injustice, sweltering with the heat of oppression, will be transformed into an oasis of freedom and justice.

I have a dream that my four little children will one day live in a nation where they will not be judged by the color of their skin but by the content of their character.

I have a dream today!

I have a dream that one day, down in Alabama, with its vicious racists, with its governor having his lips dripping with the words of "interposition" and "nullification"—one day right there in Alabama little black boys and black girls will be able to join hands with little white boys and white girls as sisters and brothers.

I have a dream today!

I have a dream that one day every valley shall be exalted, and every hill and mountain shall be made low, the rough places will be made plain, and the crooked places will be made straight; "and the glory of the Lord shall be revealed and all flesh shall see it together."[2]

This is our hope, and this is the faith that I go back to the South with.

With this faith, we will be able to hew out of the mountain of despair a stone of hope. With this faith, we will be able to transform the jangling discords of our nation into a beautiful symphony of brotherhood. With this faith, we will be able to work together, to pray together, to struggle together, to go to jail together, to stand up for freedom together, knowing that we will be free one day.

And this will be the day—this will be the day when all of God's children will be able to sing with new meaning:

> My country 'tis of thee, sweet land of liberty, of thee I sing.
> Land where my fathers died, land of the Pilgrim's pride,
> From every mountainside, let freedom ring!
> And if America is to be a great nation, this must become true.
> And so let freedom ring from the prodigious hilltops of New Hampshire.
> Let freedom ring from the mighty mountains of New York.
> Let freedom ring from the heightening Alleghenies of Pennsylvania.
> Let freedom ring from the snow-capped Rockies of Colorado.
> Let freedom ring from the curvaceous slopes of California.
> But not only that:
> Let freedom ring from Stone Mountain of Georgia.
> Let freedom ring from Lookout Mountain of Tennessee.
> Let freedom ring from every hill and molehill of Mississippi.
> From every mountainside, let freedom ring.

And when this happens, when we allow freedom to ring, when we let it ring from every village and every hamlet, from every state and every city, we will be able to speed up that day when all of God's children, black men and white men, Jews and Gentiles, Protestants and Catholics, will be able to join hands and sing in the words of the old Negro spiritual:

> Free at last! Free at last!
> Thank God Almighty, we are free at last![3]

[1] Amos 5:24 (rendered precisely in The American Standard Version of the Holy Bible)

[2] Isaiah 40:4–5 (King James Version of the Holy Bible). Quotation marks are excluded from part of this moment in the text because King's rendering of Isaiah 40:4 does not precisely follow the KJV version from which he quotes (e.g., "hill" and "mountain" are reversed in the KJV). King's rendering of Isaiah 40:5, however, is precisely quoted from the KJV.

[3] "Free at Last" from *American Negro Songs* by J. W. Work.

Activity 3.1 • Use Microsoft's Comment Feature to Annotate a Text

If you download Dr. Martin Luther King, Jr.'s speech from *American Rhetoric* (www.americanrhetoric.com), you can make use of Microsoft's Comment feature to annotate the speech with your comments, as is done in the example below. In Microsoft Word, highlight the text you want to annotate, go to the "Insert" pull-down menu, and select "Comment." A box will appear where you can enter your comment.

> I am happy to join with you today in what will go down in history as the greatest demonstration for freedom in the history of our nation.
>
> Five score years ago, a great American, in whose symbolic shadow we stand today, signed the Emancipation Proclamation, This momentous decree came as a great beacon light of hope to millions of Negro slaves who had been seared in the flames of withering injustice. It came as a joyous daybreak to end the long night of their captivity.
>
> But one hundred years later, the Negro still is not free. One hundred years later, the life of the Negro is still sadly crippled by the manacles of segregation and that chains of discrimination. One hundred years later, the Negro lives on a lonely island of poverty in the midst of a vast ocean of material prosperity. One hundred years later, the Negro is

Comment [1]: Reference to Lincoln's Gettysburg Address

Activity 3.2 • Discuss "I Have a Dream"

Read the "I Have a Dream" speech by Dr. Martin Luther King, Jr., and, if possible, watch the speech. It is archived at *AmericanRhetoric.com*, where it is listed as the most requested speech and is #1 in the website's list of the top 100 American speeches.

Discuss the *kairos* of Dr. King's speech. What was the occasion? Who was his audience, both present and absent? What were the issues he spoke about?

How did Dr. King take advantage of the *kairos* of the situation in the wording of his speech?

Why do you think the speech continues to be so popular and influential?

Collaborate

Activity 3.3 • Identify the *Kairos*

Identifying the *kairos* in Dr. Martin Luther King, Jr.'s speech in front of the Lincoln Memorial is easy. In some speeches, however, identifying the *kairos* is more difficult. Every speech and every text has a *kairos*, but some rhetors are better at identifying it and utilizing it than others. Identify the *kairos* in the following readings that have appeared thus far in the text. Then discuss in your group how the writer or speaker does or does not utilize *kairos* to maximum effect.

- " 'Columbusing': The Art of Discovering Something that is Not New," Chapter 1, p. 18.

- "Microsoft Just Laid Off Thousands of Employees with a Hilariously Bad Memo," Chapter 1, p. 25.

- "The Sleepover Question," Chapter 1, p. 30.

- "Do You Know How Your Mascara is Made?" Chapter 2, p. 68.

- "The Web Means the End of Forgetting," Chapter 2, p. 88.

- "The Point When Science Becomes Publicity," Chapter 2, p. 93.

- "Why Has Godzilla Grown?" Chapter 2, p. 104.

Compose

Activity 3.4 • Analyze an Audience

Select a group that you do not belong to, and analyze it as a potential audience. To begin your analysis, you might locate a blog on the internet that advocates a point of view different from your own. For example, if you agree with theories about climate change, read a blog frequented by those who do not share your perspectives. If you are a Democrat, look for an Independent or Republican blog. Find a yoga blog if you are a football fan. Read a week's worth of blog entries, and write a one-page analysis, including the answers to these questions.

1. What are the two or three issues of primary interest to the group? What is the group's general position on each issue?

2. Who are these people? Where do they live? What is their educational level?

3. What is the extent of their knowledge about the issues of primary interest? Are they familiar with the evidence, or do they just repeat opinions?

Project: Rhetorical Analysis: Martin Luther King Jr.'s "I Have a Dream"

By N. Fox Edele

References

- Read this article about King's speech at History.com for historical context.

- "I Have a Dream": Review the speech and its text in this 50th-anniversary article from 2013. (Copy of speech in course text)

YOUR MISSION

Drawing from "I Have a Dream" and the rhetorical situation you studied in 1101 and reviewed in readings "Rhetoric and Writing," you are asked to write a 4-5-page rhetorical analysis (double-spaced) that focuses on **one** of the following strategies:

- *logos*: how does the author use material and/or data and evidence to create this speech?

- *pathos*: how does the author establish an emotional connection between the audience and the speech?

- *ethos*: how does the author present a trustworthy picture of himself as speaker/leader?

- *kairos*: in what ways is this story relevant to its particular time (1963) and today?

YOUR TASK

Your task in this paper is to address the following specific points, with direct reference to your text (paraphrase and quotation). Your rhetorical analysis will gain its *ethos* (credibility, as you know) and value from your source material. You always want to show that you've consulted sources. Remember that all your writing needs to demonstrate the answer to two crucial questions:

- what do you know?

- how do you know it? (That's why you need citations)

You may include a visual quotation as well (no larger than 3"). Your paper should be formatted in APA, MLA, or Chicago style and show evidence of careful proofreading.

1.   Provide a complete **identification of your text** (title, author, and genre).

2.   Explain what the **purpose** and **argument** of the text are.

3.   Provide the **historical context** for this speech.

4.   What **strategy** is the particular focus of your project here? Define the strategy and its power to communicate the message of this narrative to us, the audience.

5.   You want to move toward **a statement of the stakes involved**: Who wins? Who loses? What is the risk, the gain, or the loss? What's the significance of this text and its argument?

6.   How and why is the argument of the story **effective**? This question is not entirely personal—you are part of the intended audience here. Why do you think this material appeals to you? **What is the exigence of this story? What does it prompt us to think about or inspire us to do**?

Rhetorical Analysis of an Argument: What Your Paper Should Talk About

Construct an account of the argument in "I Have a Dream." Your goal is to *show how King's use of a specific rhetorical strategy serves to support the claims* in the text and to explain *how the argument is effective in terms of the author's use of this rhetorical strategy.* Your paper should respond to these specific questions in the following order:

Part 1. The intro should answer these questions, after you provide a full ID of the text and author:

•   What is the author's project? What is the author doing (investigating, researching, comparing, defending, proposing, challenging, etc.)?

•   What is the author's argument? What is the author trying to persuade us to believe?

•   What are YOU going to talk about in this paper? What do you intend to show us? (For example, "In my analysis of this text, I will examine [what?] and show [what?]").

Part 2. *The central analysis should include this information*:

- In your own words—with additional paraphrases or quotes from History.com or another historical source, provide the historical context for this speech.

  - What was the *kairos* of this speech—what was it responding to—why was it necessary and important?
  - Is it an important message for our culture, our world, over 50 years later?

- What rhetorical strategy does the author employ in presenting this message? Does the author rely most powerfully on emotion (*pathos*), reason (*logos*), moral authority (*ethos*), or historical context (*kairos*)?

  - What evidence does the author use to persuade us?
  - Why is this chosen evidence, in the form of a quote, useful here? What are you showing us?
  - How does this strategy in this situation serve to advance the author's theme or idea?

- What further evidence of this strategy do you discern in this text? Provide the answer in 2 or 3 additional sections, connected smoothly to the first example.

  - Same questions for writing about these examples.

Part 3: *The conclusion should tell us, "So what?"*:

What are the stakes of this speech, this argument? Does the author "make it work"? Do the author's claims enable you to comprehend the issue addressed here more clearly? Has your thinking on this issue changed as a result of your experience with this text? Please explain the conclusions you've drawn based on the strategy employed to empower this argument or this text.

The analysis should be 4-5 pages in length and in either APA, MLA, or Chicago format (title page, 1-inch margins, double-spaced, 12-point Times Roman font).

ENC 1102 Essay Award Winner

Teacher's Note by N. Fox Edele

Mary Oglesby's "The Bridge Builder" explores the *pathos* appeal in Martin Luther King Jr.'s speech, "I Have a Dream." King's speech, in Oglesby's view, is designed to evoke feelings of hope in the audience whose suffering he seeks to assuage and channel as a force for change. Thus, this analysis serves as argument as well: Oglesby coins the phrase "American cohesion" to describe King's purpose in extending his "Dream" beyond himself and his immediate audiences, to those who exclude them. Oglesby opens and closes her analysis with King's message of unity: her emphasis on unity as the central theme of King's speech also ties her own text together, from the epigraph and visual that foreground it to her final remarks. It is Oglesby's conclusion that King presents himself as a "bridge" that unifies America despite perceived separations of class, culture, race, religion, and time.

ENC 1102 Essay Award

The Bridge Builder

Mary Oglesby

What we need in the United States is not division; what we need in the United States is not hatred; what we need in the United States is not violence and lawlessness, but is love and wisdom, and compassion toward one another, and a feeling of justice toward those who still suffer within our country, whether they be white or whether they be black.

—Robert F. Kennedy

Martin Luther King Jr.'s opening line of his "I Have a Dream" speech suggests that his address, alongside others, would be "the greatest demonstration for freedom in the history of our nation" (King). The civil

Figure 1. "Estate of Leonard Free". *Goodnet*. Web.

rights movement, led most famously by King, was just that: a call to acting justly and civilly towards the rights of every citizen, black or white. These challenges to act came through the means of marches, sit-ins, and rallies. The key was King's use of peaceful protests, aimed at making resounding statements, not causing profound harm: "While others were advocating for freedom by 'any means necessary,' including violence, Martin Luther King, Jr. used the power of words and acts of nonviolent resistance, such as protests, grassroots organizing, and civil disobedience to achieve seemingly-impossible goals," ("About Dr. King"). This fact alone gives his argument an edge up because the once unreachable white population finally listened, and they heard the first person who urged non-violent action.

King's opportunity to speak on behalf of the black community was the pinnacle of his career as a fighter of injustices done to his people, and he rose to the occasion accordingly. In late August of 1963, King may have been standing above everyone else when he gave his deliverance on the steps of the Lincoln Memorial, but he placed himself beside every suffering African American man, woman, and child when addressing the need for equality in the United States. Standing where he was, faced with the challenge to rise up to the standard he was subject to in those few moments, in no way changed from where he came. His new position did not change the exile he felt as an American citizen encumbered by the weight of a country split into two dimensions. He tapped into every

American heart, no matter the race or social stature, and lit a fire under the civil rights movement that got a ball rolling into a future composed of change. He, in all his courage, stood before a crowd of 250,000 listeners arguing for equity and voting rights, and for an end to racial segregation and discrimination ("King Speaks"). In this analysis, examine King's use of the rhetorical device of *pathos* by showing how he invokes emotion through powerfully depicting the need for change in the United States in sharing his dream of American cohesion with a message that affects every person, past and present.

In the first segment of his speech, King creates an image that displays the need for a change, and by artfully constructing this picture for his audience, he spurs the *pathos* of deserved sympathy for the grievances carried by the African American society. The anaphora of "One hundred years later" presents itself four times successively in King's speech, with each stem followed by an unfortunate circumstance that black people still find themselves victim to, even one hundred years after being promised citizenship equality. These circumstances include the injustices of oppression, purposeful exile, segregation, discrimination and poverty. King designs this portion of his argument to emphasize that even though he and his people were guaranteed freedom and citizenship through the emancipation proclamation and the 13th and 14th amendments that were put into place over one hundred years ago, they are still being treated as if they had never progressed from the chains of slavery. This musters up a realization amongst those not receiving discriminatory treatment the reality of the situation, and creates the *pathos* of empathy for the transgressions experienced by blacks. Because of this treatment, King symbolizes the false promises of the prior centennial as a "bad check, a check that has come back marked 'insufficient funds'" (King). He goes on to assure the writers of this note that he will not accept the idea that there is no desire to right the wrongs, and demands a check backed up by "the riches of freedom and the security of justice" (King). In this way, he portrays to government leaders and every person playing on the oppression of his community the message that they will no longer stand for a metaphorical bankrupt bank of justice (King).

Using this symbolic metaphor, he makes another proposition of advocating for leaders to act upon the ideals once promised to the people of color, not having them ignored and abused for a greater multitude of years. Though the community he addresses has been tirelessly fighting for justice, he urges his people: "Let us not seek to satisfy our thirst for freedom by drinking from the cup of bitterness and hatred" (King). In making that statement he characterizes his movement as a peaceful one, and paints himself as a peaceful activist only seeking positivity as an outcome. Honestly expressing his motives for tranquil change summarizes his message to the people who have not been in agreement with him that he only seeks the good in a way beneficial and fair to all people, not in a way of stirring up violence and furthering the pain of the torn country. These points made by King illustrate that blacks had been "victims of creative suffering," and activate King's genius use of *pathos*. His meticulously designed images force the guilty population into feelings of remorse and regret for their actions, which indeed jumpstarted the agents of change as promptly as King has wished.

In addition to shedding a light on the discouragement of the black community, the second portion of King's speech foretells a future that harnesses his dream of American unity, eliciting the powerful *pathos* of hope in the public. He ends his portrayal of inequities by stating that even through the heartbreaks and trials forced on his people, that he still has a dream. He projects a bright light of optimism to every American, black or white, that they can progress as brothers and sisters of the same nationality joined in unity, and he makes every person truly believe, for the first time, that it is a real possibility. He points out, "the sons of former slaves and the sons of former slave owners will be able to sit down together at the table of brotherhood" (King). In the early 1960s, black men and white men congregating together would have never been an acceptable action, but King brought the possibility of union to life. This point sheds a light on a thought never before presented to the American citizens, and for once, the idea of coming together encompasses the general population as a whole. He introduces the *pathos* of love for one another, a notion held impossible to perceive before, and begins to formulate an invisible glue between all members of the country.

One of the most emotion-filled parts of his speech begins with, "This is our hope," (King). Following his proclamation of hope is the repetition of the phrase, "With this faith," and after that reoccurring stem, he proceeds to share all the change that could happen if faith remains. These include changes of despair to hope, separation to brotherhood, and the change of acting as one entity in every aspect of life; from working together to praying together (King). He utilizes the *pathos* of hope yet again in this motivational stanza that speaks to all races of people, manifesting a dire need of perseverance through the progress of change, no matter how difficult. This part of his speech holds the promise that if a collected faith remains, chances are that humankind will find the cohesion needed to rid the toxic division, that the harnessed hope will create the first opening of freedom for African Americans.

Throughout his oration, the most emphatic point is that he does have a dream for a better America. This demonstrates the *pathos* of love for his country and his fellow Americans, an admirable set of characteristics at the time. Though he is downtrodden by discrimination and pain, he remains optimistic in his pursuit of freedom. As solely a man with an unfailing confidence in his dream, just being himself is the true definition of bringing about *pathos*. Standing up for what is right in the face of adversity and criticism is an honorable trait, and America witnessed a man who truly was authentic and caring for the well-being of every living entity. The United States had the privilege to live with a man who, treated as a second-rate citizen, brought a beam of light to a lost and dying world. Martin Luther King Jr. is the real symbol of hope and unity, and he is the reason we saw the most dramatic change in our country's disposition towards one another.

As it turns out, King was correct in his initial claims. He was correct that his speech ended up being the greatest stand for freedom in American history. We see his demonstration in present day classroom settings, on televisions, and even in January on the holiday dedicated to him and the legacy he left behind. It was a speech that made an impact, so much of one that it changed the mindset of a nation in 1963, and it still resounds through the decades to follow as a life-changing message. He was also affirmed by all races of people coming together, gradually, but together all the same, to live more harmoniously in American society. Though individuals may need to be periodically reminded of the desideratum of unity to have a healthy nation, we still fall back on King's speech from fifty-three years prior to exemplify the need to mend the tears between one another. King is the filler of all gaps: past and present, black and white, love and hate, riches and poverty, discord and unity. He built a bridge between the races, one that allows us to travel freely to each other and live in a world no longer segregated from one another. He restored our country back into peace in the 1960s, and he accomplished that through his use of *pathos* to help United States citizens of every race realize the imperativeness of strong bonds between each other, and the beautiful America that would result because of that.

Works Cited

"About Dr. King." *The King Center*, 2014. Web. 6 October 2016.

"King speaks to the March on Washington." *A+E Networks*, 2010. Web. 5 October 2016.

King, Martin Luther. "I Have A Dream." in Reilly, Mollie, ed. "Martin Luther King Jr. Delivers his 'I Have A Dream' Speech 52 Years Ago Today." *The Huffington Post,* 28 August 2015. Web. 3 October 2016.

"Women's March Address" Introduction

By Laura Herbek

Like King's "I Have a Dream," Kelly Bushnell's "Women's March Address" advocates peaceful assembly as a means of achieving justice. On January 21, 2017, a crowd of 2,000 demonstrators gathered in downtown Pensacola's Plaza de Luna during an organized march in support of women's rights. Bushnell began her address to the crowd by submitting the words of fellow demonstrators, who were marching because "if we don't now, we might not get another chance" and because "sexual assault has become a rite of passage for women in this country."

Bushnell's speech is powerful in part because of its kairotic moment. Bushnell reminded her audience of Pensacola's "difficult and even violent history" by referencing events such as "the lynchings of black men just blocks away in Plaza Ferdinand" and "the arson of the women's clinic on 9th Avenue just five years ago this week." Bushnell acknowledged that marching in Pensacola "means more. It demands more courage." This concept was further amplified by the rainy weather that speakers and demonstrators alike endured that day.

The Pensacola Women's March occurred in solidarity with the larger Women's March on Washington. As an official "sister march," Pensacola's event demonstrated *ethos* by following the general guidelines outlined by Women's March DC organizers. Out of respect for these guiding principles, Bushnell stressed hope, inclusiveness, and unity in her speech. Though some audience members expressed anger and frustration at the rhetoric of the newly-formed Trump administration, "Women's March Address" avoided confronting President Trump by name in favor of emphasizing social justice and grassroots activism.

Pensacola Women's March Address

By Kelly Bushnell

21 January 2017

I want to begin not with my own words, but with yours. One of the best things about organizing this march is that Janet and I have gotten to meet so many women and allies in this community and learn their stories. Sarah says she is marching so her LGBT, nonwhite, and non-Christian friends know they have an ally in her. Carol is marching for her wife, sisters, students, for access to healthcare, and because Black Lives Matter. Karen wrote to say she is marching because she's 67 and doesn't want to see us go backwards. And Margaret commented simply, "Same age! Same reason!" Sandra is marching "because if we don't now, we might not get another chance." Azura is marching for her missing and murdered trans and Native sisters, because if we don't keep them in our memory they will find no justice. Vickie is marching for those who can't: the hardworking single moms and dads, our undocumented neighbors, the differently abled, the tired, the poor. Nancy is marching because she hopes this will be her last march. Jessica is marching because surviving sexual assault has become a rite of passage for women in this country. Amanda says she is marching because she has feet!

And here in Pensacola is a particularly historic place to march. Only a hundred years separates us from the lynchings of black men just blocks away in Plaza Ferdinand under Jim Crow. There are people here today who remember a legally racially segregated Pensacola. There are people here today who remember the police raids on local gay bars in the 1970s and who remember the clinic bombings of 1984 and the doctors and escorts murdered in the early 1990s. And many of us remember the arson of the women's clinic on 9th Avenue just five years ago this week.

But there are also people here today who remember the lunch counter sit-ins of the 1960s on Palafox. Or that those raids on the gay bars in the 1970s led to Pensacola's being an LGBT vacation destination on Memorial Day weekend. There are people here today who marched with the National Organization for Women after the clinic murders and who marched for immigrants' rights in MLK Plaza in 2006.

Marching here, with this city's often difficult and even violent history, is different than other places. It means more. And it demands more courage. Thank you for having the courage today to march for our sisters, and especially for our daughters and our students. Many of the veterans marching today have told me they feel it is their patriotic duty to do this, to hold this country to the ideals it stands for, and I'm reminded of a speech by President Obama in which he says that loving your country isn't just fireworks on the fourth of the July: "Loving your country must mean accepting your responsibility to do your part to change it. If you do," he says, "your life will be richer, and our country will be stronger." We are already 2,300 voices stronger together, to add to the 1 and a half million others doing this very same thing today.

As you heard—and certainly already knew—being a woman is not a monolithic identity. Though unity is our goal, it is just as important to celebrate our intersectionality and the incredible diversity of women's roles in their communities, because it is our differences which make our unity meaningful, and our willingness to fight for our sisters from all communities.

We must remember, for instance, that the 19th Amendment in 1920 only granted white women the right to vote. For Native women, it was 1924. For Asian women: 1952. For black women: not until 1964. The march toward equality must not leave any women behind again. As Audre Lorde writes, "I am not free while any woman is unfree, even when her shackles are very different from my own."

I have also heard the anger in your voices as you tell us why you march. As a woman and an American, I am angry too. The most vulnerable among us have not only been insulted and threatened by the rhetoric of the past year, but that rhetoric has been normalized as permissible political discourse. I don't accept that. And if you're here, I don't think you do either. It's a tall order to turn anger into empowerment and empowerment into real change. We can only do it together, and not by putting aside our differences but by embracing them.

I'm still angry—but for the first time in a long time, looking at this incredible gathering of powerful women and allies, seeing your kids over there playing in the puddles, for the first time in a long time I also feel hopeful. I see a sea of women and allies who are ready for the fight: to stand in solidarity with women and marginalized communities for our rights, our health, and our safety, especially those most targeted by current or proposed legislation. Trans women and men: we will be with you—and pee with you—in any bathroom in this country. Muslim friends: if they try to register you, they'll have to register us all. Immigrant neighbors: welcome to your new home. It needs some work, but that's what friends are for, and you have a lot of friends. And they—we—are ready to make history in Pensacola and across our country. I'm so proud to make history with you today.

Aristotle's Persuasive Appeals

Some theorists associate the rhetorical triangle directly with Aristotle's **appeals** (or proofs): *ethos, pathos,* and *logos*. **Ethos** refers to the writer's (or speaker's) credibility; **pathos** refers to emotion used to sway the audience; and, finally, **logos** refers to the writer's purpose (or subject), for an effective argument will include evidence and other supporting details to back up the author's claims.

Aristotle wrote:

> Of those proofs that are furnished through the speech there are three kinds. Some reside in the character [*ethos*] of the speaker, some in a certain disposition [*pathos*] of the audience and some in the speech itself, through its demonstrating or seeming to demonstrate [*logos*].

Contemporary theorist Wayne C. Booth said something similar:

> The common ingredient that I find in all writing that I admire—excluding for now novels, plays, and poems—is something that I shall reluctantly call the rhetorical stance, a stance which depends upon discovering and maintaining in any writing situation a proper balance among the three elements that are at work in any communicative effort: the available arguments about the subject itself [*logos*], the interests and peculiarities of the audience [*pathos*], and the voice, the implied character of the speaker [*ethos*].

Arguments from *Logos*

Logos, or reason, was Aristotle's favorite of the three persuasive appeals, and he bemoaned the fact that humans could not be persuaded through reason alone, indeed that they sometimes chose emotion over reason. Aristotle also used the term *logos* to mean rational discourse. To appeal to *logos* means to organize an argument with a clear claim or thesis, supported by logical reasons that are presented in a well-organized manner that is internally consistent. It can also mean the use of facts and statistics as evidence. However, *logos* without elements of *pathos* and *ethos* can be dry, hard to understand, and boring.

Consider the following logical argument that advocates televising executions.

Reading 3.2

In this opinion piece published in The New York Times, *Zachary B. Shemtob and David Lat argue what they know is going to be an unpopular position in the United States—that executions should be televised. Shemtob is an assistant professor of criminal justice at Connecticut State University, and Lat is a former federal prosecutor who also founded a legal blog,* Above the Law. *They reason, "democracy demands maximum accountability and transparency." Knowing that their position contradicts present policy, they carefully address possible objections to their position, such as the idea that executions are too gruesome to put on television.*

Executions Should Be Televised
by Zachary B. Shemtob and David Lat

[In July of 2011], Georgia conducted its third execution of the year. This would have passed relatively unnoticed if not for a controversy surrounding its videotaping. Lawyers for the condemned inmate, Andrew Grant DeYoung, had persuaded a judge to allow the recording of his last moments as part of an effort to obtain evidence on whether lethal injection caused unnecessary suffering.

Though he argued for videotaping, one of Mr. DeYoung's defense lawyers, Brian Kammer, spoke out against releasing the footage to the public. "It's a horrible thing that Andrew DeYoung had to go through," Mr. Kammer said, "and it's not for the public to see that."

We respectfully disagree. Executions in the United States ought to be made public.

Right now, executions are generally open only to the press and a few select witnesses. For the rest of us, the vague contours are provided in the morning paper. Yet a functioning democracy demands maximum accountability and transparency. As long as executions remain behind closed doors, those are impossible. The people should have the right to see what is being done in their name and with their tax dollars.

This is particularly relevant given the current debate on whether specific methods of lethal injection constitute cruel and unusual punishment and therefore violate the Constitution.

There is a dramatic difference between reading or hearing of such an event and observing it through image and sound. (This is obvious to those who saw the footage of Saddam Hussein's hanging in 2006 or the death of Neda Agha-Soltan during the protests in Iran in 2009.) We are not calling for opening executions completely to the public—conducting them before a live crowd—but rather for broadcasting them live or recording them for future release, on the Web or TV.

When another Georgia inmate, Roy Blankenship, was executed in June, the prisoner jerked his head, grimaced, gasped and lurched, according to a medical expert's affidavit. The *Atlanta Journal-Constitution* reported that Mr. DeYoung, executed in the same manner, "showed no violent signs in death." Voters should not have to rely on media accounts to understand what takes place when a man is put to death.

Cameras record legislative sessions and presidential debates, and courtrooms are allowing greater television access. When he was an Illinois state senator, President Obama successfully pressed for the videotaping of homicide interrogations and confessions. The most serious penalty of all surely demands equal if not greater scrutiny.

Opponents of our proposal offer many objections. State lawyers argued that making Mr. DeYoung's execution public raised safety concerns. While rioting and pickpocketing occasionally marred executions in the public square in the 18th and 19th centuries, modern security and technology obviate this concern. Little would change in the death chamber; the faces of witnesses and executioners could be edited out, for privacy reasons, before a video was released.

Of greater concern is the possibility that broadcasting executions could have a numbing effect. Douglas A. Berman, a law professor, fears that people might come to equate human executions with putting pets to sleep. Yet this seems overstated. While public indifference might result over time, the initial broadcasts would undoubtedly get attention and stir debate.

Still others say that broadcasting an execution would offer an unbalanced picture—making the condemned seem helpless and sympathetic, while keeping the victims of the crime out of the picture. But this is beside the point: the defendant is being executed precisely because a jury found that his crimes were so heinous that he deserved to die.

Ultimately the main opposition to our idea seems to flow from an unthinking disgust—a sense that public executions are archaic, noxious, even barbarous. Albert Camus related in his essay "Reflections on the Guillotine" that viewing executions turned him against capital punishment. The legal scholar John D. Bessler suggests that public executions might have the same effect on the public today; Sister Helen Prejean, the death penalty abolitionist, has urged just such a strategy.

That is not our view. We leave open the possibility that making executions public could strengthen support for them; undecided viewers might find them less disturbing than anticipated.

Like many of our fellow citizens, we are deeply conflicted about the death penalty and how it has been administered. Our focus is on accountability and openness. As Justice John Paul Stevens wrote in *Baze v. Rees*, a 2008 case involving a challenge to lethal injection, capital punishment is too often "the product of habit and inattention rather than an acceptable deliberative process that weighs the costs and risks of administering that penalty against its identifiable benefits."

A democracy demands a citizenry as informed as possible about the costs and benefits of society's ultimate punishment.

Collaborate

Activity 3.5 • Analyze an Argument from *Logos*

In your small group, discuss the following points, and prepare to present and defend your responses to the class.

1. Go over the Checklist of Essential Elements in an Argument (Chapter 2, p. 81), and decide if the authors of this article fulfill each one.

2. Shemtob and Lat present a logical argument about why executions should be televised. Ignoring your own reaction to their editorial, outline the main points.

3. Explain how the authors handle their audience's possible emotional objections to their argument.

4. What is your reaction to the argument that executions should be televised? Did reading and evaluating the article cause you to see the issue differently? If so, in what way?

Explore

Activity 3.6 • Find an Argument from *Logos*

Find an essay or article in print or on the internet that uses *logos* as its primary appeal. Make a copy, and bring it to class. In your small group, discuss the texts the group members brought in, and decide which one contains the strongest argument based on *logos*. Describe the argument for the class.

Deductive Reasoning

Aristotle was the first person in Western culture to write systematically about logic, and he is credited with developing and promoting syllogistic or **deductive reasoning** in which statements are combined to draw a **conclusion**. He wrote that "a statement is persuasive and credible either because it is directly self-evident or because it appears to be proved from other statements that are so." This logical structure is called a **syllogism**, in which premises lead to a conclusion. The following is perhaps the most famous syllogism:

> Major premise: All humans are mortal.
>
> Minor premise: Socrates is human.
>
> Conclusion: Socrates is mortal.

The **major premise** is a general statement accepted by everyone that makes an observation about all people. The second statement of the syllogism is the **minor premise,** which makes a statement about a particular case within the class of all people. Comparison of the two premises, the general class of "all humans" and the particular case of "Socrates" within the class of "all humans" leads to the conclusion that Socrates also fits in the class "mortal," and therefore his death is unavoidable. Thus, the logic moves from the general to the particular.

Similarly, if you try the pumpkin bread at one Starbucks and like it, you may infer that you will like the pumpkin bread at another Starbucks. The argument would look like this:

> Major premise: Food products at Starbucks are standardized from one Starbucks to another.
>
> Minor premise: You like the pumpkin bread at one Starbucks.
>
> Conclusion: You will like the pumpkin bread at another Starbucks.

Often in deductive reasoning, one of the premises is not stated, resulting in what is called a truncated syllogism or **enthymeme.**

For example, in the above syllogism about pumpkin bread, an enthymeme might leave out the major premise, "Food products at Starbucks are standardized from one Starbucks to another." In that case, the syllogism could be shortened to this:

| Enthymeme: | If you like the pumpkin bread at one Starbucks, you will like it at another Starbucks. |

However, if your major premise is wrong (whether it is stated or not) because the owner of one Starbucks substitutes an inferior stock of pumpkin bread, then your conclusion is wrong.

An enthymeme also relies upon common experience between speaker and audience. If your audience has never tasted pumpkin bread at Starbucks, then they are less likely to believe your enthymeme.

Deductive reasoning is dependent upon the validity of each premise; otherwise the syllogism does not hold true. If the major premise that food products are standardized at all Starbucks franchises does not hold true, then the argument is not valid. A good deductive argument is known as a valid argument and is such that if all its premises are true, then its conclusion must be true. Indeed, for a deductive argument to be valid, it must be absolutely impossible for both its premises to be true and its conclusion to be false.

Collaborate

Activity 3.7 • Develop a Deductive Argument

In your small group, develop a deductive argument by creating a major premise, a minor premise, and a conclusion for a topic of your group's choice. Present the argument to the class.

Inductive Reasoning

Aristotle identified another way to move logically between premises, which he called "the progress from particulars to universals." Later logicians labeled this type of logic **inductive reasoning**. Inductive arguments are based on probability. Even if an inductive argument's premises are true, that doesn't establish with 100 percent certainty that its conclusions are true. Even the best inductive argument falls short of deductive validity.

Consider the following examples of inductive reasoning:

| Particular statement: | Milk does not spoil as quickly if kept cold. |
| General statement: | All perishable foods do not spoil as quickly if kept cold. |

| Particular statement: | Microwaves cook popcorn more quickly than conventional heat. |
| General statement: | All foods cook more quickly in a microwave. |

In the first example, inductive reasoning works well because cold tends to pro-long the useable life of most perishable foods. The second example is more problematic. While it is true that popcorn cooks more quickly in a microwave oven, the peculiarities of microwave interaction with food molecules does not produce a uniform effect on all food stuffs. Rice, for example, does not cook much, if any, faster in a microwave than it does on a stovetop. Also, whole eggs may explode if cooked in their shells.

A good inductive argument is known as a strong (or "cogent") inductive argu-ment. It is such that if the premises are true, the conclusion is likely to be true.

Activity 3.8 • Develop an Inductive Argument

In your small group, develop an inductive argument by creating a particular state-ment and a general statement for a topic of your group's choice. Present the argu-ment to the class. Be sure that your inductive argument is strong or "cogent."

Collaborate

Logical Fallacies

Generally speaking, a **logical fallacy** is an error in reasoning, as opposed to a factual error, which is simply being wrong about the facts. A **deductive fallacy** (sometimes called a *formal fallacy*) is a deductive argument that has premises that are all true, but they lead to a false conclusion, making it an invalid argu-ment. An **inductive fallacy** (sometimes called an *informal fallacy*) appears to be an inductive argument, but the premises do not provide enough support for the conclusion to be probable. Some logical fallacies are more common than others and, thus, have been labeled and defined. Following are a few of the most well-known types.

Ad hominem (Latin for "to the man") arguments attempt to discredit a point of view through personal attacks upon the person who has that point of view. These arguments are not relevant to the actual issue because the character of the person that holds a view says nothing about the truth of that viewpoint.

> *Example*: Noam Chomsky is a liberal activist who opposes Ameri-can intervention in other countries. Noam Chomsky's theory of

transformational grammar, which suggests that humans have an innate ability to learn language, is ridiculous.

Non sequitur (Latin for "it does not follow") arguments have conclusions that do not follow from the premises. Usually, the author has left out a step in the logic, expecting the reader to make the leap over the gap.

> *Example*: Well, look at the size of this administration building; it is obvious this university does not need more funding.

Either/or or **false dichotomy** arguments force an either/or choice when, in reality, more options are available. Issues are presented as being either black or white.

> *Example*: With all the budget cuts, we either raise tuition or massively increase class size.

Red herring arguments avoid the issue and attempt to distract with a side issue.

> *Example*: Why do you question my private life issues when we have social problems with which to deal?

Ad populum (Latin for "appeal to the people") arguments appeal to popularity. If a lot of people believe it, it must be true.

> *Example*: Why shouldn't I cheat on this exam? Everyone else cheats.

Ad vericundiam (Latin for "argument from that which is improper") arguments appeal to an irrelevant authority.

> *Example*: If the President of Harvard says it is a good idea, then we should follow suit. Or, That is how we have always done it.

Begging the question arguments simply assume that a point of view is true because the truth of the premise is assumed. Simply assuming a premise is true does not amount to evidence that it *is* true.

> *Example*: A woman's place is in the home; therefore, women should not work.

Confusing cause and effect is a common problem with scientific studies in which the fact that two events are correlated implies that one causes the other.

> *Example*: Obese people drink a lot of diet soda; therefore, diet soda causes obesity.

Post hoc (from the Latin phrase *Post hoc, ergo proper hoc,* or "after this, therefore because of this") is a fallacy that concludes that one event caused another just because one occurred before the other.

> *Example*: The Great Depression caused World War II.

In a **straw man** fallacy, a position of an opponent is exaggerated or weakened, so that it is easier for the opponent to argue against it.

> *Example*: Pro-choice advocates believe in murdering unborn children.

A **slippery slope** argument asserts that one event will inevitably lead to another event.

> *Example*: This Dilbert cartoon:

DILBERT © 2008 Scott Adams. Used by permission of UNIVERSAL UCLICK. All rights reserved.

Table 3.1 • Descriptions and Examples of Logical Fallacies

Fallacy	The Error in Reasoning	Example
Ad populum	When we attempt to persuade people by arguing our position is reasonable because so many other people are doing it or agree with it.	"Why shouldn't I cheat on this exam? Everyone else cheats."

Ad vericundiam	An appeal to persuasion based on higher authority or tradition.	"If the president of Harvard says it is a good idea, then we should follow suit." Or, "That is how we have always done it."
Begging the question	When a speaker presumes certain things are facts when they have not yet been proven to be truthful.	"Oh, everyone knows that we are all Christians."
Confusing cause and effect	A common problem with scientific studies in which the fact that two events are correlated implies that one causes the other.	"Obese people drink a lot of diet soda; therefore, diet soda causes obesity."
Either/or	Presents two options and declares that one of them must be correct while the other must be incorrect.	"We either raise tuition or massively increase class size."
Non sequitur	When you make an unwarranted move from one idea to the next.	"Well, look at the size of this administration building; it is obvious this university does not need more funding."
Post hoc	Assumes that because one event happened after another, then the preceding event caused the event that followed.	"Every time Sheila goes to a game with us, our team loses. She is bad luck."
Red herring	When a speaker introduces an irrelevant issue or piece of evidence to divert attention from the subject of the speech.	"Why do you question my private life issues, when we have social problems with which to deal?"
Slippery slope	Assumes that once an action begins it will follow, undeterred, to an eventual and inevitable conclusion.	"If we let the government dictate where we can pray, soon the government will tell us we cannot pray."

Activity 3.9 • Identify Logical Fallacies

Explore

Match the following types of logical fallacies with the examples below.

Types:

Ad hominem

Begging the question

Confusing cause and effect

Post hoc

Straw man

Slippery slope

Examples:

1. Legalization of medical marijuana will lead to increased marijuana use by the general population.

2. Twenty-one is the best age limit for drinking because people do not mature until they are 21.

3. If you teach birth control methods, more teenage girls will get pregnant.

4. The culture wars of the 1960s were a result of parents being unable to control their children after the post–World War II baby boom.

5. Al Gore claims that climate change is a dangerous trend. Al Gore is a liberal. Therefore, there is no climate change.

6. Immigration reform advocates want to separate families and children.

Activity 3.10 • Create Examples of Logical Fallacies

Collaborate

In your small group, work through the chart of logical fallacies above and create a new example for each type of fallacy. Then report to the class, one fallacy at a time, with the instructor making a list of each group's examples on the chalk board. Discuss any examples that are not clear cases of a particular fallacy.

Arguments from *Pathos*

Pathos makes use of emotion to persuade an audience.

Aristotle wrote:

> Proofs from the disposition of the audience are produced whenever they are induced by the speech into an emotional state. We do not give judgment in the same way when aggrieved and when pleased, in sympathy and in revulsion.

Effective rhetors know their audiences, particularly what emotions they hold that are relevant to the issue under consideration. What motivates them? What are their fears, their hopes, their desires, and their doubts? If the audience has the same emotions as you do, fine. However, if they do not already hold those emotions, you need to bring them to share the hurt, the anger, or the joy that will persuade them to share your viewpoint—through the stories you tell, the statistics you cite, and the reasoning you offer.

For example, when Dr. Martin Luther King, Jr., in his "I Have a Dream" speech referred to the "hallowed spot" of the Lincoln Memorial, he was appealing to his audience's feelings of patriotism and reverence for the accomplishments of President Lincoln. Subtly, he was also garnering this emotion toward Lincoln in contemporary support of civil rights. Lincoln had issued the Emancipation Proclamation that declared all slaves to be free, yet, according to King, America had not lived up to Lincoln's promise.

Reading 3.3

E. Benjamin Skinner has written on a wide range of topics. His articles have appeared in Newsweek International, Travel and Leisure, *and other magazines. This essay was adapted from* A Crime So Monstrous: Face-to-Face with Modern-Day Slavery *and appeared in* Foreign Policy.

People for Sale

by E. Benjamin Skinner

Most people imagine that slavery died in the nineteenth century. Since 1810, more than a dozen international conventions banning the slave trade have been signed. Yet today there are more slaves than at any time in human history.

And if you're going to buy one in five hours, you'd better get a move on. First, hail a taxi to JFK International Airport and hop on a direct flight to Port-au-Prince, Haiti. The flight takes three hours. After landing, take a tap-tap, a flatbed pickup retrofitted with benches and a canopy, three-quarters of the way up Route de Delmas, the capital's main street. There, on a side street, you will find a group of men standing in front of Le Réseau (the Network) barbershop. As you approach, a man steps forward: "Are you looking to get a person?"

Meet Benavil Lebhom. He smiles easily. He has a trim mustache and wears a multicolored striped golf shirt, a gold chain, and Doc Martens knockoffs. Benavil is a courtier, or broker. He holds an official real estate license and calls himself an employment agent. Two-thirds of the employees he places are child slaves. The total number of Haitian children in bondage in their own country stands at 300,000. They are restavèks, the "stay-withs," as they are euphemistically known in Creole. Forced, unpaid, they work in captivity from before dawn until night. Benavil and thousands of other formal and informal traffickers lure these children from desperately impoverished rural parents with promises of free schooling and a better life.

The negotiation to buy a child slave might sound a bit like this:

"How quickly do you think it would be possible to bring a child in? Somebody who could clean and cook?" you ask. "I don't have a very big place; I have a small apartment. But I'm wondering how much that would cost? And how quickly?"

"Three days," Benavil responds.

"And you could bring the child here?" you inquire. "Or are there children here already?"

"I don't have any here in Port-au-Prince right now," says Benavil, his eyes widening at the thought of a foreign client. "I would go out to the countryside."

You ask about additional expenses. "Would I have to pay for transportation?"

"Bon," says Benavil. "A hundred U.S."

Smelling a rip-off, you press him, "And that's just for transportation?"

"Transportation would be about 100 Haitian," says Benavil, "because you'd have to get out there. Plus, [hotel and] food on the trip. Five hundred gourdes"—around $13.

"OK, 500 Haitian," you say.

Now you ask the big question: "And what would your fee be?" Benavil's eyes narrow as he determines how much he can take you for.

"A hundred. American."

"That seems like a lot," you say, with a smile so as not to kill the deal. "Could you bring down your fee to 50 U.S.?"

Benavil pauses. But only for effect. He knows he's still got you for much more than a Haitian would pay. "Oui," he says with a smile.

But the deal isn't done. Benavil leans in close. "This is a rather delicate question. Is this someone you want as just a worker? Or also someone who will be a 'partner'? You understand what I mean?"

You don't blink at being asked if you want the child for sex. "Is it possible to have someone who could be both?"

"Oui!" Benavil responds enthusiastically.

If you're interested in taking your purchase back to the United States, Benavil tells you that he can "arrange" the proper papers to make it look as though you've adopted the child.

He offers you a 13-year-old girl.

"That's a little bit old," you say.

"I know of another girl who's 12. Then ones that are 10, 11," he responds.

The negotiation is finished, and you tell Benavil not to make any moves without further word from you. You have successfully arranged to buy a human being for 50 bucks.

It would be nice if that conversation were fictional. It is not. I recorded it in October 2005 as part of four years of research into slavery on five continents. In the popular consciousness, "slavery" has come to be little more than just a metaphor for undue hardship. Investment bankers routinely refer to themselves as "high-paid wage slaves." Human rights activists may call $1-an-hour sweatshop laborers slaves, regardless of the fact that they are paid and can often walk away from the job.

The reality of slavery is far different. Slavery exists today on an unprecedented scale. In Africa, tens of thousands are chattel slaves, seized in war or tucked away for generations. Across Europe, Asia, and the Americas, traffickers have forced as many as 2 million into prostitution or labor. In South Asia, which has the highest concentration of slaves on the planet, nearly 10 million languish in bondage, unable to leave their captors until they pay off "debts," legal fictions that in many cases are generations old.

Few in the developed world have a grasp of the enormity of modern-day slavery. Fewer still are doing anything to combat it. . . . Between 2000 and 2006, the U.S. Justice Department increased human trafficking prosecutions from 3 to 32, and convictions from 10 to 98. By the end of 2006, 27 states had passed anti-trafficking laws. Yet, during the same period, the United States liberated only about 2 percent of its own modern-day slaves. As many as 17,500 new slaves continue to enter bondage in the United States every year . . . Many feel that sex slavery is particularly revolting—and it is. I saw it firsthand. In a Bucharest brothel, I was offered a mentally handicapped suicidal girl in exchange for a used car. But for every woman or child enslaved in commercial sex, there are some 15 men, women, and children enslaved in other fields, such as domestic work or agricultural labor.

Save for the fact that he is male, Gonoo Lal Kol typifies the average slave of our modern age. (At his request, I have changed his name.) Like a majority of the world's slaves, Gonoo is in debt bondage in South Asia. In his case, in an Indian quarry. Like most slaves, Gonoo is illiterate and unaware of the Indian laws that ban his bondage and provide for sanctions against his master. His story, told to me near his four-foot-high stone and grass hutch, represents the other side of the "Indian Miracle."

Gonoo lives in Lohagara Dhal, a forgotten corner of Uttar Pradesh, a north Indian state that contains 8 percent of the world's poor. I met him one evening in December 2005 as he walked with two dozen other laborers in tattered and filthy clothes. Behind them was the quarry. In that pit, Gonoo, a member of the historically outcast Kol tribe, worked with his family 14 hours a day. His tools were a hammer and a pike. His hands were covered in calluses, his fingertips worn away.

Gonoo's master is a tall, stout, surly contractor named Ramesh Garg. He makes his money by enslaving entire families forced to work for no pay beyond alcohol, grain, and subsistence expenses. Slavery scholar Kevin Bales estimates that a slave in the 19th-century American South had to work 20 years to recoup his or her purchase price. Gonoo and the other slaves earn a profit for Garg in two years.

Every single man, woman, and child in Lohagara Dhal is a slave. But, in theory at least, Garg neither bought nor owns them. The seed of Gonoo's slavery, for instance, was a loan of 62 cents. In 1958 his grandfather borrowed that amount from the owner of a farm where he worked. Three generations and three slave masters later, Gonoo's family remains in bondage.

Recently, many bold, underfunded groups have taken up the challenge of tearing out the roots of slavery. Some gained fame through dramatic slave rescues. Most learned that freeing slaves is impossible unless the slaves themselves choose to be free. Among the Kol of Uttar Pradesh, for instance, an organization called Pragati Gramodyog Sansthan (PGS)—the Progressive Institute for Village Enterprises—has helped hundreds of families break the grip of the quarry contractors.

The psychological, social, and economic bonds of slavery run deep, and for governments to be truly effective in eradicating slavery, they must partner with groups that can offer slaves a way to pull themselves up from bondage. One way to do that is to replicate the work of grassroots organizations such as the India-based MSEMVS (Society for Human Development and Women's Empowerment). In 1996 the group launched free transitional schools where children who had been enslaved learned skills and acquired enough literacy to move on to formal schooling. The group also targeted mothers, providing them with training and start-up materials for microenterprises. . . . In recent years, the United States has shown an increasing willingness to help fund these kinds of organizations, one encouraging sign that the message may be getting through.

For four years, I encountered dozens of enslaved people, several of whom traffickers like Benavil actually offered to sell to me. I did not pay for a human life anywhere. And, with one exception, I always withheld action to save any one person, in the hope that my research would later help to save many more. At times, that still feels like an excuse for cowardice. But the hard work of real emancipation can't be the burden of a select few. For thousands of slaves, grassroots groups like PGS and MSEMVS can help bring freedom. Until governments define slavery in appropriately concise terms, prosecute the crime aggressively in all its forms, and encourage groups that empower slaves to free themselves, however, millions more will remain in bondage. And our collective promise of abolition will continue to mean nothing at all.

Activity 3.11 • **Write about an Argument from** *Pathos*

After reading Skinner's essay on slavery, reread the passage in which he negotiated to buy a child slave. Then freewrite for five minutes about how that negotiation made you feel.

Compose

Activity 3.12 • **Analyze an Argument from** *Pathos*

Most people feel emotional when they read about a child in distress, and Skinner further highlights that emotional effect by putting this particular episode in dialogue, always a point of emphasis in an essay. Discuss these questions in your small group.

Collabora

1. Do you think Skinner deliberately appealed to *pathos* in this part of his essay?

2. List other areas where the essay evokes an emotional response. Consider why, and freewrite on the feelings and beliefs that are brought into play on your own. Discuss with your group your responses and how you think the author knew you would probably react this way.

3. Although much of Skinner's argument relies on *pathos*, he also provides statistics and references to authorities to bolster his argument. Identify the paragraphs which provide statistics or other evidence that would qualify as *logos*.

Activity 3.13 • **Find an Argument from** *Pathos*

Find an essay or article in print or on the internet that uses *pathos* or emotion as its primary appeal. Make a copy and bring it to class. In your small group, discuss the texts that the group members brought in, and decide which one contains the strongest argument based on *pathos*. Describe the argument for the class.

Explore

Teacher's Note by Jasara Norton

Anastasija Cumika's and Caitlyn Waters' award winning essays are from an ENC 1102 course in which students rhetorically analyzed a local text. Students were asked to restrain their rhetorical analysis to no more than two of Aristotle's appeals for a focused final argument. Cumika's and Waters' varied interpretation of the assignment demonstrates an ability to make context-driven rhetorical distinctions.

Focusing on *pathos* and *logos*, Cumika argues in "How to Persuade Students with a Video" that the UWF library's plagiarism video both informs and persuades. Cumika examines the interplay of emotions at work in the video and how the logical structure of the video reinforces key concepts. With her argument in mind, watch the library's plagiarism video. Do you agree with Cumika's analysis? One assignment criterion was that students use visuals to help make their arguments. Do the visuals contribute to Cumika's analysis? How so?

In "The Reality of Modern Day Slavery," Waters analyzes a more traditional text, an essay in the *Rhetoric and Writing* textbook. The topic of this essay warrants a different set of rhetorical emphases, and Waters intuits this context. According to Waters, the essay is compelling because the author's appeal to *pathos* is substantiated by his *ethos*—evidence of his extensive first-hand experience researching and reporting on modern day slavery. In places, Waters relies on textual nuances to prove her analysis. This kind of close read is a valuable rhetorical skill across writing genres and applications. Can you identify the places in which Waters conducts a close read of her selected text? Finally, were you aware of modern day slavery before reading this essay? How does Waters' discussion of the issue change your views?

ENC 1102 Essay Award

The Reality of Modern Day Slavery

Caitlyn Waters

As of 2016, there are an estimated 29.8 million people living as slaves in the world (Fisher). Many people in the United States and other developed countries in the world are unaware of the number of people who are trapped by slavery. Even the United States is still affected by slavery; an estimated 60,000 people are in some form of slavery (Fisher). I became aware of this fact through the research I conducted after reading E. Benjamin Skinner's "People for Sale" in our *Rhetoric and Writing* textbook. The essay helps people realize that slavery exists today despite modern society's belief that it was abolished years ago. Skinner discusses his own account of meeting someone who is a part of the slave trade, and gives statistics about slavery along with a personal story about a man who is enslaved in India. Skinner's essay is persuasive because he establishes his *pathos* by including chillingly detailed stories of slavery in second-person and strengthens his *ethos* through facts and research.

In order for Skinner to grab readers who want to learn more about modern-day slavery, he tells a disturbingly personal story about slavery. Skinner is doing research about slavery and wants to learn about the process of buying someone, so he met a slave broker by the name of Benavil Lebhom in Haiti. Lebhom sells children, and Skinner carried out a mock exchange with Lebhom for a child slave. Skinner asks many questions as if it were a business exchange, such as "How quickly do you think it would be possible to bring a child in? Somebody who could clean and cook?" (Skinner 116) The tone of the exchange is formal which is discomforting for the reader because they are talking about buying a human being as if he or she were an object. Skinner's incorporation of this frightening, real experience invokes *pathos* because the readers know it is morally wrong to sell a human being, let alone a child. The incorporation of the exchange is persuasive because, as the *Rhetoric and Writing* textbook states, people who are emotionally invested in a topic are eager to act out for that cause. This true story lures readers in and makes them feel emotional about slavery because they are faced with evidence of a horrifying crime, which makes the readers want to take action.

As the exchange goes on, Benavil asks Skinner if he would want "someone who will be a 'partner'" and proceeds to offer Skinner a thirteen-year-old girl, to which he replies with "that's a little bit old" (Skinner 117). The exchange between the two pertaining to the child sex slave makes readers feel disgust because a child is being sold to a grown man for sex and labor. When Skinner says that a thirteen-year-old girl is too old for him, this detail confronts the readers to the horrors of slavery. By showing this part of his story, he is using *pathos* to convince readers to understand that this horrible crime still occurs and that this crime of slavery should be prevented. Thus, his mock exchange of buying a child slave is persuasive because it makes the readers realize that this situation is not the only exchange happening in the world, and many of these exchanges are happening with no one there to stop it.

The way Skinner words his personal exchange invokes *pathos* in readers because he uses second person. For example, he says, "[y]ou don't blink at being asked if you want the child for sex," and "[y]ou have successfully arranged to buy a human being for 50 bucks" (Skinner 117). Since he uses the words "you" throughout the story, it makes the readers feel as if they are a part of the story and that they are the ones buying the slave. This usage of the word "you" invokes *pathos* because it makes the readers feel as if they are a part of buying a human being and makes them feel uncomfortable. Skinner's use of second-person pronouns is persuasive because it makes the readers feel as if they are there, so they feel the urgency to do something to prevent slavery from continuing.

To show another side of modern slavery, Skinner introduces the story of Gonoo Lal Kol. Gonoo is a slave in India and represents people who are enslaved in the modern age. Skinner explains that Gonoo works in an "Indian quarry with his family 14 hours a day" to pay off a "loan of 62 cents that his grandfather borrowed in 1958" (Skinner 118). The tragic story of Gonoo invokes *pathos* because it confronts readers to the reality of slavery in which something as small as borrowing sixty-two cents can lead to the enslavement of a family for generations. It is hard for people of developed countries to fathom that he is enslaved because of a mere sixty-two cents that was borrowed a half-century ago because to modern society, sixty-two cents is a small amount of money. The story makes readers realize that slavery takes advantage of poor and illiterate people who are unable to defend themselves and that Gonoo's story is not the only story of debt bondage. Skinner incorporates Gonoo's story because it persuades readers to recognize that despite being in the modern age people who are born into the wrong circumstances can become trapped by slavery.

Moreover, Skinner establishes his own credibility through his personal experiences with the slave trade. He shows his readers that he is able to discuss this matter because he has conducted research on how to buy a human being. In his story about buying a child sex slave, he explains that Lebhom is a "broker... [and that he is an] informal trafficker who lures these children from desperately impoverished rural parents" (Skinner 116). He establishes that he knows how the trade works; therefore, he establishes his *ethos* in that he knows the different areas of selling slaves. Further, from his know-how about buying the girl, readers can conjure that he has experience dealing with actual accounts of slavery which gives him the credibility to discuss this topic. He persuasively tells his exchange experience because it represents proof that he has experience in the slave trade in order for him to discuss it in detail.

Skinner also discusses his research and uses facts to build his credibility to his readers. He says that the exchange he had with Lebhom is a part of his "four years of research into slavery on five continents" (Skinner 117). The exchange is proof of the research he has conducted, and he shows readers that he has been doing his research for a long period of time. Additionally, he also says that his research has been conducted on five continents, which furthers his credibility with readers because he shows that he has investigated different groups of enslaved people all around the world. Slavery is a global problem, and by telling his readers that he studies slavery across the world, he makes the information more reliable. He goes on to give facts, such as "17,500 new slaves continue to enter bondage in the United States every year" (Skinner 118). The facts that he uses persuade readers to believe that he has done extensive research in order to discuss these facts. Skinner persuasively uses *ethos* in the form of facts and his own experiences from his research to make readers know that he is a credible source and to take his information seriously.

Skinner's essay, "People for Sale," shows the dark side of humanity and the atrocities that humanity can inflict on others. Skinner uses *pathos* by incorporating disturbing details of slavery stories and proves his credibility through his use of facts and his research to support his claim that slavery is still a significant problem in the world. Even though I have not been personally affected by slavery, it is inhumane to sell people as objects. People are born with unalienable rights which include freedom and equality, and slavery infringes upon people's natural-born rights. After reading Skinner's essay, I have come to the conclusion that slavery is a world problem and that in the modern society that we live in, slavery should be eradicated. Skinner's goal for his essay is to bring awareness to slavery and successfully convince his readers that the public and government must work together in order to stop slavery.

Works Cited

Fisher, Max. "This map shows where the world's 30 million slaves live. There are 60,000 in the U.S." *Washington Post*. Washington Post, 17 October 2013. Web. 27 February 2016.

Skinner, E. Benjamin. "People for Sale." *Rhetoric and Writing*. Ed. Bre Garrett. Pensacola: Fountainhead Press, 2016. 116-119. Print.

Arguments from *Ethos*

No exact translation exists in English for the word *ethos*, but it can be loosely translated as the credibility of the speaker. This credibility generates goodwill which colors all the arguments, examples, and quotes the rhetor utilizes in his or her text. Rhetors can enhance their credibility by providing evidence of intelligence, virtue, and goodwill and diminish it by seeming petty, dishonest, and mean-spirited. In addition, a speaker or writer can enhance his or her own credibility by incorporating references to quotes or the actions of authorities or leaders.

Aristotle wrote:

> Proofs from character [*ethos*] are produced, whenever the speech is given in such a way as to render the speaker worthy of credence—we more readily and sooner believe reasonable men on all matters in general and absolutely on questions where precision is impossible and two views can be maintained.

For example, Dr. Martin Luther King, Jr., pointed out in his "I Have a Dream" speech, that, according to the framers of the Constitution and the Declaration of Independence, "unalienable Rights" of "Life, Liberty and the pursuit of Happiness" apply equally to black men and white men. He was, in effect, borrowing the *ethos* of Thomas Jefferson and the framers of the Constitution in support of the unalienable rights of black people.

Consider the following article and how the author's credibility or *ethos* enhances the appeal of his arguments.

Reading 3.4

Ray Jayawardhana, the author of "Alien Life Coming Slowly into View," which was originally published in The New York Times, *is a professor of astronomy and astrophysics at the University of Toronto. He is also the author of* Strange New Worlds: The Search for Alien Planets and Life Beyond Our Solar System.

Alien Life Coming Slowly into View

by Ray Jayawardhana

I remember the first time the concept of another world entered my mind. It was during a walk with my father in our garden in Sri Lanka. He pointed to the Moon and told me that people had walked on it. I was astonished: Suddenly that bright light became a place that one could visit.

Schoolchildren may feel a similar sense of wonder when they see pictures of a Martian landscape or Saturn's rings. And soon their views of alien worlds may not be confined to the planets in our own solar system.

After millenniums of musings and a century of failed attempts, astronomers first detected an exoplanet, a planet orbiting a normal star other than the Sun, in 1995. Now they are finding hundreds of such worlds each year. Last month, NASA announced that 1,235 new possible planets had been observed by Kepler, a telescope on a space satellite. Six of the planets that Kepler found circle one star, and the orbits of five of them would fit within that of Mercury, the closest planet to our Sun.

By timing the passages of these five planets across their sun's visage—which provides confirmation of their planetary nature—we can witness their graceful dance with one another, choreographed by gravity. These discoveries remind us that nature is often richer and more wondrous than our imagination. The diversity of alien worlds has surprised us and challenged our preconceptions many times over.

It is quite a change from merely 20 years ago, when we knew for sure of just one planetary system: ours. The pace of discovery, supported by new instruments and missions and innovative strategies by planet seekers, has been astounding.

What's more, from measurements of their masses and sizes, we can infer what some of these worlds are made of: gases, ice or rocks. Astronomers have been able to take the temperature of planets around other stars, first with telescopes in space but more recently with ground-based instruments, as my collaborators and I have done.

Two and a half years ago, we even managed to capture the first direct pictures of alien worlds. There is something about a photo of an alien planet—even if it only appears as a faint dot next to a bright, overexposed star—that makes it "real." Given that stars shine like floodlights next to the planetary embers huddled around them, success required painstaking efforts and clever innovations. One essential tool is adaptive optics technology, which, in effect, takes the twinkle out of the stars, thus providing sharper images from telescopes on the ground than would otherwise be possible.

At the crux of this grand pursuit is one basic question: Is our warm, wet, rocky world, teeming with life, the exception or the norm? It is an important question for every one of us, not just for scientists. It seems absurd, if not arrogant, to think that ours is the only life-bearing world in the galaxy, given hundreds of billions of other suns, the apparent ubiquity of planets, and the cosmic abundance of life's ingredients. It may be that life is fairly common, but that "intelligent" life is rare.

Of course, the vast majority of the extra-solar worlds discovered to date are quite unlike our own: many are gas giants, and some are boiling hot while others endure everlasting chills. Just a handful are close in size to our planet, and only a few of those may be rocky like the Earth, rather than gaseous like Jupiter or icy like Neptune.

But within the next few years, astronomers expect to find dozens of alien earths that are roughly the size of our planet. Some of them will likely be in the so-called habitable zone, where the temperatures are just right for liquid water. The discovery of "Earth twins," with conditions similar to what we find here, will inevitably bring questions about alien life to the forefront.

Detecting signs of life elsewhere will not be easy, but it may well occur in my lifetime, if not during the next decade. Given the daunting distances between the stars, the real-life version will almost certainly be a lot less sensational than the movies depicting alien invasions or crash-landing spaceships.

The evidence may be circumstantial at first—say, spectral bar codes of interesting molecules like oxygen, ozone, methane and water—and leave room for alternative interpretations. It may take years of additional data-gathering, and perhaps the construction of new telescopes, to satisfy our doubts. Besides, we won't know whether such "biosignatures" are an indication of slime or civilization. Most people will likely move on to other, more immediate concerns of life here on Earth while scientists get down to work.

If, on the other hand, an alien radio signal were to be detected, that would constitute a more clear-cut and exciting moment. Even if the contents of the message remained elusive for decades, we would know that there was someone "intelligent" at the other end. The search for extraterrestrial intelligence with radio telescopes has come of age recently, 50 years after the first feeble attempt. The construction of the Allen Telescope Array on an arid plateau in northern California greatly expands the number of star systems from which astronomers could detect signals.

However it arrives, the first definitive evidence of life elsewhere will mark a turning point in our intellectual history, perhaps only rivaled by Copernicus's heliocentric theory or Darwin's theory of evolution. If life can spring up on two planets independently, why not on a thousand or even a billion others? The ramifications of finding out for sure that ours isn't the only inhabited world are likely to be felt, over time, in many areas of human thought and endeavor—from biology and philosophy to religion and art.

Some people worry that discovering life elsewhere, especially if it turns out to be in possession of incredible technology, will make us feel small and insignificant. They seem concerned that it will constitute a horrific blow to our collective ego.

I happen to be an optimist. It may take decades after the initial indications of alien life for scientists to gather enough evidence to be certain or to decipher a signal of artificial origin. The full ramifications of the discovery may not be felt for generations, giving us plenty of time to get used to the presence of our galactic neighbors. Besides, knowing that we are not alone just might be the kick in the pants we need to grow up as a species.

Activity 3.14 • Analyzing an Argument from *Ethos*

Ray Jayawardhana draws upon the *ethos* of his position as a professor of astronomy and astrophysics to formulate a convincing argument for the strong possibility of the existence of alien life. In your group, discuss how Jayawardhana's profession increases the credibility of his argument.

Collabor

1. How do you think this essay would compare to essays by people with greater credentials who argue that no alien life exists? What kinds of additional evidence could Jayawardhana have offered that would strengthen his argument?

2. Is Jayawardhana appealing to *pathos* with his opening narrative? What effect does he want to have on his audience by describing this childhood memory?

Activity 3.15 • Find an Argument from *Ethos*

Find an essay or article in print or on the internet that uses *ethos* or the credibility of the author as its primary appeal. Make a copy and bring it to class. In your small group, discuss the texts that the group members brought in, and decide which contains the strongest argument based on *ethos*. Describe the argument for the class.

Explore

Combining *Ethos*, *Pathos*, and *Logos*

The *ethos*, *pathos*, and *logos* appeals are equally important and merit equal attention in the writing process. No text is purely based on one of the three appeals, though more of the argument in a particular text may be based on one appeal rather than another. In each writing situation, however, an effective rhetor will think about how each plays into the structure of the argument.

Today, for example, a public speaker's effectiveness is influenced by his or her ability to use a teleprompter, or, if one is not available, to memorize a speech well enough so he or she can speak without frequently referring to notes. If a speaker's eyes flit from left to right across the text of a teleprompter, it shows on television. This reduces the credibility, or *ethos*, of the speaker, no matter how well the other appeals are executed in the speech. The equivalent of strong public speaking skills for a written text would be to produce a document that is essentially free from grammatical errors, spell-checked, and printed on good paper stock with the correct margins and type size. If the document does not look professional, it will lose credibility or *ethos* no matter what it says.

To give another example, E. Benjamin Skinner's essay, "People for Sale," relies on the highly emotional image of a child being sold into slavery for its major appeal. However, if you read back through the essay, you will see that it has a clear thesis, which could be stated as the following: Slavery exists in the present time, even in the United States, and it is not even that difficult to buy a slave. The essay is well organized and offers a variety of evidence, including statistics and first-person observation. *Logos* may not stand out as the primary appeal in Skinner's essay, but it is nevertheless strong in its appeal to *logos*.

If you want to develop your writing skills, it is essential that you pay attention to each of Aristotle's appeals—*ethos, pathos,* and *logos*.

Compose

Activity 3.16 • Identify *Ethos, Pathos,* and *Logos*

Choose one of the texts in Chapters 1, 2, or 3, and identify in your small group the *ethos, pathos,* and *logos* of the particular text. Then discuss how the three appeals together are used by the author to produce an effective essay. Alternatively, discuss which of the appeals is weak in the particular essay and how that affects the effectiveness of the essay.

Photos Heighten *Ethos*

Caitlyn Jenner, formerly Bruce Jenner, asserted her visual *ethos* as a transgender woman when she accepted the Arthur Ashe Courage Award at the ESPY Awards in Los Angeles in July 2015. News outlets worldwide carried videos

Caitlyn Jenner wore a feminine Versace evening gown at the ESPY Awards.
Photo Credit: Getty Images.

A transgender woman posted her own magazine "cover" on the internet.
Photo Credit: Tumblr/ missinginanus

or photos of Jenner wearing a stunning white Versace gown as she received a standing ovation from some of sport's greatest stars and celebrities. The same month, further enhancing Jenner's *ethos* as a transgender woman, *Vanity Fair* featured her on its cover in a traditionally female pose, wearing a glamorous white swimsuit. The *Vanity Fair* cover received both praise and criticism, with some bloggers saying Jenner's photos perpetuated white female beauty stereotypes. However, other transgender women were inspired to create their own "covers" and post them on the internet. Thus, having a "cover" photo became a new way for transgender women to establish their gender *ethos*.

Activity 3.17 • Locate a Photo that Presents an Argument from *Logos, Ethos,* or *Pathos*

Explore

Locate and print or photocopy a photo that presents an argument from *logos, ethos,* or *pathos*. In one sentence, state the photo's argument, identifying whether it is from *logos, ethos,* or *pathos*. Bring the photo and your sentence to class, and share them with your group. Then the group will select one photo and sentence to present to the class.

Activity 3.18 • Focus on Rhetorical Analysis

Compose

Practice and play a rhetorical game of *copia,* a Greek term defined by Cicero as *abundance*. Read Williams' and Hassan's full rhetorical analysis essays.

- Re-write their introductions in different ways. What other options work for the opening paragraphs of these essays? Perhaps other options exist at other places in the essay? Try re-arranging another paragraph to serve as a new introduction.

- Re-write five different versions of the thesis statements to practice different possibilities for how to mark for readers a precise articulation of each essay's focus.

Chapter Exercises

Compose

Activity 3.19 • *Logos* Activity: Write a Letter to the Editor

In the following letter to the editor of *The Baltimore Sun* (published in the Readers Respond section), the author takes exception to the new city policy of equipping police officers with body cameras. The cameras are not being deployed as a crime deterrent but rather to collect data to be used in lawsuits alleging police brutality and misconduct.

Be Prudent with Police Cameras

Though I understand the rush to hold police officers accountable for their behavior, I do not understand placing body cameras on all cops ("Police Body Cameras Will Yield Important Data, Baltimore Task Force Says," Feb. 21 [2015]). This would be like putting every citizen who commits a crime on supervised probation. It is not necessary for all folks, but some need the extra incentive to remain lawful.

I suggest we treat cops like society in general. If one's behavior merits extra scrutiny, then by all means place a camera on him or her. If, however, an officer is honoring the oath and not acting outside of legal authority, leave him or her alone. The cost to place a camera on thousands of police officers is not a great way to spend tax dollars.

I believe this rational response is more prudent than an overreaction. I also believe that facts, not emotion, should dictate how we react to issues that matter.

Mike Snyder, Havre de Grace

1. Choose one of your favorite newspapers or magazines and write a letter to the editor. Express your opinion about an issue profiled in a recent article published in the periodical, as the writer does in the above sample letter to the editor, or about a recent editorial or op-ed. Your letter does not need to be long, but you need to make your argument clear and support it with specific examples.

2. After you have written your letter to the editor, write a paragraph describing your target publication, what you have written in your letter, and why your letter is an illustration of *logos*. Turn in your paragraph with your letter to the editor.

Activity 3.20 • *Pathos* Activity: Portray an Emotion in a Collage

Think of an emotion that you've been feeling lately and that you are willing to explore. Create a collage to express that emotion. Use these criteria.

▓ You can create your collage with cut and paste paper or you can create it through a computer program.

▓ Have little white space. Use colors with emotional connotations (blue for calm, for example).

▓ Have at least three images. You can find these on the internet or in magazines, or take your own photos.

▓ Before you begin your collage, write down the emotion you are trying to explore, and describe how you plan to represent it. In other words, make a plan, even though you will likely deviate from it.

▓ When you finish, write a paragraph describing the experience of creating the collage. Turn your paragraph in with your collage.

Activity 3.21 • *Ethos* Activity: Create a Professional LinkedIn Page

LinkedIn, the world's largest professional network, provides a unique opportunity for aspiring professionals. Using several basic steps, you can create a page on LinkedIn that projects your professional *ethos*—the "you" that you want others in your field to see—so you can find opportunities and make meaningful connections with other LinkedIn participants.

Stephanie Laszik, a M.A. student and instructor at the University of Texas at Tyler shares these tips for creating your own LinkedIn page.

* * *

(continued on next page)

Explore

Compose

Remember that LinkedIn is a social media network in which both employers and employees create user profiles and establish professional connections. LinkedIn provides users with the opportunity to present their educational and professional accolades, seek and post potential jobs, follow companies and employees of companies, maintain supportive professional relationships, and network with other users in similar professions.

For this assignment, create a professional-looking LinkedIn page similar to the one shown here. Discuss in your small group what information and photos you want to use on a page intended for networking with others in your professional field. In effect, you are creating an *ethos* for yourself by these choices.

   ▌ Access LinkedIn at www.LinkedIn.com and complete the free registration using a reliable email account and password.

   ▌ Be sure to include a professional head shot as your identity photo. This is often the first component potential employers and connections will see when they browse LinkedIn.

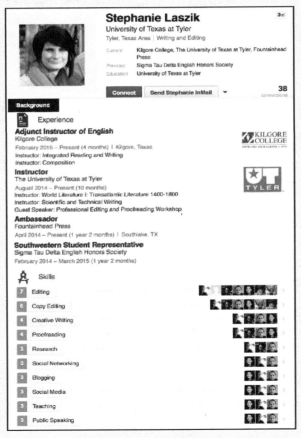

(continued on next page)

▌ The key to a strong LinkedIn profile and relevant connections is thoroughly documenting your education and job experiences. LinkedIn allows you to include current and previous positions, skills you possess in your field, your education, and volunteer experiences.

▌ When completing each section, be as thorough as possible. The more relevant information you include under each section of your profile the better the network will be able to match you with companies and connections.

▌ While LinkedIn communicates information in a similar manner as traditional employment documents, the site is also live and interactive. After you complete your profile, LinkedIn will recommend connections, often within the companies and fields of employment you have added to your profile. Your connections are able to endorse you and suggest skills to be added to your profile.

▌ As you build a database of connections on your LinkedIn profile, you will notice the site enables you to track your profile views, gauge your ranking among other profiles from your companies, and observe trends in member traffic to your profile.

▌ For up-to-date maintenance of your profile and connections, the LinkedIn app can be downloaded to your devices such as a smart phone or tablet computer.

After you have completed your LinkedIn page, write a paragraph that explains the *ethos* you wanted to project in your page and how your content projects that *ethos*.

Compose

Activity 3.22 • Write a Rhetorical Analysis

In this assignment, you will make use of rhetorical vocabulary to analyze a text or combined text and images. You can analyze a speech archived on the *American Rhetoric* website (www.americanrhetoric.com), which features many presidential and other prominent speeches. Alternatively, you can write a rhetorical analysis of a Facebook page, a newspaper or magazine article, or website of your choice.

In your analysis, apply several of the rhetorical concepts you have studied this semester.

▪ Speaker or writer—Does the speaker's identity affect the text?

▪ Purpose—What was the speaker or writer trying to achieve?

▪ Audience—Who was the speech/text directed to? Are there multiple audiences?

▪ Rhetorical appeals—How does the speaker or writer use *ethos, pathos,* and *logos*?

▪ *Kairos*—What is special about the rhetorical moment of the text/speech in terms of place and time?

Activity 3.23 • Reflect on Your Rhetorical Analysis

Freewrite for five minutes about the writing of a rhetorical analysis. You can answer one or more of these questions or comment about something else related to the writing of the essay. What made you choose this particular essay to analyze? Was it easy or difficult to identify the rhetorical concepts? Why or why not? How did you choose to organize your essay? Did the writing of this essay further your understanding of rhetorical concepts?

If your instructor directs, revise your freewriting into a coherent paragraph with a topic sentence and points to support the thesis.

Compo:

Image credit: "Public Writing: UWF Nature Trail" by Alden David Martinez

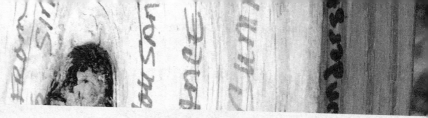

chapter 4
Inventing Rhetorically

Praxis in Action

My Invention Strategies

Jenelle Clausen
M.F.A., Creative Writing
Bowling Green State University

The key to writing based on research is to begin with an open mind. When I start thinking about topic ideas for a paper, I try not to solidify my opinion on a topic until I've researched the subject widely. The impulse I feel is often the exact opposite—I know enough about my topic that I know what angle I want to take, so now I just need sources to confirm that, right? Wrong! That kind of thinking limits topic options and inhibits learning. I want my writing to benefit me as well as my readers. If I want my readers to listen to me, I should listen to others who have already been part of the conversation concerning my topic.

I like to take time to explore a broad topic. If I start early on an assignment, then I have time to meander the internet, search library databases, read books and talk to friends, librarians, and experts. I bookmark sources, physically and electronically, and keep a separate Word document with notes about sources, so I can later trace my way back to the information I need. Though I won't use all of my research as I narrow down my topic, it is helpful, since it immerses me in my subject and exposes me to diverse perspectives.

As I narrow down my topic, I also need to determine the audience for and purpose of my essay. When writing for class, the instructor is an audience, of course, because he or she wields the red grading pen. But it's important also to think outside the context of the classroom and consider whom I might want to reach in a larger or "real-world" context. What do I want to persuade this broader audience to think, feel, or do? How do I effectively communicate with this audience ("with" is important since a writer has to anticipate a reader's response(s), not just throw assertions at him or her)? And what is the answer to the looming question, "So what?" In other words, I need to clarify why others should also care about my topic. All of this will further guide my research and drafting.

Aristotle's Classification of Rhetoric

Aristotle, in *The Art of Rhetoric* (or *Rhetoric*), laid the groundwork for today's persuasive writing by being the first to write systemically about how to teach rhetoric. In contrast, his teacher, Plato, distrusted rhetoric. Plato deplored the way rhetoricians (or politicians) of his era skillfully manipulated the people of Athens, particularly the masses of up to 10,000 voters in the Assembly or 500 in the juries of the law courts. Aristotle, on the other hand, perceived great potential in rhetoric, when taught properly. Rhetoric, as he envisioned it, could be both persuasive and ethical, and in *The Art of Rhetoric* he laid out an organization and classification of rhetoric as he believed it should be taught.

Aristotle divided the process of writing and delivering a composition into five parts. The first of these was **invention**, during which the writer or speaker expanded a topic into ideas that were later arranged into a text or speech. According to the ancient Greeks, the rhetor *invented* these ideas, though they may have mirrored or adapted thoughts presented by previous rhetors. Today, we call this the **prewriting stage** of the writing process, an adaptation of Aristotle's invention stage.

The Five Canons of Rhetoric

Greek and Roman teachers of rhetoric divided rhetoric into five parts or canons. These canons corresponded to the order of activities in creating a speech, as they perceived the process: invention, arrangement, style, memory, and delivery. These five parts are described in many handbooks of rhetorical instruction, including the *Rhetorica ad Herennium*, which was composed by an unknown author between 86 and 82 CE:

> The speaker. . .should possess the faculties of Invention, Arrangement, Style, Memory, and Delivery. Invention is the devising of matter, true or plausible, that would make the case convincing. Arrangement is the ordering and distribution of the matter, making clear the place to which each thing is to be assigned. Style is the adaptation of suitable words and sentences to the matter devised. Memory is the firm retention in the mind of the matter, words, and arrangement. Delivery is the graceful regulation of voice, countenance, and gesture.

Today, classes in composition or writing studies still emphasize the necessity of **invention**, now interpreted as prewriting activities that enable writers to develop the logic and words needed for effective arguments. **Arrangement** involves organizing an argument into a logical format that leads the reader easily from the thesis to the conclusion. **Style** has to do with the author's voice and tone and the structure of sentences and paragraphs. **Memory** is used somewhat differently today, as students are no longer required to memorize compositions for oral presentation. Instead, memory is utilized in ways such as remembering how and where to retrieve information from the internet, books, and other reference materials. Finally, **delivery**, which once involved gestures and tone of voice in an oral presentation, today has to do with document design, so that the final product is presented in a professional manner according to Modern Language Association (MLA) or American Psychological Association (APA) style. Delivery also involves grammatical accuracy because surface errors detract from the effective impact of a document. See Table 4.1 for a summary of the five parts of rhetoric.

Table 4.1 • The Five Parts (or Canons) of Rhetoric

English	Greek	Latin
invention	*heuresis*	*inventio*
arrangement	*taxis*	*dispositio*
style	*lexis*	*elocutio*
memory	*mneme*	*memoria*
delivery	*hypocrisis*	*actin*

The Modern Writing Process Overview

Prewriting (Inventing)

Writing is not only about putting the pen to paper. As did rhetors in ancient Greece and Rome, you have to think deeply and critically about a subject before you begin a composition. The "invention" step of the writer's process is designed to help you find a worthwhile topic and develop your ideas about that topic before you start to write a draft. It includes writing, discussion, and research, as well as informal writing to help you explore your thoughts and feelings about a subject. Whatever method you choose, keep a record of your thoughts and discoveries as you spend this time in close examination of your subject.

Drafting

It may seem odd that writing a draft should come in the middle of the writer's process. However, research has shown that students and professionals alike write more effective essays when they don't reach for the pen too quickly. If you have spent enough time in the invention stage, the actual drafting stage may go more quickly. After writing the first draft, in succeeding drafts you can add details, observations, illustrations, examples, expert testimony, and other support to help your essay entertain, illuminate, or convince your audience.

Revising

Today, we talk more about the revision stage of writing than did ancient rhetoricians. If you are a student who tends to write assigned essays at the last minute, you may have missed this step entirely, yet many writers claim this is the longest and most rewarding step in the writing process. To revise, you must, in a sense, learn to let go of your writing. Some students think their first drafts should stay exactly the way they are written because they are true to their feelings and experience. Many writers find, however, that first drafts assume too much about the reader's knowledge and reactions. Sometimes readers, reading a first draft essay, are left scratching their heads and wondering what it is the writer is trying to convey. Writers who revise try to read their writing as readers would, taking note of gaps in logic, the absence of clear examples, the need for reordering information, and so on. Then they can revise their content with the reader in mind.

Editing and Polishing

Once writers have clarified their messages and the methods by which they will present those messages, one more step must be taken. Particularly because their compositions are written, rather than presented orally, writers must go over their work again to check for correct spelling, grammar, and punctuation, as well as the use of Standard Written English. Some students finish with an essay, print it, and turn it in without ever examining the final copy. This is a critical mistake, because misspelled words and typographical and formatting errors can make an otherwise well-written essay lose its credibility. The five canons of rhetoric and the modern writing process are summarized in Table 4.2.

Table 4.2 • The Five Canons of Rhetoric and the Modern Writing Process

Five Canons of Rhetoric	Modern Writing Process
Invention—Devising the arguments that will make the case convincing, often basing them on models of famous speeches.	Prewriting—Determining the thesis, points of argument, counterargument, and rebuttal. Researching evidence to support the argument.
Arrangement—Ordering the argument into a logical format.	Drafting, revising, and editing—Putting ideas and prewriting into a useable form through a recursive process of drafting, revising, and editing.
Style—Finding suitable words and figures of speech. [Note: This may have been a recursive process, but the ancients did not consider that aspect important.]	
Memory—Retaining the argument in the mind, including its content and arrangement.	Knowing how and where to retrieve information from the internet, books, and other reference materials.
Delivery—Effective use of voice and gestures to present argument.	Publication—Putting text, images, and other elements in a suitable format and releasing the document to an audience.

Activity 4.1 • Compare the Five Canons of Rhetoric and the Modern Writing Process

Collaborate

In your group, reread the discussions in this chapter on the five canons of rhetoric and the modern writing process and review the table above. What parts of the five canons correspond to the modern writing process? What step in the five canons is not included in the contemporary writing process? If the similarities and differences are not clear to you, consult the internet. If you search for either "Five Canons of Rhetoric" or "Writing Process" you will find resources. What explanations can you offer for the differences? The similarities?

Inventing Topics in Academic Writing

By Justin McCoy

For your final writing project in ENC 1101, you will produce an academic research paper on a topic of your choice. There are numerous recursive stages involved in the production of a polished writing project, but the first step is inventing a topic. This step is very important because it not only launches your research but also impacts—either positively or negatively—your level of interest and investment in the development of your writing project.

First, determine a general topic by reflecting on your interests and experiences. Consider your passions and personal memories. For instance, if hunting was part of your family tradition growing up, then perhaps you are interested in gun control. Or, if you or someone you know has been the victim of bullying, you may consider selecting that topic. If you are a college athlete, then the topic of college athletics may generate some significant interest from you. If after you have reflected on your interests and passions but still have not gravitated toward a topic, conduct a cursory search online to locate topics others discuss that may resonate with you and your experiences. In addition, to assess your level of investment in a topic, you may write an exploratory paper in which you connect a personal memory to a topic you are interested in. The ultimate aim here is to locate a topic you care about. Often, understanding your level of investment in a topic is not evident until you have explored your connection to the topic through exploratory writing.

But how do you know if your topic meets the criteria for a writing project? In your academic research paper, you will take a stance on a topic in your thesis statement. In order to meet this objective, you must ensure there is a debate surrounding your topic, one on which you can weigh in. You will locate a contentious issue within your topic, a facet of your topic that has a conversation with at least two opposing viewpoints attached to it. For example, if you are interested in race as your general topic, you would not simply write a "racism is bad" paper because this viewpoint does not contribute to an existing conversation on the topic of race. In other words, no one is saying that racism is good, so the "racism is bad" paper does not join an existing conversation on the topic of race. If you are interested in writing about race, focus this topic by locating an issue that is attached to, or sparks a debate on, race, such as any of the multiple police brutality stories in the news.

You must assess what others say about your chosen topic in order to locate a popular debate related to the topic. To familiarize yourself with the popular debates surrounding your topic, consult credible media sites, which do a great job of characterizing the conversation relevant to an issue by emphasizing the points of contention, or the areas in which people disagree. Topics that have search results on credible media sites typically meet the criteria for an approvable paper topic. News stories from these sites will help you determine the different stances on your topic and will assist you in identifying specific prominent voices on each opposing side. The following media sites are a few places where you can explore the conversations attached to diverse topics:

- *Politico*
- *ABC News*
- *USA Today*
- *The New York Times*
- *Fox News*
- *MSNBC*
- *CNBC*
- *CNN*
- *ABC News*
- *The Washington Post*
- *Mother Jones*
- *The Nation*
- *Salon*
- *The Associated Press*
- *NPR*
- *Slate*
- *CBS News*
- *The Guardian*

In addition, another avenue to explore, and likely your primary avenue for expert opinions that you will incorporate in your final writing project, is the UWF libraries online databases. Among the most helpful databases for inventing and focusing topics include the following:

- *Academic OneFile*
- *CQ Researcher*
- *Opposing Viewpoints in Context*

The last database in the above list, *Opposing Viewpoints in Context*, is comprehensive in its scope, providing both a list of hot-button issues and resources on these issues that are organized by opposing viewpoints.

Remember that in order to locate a controversial topic with contemporary relevance, specificity is key. One of the pitfalls of not focusing on a facet of a topic that is popularly debated is that your paper will not contribute to an ongoing conversation, the primary aim of academic writing.

Focal Topic Scavenger Hunt

By Bre Garrett

The first part of writing an academic research essay involves inventing and selecting a meaningful topic. To find possible topics, engage in a focal topic scavenger hunt. Think of this activity as a process of creation and discovery, the two main acts of invention. You are not entering or beginning this activity with a topic already selected. Rather, the goal is the searching—finding a topic by going through the steps of the scavenger hunt.

Part 1: Abundance—*Thinking Wide and Open Searching*

The goal here is to locate and identify several possible topics. Try to locate at least five possible topics for Part 1. For each step, document your findings by showing the path that led you to the topic. You can document with written words and descriptions, or you might take photos or screen caps, or include sound files.

- Search the NRP website, and other news sites, for timely, kairotic topics. Conduct a basic search of NPR's site, reading multiple headlines and searching different programs. Create a list that documents the topics you discovered and where you found them.

- Search and find topics that stem from TED Talks (either via ted.com/talks or on NPR's TED Radio Hour.

- Search your personal, local community, the UWF and Pensacola area. What topics/subjects do you observe around you on campus, in Pensacola, or in the regional community? Search campus newspapers, local websites, campus lectures, flyers/advertisements, etc. Collect evidence to document your search. For example, take pictures of flyers.

- Search for possible topics/subjects/issues by investigating conversations in an academic discipline (your major or an area that interests you). Search particular department websites as well as the UWF website. Read about "news" or highlighted events and faculty grants and publications. What are areas of research in and across different disciplines?

Part 2: *Narrowing your Focus*

Once you have selected five possible topics, narrow your focus to 1-2 topics and conduct additional research. To complete Part 2 of the scavenger hunt, complete the following tasks:

- Search your topic online and play with word variation. For example, if your topic is ocean pollution, you might search "plastic pollution" or "zero waste culture." Here, word variation is critical and deliberate.

- Search the library catalog for articles about your topic(s): go to "Databases" and explore both Database by Subject and A-Z Database list. See what articles you can locate.

- Have a conversation and inquire what others know about your topic. Have a conversation with at least three people. Document who you talk with and their differing views. Also, document what you learn about your topic from conversation. How is conversation a type of research?

- Locate both historical and cultural context(s) for your topic(s). Find texts, websites, newpapers, or other sources. For example, if your topic is about the #metoo movement, you might explore the 2018 *Time* magazine article and cover: "The Silence Breakers," which would provide a cultural example. But, for historical context, you might research #metoo founder, Tarana Burke.

What's next?

- In-class or on an online forum, generate a list of all possible topics. Use the list to discuss timely topics and historical and cultural context.

- Workshop additional, more focused invention activities to help you narrow your topic and move from topic to argument. Try the "stasis activity" to break your topic into parts, or find an article about your topic and use "reading as invention."

Stasis Theory

Stasis theory presents a series of four questions that were developed by Greek and Roman rhetoricians, primarily Aristotle, Quintilian, and Hermagoras. Answering these questions for an issue enabled rhetors to determine the critical (or stasis) point in a disagreement. This was a technique the ancients developed for the law courts to enable advocates to focus their arguments on the crux of the case. Quintilian, the great Roman teacher of rhetoric, explained in regard to a defendant:

> By far the strongest mode of defense is if the charge which is made can be denied; the next, if an act of the kind charged against the accused can be said not to have been done; the third, and

most honorable, if what is done is proved to have been justly done. If we cannot command these methods, the last and only mode of defense is that of eluding an accusation, which can neither be denied nor combated, by the aid of some point of law, so as to make it appear that the action has not been brought in due legal form.

Marcus Fabius Quintilianus (Quintilian) was a Roman orator from Spain who taught stasis theory.

In other words, Quintilian is saying that in law cases, advocates have four choices in developing a focus for their arguments. You have probably watched a courtroom drama on television or film and can recall various defenses made on behalf of defendants. The strongest and most obvious defense is that the defendant is not guilty, that is, he or she did not do the deed in question. The same was true in Quintilian's day. However, sometimes an argument of innocence is not possible, perhaps because it seems obvious that the defendant did perform the deed in question. Thus, the advocate must develop a different strategy. For example, in defense of one accused of murder, the attorney may argue self-defense or mitigating circumstances (such as that the killing was an act of war). In rare cases, other defenses are offered; for example, if the supposed victim's body has not been found, the advocate can argue that the victim may still be alive. An attorney can discover these possible defenses by using stasis theory to analyze the situation.

Another great advantage of stasis theory is that, if pursued diligently, it prevents the rhetor from making the mistake of organizing an argument by simply forwarding reasons why he or she is correct and the opposition is wrong. That approach may please people who agree with the rhetor, but it will not likely gain any support from the opposition. Answering the stasis questions carefully forces the writer to consider aspects of the issue that may have been overlooked but are crucial to an effective argument.

The wording of the four questions has varied somewhat over time, but essentially they are questions of fact, definition, quality, and policy. The same questions can be applied to any issue, not only issues of law. The four stasis questions are as follows:

1. What are the facts? (conjecture)

2. What is the meaning or nature of the issue? (definition)

3. What is the seriousness of the issue? (quality)

4. What is the best plan of action or procedure? (policy)

Many writers prefer stasis theory to other prewriting techniques because answering the questions determines whether or not the different sides of an argument are at stasis. Being at **stasis** means that the opponents are in agreement about their disagreement—the stasis point—which can be identified by one of the four stasis questions. If the sides are at stasis, they have common ground to build upon, for they are arguing the same issue. There is, thus, a greater chance the sides can reach a workable consensus or compromise. If opponents are not at stasis, there is much more work to be done to reach consensus.

For example, in the argument about the teaching of evolution and/or intelligent design in schools, the two sides are not in agreement about how to discuss the issue. Those in favor of teaching evolution claim intelligent design should not be called science, which is an issue of definition. Those who propose teaching intelligent design along with (or instead of) evolution tend to focus on "proving" evidence, an issue of fact. Until the two sides can agree upon what is the stasis point, or crux of the issue, they cannot debate effectively. They are not presenting arguments about the same question.

The four stasis questions can be broken into the subquestions listed in Table 4.3 on the following page. If you want to find the stasis point, work through the list for your issue, answering all of the subquestions. However, for each question, you must identify not only how *you* would answer the question but also how the opposing side or sides would answer. For example, if you are considering the issue of climate change, people with different positions will not agree on the facts. Thus, you must identify the basic facts of climate change represented by your side, and then identify the facts that might be presented by the opposing side.

Table 4.3 • Stasis Questions

Fact
• Did something happen? • What are the facts? • Is there a problem/issue? • How did it begin, and what are its causes? • What changed to create the problem/issue? • Can it be changed? It also may be useful to ask the following critical questions of your own research and conclusions: • Where did I obtain my data, and are these sources reliable? • How do I know they're reliable?

Definition
• What is the nature of the problem/issue? • What exactly is the problem/issue? • What kind of a problem/issue is it? • To what larger class of things or events does it belong? • What are its parts, and how are they related? It also may be useful to ask the following critical questions of your own research and conclusions: • Who/what is influencing my definition of this problem/issue? • How/why are these sources/beliefs influencing my definition of the issue?

Quality
• Is it a good thing or a bad thing? • How serious is the problem/issue? • Who might be affected by this problem/issue (stakeholders)? • What happens if we don't do anything? • What are the costs of solving the problem/issue? It also may be useful to ask the following critical questions of your own research and conclusions: • Who/what is influencing my determination of the seriousness of this problem/issue? • How/why are these sources/beliefs influencing my determination of the issue's seriousness?

Policy
• Should action be taken? • Who should be involved in helping to solve the problem/address the issue? • What should be done about this problem? • What needs to happen to solve this problem/address this issue? It also may be useful to ask the following critical questions of your own research and conclusions: • Who/what is influencing my determination of what to do about this problem/issue? • How/why are these sources/beliefs influencing my determination of what to do about this issue?

Adapted from Brizee, Allen. "Stasis Theory." *OWL Purdue Online Writing Lab,* Purdue University, 1 Mar. 2013, owl.english.purdue.edu/owl/resource/736/1/.

Using Stasis Questions

To illustrate the use of stasis questions, a team of writers working together to compose a report on racism in America might use the stasis questions to talk through information they will later use in their report. In the following sample dialogue, team members disagree about what actions are racist.

"Flying the Confederate battle flag is racist."

"Flying the Confederate battle flag is *not* racist."

"Yes, it is, because it represents the Confederate states that supported slavery, and it's generally accepted that slavery in America was racist."

"Flying the Confederate battle flag is not racist, because it's a part of American history and Southern heritage."

"After the June 2015 shooting in the Charleston church, more people have come to see flying the Confederate flag as a racist act."

"Yes, but flying the flag is still protected by the First Amendment as free speech."

These two team members disagree about whether or not flying the Confederate battle flag is a racist act. This sort of disagreement might lead to a complete breakdown of group work if common ground cannot be found.

In this example, the team members go on to agree that some people still exhibit the Confederate battle flag (*fact*) on their vehicles and on their clothes, and that the flag is also displayed in museums (*fact*).

The group members agree that the issue is still very important to many people, since a number of American states have recently debated the flag in legislatures and assemblies. For example, the South Carolina Legislature voted in 2015 to remove the Confederate battle flag from the state capitol grounds, while some opposed to the change said the removal disrespected the state's Confederate history (*quality*).

Moreover, a number of legal suits have been filed for and against the display of the flag in public places. For example, the Supreme Court in 2015 decided that Texas's refusal to allow specialty license plates to bear the Confederate flag did not violate the First Amendment. However, those selling and displaying the flag have suggested that the flag does not represent an endorsement of slavery but, rather, regional pride (*quality*).

In this sense, the team members have achieved stasis on two of the four stases—*fact* (people still display the flag) and *quality* (it's a very important issue). Where the team members disagree, however, is in the stases of *definition* (is the display of the flag "racist"?) and *policy* (what should we do about this?).

Thinking about this disagreement using stasis theory allows people to build common ground so that parties who disagree can move toward resolution and action even if they can't agree on all levels. For example, team members who disagree about whether or not flying the Confederate battle flag is racist might still be able to agree on what to do about it.

> "Okay, we disagree about whether flying the flag is racist, but we can agree that flying the flag is probably protected under the First Amendment to the United States Constitution—that flying the flag is protected by our freedom of speech."
>
> "Yeah."
>
> "So, people are free to display the flag on their vehicles, on their clothes, and on their property, as well as in museums. But, state

Figure 4.1 • Disallowed Texas License Plate

License plate that Texas refused to allow because of its incorporation of the Confederate flag.

legislatures and assemblies, like the one in South Carolina, will have to debate and vote on whether or not the flag can be displayed on publicly funded property or in public symbols, such as state flags and seals. And it may be that the courts may sometimes need to be involved, like in the case of the Supreme Court decision about license plates in Texas.

"That sounds pretty democratic. Sure."

Not every team situation is going to end this amicably; however, by using the stasis questions to help keep the dialogue going—on a reasonable course—team members can find common ground and work toward action that is acceptable to most, if not all, of the group members.[1]

Stasis Theory and Kairos

As you will remember from Chapter 3, the *kairos* of an argument is the context, opportune moment, or point in time in which the rhetor, the audience, the issue, and the current situation provide opportunities and constraints for an argument. If you keep *kairos* in mind as you analyze an issue, you take advantage of timeliness. For example, if you want to write an argument about the death penalty, you might consider that United States courts are increasingly questioning the validity of eyewitness testimony, evidence which has been the deciding factor in many death penalty cases.

As part of your use of stasis theory, consider the four questions in relation to *kairos*.

---

1. Adapted from Brizee, Allen. "Stasis Theory for Teamwork." *OWL Purdue Online Writing Lab,* Purdue University, 17 Apr. 2010, owl.english.purdue.edu/owl/resource/736/03/.

1. How do recent developments (new facts) or the local situation affect the issue? Will it change your audience's perception of the facts?

2. Does the current situation affect your audience's definition of the issue? Is it defined differently by an audience in this location than elsewhere?

3. Have recent events made the issue more or less important to your audience? Is it more or less important in your location than elsewhere?

4. Do recent events, locally or widely, affect the need or lack of need for action in your audience's perception?

As a rhetorician, it is important for you to be aware of the history of a controversy. But it is equally important to have an awareness of the *kairos* of the argument. Such an awareness enables you to adopt a "ready stance" and adjust your argument, so that it reflects an awareness of your audience's position and interests, as well as contemporary developments in the issue. Such a flexible stance may afford you an opportunity to be persuasive that you might otherwise miss.

Explore

Activity 4.2 • Identify the Defense in a Television or Film Courtroom Drama

As your instructor directs, watch a courtroom drama on television or film and decide what defense the defendant's attorney is offering. Report your conclusion to your small group or the class. Then, after you have discussed the stasis questions, identify which of the four questions the attorney in the drama is focusing upon as the crux of the defense. Discuss with your group or the class.

Explore

Activity 4.3 • Use Stasis Theory to Explore Your Topic

Choose an issue that interests you and answer all the stasis questions in Table 4.3 on pp. 182–83, both for your position and for the opposing argument. Elaborate with three or four sentences for each subquestion that is particularly relevant to your topic. Is your issue at stasis for any of the questions? Report to your group or to the class.

Compose

Activity 4.4 • Evaluate a Public Debate

Locate a public debate that has been reported recently in newspaper editorials, television programs, or other media that can be analyzed by using stasis theory. In a paper of 350 to 500 words, address these points.

- Describe the context (*kairos*).
- Identify the sides of the argument and their main points.
- Decide which stasis question each side is primarily addressing.
- Determine whether or not the issue is at stasis and explain your answer.
- Include a citation in MLA or APA format for your source or sources.

Other Invention Strategies

Great myths have grown up around writers who can supposedly sit down, put pen to paper, and write a masterpiece. If these myths had developed about any other type of artist—a musician or a painter—we would scoff about them and ask about the years of study and practice those artists had spent before they created their masterpieces. Since all of us can write to some degree, perhaps it seems more feasible that great authors simply appear magically amongst us. Alas, it is not so; like all talented artists, good writers must learn their craft through consistent and continuous practice. Similar to how the ancient Greeks used **stasis questions** or *topoi* (a strategy or heuristic made up of questions about a topic which allows a rhetor to construe an argument) to generate raw material for their compositions, many writers today use the following invention strategies as prewriting activities.

"Inventing an Argument Stance: Four Corners Exercise"

By Bre Garrett

In-class activity for developing argument stance and negotiating common ground.

Select a timely topic for class discussion, or extrapolate a topic from one of the ENC 1101 student essays in this textbook or from an assigned class reading. Choose a topic that lends itself to debate—a topic that has clear pro and con viewpoints. Local, campus issues provide easily debatable topics: for example, the Smoking Ban that UWF implemented in 2016.

Present the topic to students and open class discussion about the issue. Have students freewrite for 5 minutes about their positions and views regarding the topic. Give students an arguable statement that derives from class discussion.

Assign four different classroom locations (the four corners of the classroom)—clearly demarcated places—to the following standpoints: **Strongly Agree, Agree, Disagree, Strongly Disagree**. Ask students to go to the corner and stance that best represents their opinions. Undecided students can stand in the middle.

Have students from each of the four groups try and convince other students and those in the middle to join their positions. This exercise makes literal the concept of locating and positioning yourself in relation to your beliefs. Students practice articulating the differences among various sides of an issue and engage in public discourse as conversation.

As a follow-up, write a reflection about what you learned about the issue, about argument as conversation, and about where you stand on the issue. The following questions can guide your thinking:

- Did your beliefs change, or did you feel more strongly about your original stance?

- What did you learn about the other side?

- What did you observe about your argument style? For example, did you remain calm despite differences of opinion? Did you get agitated and heated? Are you able to listen across difference?

Freewriting

One practice method developed in the 1970s and often attributed to Peter Elbow, author of *Writing without Teachers*, is called freewriting. This method is just what it sounds like—writing that is free of any content restrictions. You simply write what is on your mind. This method is freeform, but there is some structure—you must set a time limit before you begin, and once you begin, you must not stop. The time period is usually 10 to 20 minutes, and you must keep your pen or pencil moving on the page—no hesitations, no corrections, no rereading. Don't worry about spelling, or punctuation, or grammar—just download onto the paper whatever comes to mind. It will seem awkward at best; some have said it is downright painful. But after a few weeks of practice, you will realize it is effective and a wonderful individual method of getting at your thoughts on a subject.

Invisible Freewriting

If you just cannot stop paying attention to your spelling and grammar, or if you find yourself always stopping to read what you have written, you can freewrite invisibly. To do this, you will need carbon paper and a pen that is retracted or out of ink. You sandwich the carbon paper, carbon side down, between two sheets of paper and write on the top sheet with your empty pen. You cannot see what you are writing, but it will be recorded on the bottom sheet of paper. If you prefer to work on the computer, you can easily modify this technique by taping a blank sheet of paper over the monitor while you type.

Focused Freewriting

When freewriting, you are writing without sticking to any particular topic. You are exploring many ideas and your sentences may roam from your day at work, the letter you just got from your sister, or a story you read in the paper about a man who tracks the nighttime migrations of songbirds. With focused freewriting, you are trying to concentrate on one particular subject. You can write the name of that subject at the top of the page to remind you of your topic as you write. The rules are the same as the other types of freewriting, but you are focusing on one question or idea and exploring it in depth.

One drawback of focused freewriting is that students sometimes confuse it with a different step in the writing process: drafting. Remember that freewriting is "invention" work, intended only to help you explore ideas on paper. Drafting takes place only after you have explored, analyzed, and organized those ideas. Freewriting helps you think and write critically about a topic while drafting occurs once you have done the critical thinking necessary to come up with a unified, cohesive, and organized plan for an essay.

Listing/Brainstorming

This method of mapping is the least visual and the most straightforward. Unlike freewriting, where you write continuously, with listing you write down words and/or phrases that provide a shorthand for the ideas you might use in your essay, much as you would a grocery or "to-do" list. Brainstorming is a bit looser. Lists usually follow line after line on the page; brainstorming consists of words and phrases placed anywhere you want to write them on the page.

Example of Brainstorming about Climate Change

Global warming

Polar ice caps melting

Cities underwater as water rises

Natural process or human caused?

People will lose homes when in places where ocean will rise

UK built Thames barrier

How much will preventative measures cost, and who pays for them?

Clustering

When you think of a cluster, you think of several like things grouped together, often with something holding them together. Peanut clusters, a type of candy, are peanuts joined together with milk chocolate. Star clusters are groupings of stars, like the Pleiades or the Big Dipper, connected by their relative positions to each other in space. You can create clusters of like ideas by grouping your ideas around a central topic on a blank sheet of paper. Figure 4.2 shows a sample clustering exercise.

Figure 4.2 • Sample Clustering Exercise

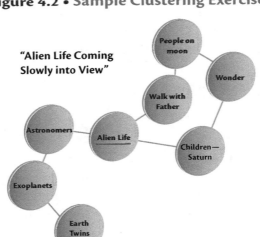

Activity 4.5 • **Try Different Prewriting Techniques**

Choose a topic, and try each of the prewriting techniques listed below. Save your work. Then, in your group, discuss which technique or techniques you prefer.

- Freewriting

- Invisible Freewriting

- Focused Freewriting

- Listing

- Clustering

Activity 4.6 • **Organize or Arrange Your Prewriting**

The "invention" process is intended to get our ideas out of our heads and onto a piece of paper, but rarely do these ideas arrive in the most logical or effective order. Take some time to analyze the material that you produced when you completed the previous activity. Make a list, placing all the ideas in a logical order, and combine similar ideas.

Next, look for your most significant point, the most important thing you want to say about your subject. This may become your tentative thesis.

Then, identify which of the other items will help you communicate your thesis, and delete items that are irrelevant to it. Keep organizing and deleting until you are satisfied with your list of topics or main points.

Reading as Invention

By Jasara Norton

Focused freewriting and group discussions can be effective ways of developing a topic, but what happens if you try those techniques and still can't locate a topic that interests you? Reading is another means of finding a starting point for your writing project. In fact, when students encounter writer's block or are unsure how to add relevant content to a draft, instructors often tell them to return to the research: essentially, to read more.

This method makes sense when we revisit the idea of writing and research as joining a conversation. A strong topic choice is measured, in part, by its cultural significance. The question is, how do we know what topics are culturally significant? We know by listening. Reading is a way of listening to others and hearing other voices. Reading is also a way of stimulating ideas and responses that might not have surfaced if you hadn't joined the conversation. The key to reading as invention is to actively engage with what you're reading as you're reading it.

The following article is about the next generation of college students and the issues and interests that are important to them. Depending on your age, you might be the subject of this article. Either way, you will notice that the author presents many current issues. Actively read the article by annotating it and then consider the following prompts.

1.   How does the author describe Generation Z? Do you agree? Disagree? Provide examples to support your opinion.

2.   What questions does this article generate? Write them down and begin exploring the answers by using Adam Webb's "reading around" method.

3.   Consider *kairos*. Generational cohorts are distinct because of *kairos* rather than arbitrary date ranges. What issues are you facing that are particularly relevant to your generation? What are the events that give rise to those issues?

4.   Follow the links the author provides for more ideas or support for your ideas. Reputable articles always come with built-in research material.

Link to article: http://www.nytimes.com/2015/09/20/fashion/move-over-millennials-here-comes-generation-z.html?_r=0

Take a Leap into Writing

by Craig Wynne

Reading 4.1

Craig Wynne is an Assistant Professor of English and Modern Foreign Languages at Hampton University who also consults professionals on overcoming writing anxiety. In this article, Wynne uses skydiving as both a figurative and literal representation of "jumping" into the writing process. As you read, think about the times in your academic career when you have had hesitations about writing and how that affected your writing process.

When I was working at Berkeley's College Academic Support Center, I often tutored second-language learners who struggled with sentences that had awkward constructions. Sometimes, I would say to a student, "What is it you're trying to say here?" The student inevitably could state the point orally with accuracy and clarity. I would then say to the student, "Write down what you just said." The student would write it down with pen and paper. Then I'd say, "Okay, pretend you're the professor. Which do you think is the easier sentence to understand: what you wrote or what you typed?" The student would say, "What I wrote. Whenever I type, I'm always afraid of what the professor will say."

Craig Wynne says, "When jumping out of an airplane, you don't have time to think about consequences. You just have to do it. [. . .] The same principle applies to writing."

Photo Credit: Craig Wynne

Around that time, I read an article in *Writer* magazine entitled "Forget the Rules and Take a Leap," by an author named Deanna Roy. In this article, Roy had been suffering from writer's block, and she found that skydiving was a way for her to release her thoughts without fear of saying the "wrong thing." So I decided to put this idea into practice myself for the purposes of teaching my students about overcoming their inhibitions when it came to writing.

When jumping out of an airplane, you don't have time to think about consequences. You just have to do it. You can see from the photo, jumping wasn't an easy thing for me to do, but afterwards I was glad I had gone through with taking that leap.

The same principle applies to writing. You need to find a way to write without thinking about whether your words are spelled correctly or whether the professor won't like the idea. Those thoughts get in the way with your writing process. Some students can write with that kind of freedom on a computer, but others find that with the computer comes an uninvited editor who looks over their shoulder and criticizes. Yet, they can escape that editor by talking out their thoughts and then writing with pen and paper. Whatever works. This doesn't mean that writing is ever going to be easy. It's just easier if you can get your thoughts down on a piece of paper before that internal editor starts looking for errors.

A professor named Peter Elbow developed a process called freewriting, which helps writers take that leap from thoughts into words. To freewrite, you put your pen to paper and just write. You don't want to think about whether something is spelled incorrectly or whether the professor will like an idea. Freewriting is the chance for you to get your ideas down on paper (or on the computer). When you freewrite, you don't stop. You just write. Even if you have an idea you think sounds completely stupid or off-the-wall, just write it down. You never know. Sometimes, those "silly" ideas could contain something you might be able to use for your assignment. When I start a project, I begin by letting all my ideas out in words in a row, even if they don't sound quite right. Professor Elbow remarked that freewriting results in a lot of words that are garbage. That's true. However, eventually, I come to words that express an idea I like. In order to get to the point of liking my words, I have to take that leap onto the page. Eventually, I have to worry about grammar, structure, and the end product, but not while I'm freewriting.

Activity 4.7 • Consider "Take a Leap into Writing"

In your small group or on your own, consider and answer the following questions.

1. How do you write most easily? On a computer? With pen and paper? Share your experience getting words onto a page.

2. What do you think of Wynne's comparison of writing to skydiving? What do the two things have in common?

3. Do you have an internal editor that keeps you from writing freely? Can you describe your editor? What does it do?

Collaborate

Activity 4.8 • Focused Freewriting

Practice doing some focused freewriting by following these steps.

1. Write your topic at the top of a blank sheet of paper.

2. Write a list of at least 10 aspects or characteristics of your topic.

3. Choose two or three items from your list, and do a focused freewriting on each item for five to eight minutes.

4. Add more items to your list if you have discovered new ideas during your freewriting.

Compose

Creating a Research lino Canvas

By Laura Herbek

Begin by browsing procon.org in search of a controversial research topic. This nonprofit, nonpartisan website covers a range of polarizing issues sorted into categories like health and medicine, education, and politics. As a group, you must agree on one topic to focus on for this activity. Don't waste time hashing out the issues with your group members; your job is not to develop a stance for or against any issue, but to explain why others hold these views.

Your group will be using linoit.com to create a lino canvas based on your research. lino canvases are a great way to store information and share it visually. If you haven't used lino before, check out one of the website's tutorials. All

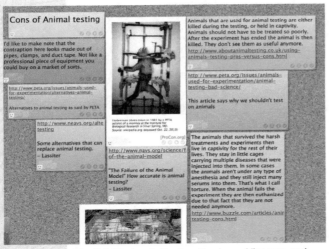

"Animal Testing" by Erik Blackwell, Ben Lassiter, Jenny Nhauyen, and Lauren Weiss. Printed with permission.

students need to create free accounts in order to use the site. One group member must volunteer to create a public canvas and share the information with all group members so that everyone can access the group canvas.

Once you have selected a topic, your group needs to develop two or three guiding research questions to offer some direction as you investigate this debate (see "Research as Inquiry: Guiding Research Questions"). Make sure someone in your group posts these questions to the lino canvas.

Next, use procon.org and other credible sources to research the debate surrounding this subject. Examine the history of the debate, such as how and when it came about and any important developments since that time. Also

study the arguments that object to or support this issue, as well as the evidence typically used to support these arguments. Don't forget to look for answers to your guiding research questions along the way!

As you research, post your findings to the lino canvas. Many students choose to share pictures, videos, and relevant articles. It's useful to post important quotes from the works that you present to help others understand the material better. You can also use lino

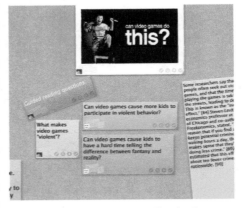

"Violent Video Games" by Becca Bocchinfuso, Donald Caudill, Sammy Cordova, and Jessica Doyle. Printed with permission.

to share your personal observations. Remember that your professor will be able to identify the author of each post, so it's essential that you contribute to the canvas.

Finally, your group should spend a little time organizing and arranging your canvas. Don't hesitate to rotate stickies or move them around. You might decide to group your research under headings like "Pros" and "Cons," or use a particular corner of the canvas for guiding research questions and answers. Your group can also change the colors of sticky notes for particular topics or group members and add stickers to the canvas. You want to make sure that the canvas is easy for others to read and understand, and that there is plenty of information for each category of research.

Finally, groups should share their canvases with the class. At the project's end, you will have access to shared research on a number of controversial debates as well as explanations of the positions people take within those debates.

Artistic and Inartistic Proofs

In the previous chapter, we discussed the three appeals or means that a rhetor can use to persuade an audience: *ethos, pathos,* and *logos.* In *The Art of Rhetoric,* Aristotle divides these appeals or means of persuasion into two types of proofs: artistic and inartistic. Today, these proofs are still part of the writing process though we call them by different names.

Artistic proofs are logical arguments constructed by rhetors from ideas plucked from their minds. An individual then develops these thoughts into a line of reasoning and, in the process, explores and narrows the topic, creates a thesis, and determines the ideas that need to be conveyed to the audience. These proofs are the ones that Aristotle and other ancient rhetoricians believed were critically important, for they are the ones developed from the *rhetor's own mind* and, thus, *invented.* These ideas can be shaped into two types of arguments—deductive and inductive—which we will discuss in the next few pages.

Inartistic proofs are direct evidence that the speaker might use to support the argument, such as testimony, documents, and anything else that rhetors do not invent through their own thinking. Today, we would call these proofs research. They, also, are essential to writing, but they should *support* the writer's ideas, rather than lead them.

For Aristotle's students, the use of artistic and inartistic proofs might not have been a two-step process—first one and then the other, though the proofs are arranged that way in *The Art of Rhetoric,* as they are in this book. Rather, they might have developed both proofs in an alternating or recursive process. After developing basic ideas for a composition through invention, these students would then collect information from authorities (testimony). Then they would return to inventing artistic proofs about the project, followed by more references to inartistic proofs. Today, we have more resources for research than did the ancient Greeks, but this does not make artistic proofs any less important. The differences between artistic and inartistic proofs are summarized in Table 4.4.

Table 4.4 • Aristotle's Artistic and Inartistic Proofs

Artistic	Inartistic
Ideas from the rhetor's own mind, thus *invented*	Information gained from external sources
Personal knowledge	Authorities
Observation	Testimony
Patterns of reasoning	Documents

Collaborate

Activity 4.9 • **Begin with What You Know**

In your small group, make a list of controversial topics that you already have some knowledge about because of personal experience or course work. For example, one of you may be among the millions of Americans without health insurance or you may know someone else in this position. If so, you probably know about some of the failings of the American health care system. Alternatively, you may have lost a job during the Great Recession or been unable to find a job when you needed one. If so, you probably have some thoughts about the efforts of the federal government to deal with the economic crisis. These personal experiences give you knowledge which you can use as artistic proofs in an essay. Share your group's list with the class.

Develop Artistic Proofs through Observation

Close observation for descriptive detail can enhance almost any topic. If you are writing a paper on the effectiveness of recycling in your community, you might take a trip to your community's processing area for recycled glass. There you could gather information through observing the glass recycling process. Good observations become personal knowledge which makes them artistic proofs.

You may need to call to get permission to visit certain places. You'll need to identify yourself and your topic. Usually you can get permission to visit and observe. However, if you cannot get permission to visit an area, you can ask your contact if there is a similar area nearby. Again, look at your research questions before you visit to decide which questions might be answered by your observations. For example, if you have read about recycling centers in other communities, during your visit to the local center, you could observe the similarities and differences in their procedures. Good writers always gather more detail than they actually use so they have choices about what to include.

The key to successful observation is tuning the senses. Can you remember what your room smelled like when you woke up this morning, the first thing you saw when you opened your eyes, the way your sheets or blanket felt against your skin, the sounds in the room after you turned off your alarm, or the taste of the orange juice or coffee you had with breakfast? Our minds are trained to ignore seemingly unimportant information, so if you can't remember any sensory details from your morning, you're not alone. When conducting an observation, however, those sensory responses are an important part of your research. Sitting in the place you're observing, freewrite for at least five minutes on each of the senses: touch, taste, smell, sight, and sound. You might even freewrite on each of the senses from several different vantage points, depending on the size of the place or the event you're observing. Take notes on the responses given by those you speak with.

Within fifteen minutes of leaving the place you have been observing, take a few minutes to read over your notes and write a few overall impressions or add details you missed in your description. Look again at your research questions, and decide which ones have been answered by your visit.

Activity 4.10 • Observation Exercise to Develop Artistic Proofs

In this exercise, describe your classroom. Alternatively, go to another setting such as a museum, restaurant, or library and describe that space and the people in it.

Explore

- How large is the space, approximately? Describe the shape of the room, and the color and texture of the walls, the ceiling, and the floor.
- How is the space furnished? Describe the color, shape, and style of the furnishings.
- What about representing the other senses? Is the room silent or noisy? Does it have a characteristic smell? Describe.
- How many people are in the room? What are they doing? Describe their ages, general style of dress, and possessions such as computers, backpacks, or purses.
- Pick two or three people that stand out in some way from the other occupants and write a sentence or two about each, describing what it is about each person that caught your attention.

Reading 4.2

Dan Neil, auto columnist for the Wall Street Journal, *reviewed the new Porsche Macan S in his weekly column "Rumble Seat." He calls the vehicle Barbie's dream car, meaning that Porsche has designed it with well-to-do, fashion-conscious women in mind. See if you think that stereotype fits the car.*

As you read the article, pay attention to how the author uses details from his personal knowledge of the auto world, as well as his close observation from driving and inspecting the Porsche, to enrich his writing. Notice, also, how some details—such as the $500 million Porsche spent to build an assembly line for the car in Leipzig, Germany—likely came from promotional materials or interviews with Porsche personnel.

Porsche Macan S: Is This Compact Crossover Barbie's Dream Car?

By Dan Neil

You just knew when Porsche decided to build Barbie's Dream Car it was going to be awesome.

And it is. The 2015 Macan S ($49,900 MSRP) is Porsche's entry to the exploding luxury compact crossover segment, and it is a dram of excelsior, a proud, darling thing: quick off the line (5.0 seconds to 60 mph, with the optional launch control engaged) and nimble at the helm, with a steel-spring suspension (wishbone front and trapezoidal-link rear) that's as tight as a speed skater's buttocks. Actually, the Macan S drives shockingly well considering it weighs in around 4,500 pounds and is a foot taller than a 911. More on that later.

Curb appeal? Forget about it. Among the details to savor is the clamshell hood that extends to the front wheel arches, so that the hood shut lines go away. The Macan isn't dripping in aggression, design-wise, with soft,

Sexy Beast. The Porsche Macan S has a leg up in the luxury compact crossover market with soft contours and the best interior among its rivals.

Photo Credit: Porche Cars North America

rounded corners inherited from the 911 and an open, expressive face. It has nothing like the Range Rover Evoque's narrow, predatory stare. And yet the Macan is low, wide and stance-y, with staggered tires (a wider set in back) and heavy haunches. It's a Cayenne in short pants.

Porsche has made no secret of the desire to expand the brand to more women. Translating that desire into product design is a perilous business, especially for such a macho brand. But I think the Porsche design team, led by Michael Mauer, got exactly what it was looking for. The Macan hits a mall parking lot like a fishing lure hits the water, if smartly dressed women were largemouth bass.

The category, Alex, is premium/luxury compact crossovers and/or sport-utilities. The yard marks are wide, but you are going to shell out anywhere from about $40,000-$70,000—I recommend leasing such nonsense—and the competitive set includes the cream of the world auto-making crop: Acura RDX, Audi Q3, BMW X3, Land Rover Discovery Sport, Mercedes-Benz GLA, the Evoque and a few others.

In this category you are free to spend like you are on cocaine. There is such a thing as a Macan Turbo (with a 3.6-liter, 400-hp version of the V6) that starts at $72,300 and can top six figures when you start adding carbon-ceramic brakes ($8,150) and air suspension ($1,385).

Our Macan S test car—painted ermine-white with beige leather interior—came in at $72,620 and included 20-inch alloy wheels ($1,260), the active dampers ($1,360), the upgraded Bose stereo ($1,400) and infotainment package ($2,990) and the Premium Package Plus ($5,990). Oof!

The powertrain is a thing of beauty, starting with the all-aluminum, 90-degree, 3.0-liter direct-injection twin-turbo V6, producing a nicely focused 339 pound-feet, from 1,450 rpm all the way to 5,000 rpm, and peak horsepower from 5,500-6,500 rpm. Golly, what a sewing machine. When you switch to Sport + mode and add some throttle, the engine bawls, it purrs, it chuckles. Hot, guttural overrun sounds come courtesy of the active exhaust valve. But the symphony is turned way down in volume, a bit too far to seem threatening, just adorable. Growl, kitty, growl!

Downstream of the engine is Porsche's seven-speed dual-clutch PDK automatic transmission and the full-time all-wheel drive system, based around a digitally managed multi-plate center differential. The Macan's front diff is open and the rear is limited-slip, with the option of the Porsche Torque Vectoring Plus on the rear diff, slewing torque left or right as needed to help the car turn harder and accelerate sooner.

Romp it and all this actuates with greased flawlessness one might expect in a late-model Porsche, even to a fault. There isn't a sharp edge to be found is this car. Even in Sport + mode, the PDK acts like/drives like any other high-tech, torque-converter based automatic transmission, with upshift events that flutter among the ratios, never bang.

Honestly, Porsche. If the camera could zoom into the ghostly face of Ferdinand Porsche as he surveyed his legendary sports-car empire, now building glammy luxe crossovers for the recently divorced in West Palm Beach, would he have a single tear, like Iron Eyes Cody?

Oh, I've had it all explained to me: Porsche, now a holding of Volkswagen AG, has been fully entrained into the group's product slipstream. The Macan is a platform cousin to the Audi Q5, sharing VW's MLB platform, for light-duty vehicles with front-longitudinal engine orientation and all-wheel drive.

About a third of the Porsche's structure is common to the Audi, but Macan gets Porsche-proprietary engines and the PDK gearbox; exterior and interior; suspensions and dynamics software. Porsche AG also spent more than $550 million to construct the Macan assembly line in Leipzig, Germany—where car-building counts—with an annual capacity of 50,000 cars. So pedigree really isn't an issue.

And yet, I can't help thinking the Macan would have been a lot—what's the word?—lighter, had it not been born to share the girdle of the corporate platform.

If the Macan wins, it's to the credit of Porsche's interior-trim department. This is the best interior of any in the competitive set: clean and Nordic in design, wintry with polished alloy, rich with skins, with lots of very nice parts from the company's bins, including Porsche's new, three-spoke steering wheel, like the one in the 918 Spyder. The seats are terrific, and the fully upholstered rear cargo space large and useful (17.7 cubic feet). My kids had no problems riding in the back seat. The whole thing is surprisingly undiminished by the price point.

If the Macan stumbles, it might be because it feels a bit soft to enthusiasts. This truckette is well over two tons, and all the adaptive suspension, torque vectoring and sport tires only defray the costs of that mass. Yes, it has good road-holding in corners, considering, but the weight makes it feel antsy. Yes, the electric-assist steering is tactile and responsive, but it could be more of both. The short-stroke engine of the Macan S (69 mm stroke and 96 mm bore) spins like a bandit, but it's all so at a distance, so muted and isolated. The Macan's missing piece is driver involvement.

But maybe you don't feel like driving at the moment. In that case, switch on the Macan's optional Lane Keeping Assist, a ghost-in-the-machine system that will keep a car heading down a road with minimal input from the driver. Now you can smile. And don't forget to wave, Barbie.

Activity 4.11 • Find Artistic and Inartistic Proofs in a Reading

Explore

Much of the information for Dan Neil's column, "Porsche Macan S: Is This Compact Crossover Barbie's Dream Car?" comes from his own personal experience and observation. For example, his description of the car: "[I]t is a dram of excelsior, a proud, darling thing: quick off the line…with a steel-spring suspension (wishbone front and trapezoidal-link rear) that's as tight as a speed skater's buttocks," is his own evaluation or thought and, thus, an artistic proof. So is the sentence, "Porsche has made no secret of the desire to expand the brand to more women. Translating that desire into product design is a perilous business, especially for such a macho brand." That knowledge comes from his long experience with reviewing the automobile market.

However, the numbers Neil uses to describe the powertrain—"all-aluminum, 90-degree, 3.0-liter direct-injection twin-turbo V6, producing a nicely focused 339 pound-feet, from 1,450 rpm all the way to 5,000 rpm, and peak horsepower from 5,500-6,500 rpm"—may have come from the manufacturer's promotional literature or an interview, though the conclusion of "nicely focused" may be his own.

For this activity, go through the reading and highlight (or underline) the parts that you think come from Neil's own knowledge or observation. These are the artistic proofs. Information he has obtained from other sources (such as the car company) would be inartistic proofs.

If you aren't sure whether or not a sentence is Neil's own knowledge or observation, make a note of that in the margin. Discuss this as a class.

Explore

Activity 4.12 • **Develop Criteria for Reviews**

In your small group, discuss these questions in response to Neil's article about the Porsche Macan S.

1. What criteria did Dan Neil use in evaluating the Porsche Macan S? Share your answers with the class.

2. What reviews do you plan to write for Activity 4.13? Discuss in your group how each of you plans to develop criteria to evaluate your topics.

Individually, make a short list of criteria you will use to evaluate your topic for Activity 4.13.

Compose

Activity 4.13 • **Write a Product Review**

Choose a new product in a category you know well, such as a computer or a motorcycle, and write a review as if you were a columnist for a newspaper, magazine, or blog. Using the techniques explained in this chapter, such as freewriting or brainstorming, prewrite to elicit what you know about the product and the product category. Then, observe the product and try it out, so that you can review its positives and negatives. If you need specific information that you do not know, consult the product advertising, packaging, or instruction manual.

Like Dan Neil's auto product review, you can use vivid language and insider slang in order to provide an enjoyable experience for your reader. Remember, however, that this is an argument. You need to evaluate whether the product is a good or bad selection for its target audience and why.

Reading 4.3

Guardians of the Galaxy's Happy Satire of the Sad Origin Story

by Katie Kilkenny

Katie Kilkenny's film review, published on theatlantic.com, makes use of the superhero origin story plot format to review Guardians of the Galaxy. *Superhero origin stories, according to Kilkenny, are not generally very original. However,* Guardians *adds a satire twist to the plot pattern because the deep trauma's of the film's heroes has not endowed them with any nobility, as it usually does in an origin story; rather, they are misfit sell-outs who are, nevertheless, called upon to save the galaxy.*

Superhero origin stories, for the most part, aren't very original. They all to some extent involve a young child or particularly immature man falling prey to a terrible crime, accident, experiment, or, alternately, reluctantly getting chosen by higher powers. Then comes a period of shock swiftly followed by a period of combat training—for, as all comic lovers understand, a true hero directs his mournful energies toward coordinating outfits, gadgets, and crime-fighting prowess around a theme. The takeaway: Superheroes are just like you and me until something genuinely terrible befalls them—then, an inhumanly noble hunger to fight crime takes over.

On the surface, *Guardians of the Galaxy,* Marvel's latest movie, is an origin story, too. Given the obscurity of the source comic, it has to be: Our heroes, a bunch of alien rogues, were introduced briefly in a 1969 issue of *Marvel Superheroes,* played benchwarmers to the likes of the Avengers for about 50 years, then were revived by writers Dan Abnett and Andy Lanning in 2008 to middling sales. To counteract the risk of the venture we follow recognizable white male Chris Pratt, newly buff and emotional, playing Peter Quill, a boy who was abducted by aliens and now calls himself "Star-Lord."

Sensibly, Peter's chosen alias is roundly mocked by his fellow Guardians in the film—as is his masculinity, wooing capabilities, general leadership, and other qualities that usually endorse newbie heroes in tights. Pratt is at the point in his career when critics would label him an "unlikely leading man"; here he actually plays one to his scrappy, squabbling intergalactic crew. As the title suggests, they're the real heroes of this kinda-sorta-superhero movie. If *Guardians of the Galaxy* is an origin story, it is also a satire of the origin story, one that emphasizes the power of the "We" over that of the "Chosen One."

Photo Credit: Everett Collection, Inc.

Every member of the Guardians has known deep trauma. Chris Pratt's lead Peter Quill lost his mom (cancer); Zoe Saldana's Gamora is practically dead to the last surviving member of her family Nebula (Karen Gillan); her previous colleague-in-crime Ronan (Lee Pace) slaughtered the family of Dave Bautista's Drax; and Rocket Raccoon (Bradley Cooper) doesn't even have a family since, as a human experiment in anthropomorphization gone wrong, he's basically a lab animal. As for his pet, the sentient tree Groot (Vin Diesel), who knows? He can only string together three words (the innocuous truth, "I am Groot"). Judging by the way he tortures his adversaries—pushing his roots into their nostrils, out other orifices—it's safe to assume the tree has issues, too.

But in contrast to the rest of the genre, these sob stories don't bestow nobility. No one's particular woes are more "super" than another's. In fact, any attempt at tragedy one-upmanship would counteract the movie's shaggy, communal comedy. The Guardians aren't superheroes so much as they are a heterogeneous mix of losers, bandits, and outlaws who know just how unexceptional they are. As Chris Pratt's character says to rally the troops, "I look around and I see losers. Like, people who have lost something."

The real reason they connect is because they're all lucky sellouts, not Chosen Ones. The point of their big entrée into superherodom is to scrape together some prize money by selling the mysterious Infinity Stone, this franchise's equivalent of the equally irrelevant MacGuffin in *The Avengers,* the Cosmic Cube. The film then becomes a series of encounters that all lead up to the faceoff with the slithery highest bidder. While *Guardians* welcomes comparisons to *Star Wars*, there's no Luke, paragon of high-minded heroic ideals—our heroes are all a bunch of opportunistic Hans, ineloquent Wookies, and cowardly C-3POs. Yes, they're a strong, sad bunch, but in total it's a managerial nightmare to corral a team around a single crime-fighting objective sans incessant arguments.

In fact, *Guardians of the Galaxy* makes the case that a hero's individual strength amounts to merely a culturally acceptable form of pigheadedness. Take the movie's portrayal of Drax, a conflicted vigilante with only one thing on his mind—avenging his murdered wife and child. It's a generic motivation, and another movie might try to use him to bring us to tears. But here he nearly dies in the attempt for revenge, thus endangering the greater mission, to make money. "We've all got dead people!" his compatriot Rocket Raccoon scoffs. And for one moment of wonderful lucidity a Marvel movie makes sport of Marvel's big, profitable trope: the prolonged mourning of buff guys in tights.

The lampooning is more playful than genuinely threatening to the Marvel universe, though. For however much *Guardians* critiques the usual fare, it's still bookended by Chris Pratt's tragic flashbacks, a technique reminiscent of Christopher Nolan's super-serious *Batman Begins*. The flashbacks are the movie's least convincing moments, either because they're too earnest for the self-conscious flick or the actor isn't as good at shedding tears as he is at acting a buffoon on *Parks and Recreation.*

The origin story isn't some morally fraught trope that needs toppling, either. In fact, psychologist Robin Rosenburg has noted that superhero origin stories teach us "how to be heroes, choosing altruism over the pursuit of wealth and power."

But if we're going to take them seriously as instructions for how to be altruistic super-individuals, origin stories could also teach teamwork. This is where *Guardians of the Galaxy,* at its most delightfully self-aware, has a new take. It doesn't pretend like its heroes are not all mortals with an interest in pursuing that plebeian concern, money. Even so, it does show that a group of flawed losers can take down a planetary dictator with an enchanted stone if, for one moment, they forget their own baggage and hack out a semblance of a plan first.

Collaborate

Activity 4.14 • **Discuss Review of *Guardians of the Galaxy***

Katie Kilkenny describes *Guardians of the Galaxy* as a superhero origin story. In your small group, discuss the following points and share your responses with the class.

1. Make a list of other superhero origin movies. In what ways do they fit the pattern Kilkenny lays out in her first paragraph? In what ways do they deviate from Kilkenny's pattern?

2. How does Kilkenny say *Guardians* fits the pattern, and in what ways does it not? What is the main strength of the movie, and how is it a new take on the superhero origin story?

3. Is Kilkenny's review effective? Why or why not?

Explore

Activity 4.15 • **Develop Criteria for Film Reviews**

In your small group, discuss the following points.

1. How does Katie Kilkenny employ the use of the superhero origin story movie plot pattern to create her criteria for reviewing *Guardians of the Galaxy*?

2. What film reviews do you plan to write for your next assignments? Is there a plot pattern such as a love story or buddy film that you can apply to your chosen movies? Perhaps there is an outstanding performance by an actor or an excellent rendering of a book into film. What other criteria might you employ? How would you evaluate a film based on your chosen criteria?

Individually, search the internet for reviews of your chosen film to use as resources to back up you evaluation. Be sure to cite any quotes or paraphrases from other reviews you incorporate into your review. Then, write down the criteria you plan to use to review your film. Discuss these criteria with your group, and, if requested, turn in your writing to your instructor.

Activity 4.16 • **Write a Film Review**

In this assignment, you are a film critic. Write a review that could appear in a newspaper, magazine, or blog. Your style and tone will be dictated by your audience, so identify the publication just under the title of your review by saying something like this: "Written for Undergroundfilms.com." Be sure to read several reviews published in your chosen media outlet.

Compose

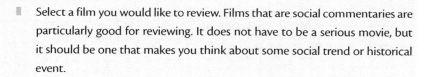

- Select a film you would like to review. Films that are social commentaries are particularly good for reviewing. It does not have to be a serious movie, but it should be one that makes you think about some social trend or historical event.

- After you decide on a film, learn about its context. Who is the director, producer, and primary actors? What films have these individuals worked on before? Have they won awards? Are they known for a certain style? Read and annotate other reviews of the film, marking sections that you might paraphrase or quote to support your opinions.

- Employ the criteria you developed in the previous activity to write a working thesis that makes an argument about your chosen film.

- Create a working thesis that makes an argument about the film. You can modify this thesis later, but it helps to identify early on what you want to argue.

- Use some of the invention strategies from this chapter to help you articulate what proofs you can use to support your argument.

- Near the beginning of your draft, briefly summarize enough of the film that your review will be interesting to those who have not seen it. However, don't be a "spoiler." Don't ruin the film for potential viewers by giving away the ending.

- Organize your essay into three main points that support your thesis and at least one counterargument that complicates or disagrees with your argument.

- Write a compelling introduction that uses one of the approaches discussed in Chapter 6. You want your reader to be interested in what you have to say. For example, you might begin with a startling quote from the film or a vivid description of a pivotal scene.

- Be sure to include specific examples and colorful details. These are essential to make your review interesting to the reader.

Compose

Activity 4.17 • **Reflect on Your Film Review**

Freewrite for five minutes about the movie review you just wrote. Answer one or more of the questions in the previous activity, or write about something else related to your product review. Why did you choose that particular film? What was it like combining your personal knowledge, observation, and information you obtained from the movie website or another review?

If your instructor requests, turn your freewriting into a polished paragraph with a thesis and supporting sentences.

Image credit: "CompCon: UWF Student Composition Conference" by a UWF Photographer.

chapter 5
Researching Rhetorically

How I Research

Rosalie Krenger
M.A. Student, Emporia State University
Assistant to the Director of Creative Writing and Teaching Associate

When I research, I always try to be open, unbiased, and prompt. I start off with a good, open-ended research question. I like questions that provide me with direction in my research but are open enough that I might find information I hadn't considered or be led to other questions I could investigate. I also make sure I look at issues from as many sides as possible. Knowing multiple sides of an issue allows me to make a convincing argument by giving me the opportunity to rebut or concede argument points where appropriate, which adds to my *ethos* as a writer. Thus, I resist the urge to only search for sources that support my thesis.

Actually, doing the research can sometimes be frustrating for me because it doesn't immediately produce tangible results, i.e. words on a page. So it's often tempting to put it off until a deadline draws near. However, starting my research as soon as I learn of an assignment makes for an easier writing process and a better paper in the end. It gives me not only enough time to thoroughly investigate my topic but also to change my thesis if need be. Moreover, I have time to submit an interlibrary loan request if I discover an important book on my topic that my college library doesn't have.

In addition to books in the library, I like to use databases like *JSTOR* and the *MLA International Bibliography* that are accessible through the library's webpage. I start with keywords or phrases and begin weeding out sources that aren't appropriate to my research, aren't credible, or weren't published recently. Also, I check the reference pages of my selected journal articles, as they often lead me to other relevant books or articles. I make sure to save as many of the sources as possible on my computer, so I can revisit them as I write. I also create my works cited page as I go, which saves a lot of time later.

Approaching research in this way strengthens my writing, lends to my *ethos*, and makes the process much smoother because I feel confident that I know my subject.

Research Provides Inartistic Proofs

As discussed in Chapter 4, ancient Greeks began the writing process with invention, a stage in which they searched their memories for data related to the topic at hand. This information constituted artistic proofs, knowledge that rhetors invented from their own minds, emotions, and observation. However, rhetors also supplemented their invented proofs with information that was gleaned from other sources such as the testimony of witnesses, evidence given under torture, and written contracts. Yes, evidence given under torture was considered a legitimate proof. None of these inartistic proofs were generated from the rhetor's mind or "invented." As such, the Greeks considered these sources of information to be inartistic proofs.

Today, the range of inartistic proofs available to writers and speakers is vastly expanded—scientific studies, opinions from authorities, videotapes of events, government documents, and so on. You can locate these in the traditional way—library books and print periodicals—but more likely you will begin your search with the internet, a resource the ancients could not have imagined. However, as in ancient times, it is still the task of today's rhetor to locate available resources, sift through them to locate those that are relevant, evaluate their reliability and validity, and incorporate them into a text to support an argument.

Researching rhetorically, the title of this chapter, refers to making use of your *ethos* or credibility as a writer by incorporating your expert knowledge gained from everyday experiences and the subjects you have studied. You may decide, like Shanna Farrell, author of Reading 5.2, "What Does It Mean to Drink Like a Woman?", to write about a topic that has immediate relevance to your own life. Farrell uses her own experience to challenge the conventional wisdom that women like "girlie" drinks that use fruity flavors to disguise the flavor of alcohol.

Researching rhetorically also involves maximizing as well as "borrowing" the credibility of source materials you quote or paraphrase in your text. When you quote or paraphrase an expert, your paper gains authority that it would not otherwise have. For example, if you are the parent of a child with attention deficit hyperactivity disorder (ADHD), your experiences caring for that child and interacting with the health care and educational systems, as well as the reading you have done to seek out effective treatment, qualifies you to speak with authority about what it is like to raise such a child. If you are writing a paper about educational options for children with ADHD, you can cite some of your own experiences, but you will also want to quote or paraphrase opinions of authorities about the best ways to provide a quality educational environment for these children. These expert opinions can be found in books, periodicals, and possibly government documents, and including them will increase your power to convince an audience.

You Do Research Every Day

Although the words "research paper" sound imposing to many students, research is really a natural part of your experience. You do research every day, often without being aware of the process, whether it is determining the calorie count of a serving of sugar-free ice cream or calculating the dollar amount you will spend on gasoline for a weekend trip.

Ideally, a research paper grows out of questions you have about the way the world works—issues or things that you have thought about that intersect your own life. For example, you may worry about how your student loan debt will affect you after you graduate, and you know that many other college students face the same issue. A research paper about the effects of student loan debt would be a more formal response to a question that already interests you. Because of your personal connection, you find the topic interesting enough to consider researching the issue to find out real answers to your questions about that topic.

The information gathering you do for a research paper builds on the informal research skills you already have by adding additional places to look for information and additional tools to use in that search.

How do you go about finding the best reference sources to support your general knowledge? A key factor to keep in mind is the credibility of each of the sources you choose. Citing information from a source written in the last three years is generally more credible than a source published ten years ago because the information is obviously more current. Peer-reviewed journals and books published by reputable publishers are probably the most credible sources. Information from a news magazine such as *Time* has more credence than material found in popular magazines such as *Glamour* or *People,* which are designed for entertainment rather than covering the news. Indeed, many instructors will forbid the use of *Wikipedia* as a source, not because all the information is inaccurate (because it is not), but because the reader has no way of evaluating whether information is correct or not since the entries were written by volunteers and the content has not been vetted by a reputable publisher or other authoritative organization.

Don't be reluctant to ask for help. Your instructor may be willing to suggest resources on your topic, as will librarians. Some instructors may refer you to specific books or authors. Others may demonstrate a journal search for you, in the process finding you valuable sources. Librarians can be valuable allies in your search, as their job is to serve your needs as a library patron. If you ask for help, a librarian will often run a search for you in the online catalog or may even walk with you into the stacks to find appropriate source materials.

Research as Inquiry: Guiding Research Questions

By Laura Herbek

Guiding research questions are inquiries you attempt to answer or understand better over the course of your research. They can be broad, such as "Why are so many people opposed to the death penalty?" or more specific, like "Are many illegal immigrants actually receiving welfare benefits?" Don't be discouraged if your guiding research question seems difficult or even impossible to answer definitively. Getting closer to the answer is still a worthwhile endeavor.

Primary and Secondary Research

If you've ever purchased a major consumer product, say a computer, chances are you already knew quite a bit about what was available before you took out your charge card. For example, many of your friends probably have computers as well as definite opinions about what brands and models are preferable, and they have shared those opinions with you. Perhaps you already own a computer and like it so much that you want to upgrade to the next model, or maybe you have complaints about its performance. Still, before you made your purchase, you probably did some research on the internet, reading product specifications and reviews. Maybe you tried out a computer or two at the local Apple Store or another retailer. If you went through this sort of process before buying a computer or another consumer product, you already know the basics of primary and secondary research.

Primary research involves personal interaction with your subject. Interviews with people on the scene of an event and questionnaires are all primary sources. Novels, poems, diaries, and fictional films are also primary sources because they stand alone and are not interpreting anything else. To return to the computer purchase analogy, when you visited the Apple Store or other retailers to examine computers, you were doing primary research. When you looked at product reviews in magazines, you were doing secondary research. Similarly, when you read a *Time* magazine article that analyzes climate change and quotes prominent experts in the field, you are conducting secondary research.

A little later in this chapter, an activity asks you to interview someone who has had an unusual life experience and write a profile of that person. You may be able to gather all the information you need for this assignment by doing an interview, though it might be a good idea to revisit the observation exercise (Activity 4.10) in Chapter 4. If you know the person personally, you can also utilize that prior knowledge.

Secondary research sources analyze, collate, or synthesize existing primary research. An author doing secondary research collects primary sources and interprets what the primary research means.

The majority of your sources in a research paper may be secondary research. You should choose your sources carefully because the credibility of information from secondary research depends on the validity of the primary research being discussed, the qualifications of the writer, and the reputation of the publisher. Your writing will be stronger if it also includes discussion of primary research, when that is possible, along with the findings from secondary research.

Many writing assignments ask you to combine your own experience or primary research with information gained from secondary research in books or periodicals. For example, you might be asked to write an essay about recycling. You can include your own experience with recycling or visit a recycling center in your community and report what you see. You can also support this primary research with secondary research in books or periodicals in which authorities offer facts and opinions about the effectiveness of recycling. In addition, you can interview an authority on recycling, perhaps a professor or chairperson of a community committee, as an additional secondary source.

You may notice that many magazine articles or books refer to other books, statistical studies, or additional evidence but do not document sources in the text or give a bibliography. In this course, however, your instructor will probably ask you to document outside references following the Modern Language Association (MLA) or American Psychological Association (APA) format. The purpose is to train you in academic writing, which differs from journalism or popular writing in that all sources are credited both in the text and in a works cited page. Documentation also benefits those who read your essays and might want to use the same sources for additional research of their own. It is, therefore, not a check against plagiarism but an important tool for other researchers.

In this article, Alexander L. Ames argues that primary sources add depth and help bring a research topic to life. Ames is a Ph.D. student in the history of American civilization at the University of Delaware.

Bringing History to Life with Primary Sources

by Alexander L. Ames

History sometimes bores because of the way it is taught. Often, educators merely present students with information they are supposed to remember, rather than encourage students to explore historic documents and draw conclusions. As a Museum Studies intern at Mystic Seaport, a maritime history museum in Mystic, Connecticut, I worked with other interns to create history education programs targeted at high school audiences. We presented students with primary sources and asked them to think critically about the documents, to develop their own ideas about history.

My favorite program we developed related to the Temperance Movement, a mid-nineteenth century social reform movement that aimed to put an end to alcohol consumption. Members of the Greenman family, prominent shipbuilders and storeowners who lived in Mystic, became involved in Temperance as the movement gained national momentum. We traced the development of their beliefs through historic documents relating to their business and civic activities. For example, we showed students pages from the 1840s account books of the family-owned Greenman General Store that had frequent references to the sale of alcohol. By the 1850s, those references had vanished. Also, we gave students newspaper articles from the 1870s in which the Greenmans publicly stated their support of Temperance, indicating the passion with which the Greenmans advocated against alcohol. The text of the education program encouraged students to discover the Greenmans apparently stopped selling alcohol, a decision that affected the company's profits, *before* their public announcement of their change in attitude toward alcohol.

Students going through the educational program realized they would not know this fascinating detail, which hints the Greenmans were willing to lose company revenue in support of their beliefs, if they had not scrutinized account books from the nineteenth century. Moreover, we asked students to think about whether they could cite negative evidence—that is, the *absence* of liquor sales in the 1850s account books—as sufficient grounds for assuming the Greenmans changed their business practices by that decade? What other evidence would help support this conclusion—an open ended question students can answer in a variety of ways.

Focusing on historical evidence allows us to ask deeper questions about our conclusions. The questions we encouraged the students at Mystic Seaport to think about show the debatable nature of historical conclusions based on primary sources. While applied here to a museum activity, this strategy of poring over primary sources can be used in almost any research context. Original documents get us as close as possible to whatever subject we are studying. They also add depth to our interpretations by encouraging critical analysis of sources.

Reading 5.2

What Does It Mean to Drink Like a Woman?

by Shanna Farrell

I am a woman who likes whiskey. I order Manhattans. I drink Old Fashioneds. And nearly every time I announce this request to a bartender, I get the knowing nod—the unvoiced approval and the respect that comes along with defying the expectations of what a woman usually drinks.

And usually this approving bartender is a male. By nature of its history, bartending is a male-dominated industry, one in which women tend to work a little harder to earn the same credibility bestowed upon our dark-spirits willing counterparts.

One of the familiar ways to begin an essay or article is to tell an anecdote that illustrates the topic being discussed in the text. In "What Does It Mean to Drink Like a Woman?" Shanna Farrell tells an anecdote, but it is about her own experience, not someone she has interviewed. A writer's decision to include herself in the text only works well when the writer is an authority on the subject. In this case, the essay is about what women drink, and the writer uses her own experience to challenge the conventional wisdom that women like "girlie" drinks that use fruity flavors to disguise the flavor of alcohol. Though she does not have a graduate degree or other scholarly qualification, she is, for this topic, an authority.

"What It Means to Drink Like a Woman?" was first published at Punch, *an online magazine that publishes narrative journalism about wine, spirits, and cocktails.*

"It's kind of a thrill when a woman orders whiskey," says Toby Cecchini, a longtime bartender and the owner of New York's Long Island Bar. "You serve three hundred white wines to women and when a female comes in and asks for a single malt, it blows my mind. Red carpet for you, ladies." As a woman, ordering a Manhattan or an Old Fashioned affords more attention from the bartender and, admittedly, I find it empowering.

But why? Why do I get more attention for ordering a spirit-forward drink, and why do I—why does any woman—find this empowering? In a sense, by ordering whiskey with confidence, I'm challenging the stereotype that women have dainty palates while disproving the assumption that I'm not interested in spirits—a stereotype that, in part, stems from historic mores that are deeply woven into the cultural fabric that dictates gender roles.

While there have long been behavioral codes, Emily Post was the first to formalize them in 1922 with her highly influential book *Etiquette*. The book gave explicit instructions for the conduct of women, which proclaimed that she be passive and not draw attention to herself, take a man's arm after dark because she might trip, not allow a drunk man into her house and—my personal favorite—"never pay a party call on a gentleman."

These rules enabled stereotypes about the fragility of women, which translated into drink trends assuming women prefer cocktails that disguise the taste of alcohol, because, well, alcohol can be aggressive. In the 1950s the Pink Lady became popular, which, according to The Bartender's Book, was considered a both inoffensive and visually appealing choice for "that nice little girl who works in files." Gender stereotypes were further perpetuated by the Lemon Drop, which was first introduced in the 1970s, likely at Henry's Africa in San Francisco. Henry's Africa was a classic singles bar where the Lemon Drop—a sweet drink that masked the taste of alcohol—was marketed to women to lure them inside. In 1988, Cecchini created the Cosmopolitan specifically for women. "I literally invented the Cosmo for waitresses who were on my staff," he says. "I understood a bit about how women drank." Some women do genuinely prefer lighter drinks to more spirituous cocktails. But so do some men. However, it became widely accepted that all women cleave to innocuous concoctions.

Before I earned a reputation as a whiskey drinker, there were numerous occasions when people—mostly men—would presume that I wanted something juicy or sweet. I'd sit down at a bar and be recommended anything but a spirit-forward cocktail. I'd go to a friend's place for a party and immediately be told that there were mixers—like juice or soda—for the array of spirits residing on the kitchen table while the host swirled Scotch around in his rocks glass. I'd be at a celebration and handed a shot, wherein I would ask what I was holding and be told, "It's pink; you'll like it."

The ways in which certain cocktails have been perceived, discussed and used as marketing tools reify the ideas about how women drink. They've since been embedded in our collective cultural consciousness along with ideas about women in the profession of bartending.

Prior to the women's movement in the 1970s, females struggled to be treated as equal in many professions, but the best example in bartending dates back to World War II. When men went overseas, women dominated bars as part of their patriotic duty to hold down the home front. But when men returned after the war they lobbied for ways to get their bartending jobs back and ensure that they kept them. Both Michigan and California passed laws that made it illegal for a woman to tend bar unless she was the daughter or wife of the bar owner.

Valentine Goesaert, a bar owner in Michigan, challenged this law in court but lost after the state argued that tending bar could lead to "moral and social problems" for women; this hypocrisy is highlighted by the fact that the susceptibility of men to "moral and social problems" was never mentioned. The law—which dictated, quite literally, that bartending was a male profession—stayed on the books until the early 1970s when a similar law in California was challenged and finally overturned in the federal Supreme Court.

Dale DeGroff remembers the issue lasting well after the laws had changed: "You did not see women behind the bar in the 1970s and '80s in big cities. You just didn't. It was considered a man's world." When DeGroff opened the Rainbow Room in 1986, he hired four women to tend bar. "That's probably four more women than anyone else around had hired," he says. However, management tried to put these ladies in the front of the house—where they were easier to see—causing several of them to leave.

More than 30 years later, things are finally changing. Along with updated ideas about etiquette brought to us by the women's movement, the internet is one of the primary reasons for this shift. There is an abundance of information available on spirits, which is helping to generate interest among women and allow them to challenge stereotypes. While whiskey experienced a 50% drop in sales from 1970 to 2000, it is making a comeback due, in large part, to an increase in female whiskey enthusiasts. A 2008 Nielsen survey revealed that women account for the fastest-growing segment of worldwide whiskey consumers. This is reflected in the rise of female memberships in several whiskey clubs, like the UK's Scotch Malt Whiskey Society, whose female membership doubled from 2008 to 2009, and at Seven Grand's Whiskey Society in L.A., where nearly half of its members are women.

Cecchini has noticed this shift, which is reflected in the way people order in a general sense. "In the five years since my last bar closed, things have changed," he says. "I've never made so many Manhattans and Old Fashioneds than I have in the past four months since Long Island Bar opened."

There are also more female bartenders than ever before. Julie Reiner and Audrey Saunders—now two of the most influential figures in the cocktail world—paved the way for a new generation of female bartenders, a growing population. Reiner and Saunders were doing innovative things—like featuring gin over vodka—when they came up in the New York cocktail scene in the 1990s. This garnered attention from people like DeGroff and earned them much-deserved respect by their predecessors. In fact, they trained many of the most notable male bartenders working today. Ivy Mix, one of Reiner's bartenders, co-founded Speed Rack—a female bartending competition conceived to help women establish credibility and celebrate their contributions to the cocktail world.

This sea change has served as the impetus for gender-related discussions, which is now a hot topic in the cocktail world. "It seems like every writer that is calling me wants to talk about women in bartending," says Reiner. Hopefully, these conversations will serve to further challenge gender biases and allow us to cultivate a deeper understanding of where they are rooted.

While I find the attention that I receive when I order whiskey empowering because it validates my interest in spirits, there are more ways for a female to demonstrate her knowledge about cocktails than by ordering a spirit-forward drink. I'm ordering what I like, which just so happens to be a Manhattan or an Old Fashioned. But maybe tomorrow I'll be interested in trying a new gin or vodka, regardless of what its flavor profile insinuates or what kind of reaction I get from the bartender.

Collaborate

Activity 5.1 • Analyze "What Does It Mean to Drink Like a Woman?"

1. First, annotate the essay by identifying paragraphs that come from primary sources, including the author's experience and observation and information that comes from the interview of a bartender. Second, locate information that the author found in secondary sources. Do this by making a copy of the essay and making notations in the margins. Then, in your group, consider how Shanna Farrell combines her own knowledge with secondary sources.

2. Shanna Farrell writes that she is challenging certain assumptions. What are they? What is the primary argument of the essay?

3. Farrell could have begun her essay by telling the story of another woman who ordered spirits at bars, but she chose to make the opening anecdote about herself. What do you think of that choice? Does it make her essay stronger or weaker?

4. If Farrell had wanted to expand her essay by incorporating more academic-type sources, what resource would you suggest that she consult? Notice that she does mention a Nielsen survey. Try searching for a Gallup poll (gallup.com) and/or do a *Google Scholar* search (scholar.google.com). If you locate a journal article on your topic in *Google Scholar*, you can likely find the same scholarly journal in one of your college's databases for free. Discuss what you find.

5. What topics might individuals in your group write about while using themselves as a source of information, as Farrell did, as well as incorporating research? Identify and discuss them.

Interviews

Depending on your topic, your community probably has some excellent sources sitting behind desks at the nearest college, city hall, or federal office building. If you are looking into the environment, you could contact the Environmental Protection Agency, an attorney who specializes in environmental law, a professional employee of the park system or the Bureau of Land Management, a college professor who works in the natural sciences, or a group in your area dedicated to beautification and restoration efforts. If you don't know anyone connected with these organizations, a look at several organization or local government websites should give you the information you need.

When you contact the person you'd like to interview, identify yourself and your reason for wanting to speak with him or her. Most people are happy to assist college students in their research, and almost everyone is flattered by the attention. If your first choice refuses, ask him or her if they know anyone who might be knowledgeable about your topic and available for an interview. When you get a positive response, arrange an hour and a location convenient for both of you. If the interview is scheduled more than a week from the initial contact, you can write a letter confirming your appointment, or you can call the day before the scheduled interview to confirm the time and location.

Once you've scheduled the interview, make a list of questions you will ask your interview subject. There are two types of questions you can ask your subject: open and closed. **Open questions** leave room for extended discussion because they don't have a yes, no, or specific answer:

▪   What is the most positive experience you've had with [topic]?

▪   When did you decide to study [topic]?

▪   What's the most negative experience you've had with [topic]?

Questions like these allow for extended discussions. Even if it seems your subject has finished his or her response to the question, let a few moments of silence pass before you ask another question. Silence can be uncomfortable for some people, and he or she might feel compelled to expand on the response to your question in interesting ways.

Closed questions are useful for gathering specific information. Questions such as "When did you graduate?" and "How long have you been involved in [topic]?" are closed questions. Although closed questions are important to an interview, be sure they're balanced by questions that allow your subject room to talk and expand on his or her ideas.

Before the interview, confirm the exact location of your appointment. If you are unfamiliar with the planned meeting place, go by the day before to make sure you can find it. Take several pens or pencils with you to the interview in addition to a writing tablet with a stiff back. If possible, use a recorder to record the interview, but be sure to ask your subject if it is okay. Most people will allow recording, if you assure them that the recording is only for your use in collecting information for your research paper. If you are using a recorder, test its operation before you get to the interview location so you won't have any surprises when you're with your subject or discover later that the machine was not working.

Although you've prepared a list of questions to follow, don't be afraid to ask a question that isn't on your list. If your subject mentions briefly an experience that seems relevant to your topic, you might want to ask him or her more about that experience, even though it isn't on your list of questions. Indeed, the best way to interview may be to read over your questions just before you meet your subject, then not refer to them during the interview. Before you leave, however, look over your list to see if you have missed any questions of importance.

Remember to let lulls in the conversation work for you by drawing your interview subject into further explanations or illustrations of previous comments. If you interview a talkative person who strays from the topic, try to steer him or her back to the questions you've prepared, but if you can't, don't worry. You'll probably get useful information anyway. Be courteous and attentive. Even if you're recording the interview, take notes. It makes both the subject and the interviewer feel more comfortable and serves as a backup, should your recording not work.

Within 15 minutes after leaving the interview, jot down some notes about your subject's appearance; the sights, sounds, and smells of the place where you conducted the interview; and any overall impressions of the meeting. Make sure you have the date and location of the interview in your notes because you will need it for documentation on your works cited page.

Interview Projects by C.S. Satterwhite

"Punk Rock Doc": An Interview with Dr. Bob Cross (2015)
By C.S. Satterwhite

This interview originally appeared in Pensacola's alt-weekly newspaper *Inweekly*. The interview with Bob Cross covers a scientist's efforts, as part of a large team, to stop the deadly 2014 Ebola virus outbreak in West Africa. Cross, a native of Pensacola and graduate of the University of West Florida, also performs as a musician in several bands. In 2014, *Time* named "The Ebola Fighter," the name given to a very large international group of scientists and health care workers, as its "Person of the Year." In this interview, Cross describes his work in West Africa, his education, and what he sees as their connections to DIY punk culture.

When reading this interview, consider the audience. Can you tell who the audience is by reading the questions? How does the interviewer establish his credibility (ethos) with the subject and the audience. Consider the following background research when asking questions that will be interesting for both exploring the subject and identifying the audience. Questions of authorship, shared or collective, also arise as readers see the article as not coming from one source (the interviewer) but two (the interviewer and the interviewee).

How does it feel to be among those named as *Time* magazine's "Person of the Year" for 2014?

It's a great honor to be part of the group for sure. Many have made extreme sacrifices to this cause and everyone involved, on all levels, should be applauded. This is not easy work, and nine times out of ten, you aren't getting paid any extra for the additional effort. In fact, most [of] the folks who've been working in this field for some time would do it regardless of any awards. But the recognition is certainly appreciated, if for anything, for bringing attention to parts of the world where the existing public health infrastructure isn't set up to deal with these kinds of [diseases].

Funny story: When *Time* magazine came to interview my boss, he had no idea he was to be featured in the *Time* article. None of us did! Ultimately, I'm glad it happened. The world now seems to be paying attention to how important this work is. Hopefully it will remain that way.

So tell me a little about the work you do?

I wear several hats, but I mainly consider myself a public health biologist, though much of my training and work deals with emerging viruses, specifically viral hemorrhagic fever epidemiology, pathogenesis, and development of therapeutics and vaccines against [these diseases].

What about your education? Where did you learn to become an "Ebola Fighter"?

So it takes a village right? Well, my career started in Pensacola where I worked with an epidemiologist named Samantha Rivers who got me onto a project with her when West Nile Virus first came through. It was through her that I met Drs. George Stewart, Justice Mbizo, Kendall Martin, Joe Lepo, and John Lanza through which I completed my early training in infectious disease biology and epidemiology at the University of West Florida. I got my PhD from Tulane University working on Hantavirus pathogenesis and epidemiology under Drs. Thomas Voss, Daniel Bausch, and Bob Garry.

Are you still at Tulane?

No, I'm currently a post doc at the University of Texas Medical Branch in the laboratory of Dr. Thomas Geisbert [Dr. Geisbert is one of the people featured in the *Time* magazine article. He's a recognized leader in research on emerging viruses that require Bio-Safety Level 4 containment (i.e., the spacesuit labs). In this setting, I'm working in concert with his world-class team studying pathogenic mechanisms of these viruses with the central effort of developing medical countermeasures against them.

How did that work get you to Sierra Leone fighting Ebola? Can you tell me a little about what you did in West Africa?

Sure, I was brought on as a biosafety and technical consultant to help validate a new rapid diagnostic [test] for Ebola in the field. The current state of testing and triaging patients for Ebola is complex and time consuming due to the need for stringent biosafety procedures as well as access to technical facilities that can do the molecular testing necessary. The delays for getting results [generally] vary from one to five days depending on proximity to testing centers and their respective caseload.

Five days seems like a long time considering how fast Ebola progresses. Has that changed since your mission to West Africa?

At that time, there weren't any approved rapid diagnostics available, [tests with] 10-30 minute results, so our mission was to field-test these kits in order to show the regulatory powers [such as the World Health Organization and the FDA] that we had something that could really make a difference with a disease that takes hold in three to five days after exposure. However, we just recently got word that both the WHO and the FDA have approved this diagnostic test for use, so it will be rolled out to places that need it very soon.

This trip to Sierra Leone was not your first trip to that country. Why did you go to Sierra Leone the first time?

My first mission to Sierra Leone was a research trip looking for bird-borne viruses in birds [native to] West Africa. It was also a capacity building mission where we worked with local [African] biologists to expand their ability to do disease surveillance beyond what they already had going on in-country, which was mostly rodents at the time given that the area highly endemic for Lassa Fever, a virus that is similar in disease course to Ebola.

Between your last visit to Sierra Leone and this one to fight Ebola, what differences did you see?

Probably the biggest difference was the silence throughout the country. This is a big thing. Nationwide curfews were in effect for motorcycle travel at night because it was thought that this might have been a contributing element to the outbreak's spread, and so the streets were much quieter . . . less people out.

Yeah, of course. People were scared they were going to die.

Interpersonal communication was vastly different as well. Previously, meeting a friend or colleague on the street and shaking hands was a very long and involved choreography of complex handshakes and discussion. This time, there were no handshakes from anyone. No touching, period. This was in part of the national campaign to cut transmission by altering social behaviors, not to mention the fear of not knowing who was, or was not, infected. Without the handshake, salutations were much less intimate and connected.

During [the Ebola] visit, it was clear the nation was in a critical state. Awareness of the virus was everywhere. Many, many losses on personal and cultural levels had been suffered.

Since you'd been to the affected countries, I'm sure learning about this outbreak must've been more personal. When you first heard about the Ebola crisis in West Africa, what was your first response?

Filovirus [a type of virus that tends to cause hemorrhagic fevers] outbreaks have been happening almost annually throughout Central Africa for some time now. But these were almost always in small, remote villages. When [Ebola] surfaced in West Africa, the general consensus of folks in this field was this was going to be different. Mainly because of how interconnected the cultures are in this part of the world [West Africa]. Sure there are political boundaries or borders between countries, but the heritage and culture of the people from this area don't really subscribe to these [borders] as clear-cut lines of separation between populations. Further, it's a lot easier to cover greater distances in the region [now] due to road systems that have been recently developed, owing in-part to international resource exchanges with China and other countries.

With the virus spreading quickly, what were the personal risks of going to West Africa this time?

Well, Ebola is in the area. That's clear. But you're really more likely to get malaria than Ebola just by being in the country, and even that is avoidable to an extent merely by taking antimalarial drugs prior to travel. Ebolavirus disease is mostly an incapacitating disease. Folks that are so infectious that they are capable of transmitting are *clearly* sick and really too weak to be out and about in public without great effort. Now if you are one [of the workers] in an treatment unit or otherwise treating or assisting confirmed or suspected cases, that's a whole other story. [There was] much risk in that arena, no doubt.

What was your impression of the crisis when you first got to Sierra Leone?

It was impossible to miss. Posters were everywhere, hand-washing stations were everywhere, fever check outposts were everywhere, the smell of bleach was everywhere . . . news that Ebola was in Sierra Leone was everywhere. Despite this, it was clear that there was a response in action. Ebola treatment units dotted the countryside throughout the country and any radio station was centered on new reports and informative updates on the outbreak. It's just such a big job . . . surreal.

Were you scared?

Not at all. No reason to be. Sure, this is what I do for a living, every day. And much like any public servant, like a police officer or firefighter, I've had to go through extensive training to get the confidence to make the best decisions possible when whatever challenge presents itself. No reason to be scared if you understand how transmission works and you take the proper precautions.

As people's anxiety levels grew throughout the region, they started to get very scared. There was a lot of misinformation spread about the disease, but also the healthcare workers. I read that there were riots in some of the outbreak zones, specifically in Liberia and elsewhere. Were you ever in any immediate danger?

I really don't think so. It's actually a very peaceful part of the world. Despite the stress of the outbreak . . . everyone just wants to put this thing to rest.

In your professional opinion, what were some of the reasons the Ebola virus spread so quickly?

There are a number of reasons that've surfaced as guilty culprits, but likely the most important was the lack of preparedness coupled to the delay of international response. This region has never had to deal with an Ebolavirus outbreak before. They just weren't ready. Limited diagnostics, trained personnel, and adequate equipment were not sufficiently available to act in an efficient manner enough to contain the outbreak.

As far as your African partners and their facilities, what were the West African healthcare systems like?

It's not really well developed. It exists, but you have to remember that these are not wealthy nations, unfortunately. So with limited resources, you get limited infrastructure. Outside support from international partners is nice, provided it can be sustained or leads to self-sustenance.

Often when the Western media reports about the efforts to stop Ebola, the focus is on the internationals. But you mentioned some of the local African biologists you worked with earlier. Can you tell me about the African scientists and healthcare workers you partnered with in Sierra Leone?

This time around we worked with two outstanding Sierra Leoneian scientists, both of whom I'm very proud to call friends. Augustine Goba confirmed the first case of Ebola in Sierra Leone. He and Mambu Momoh—along with other partners working from the Kenema Government Hospital's Lassa Fever Laboratory—tirelessly processed a lion share of the diagnostics for the entire country as the outbreak intensified until international assistance could arrive. And these two are just an example of the hard work, dedication, and ultimate sacrifices that have been made through the course of this outbreak. This is one [experience] that none of us are ever going to forget. Just about anyone working in this field has known and worked with some, or many, of those who have died during this effort.

When you got back to the States, how were you treated? Were you treated differently by strangers, friends, or even other scientists, knowing you were around so much death?

I would say no, I received great support from friends, colleagues, and family. They all know this is where my heart is.

How do you feel about the stigma associated with Ebola? Are you worried about that, either from your professional or personal perspective?

The stigma is real, unfortunately. Very real . . . on multiple levels. I am not a fan of it, but it exists and I think the only way to deal with it is head on. Transparency with respect to how the disease works, clear descriptions on the state-of-the-field in regard to vaccine and therapy. National preparedness is crucial to allay public fears [so people know] that it really is possible to get this thing [Ebola] under control. I am worried about [the virus and stigma] just as anyone should be worried about what dangers fear and misunderstanding are capable of producing. This is why I feel transparency throughout the process of response to this outbreak is crucial.

How is the general American perception of this Ebola crisis different than the reality, at least as you see it?

I think there was certainly cause for raised awareness on the issue. This is an important outbreak because, much like SARS did in 2002, [the virus spread] very rapidly as a result of how globally interconnected the world's become. If anything, my hopes are that the heightened state of alarm that many Americans have, regarding this particular outbreak, will help our government see how important continued support of research into understanding emerging pathogens and controlling them really is.

When Americans saw the news about Ebola and read about how dangerous it was, I know a lot of people became very scared, especially after the handful of reported cases in the US. Do you think a similar outbreak could happen in the United States? Do you think it could happen here?

I'm a firm believer that [an outbreak] could not happen on the scale that happened in West Africa. The primary reason is that the public health architecture of the US is very well developed. Response to anything like this would, and has been, comparatively swift and efficient. We simply have more resources available.

Are you satisfied with the work you and your colleagues did in Sierra Leone?

Absolutely! We put in some serious time toward helping to develop and raise awareness for an important technology [the Ebolavirus rapid test kit recently approved by the FDA] that will no doubt help in the fight. The team I worked with are all world-class scientists, and it was truly a pleasure to work alongside them.

Switching gears a bit, besides your career as an "Ebola Fighter," you also play in a few bands. Did you get to write any music while you were there or check out the music scene at all? Did you get the opportunity to see any shows or otherwise interact with the people of Sierra Leone, outside of the context of your work, while you were in Africa?

No writing, but I always try to sample new music when I'm there. West African music is some of the most amazing and intricate and downright funky stuff I've ever heard. I love it and try to soak it up as much as possible. But no shows this time. All the nightclubs have been closed due to the outbreak. But I did get to catch up with many old friends from my first trip and of course got to meet many new ones.

How do you think being a punk influenced the work you do now?

Well, I'm not sure . . . I think everybody's definition of "punk" differs. But the central theme I've always gotten out of punk was to "do what is right," regardless of societal norms or what have you. A big part of being a public health scientist is just that. By and large, most of the diseases I work on affect the poor more than any other class, if you will. Poverty, as we all know, is rife with injustices on many levels. So a big part of what I push for is giving any advantage possible to those who need it, be it developing diagnostics, vaccines, or drugs to combat infections. In my field this is done through capacity building and through technology transfer. Sure, going to an outbreak setting and helping to stop a deadly virus from taking over the world is a noble cause, but what happens when you leave? If you don't leave the people with the capacity to deal with re-emergence, the cycle will continue and more will suffer.

Are you hopeful that there will be a cure or vaccine for Ebola in the near future?

Vaccines for various strains of Ebola have existed for some time now. If I'm hopeful for anything it is the continual societal and governmental support to see that the best [vaccine] candidates become available to the public as soon as possible.

If asked, would you go back?

I have been asked, and probably will someday. But right now, much of my work against Ebola is in the lab. The central mission of our work in Dr. Geisbert's lab is to push new drugs and vaccines for Ebola and other emerging viruses out of the lab and into the places they are needed most.

Reflecting on your work as a whole, do you have any specific moments that stand out to you, either as a scientist or an American—or simply as a human being?

As a scientist and human being, if you can really separate the two . . . Well, my first experience in science was with West Nile Virus in early 2000s, doing field work. That experience really made the work real to me. Getting the opportunity to go out and see how these diseases are affecting society [and working] with people on the front lines is a real driver for me and is part of what gets me out of bed every day. The folks in every vein of this field are some of the hardest working, most passionate people I've ever met, and it's truly a pleasure to be part of the effort.

Working in a BSL4 Laboratory. Photo by Chad Mire, PhD.

Demonstrating new detection technologies to local scientists. Photo by Jessica Groves.

Kenema District Hospital. Photo by Robert Cross, PhD.

"I Paint People and their Ideas, not fruit": An Interview with Folk Artist Scott Stanton, a.k.a. Panhandle Slim

By C.S. Satterwhite

This interview with Scott Stanton, who goes by the pen name "Panhandle Slim," originally appeared in Pensacola's alt-weekly newspaper INWeekly *(inweekly. net). Stanton, a folk-artist who is known for painting portraits with quotes and paintings, gained national acclaim after the 2015 racially-charged shootings at Emanuel AME Church in Charleston, South Carolina. Prior to his painting career, Stanton was a professional skater and played in numerous punk bands. In this interview, Stanton discusses his art, the Charleston shootings, his family, and his hometown of Pensacola, Florida.*

When reading this interview, consider the audience. Can you tell who the audience is by reading the questions? How does the interviewer establish his credibility (ethos) with the subject and the audience. Consider the following background research when asking questions that will be interesting for both exploring the subject and identifying the audience. Questions of authorship, shared or collective, also arise as readers see the article as not coming from one source (the interviewer) but two (the interviewer and the interviewee).

Your paintings of celebrities are all over town, from numerous bars to my son's first grade classroom. Where did you first get the idea to paint pop icons?

I saw a Howard Finster[1] painting that I wanted but couldn't afford. I went home and made one to the best of my ability. Taking my jigsaw and cutting out the wood was the easy part for me. The painting was the new venture for me.

I painted Dolly Parton as my first painting. I had so much fun doing [that painting], I did more and more. From Hank Williams to Malcolm X, [these] were some of my first paintings. It was not until later that the voice or spirit of Wesley Willis told me to start painting lyrics and stories on the paintings. So my love for music and my days of loitering in this pop-influenced world shaped my adventure in painting.

---

1 Howard Finster (1916-2001) was a folk artist from Georgia.

What inspires you to paint?

The urge to create. The drive to learn something new everyday. The passion to spread a message from the past. The desire to connect with other people who might be thinking as I do as well as the desire to connect with people who may not think like me. The idea of creating a little piece of art that was not with us yesterday inspires me. The idea that after someone throws away some old wood, I can take that wood, paint something on it, and someone hangs that painting in their personal space: that inspires me. The smile on a person's face inspires me.

After your years as a professional skater, singer for numerous bands, why decide to go with this somewhat new persona—Panhandle Slim?

Good question. I'm not really sure, but I believe there is some psychology behind it. Maybe if I approach this as a "different person" that protects me from Scott Stanton, the real life person. [The name] allows me to be and do what I want. Real life, work, and the competitive nature of life can bring pressure upon an individual. Approaching something with the idea of having, for awhile, satisfied one's soul is very healthy to me.

Creating a new "character" gives one a clean slate to approach the river to "row, row, row your boat." I don't think "Scott Stanton" would have taken all the art chances if I didn't go at it as "Panhandle Slim." Scott Stanton might have let the fear of "you don't know how to paint" and "you are not an artist" stop this mission dead on the track. But then again, I'm not really sure. But I bet there is a good answer.

Where did you come up with the name "Panhandle Slim"?

My buddy Jody Bilinski from Pensacola, who was an old bandmate, came up to Michigan to visit me. He was wearing a western wear shirt called "Panhandle Slim," and I said, "I like that name. I'm going to sign my painting with that name." It started that day. I thought, I *am* from the Panhandle of Florida.

It suits you. Why not? So what made you venture into the folk art that you do now?

I did not really know it at the time, but punk rock, skateboarding and the spirit of doing-it-without-a-guidebook or lessons drove my paintings. Folk art spoke to me. It told me that anyone can create art, and that made me create art. Punk rock told me that anyone can create music and I did so. Skateboarding told me that there are no rules or limits in being an athlete. I don't think folk artists care at all what art coaches think. We just create what comes to our mind and folks either like it or they don't.

What about you as a performer? So much of your previous incarnations involved some aspect of performance. How does performance fit into the work of Panhandle Slim? Is it different or is it similar to you as the musician?

Yes. The music was all about playing shows, and the show was very much performance. We use to joke that [the concerts] were a show, not a listen. That's funny because my painting is so far from that. I have been asked to do events that call for "live painting" and have to kindly refuse. That is the last thing I want to do. The painting part is so personal to me and I do it alone. I enjoy watching my paint dry; I can't imagine anyone else wanting to watch. When I was a pro skateboarder, it became a job to go to demos—meaning I would go skate in front of large crowds. I did not like that at all. When I create a new painting, I very much get that feeling I would get when I created a new trick or maneuver on my skateboard. It was a new creation and only a select few would get it and appreciate it, and that satisfied my soul.

Your art is seen by many as folk art. How do you see yourself and your work in the long tradition of Southern folk art?

Well, I don't but since you asked I will try to answer. I still scratch my head that I am indeed an "artist" and more specific, I'm in a subculture called "folk artist," and even more specific a folk artist from the South. If I hadn't not lived in Kalamazoo, Michigan, for so many years, I doubt I would have fully recognized my Southern culture and the fact that I am "country," as the kids that I substitute-taught in Michigan referred to me as. They would ask, "Are you country?" I would enter the school halls at 7am and the kids in the hall would start saying, "Run, Forrest, Run!" I did not take this as mean spirited because the kids liked me. I did however realize that the way a person speaks can represent a full picture to someone else. The South influenced the way I speak and to a great deal the way I think . . . for better and for worse. My paintings help me come to terms with that. As Flannery O'Connor said, "Southern writers are stuck with the South, and it's a good thing to be stuck with." In the long tradition of folk art, I hope I leave some kind of mark while I document so much of history and pop culture with my paintings.

You gained a lot of recognition for your paintings of the nine people killed in the Emanuel AME Church in Charleston. Why did you want to memorialize these people in your paintings?

Well, like most people with any conscience, I watched the news and what happened at the church in Charleston and was filled with every emotion. I sat and thought, what can I do? The whole "Let there be peace on earth, and let it begin with me" filled my being. I can start small. I can get to know something about these nine people, and I can paint them. I can paint, then drive the paintings over to Emanuel AME in Charleston, South Carolina, because it's so close to Savannah, Georgia. Charleston is in fact Savannah's sister/brother city, so I need to do this.

I'm glad I followed through on that simple thought I had. I have made real friends today because of that decision to follow through with an idea. I simply had the nine people, their family members and their church community in mind when I did the paintings and delivered them to the church. I had no idea I would encounter the overflowing love of the people gathered outside the church as well as the people representing the church. Everyone was there, gathered in love and unity, and it was a moment I'll never forget and will always cherish.

Some of the family members got the paintings of their loved one. Some of those family members have become my friends. They are deeply spiritual and empathetic towards all humans. They pray for me, and I pray for them.

Were you concerned about any backlash from that community in particular, like maybe your art or your message would be taken the wrong way?

I was not worried about any backlash since I was doing this out of pure love for the family members, the church, and the souls of the nine who transitioned on. I prayed that my intentions would be taken as a love offering.

What do you hope will come from the paintings of the Emanuel AME Church victims, or even the coverage these paintings have received?

I hope they bring some sort of comfort to anyone who needs comfort in dealing with this horror. The coverage scared me a bit. A lot of people were contacting me from the media. I really did not know what to say at that moment as the story was breaking all over the media. The paintings said it all. The paintings gave a brief insight to the nine individuals. National Public Radio contacted me a few times for an interview, and I finally had to tell them I am not a very good speaker and do not feel a radio interview on this mass shooting is what I should be doing. The nine paintings were my statement. Social media spread these paintings, and I think that was a good thing. I believe it helped people in a small way. It helped people learn a small bit about these nine individuals from Charleston. In doing my research of these nine people and the Emanuel AME Church, I learned a great deal and gained a great deal of respect for the church and their congregation.

Outside of the Charleston paintings, back here in your hometown of Pensacola, people really love your art, too. It's all over the place. How does it feel to go back to Pensacola and see your art in so many different spots?

It feels great! This experience with my paintings has opened my mind a great deal and has led me to new people in Pensacola, my home. I have had so many great art shows in Pensacola and so many people there own my paintings. Growing up in Pensacola, I had many issues and connected them to Pensacola. The problem was Pensacola, not my mentality. I believe most people go through this journey when dealing with their hometown. Having so many great experiences in the last several years going back to Pensacola and having art shows and getting such great support from a wide range of people . . . Leaving town, I would drive over the bay bridge heading east on I-10 and think, Pensacola and the people have really changed. They are evolving.

It then hit me: they are not changing, I am changing. I am changing, I am evolving. My open mind is opening more, and I am accepting. My paintings have connected me with people I went to 2nd grade with when I first moved to Pensacola. They connected me to the Mayor. They connected me to my Mom's psychiatrist. They connected me to a kid I had a fight with in the 5th grade. He is now very successful in the world of business. They connected me to my remedial reading teacher at St. Paul's Catholic School. They connected me with my middle school art teacher. They connected me with relationships gone sour, relationships that went sour long ago.

They have connected me with people who have ideas very different from mine. They have connected me to movements I didn't know about before painting. In short, this little adventure had opened doors, and Pensacola is a very big part of this adventure. Pensacola is home, and home has showed me a great deal of love and support.

I know people love your art here, but I also see you doing exhibits elsewhere and catch snapshots of you leaving your paintings in various places. How is your art received in other places?

Very well. They are so simple, and the paintings and quotes connect with everyone. The paintings and quotes cover such a wide range of opinions. They usually connect with someone. I really like setting up random art shows outside in cities where no one is familiar with my paintings. I usually meet some interesting people, and they ask me interesting questions, like, "who are you?" "Does the city let you do this?" "Did you get permission to do this?" Then we discuss the paintings and the topics, politics, philosophy of the quotes. I usually go away learning a great deal and making a new friend or two. The internet and Facebook allow me to connect with people all over. So when I am in their hometown, all I have to do is announce it on Facebook and people show up. It is amazing, and I am grateful.

I know your son Tex paints, too. How do your kids feel about your art and having an artist for a dad?

Yes, my sons are quite talented and imaginative. My son Tex is detailed in his art, much like his uncle [musician Kent Stanton] and his great grandpa. I had a show at an art museum in Savannah, and Tex's class took a field trip to the art museum and my paintings happened to be there then. When I picked him up from school that day he had a glow on his face. I could tell he was so proud, and his friends at school wanted his autograph. He told me there was a security guard there guarding my paintings. I think that blew him away because he's used to seeing my paintings all stacked in the backyard with bird poop and other elements of nature finding a home on my paintings. But really, I don't think my boys think much of it because they are so used to seeing my paintings all day.

Is there one story about your paintings that really stands out to you as an artist and speaks to why you continue to paint?

That's a tough question. Narrowing it down to one story? I would say the Charleston 9 experience. But one thing that led me to that experience was when a person who works for the NAACP out west contacted me and asked me to paint the president of the NAACP, Cornell William Brooks. He was coming to Colorado to speak and they wanted to have a painting of him there when he came. That opened my eyes to how these simple paintings are reaching out further than I ever dreamed of. Much further. This all started with a painting or two I made to decorate my garage wall.

If someone painted you your style, what quote would you like to see by your face?

Umm, well if it was done in my style and it has my face...that would have to be a quote I said, so I will leave that to the artist and hopefully I said something or did something they feel like quoting me on. I did not really answer that, did I?

Close, but that's fine. Thank you very much!

Activity 5.2 • Reconstruct Interview Questions for "What Does It Mean to Drink Like a Woman?"

Explore

Read through "What Does It Mean to Drink Like a Woman?" and make note of the people Shanna Farrell interviewed to write the essay. Then reconstruct what interview questions she may have asked to obtain the information and quotes attributed to these individuals. For example, Farrell may have asked this question of Toby Cecchini: "What is your reaction when a woman orders whiskey?"

You can use this technique of reconstructing interview questions for other texts, which may help you in developing your own interview questions relevant to your research.

Activity 5.3 • Write Interview Questions

After you define your research project, you may decide to interview an individual who is knowledgeable about your topic. Before you go to your interview, it is a good idea to write down the major questions you want to ask your interview subject, even if you plan to record the session. At the interview, you will not necessarily ask your questions in the order you write them here, but doing this activity will help you keep the areas of inquiry in mind. Before you leave the interview, you might want to glance over the questions again, to be sure you have not missed any crucial topic.

1. Write five questions you intend to ask your interview subject.
2. After the interview, make some notes about the appearance of your subject and the setting where the interview took place.

Activity 5.4 • Summarize Your Interview

After reading through your notes from your interview and possibly listening to the recording, if you made one, summarize what your interview subject said about your topic. Remember, a summary is a distillation of the information. You are not arguing here with your subject, just trying to record his or her information as accurately as possible. Include actual quotations, properly punctuated, if you think you may want to use them in your research report. Make note of other sources or individuals that your subject may have suggested you consult.

Activity 5.5 • Write a Profile of a Person

Apply your interview and observation skills by writing a profile of a person who is unusual in some way. Your profile should include description, quotes, and whatever background explanations are needed to provide a context, so the story flows logically from one element to another. The length should be approximately 750 to 1,000 words. Answering the following questions will help you elicit information you need to write your profile.

1. History—What is the history of the person? Does the history affect the present?
2. Qualities—What qualities make this person worth writing about? Can you give examples that *show* the qualities?
3. Values and standards—What does the subject believe in most strongly? How does that shape his/her actions? Can you give specific examples?
4. Impact—How does the subject affect those around him or her? This may include both positives and negatives. Give examples.
5. Description—Write a physical description of the person, including any unusual aspects that make the person stand out in a crowd. Describe the setting where you interviewed the person or where the person works or lives.

Surveys

Comprehensive surveys that involve large populations such as the Gallup polls are conducted by many people and require large investments in time and money. A small survey involving fellow students, friends, or colleagues, can illuminate local issues or localize topics of national or international impact. For example, if you are writing using sources to write an essay about Americans' attitudes toward climate change, you can do a small survey to see if local people share the attitudes measured by the Gallup organization. However, you need to mention in your essay that your survey was indicative but unscientific because your sample size was small and the subject pool was not scientifically selected.

Activity 5.6 • Conduct a Survey

Compose

Conduct a survey by following these steps:

1. Use an online survey tool to deliver your questionnaire to your subjects, such as SurveyMonkey, Zoho Survey, or Survey Gizmo; or you can print out paper questionnaires, which you will hand out to subjects at a specific time and place.

2. Introduce your survey to your subjects by making a leveling statement that provides a context for your questions. For example, if your survey is to measure attitudes about climate change, your statement could be something like this: The United Nations' Intergovernmental Panel on Climate Change (IPCC) recently reported, "Global emissions of greenhouse gases have risen to unprecedented levels despite a growing number of policies to reduce climate change." A leveling statement makes sure your subjects have similar knowledge about your topic, but it should not influence their answers on the questionnaire.

3. Decide what information you need from your subjects, and design several closed-ended multiple choice or true/false questions (perhaps five). Also develop a small number of open-ended questions (perhaps one or two), such as "What do you think about climate change?" Open-ended questions allow participants to input more detailed responses but are more time consuming to analyze because you must code or group the responses.

4. Before you utilize your questionnaire, ask a few fellow students or friends to test it, and discuss their answers with them afterward to see if any of the survey questions were confusing or biased.

5. Use the online survey tool to analyze your mulitple choice and true/false questions. If you created open-ended questions, you can group the answers and/or use quotes from the responses.

Secondary Research Sources Expected by Professors

You have been assigned a research paper or project. What does your professor expect? First of all, you need to understand the assignment. What specifically does your professor want you to research? Do you have instructions about what kinds of sources your professor wants? Are restrictions placed on what internet or database sources you can use? Possibly, your instructor has specified that you need to use books, journals, major magazines and newspapers, and certain web-based information. This means that you are to use reputable sources to obtain a balanced, impartial viewpoint about your topic. So, how do you find these sources?

Neither you nor your professor should be surprised that you can find enough material for your research paper through the internet, even if your professor says you can use only print sources. Your library has full-text databases such as *JSTOR* and *Academic Search Complete* (*EBSCO*) that will provide you with PDF images of actual journal pages, not web pages. Moreover, *Google* and other online libraries have the full-text versions of many book chapters or entire books.

However, in many cases the latest books in a field are not online, so you need to venture into the actual library building to find some of the best sources for your research. This is also true of primary sources such as letters and maps. Moreover, librarians can aid you in finding the research materials you need.

Consider the following secondary research sources.

> **Books:** In these days of easy-to-find resources on the internet, students may wonder why they should bother with books at all. However, scholarly books treat academic topics with in-depth discussion and careful documentation of evidence. College libraries collect scholarly books that are carefully researched and reviewed by authorities in the book's field. Look for recently published books rather than older books, even if they are on your topic. Academic books or well-researched popular books often have bibliographies or lists of additional references at the end of the book. These lists are useful for two reasons. First, if such lists of books are present, it is a good clue this is a well-researched book, and, second, it gives you a ready list of other possible resources you can consult for your research project.

Scholarly journals: Just having the word "journal" in the title does not mean it is a journal. *Ladies Home Journal,* or *The Wall Street Journal,* for example, are not journals. Your instructor means peer-reviewed journals in which the authors have documented their sources. Peer-reviewed means that articles have been reviewed by experts in the field for reliability and relevance before being published. Your library should have print indexes to journals in which you can look up your topic. You may also be able to find journal articles—sometimes in full text—through the online databases offered by your college library.

Major magazines and newspapers: These publications report the news based on the actual observation of events and interviews with experts and also present informed editorial opinions. Examples are magazines such as *Time* and *Fortune* and newspapers such as *The New York Times,* the *Boston Globe, The Wall Street Journal,* and the *Washington Post.* You can locate full-text articles directly from the online versions of major print magazines and newspapers. Often, these publications charge a fee for articles not published recently. However, you can often find the same articles free through one of your library databases.

Special interest publications: These are periodicals that focus on a specific topic but are written for a wider audience than scholarly journals. Authors of articles base their articles on interviews with experts, recent scholarly books and journals, and other reputable sources. Examples include *Psychology Today* and *Scientific American.*

Government documents: Government documents present a wealth of information for many contemporary events and issues. Your library may be a federal depository, which means that users can locate many federal documents onsite. If so, you can look up government sources in the online library catalog. Government documents are also available through online databases.

Encyclopedias: Encyclopedias can be useful to browse when you are looking for topics. They are also helpful for providing background information such as dates when events occurred. However, most instructors prefer that you do not use encyclopedias as sources in your paper. This is particularly true for *Wikipedia,* the online encyclopedia that is assembled by volunteers who have specialized knowledge on topics and, thus, has no systematic vetting of the contents. However, *Wikipedia* entries often include bibliographies which can be useful in pointing you to books, articles, or other websites that can be used as references.

Web pages: The problem with web-based information is that anyone with some knowledge of computers can put up a website on the internet. Thus, information from websites must be carefully evaluated as to author, publishing organization, etc. You can follow the website review guidelines later in this chapter to determine the credibility of a site. Another option, however, is to find sources through one of the websites that screen sites and organize them by topic. Two of these that are discussed later are the *Internet Public Library,* (ipl.org), and the *Open Directory,* (dmoz.org).

As you use the categories above to find secondary sources for your paper or project, realize that your topic influences your choice of reference materials. If you are writing about a literary topic such as Shakespeare's *Othello,* you will find a number of relevant books and journal articles. If your topic is more contemporary, such as the current status of the country's housing market, you may be able to find some books or journal articles for background information, but you will need to use recent magazine and newspaper articles to find the latest information.

As you examine your sources, remember that gathering the information should help you discover what you think about your topic, not just what others think. This will enable you to create a paper based on *your* ideas and opinions, with source materials supporting your position.

Employ Computerized Library Catalogs

Public Access Catalogs (PACs) or computerized catalogs, accessed through the internet, have replaced card catalogs. A library computerized catalog provides bibliographical information about the library's collection, including thousands of books, photos, videos, journals, and other items. Generally, catalogs can be accessed by any of the following methods: keyword, subject, author, title, or call number. You may also find books that are available in digital form through the catalog. In addition, on the library home page, you will find links to other information and services such as database searches, interlibrary loans, and course reserves.

Types of Computerized Searches

Conducting a computerized search involves accessing the library's catalog using one of the following search methods.

▪ **Keyword**—Unless you know the author or title of a book, keyword is the best type of search because it finds the search word or words anywhere in the bibliographical citation.

> Example: water quality

▪ **Title**—Type the exact order of words in the title.

> Example: History of the United Kingdom

▪ **Author**—Type the author's name, putting the last name first. You don't need to include a comma.

> Example: Miller Henry J.

▪ **Subject**—Type the exact Library of Congress subject heading.

> Example: Spanish language—Grammar, Historical

▪ **Call Number**—Type the exact call number.

> Example: B851.P49 2004

If you have a general topic, you probably want to use the keyword search, for subject search actually refers to the exact Library of Congress subject-search designations, and, unless you use the precise search terms specified by that classification system, you may not get the results you want. The use of keywords, however, will lead you to hits on your topic. Then, once you have found one book that is in your topic area, you can examine the screen for Library of Congress subject headings and click on those to browse for more books.

An invaluable resource of any library is the Interlibrary Loan department. Here you can request books your library does not own, as well as journal articles from periodicals not in the library's collection or obtainable through the library's databases. Books and articles are obtained for you by the staff on a minimal or no-fee basis. This is extremely helpful because you can request books you find in bibliographies. However, it generally takes seven to 10 days to obtain books through an interlibrary loan, so you need to plan well in advance. To request an item, you simply go to the Interlibrary Loan depart-ment in your library or fill out a form on the library's website.

Activity 5.7 • Locate Books on Your Topic

Using the online card catalog at the library, locate three books about your topic. Write down the titles, authors, publishers, dates of publication, and catalog num-bers. Now, go to the stacks and find the books. While you are there, find two other books nearby on the same topic. Check the table of contents and index to see if they contain information you can use.

Utilize Electronic Library Resources

College and university libraries increasingly rely on databases to provide digi-tal versions of articles published in journals, magazines, newspapers, and gov-ernment documents, as well as other publications and materials. Generally, the databases are available to students and faculty through the internet via the library home page, though a library card and a password may be required for off-campus access.

Library databases make use of online forms similar to those of a library com-puterized catalog. Searches are by subject, title, author, and name of publi-cation. Advanced search features are available. Some databases provide the full-text versions of articles published in newspapers, journals, and magazines. Others give publication information only, such as title, author, publication, date of publication, and an abstract of the article. Popular databases include *Lexis-Nexis, Academic Search Complete* (see Figure 5.1), *Periodical Archive Online (ProQuest), Project Muse,* and *JSTOR.*

Activity 5.8 • Locate Newspaper and Magazine Articles

Go to your library's online databases, and choose one that relates to your topic. Then access it and type in your topic. Try using various key words. Jot down titles, authors, and publication information concerning any articles that look interesting. If full-text versions are available, save them to your computer or disk drive or email them to yourself. If not, find out if your library has a hard copy version or microfilm of the articles.

Figure 5.1 • Academic Search Complete

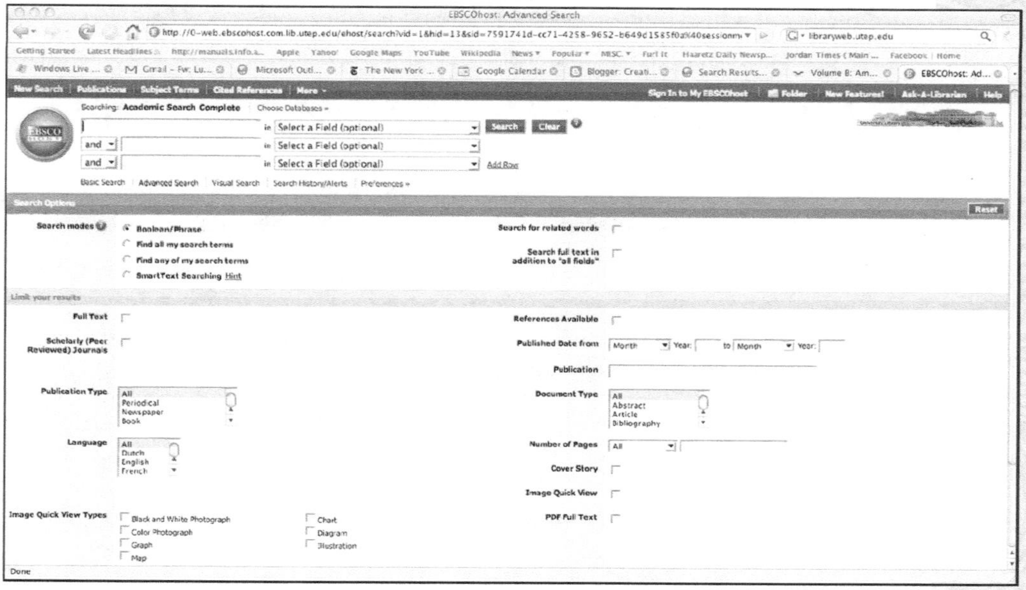

Academic Search Complete is one of *EBSCO*'s popular online databases that can be accessed by students through their library's website. The database indexes full-text articles on a wide variety of topics.

Find Internet Information

The World Wide Web is an incredible resource for research. Through it, you can find full texts of pending legislation, searchable online editions of Shakespeare's plays, environmental impact statements, stock quotes, and much, much more. Finding credible research sources is not always easy. Anyone with an internet connection and a little knowledge can put up a web page and claim to be an expert on a chosen topic. Therefore, information from the internet must be scrutinized with even more diligence than print sources. For example, if you enter the word "environment" in one of the keyword search engines, you may receive thousands of "hits," or sites that relate to that topic from all over the world. How do you sift through all of that feedback in order to find information relevant to your topic? It is a problem that has not been completely solved on the internet.

To maximize your chances of finding the information you want by using internet search engines, choose one of the major engines such as *Google, Yahoo,* or *Bing.* The big search engines browse all publically available sites and return "hits" based on your key words; these should be chosen carefully so that they are neither too broad nor too narrow. Some engines may also offer suggestions that narrow your search, such as scholarly articles, news, and related searches. Alternatively, you can do a keyword search for "best search engines" to try more specialized engines that are currently popular.

Browse through your "hits," selecting sites that look promising, going several pages deep into the search, as search engines rank "hits" based on popularity, and what you are looking for might not be on the first page. Try alternative key words for your topic, also, such as "climate change," rather than "global warming." If you are using internet sites as part of your research portfolio, read carefully the Evaluate Sources section later in the chapter.

Indexing Projects

One of the best ways to find internet resources is through indexing projects such as *Internet Public Library,* www.ipl.org (Figure 5.2), and *DMOZ* or *Open Directory,* www.dmoz.org (Figure 5.3). In both cases, librarians or volunteer researchers have personally reviewed and selected websites that are of value to academic researchers. These indexing websites are organized by subject areas but also have keyword search engines. Thus, you might quickly locate the most authoritative websites without having to wade through masses of search engine hits.

Figure 5.2 • Internet Public Library

The *Internet Public Library*'s "Resources by Subject" page, ipl.org/div/subject, offers access to authoritative internet websites by subject or keyword search.

Figure 5.3 • DMOZ

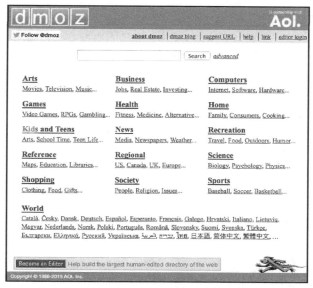

DMOZ (the Open Directory) claims to be the largest and most comprehensive human-edited directory of the Web. Volunteer researchers review and index websites of interest to academics and students.

Scholarly Journal Articles

Google Scholar, scholar.google.com, allows you to keyword search a multitude of scholarly journals. If it does not provide full text for an article, it will give bibliographic information, including the database where the article is available, such as *JSTOR* or *Academic Search Complete*. You can learn publication information for interesting articles through *Google Scholar*; then you can utilize one of your library's online databases to locate full-text of the articles.

Another resource for journal articles is the *Directory of Online Open Access Journals,* doaj.org, which allows you to search peer-reviewed online journals that offer free access. You can search either by journal or keywords.

Government Documents

Government documents and information about government services, everything from census reports to presidential speeches, can easily be found through the internet and are indexed at a variety of sites, including these:

- Gateway to government information and websites, fedworld.ntis.gov

- State and national government services and agencies, usa.gov

- United States Congress elected officials and legislation, congress.gov

- U.S. Government consumer publications, publications.usa.gov

Compose

Activity 5.9 • Compare and Contrast Media

Your instructor will select an article on a topic or event that is currently in the news. Find another article on the same subject either from the same news outlet or another major news source (*The New York Times, The Wall Street Journal, CNN, Time,* etc.). Compare and contrast how the reporting of the event is similar or different in the two texts. Note: You are not to write a report on the content of the articles themselves; instead, identify the author's perspective in each text and how it influences how the news is portrayed to readers.

Look for opinions, adjectives with positive or negative connotations, facts or evidence presented, the tone of the headline, and the text itself. Also consider the target audience.

Organize your observations in a one- to two-page report with a clear thesis that presents your evaluation of the two texts.

Make a Research Plan

Research is not something you tack on after you have completed your argument. Rather, it should be part of the writing process close to the beginning, once you have decided on a general topic. In the internet age, the problem is deciding where to start and how to sort through the information glut to find sources applicable for an academic paper.

1. Begin with the assignment. Your instructor may ask you to compare two subjects or perhaps it is to analyze cause and effect. The topic may already

be defined for you within certain parameters. Pay close attention to what you are asked to do.

2. You probably already know some things about your topic. You may even have an opinion you think you want to argue. However, to make an effective argument, you need to research the topic with an open mind and learn what experts think and studies show about the issue. First, you want to get an overview of the topic or issue, and where you start depends somewhat on the topic you choose.

   a. Current events? Recent developments in an ongoing issue? A major internet-accessible newspaper such as *The New York Times* may start you on the right track. In addition to perusing the latest edition or doing a key word search in the search box, you can look at the site index at the bottom of the page for a link to *Times Topics*, a page that leads you to collections of articles on major current topics. The *Times* charges for access after the first few articles, but you can search for free and then access articles through one of your library's databases, if necessary.

   b. What do people think about an issue? Try a polling organization such as Gallup, Inc. (www.gallup.com) or the Pew Research Center, (www.pewresearch.org).

   c. Commercial products? Companies? Look for products' and corporations' websites. Remember that you are seeing only what the companies want you to see, so be prepared to look for sources for the other side of the story.

   d. *Google* it? If you just want some background information, a quick keyword search may give you what you need. Then you can do a more careful search later.

   e. *Wikipedia* it? You may have heard that your instructor does not want you to use *Wikipedia* as a source, but you can read a *Wikipedia* article and follow links to sources the *Wikipedia* authors used. Often these sources are authoritative, and *Wikipedia* can help you get to them quickly.

3. Focus on academic sources. The previous quick and dirty approaches will give you a general perception of your topic and may have turned up newspaper articles, book references, or journal articles that you can put on your working bibliography. However, once you have a general idea of the topic or issue, you need to begin thinking about moving on to the more sophisticated research required of an academic paper.

a. Check *Google Scholar* (scholar.google.com). *Google Scholar* indexes across databases and disciplines, giving you access to journal articles, publically accessible books, and case law. Once you have a citation, you may have to locate it in one of your library's databases to obtain an article for free, but many books and other sources are freely available through *Google Scholar.*

b. Go to the college library, either online or in person. Search the library databases by discipline and the computerized catalog for books.

4. Follow the research trail. Once you locate a few good books or articles, search their bibliographies for other references.

5. Consider the dates of your sources. Unless you are using a landmark case, book, or article, your sources should be recent—preferably no more than five years old.

6. Utilize stasis theory or one of the other prewriting techniques in Chapter 4, Inventing Rhetorically, to develop your argument by discovering the critical points in an issue.

7. Develop a working thesis. Read the section in Chapter 6 about composing a thesis. A working thesis must be debatable. If you cannot state arguments on both sides, then it probably is not an arguable thesis.

8. Start outlining your argument. Read the three essay formats discussed in Chapter 6: the Toulmin model, Rogerian argument, and the general modern format. Decide which works best for your argument and draft major points.

9. Take a look at the sources you have and consider looking for additional ones if they are needed. Focus on developing your argument, rather than accumulating information. Look for at least two good sources for each of your major points. You can use a source for more than one major point, but aim for variety in your sources. Incorporate books, journal articles, surveys, and government reports. Consider interviewing an expert or observing your issue in action, if feasible.

10. Look for a counterargument. Allow your sources to disagree with each other, with you as the referee. It is much better for you to voice any objections to your argument and then answer them than to leave your readers to discover weaknesses in your argument.

11. Do not be overpowered by your sources. Remember that you carry the argument, and your source materials are there to support your major points.

At the same time, be sure your sources are all credible academic sources. If you use information from a biased source, such as a political website, be sure it is clearly labeled as such.

Evaluate Sources

Many people tend to believe what they see in print. They may think that if information is in a book or a news magazine, it must be true. If you read critically, however, you know that all sources must be evaluated. With the internet, perhaps even more than with print texts, it is important to evaluate your sources. Here are some guidelines to consider when evaluating sources.

- **Who is the author?** This question is equally important, whether the source in question is a book, a magazine, or a website. If you have the dust jacket of the book, the back flap will quickly provide you with essential information to screen the author. In the short biographical sketch, usually included along with a photo, you can learn the author's academic credentials and university affiliation, what previous books the author has published, and other qualifications that the publisher thinks qualify the author to write this particular book. If there is no dust jacket (as is often true with library books), you can try to find information about the author through an internet search engine or a reference text such as *Contemporary Authors*. A magazine or journal will often provide brief biographical information at the end of the article or on a separate authors' page. If the text is on a website, determining the authorship is more complex, as authors often are not named. In that case, you are forced to rely on the credibility of the entity publishing the website. Many websites have a link called something like "About Us" or "Mission Statement," and that page will give you some idea about the motivations of the entity sponsoring the site. Is it selling something? Is it part of an organization that has a political agenda? These are things to keep in mind when considering the bias of the site's content.

- **For what audience is the text written?** Determining this may require some detective work. In the case of a book, the preface or introduction may give you some clues. With magazines and journals, consider the demographics of the readership. With a website, a little clicking around in the site and a look at the kind of texts, graphics, and advertising used (if any) should tell you what readers the site is designed for.

- **What sources does the author rely upon?** If you are working with an academic text, the sources should be clearly cited in the text by author and page number, footnotes, or endnotes. If it is a more popular book or article, sources are acknowledged less formally; however, a credible author will still make an effort to credit sources. For example, an article might say, "According to the March issue of the *New England Journal of Medicine...*"

- **Does the text have an obvious bias?** Ask yourself if the argument is logical and if sources are mentioned for any statistics or other evidence. Are any opposing viewpoints discussed fairly? Does the author engage in name calling (a clear sign of bias)? Are there obvious holes or contradictions in the argument? For most purposes, you are looking for texts which do not appear to have been written with a biased agenda. However, in some cases, the opposite is true. If you are looking for a political candidate's position on a certain issue, then reading the candidate's book or going to the candidate's website will provide you with a biased viewpoint but one which you can analyze for the purposes of your paper. When dealing with information from sources with an obvious agenda, though, you must be careful not to represent the material as unbiased in your text.

- **What do others think of the text?** You can find reviews of books, movies, television shows, speeches, and other media by typing the word "review" along with the title in *Google* or another search engine. For a book, you can also look for a review in *Book Review Digest* or *Book Review Index*, two publications you can find in the reference section of the library. Also, *The New York Times* and other newspapers review prominent popular books. Most magazines and newspapers print letters to the editor, which may offer comments on controversial articles. *The Scout Report,* which can be found at the *Scout Project*, scout.wisc.edu/report, reviews selected websites. If you locate a review of your text, you can cite the review in your research paper to provide additional evidence of the text's credibility.

Activity 5.10 • **Locate and Evaluate a Source**

Explore

Locate one source (book, magazine or newspaper article, or website page) that you think would be a credible source for a research paper. For that source, answer the questions in the Evaluate Sources section.

Activity 5.11 • **Evaluate a Website**

Explore

Go to the internet and look up a website related to a topic you are researching. Answer these questions as fully as you can.

1. Who is the author of this source? Is the author credible on this topic? Why or why not?

2. What does the text focus on? Is it thoughtful and balanced, or does it seem one-sided? What gives you that impression?

3. When was the website last updated?

4. What is the purpose of this site? Is it to provide information? Or is it trying to persuade readers to accept a particular point of view?

5. How professional is the tone, and how well-designed is the site? How carefully has it been edited and proofread? Are there any grammatical and spelling errors that compromise its credibility?

6. What kinds of links does the site provide? Do they add to the website's credibility or detract from it?

Activity 5.12 • **Prepare an Annotated Bibliography**

Compose

An annotated bibliography is a list of bibliographical citations with a few sentences or a paragraph for each entry that offers explanatory information or critical commentary about the source. Many instructors request an annotated bibliography as a step in writing a research paper because it is an indication of the scope and direction of your research. Create an annotated bibliography by following these steps.

1. Select 10 quality sources about your topic. These should be, as your instructor directs, a mix of books, scholarly journal and magazine articles, government documents, and selected texts from websites.

2. Skim the text of each source and read portions more closely that seem relevant to your topic.

3. Write a bibliographical citation for each source in MLA or APA style. (See the appendix in the back of the book for MLA and APA style samples.)

4. Write a few sentences for each source in which you

    (a) summarize the content and purpose of the source, and

    (b) explain how you might use the source in your research paper.

Sample Annotated Bibliography in MLA Style
Topic: Double Humor in Double Consciousness

Adichie, Chimamanda Ngozi. *Americanah*. Trans. Carlos Soler. New York: Random House, 2014.

This novel addresses and critiques a Nigerian national who experiences being a member of a minority in America. Adichie critiques Africans in America who do not want to be identified as black because blacks are treated worse than other minorities. Part of Adichie's main character's argument is that immigrants from Africa lose the ability to define themselves by their home country when they come to the United States. They become black and resistance is futile.

Adichie writes from the perspective of a Nigerian living in America. She is aware of the struggle to define one's self instead of letting society do it for her. Adichie uses humor to make her point, which will provide examples for my paper.

Burciaga, José Antonio. *Drink Cultura: Chicanismo*. Santa Barbara: Joshua Odell Editions, Capra, 1993.

This collection of stories touches on the experiences of living on the US-Mexico border. Like Adichie, Burciaga uses humor to talk about the complexities of being a member of a minority in America. Being from Mexico and living on the US-Mexico Border, Burciaga's experience as a minority is different from Adichie's main character.

Burciaga wrote from the perspective of a Chicano living on the US-Mexico Border. He was born in El Paso. His essays are a product of his experiences growing up in that border city. His humor, which I will discuss in my paper, is also from a minority, but it is distinct from the African humor in Adichie's book.

Du Bois, W.E.B. "The Humor of Negroes." *Mark Twain Quarterly*, vol. 5 no. 3 (1942): 12. *JSTOR*. Web. 2 June 2015.

In this essay, nearly 40 years after the Soul of Black Folk, Du Bois writes humorously about humor and race. Drawing attention to minorities often being laughed at, Du Bois defines what is and is not funny when it comes to race.

Du Bois's landmark discussion of humor and race provides a context for discussion and examples for both Adichie's and Burciaga's humor.

---. *The Souls of Black Folk. The Project Gutenberg Ebook,* n.d. Web. 12 Oct. 2015.

In the foreword to this book, a collection of essays about race, Du Bois identifies the concept of double consciousness and "the problem of color line." Writing in 1906, Du Bois deftly addresses the tender topic of race in the United States at the beginning of the twentieth century. Part of Du Bois's goal was to start a conversation about what it was like to be a minority in the United States and the social issues associated with it.

Du Bois was the first African American to earn a doctorate and one of the founders of the NAACP. Du Bois's *ethos* comes from both his education and personal experience. His discussion of double consciousness will be the cornerstone of my paper.

Sample Annotated Bibliography in APA Style
Topic: Federal Aviation Administration User Fees

Horne, T. A. (2007, February). User fee debate. *AOPA Pilot Magazine, 50,* 27.

The author of this article is an experienced, commercial rated pilot that has flown for over 30 years. He also sits on the Aircraft Owners and Pilots Association (AOPA) board. This article explains what the Federal Aviation Administration (FAA) has proposed and what it means to pilots. Congress is cutting the budget for the FAA and in turn wants to impose fees for anyone who flies into a controlled airspace. This would have a very tragic affect on general aviation. This is huge because if anyone is flying anywhere around a decent-sized city, they are going to fly through these airspaces. Also, the FAA wants to charge for approaches into airports and landing on airport runways. This is bad because all of these charges would add up to more than $200. This would discourage people from flying, making them sell their aircraft. This would slowly dissolve the general aviation industry. I can use this article to explain what is going on and why the government wants to charge these fees.

Boyer, P. (Director) (2007, October 6). AOPA's Reasonable analysis of user fee issues at AOPA expo. *AOPA expo 2007*. Lecture conducted from AOPA, Hartford, CT.

> This lecture was given by the president of AOPA, Phil Boyer. He spoke of the fees that the FAA is trying to impose and what they would mean for general aviation pilots. He explains that the fees that the FAA wants are directed toward general aviation and not toward the airlines. He also gave some examples of what would be better for everyone, if the FAA really is in a crisis. This source is important because it provides an explanation and breakdown of these user fees and gives some examples of what could be put in place of these proposed fees.

Hedges, S. (2015, February 4). No user fees in president's budget plan. Retrieved from http://www.aopa.org/News-and-Video/All-News/2015/February/04/NO-USER-FEES-IN-PRESIDENTS-BUDGET-PLAN

> After three budgets including user fees, the Obama administration finally bowed to pressure from Congress and the Aircraft Owners and Pilots Association and did not include a provision for user fees for general aviation in the budget for 2016. AOPA's President Mark Baker described the omission of the user fees as a "big victory for the future of general aviation." Thus, this article indicates a reversal of the Obama administration's position on user fees.

Network, A. (2009, October 12). Aero-tv: airventure meet the boss—Randy Babbitt tackles user fees. Retrieved from http://www.youtube.com/watch?v=J14ut3O_j3M

> This video is from AirVenture, which is a fly-in expo. Randy Babbitt is one of the head officials for the FAA and he explains that the FAA needs money to meet the needs of the industry. He says that the planes now are more efficient, making them use less fuel which means that the fuel tax in effect now is less effective. He goes on to explain that the FAA needs to make up this deficit, but it does not know exactly where it is going to come from. This is important because it is a government official who is explaining the situation the FAA is in and what he thinks will happen.

Tennyson, E. A. (2014, March 4). White House budget contains user fee
despite opposition. Retrieved from http://www.aopa.org/News-
and-Video/All-News/2014/March/04/White-House-budget-
contains-user-fee-despite-opposition

The Obama White House's year 2015 spending plan includes a
provision of a $100-per-flight user fee to underwrite air traffic
control. The Aircraft Owners and Pilots Association continues
to oppose such a surcharge. In addition, the House aviation subcommittee sent a letter to the president, indicating bipartisan opposition of the user fee. "Your continued support for any proposal
to implement a per-flight-fee on commercial and general aviation
would only serve to undermine the strength of our aviation transportation system and the jobs that rely on this important segment
of our nation's economy," the letter warned. This article indicates
the Obama administration's continued support of user fees in the
face of substantial opposition.

Avoid Plagiarism

Plagiarism is defined as follows by the Writing Program Administrators (WPA),
a group of English professors who direct college composition programs: "In an
instructional setting, plagiarism occurs when a writer deliberately uses someone else's language, ideas, or other original (not common-knowledge) material
without acknowledging its source." A keyword here is "deliberately." Instructors, however, may have difficulty distinguishing between accidental and deliberate plagiarism. The burden is upon you as the writer to give credit where
credit is due. Review these examples of plagiarism.

- Turning in a paper that was written by someone else as your own. This
  includes obtaining a paper from an internet term paper mill.

- Copying a paper or any part of a paper from a source without acknowledging the source in the proper format.

- Paraphrasing materials from a source without documentation.

- Copying materials from a text but treating it as your own, leaving out quotation marks and acknowledgement.

The guidelines provided in Table 5.1 can help you identify when it is appropriate to give credit to others in your writing.

Table 5.1 • Choosing When to Give Credit

Need to Document	No Need to Document
• When you are using or referring to somebody else's words or ideas from a magazine, book, newspaper, song, TV program, movie, web page, computer program, letter, advertisement, or any other medium.	• When you are writing your own experiences, your own observations, your own insights, your own thoughts, or your own conclusions about a subject.
• When you use information gained through interviewing another person.	• When you are using "common knowledge"—folklore, common-sense observations, or shared information within your field of study or cultural group.
• When you copy the exact words or a "unique phrase" from somewhere.	
• When you reprint any diagrams, illustrations, charts, and/or pictures.	• When you are compiling generally accepted facts.
• When you use ideas given to you by others, whether in conversation or through email.	• When you are writing up your own experimental results.

The Online Writing Lab (OWL) at Purdue University provides an excellent handout on avoiding plagiarism, including the information about when to give credit to sources in the table above. See owl.english.purdue.edu.

Reading 5.3

In this article, originally published in The Atlantic, Megan McArdle tells the story of how a fake Martin Luther King, Jr. quote was created and posted on the internet.

Anatomy of a Fake Quotation
by Megan McArdle

Yesterday, I saw a quote from Martin Luther King Jr. fly across my Twitter feed: "I mourn the loss of thousands of precious lives, but I will not rejoice in the death of one, not even an enemy."—Martin Luther King, Jr. I was about to retweet it, but I hesitated. It didn't sound right. After some Googling, I determined that it was probably fake, which I blogged about last night.

Here's the story of how that quote was created.

It turns out I was far too uncharitable in my search for a motive behind the fake quote. I assumed that someone had made it up on purpose. I was wrong.

Had I seen the quote on Facebook, rather than Twitter, I might have guessed at the truth. On the other hand, had I seen it on Facebook, I might not have realized it was fake, because it was appended to a long string of genuine speech from MLK Jr. Here's the quote as most people on Facebook saw it:

> I will mourn the loss of thousands of precious lives, but I will not rejoice in the death of one, not even an enemy. Returning hate for hate multiplies hate, adding deeper darkness to a night already devoid of stars. Darkness cannot drive out darkness; only light can do that. Hate cannot drive out hate, only love can do that.

Everything except the first sentence is found in King's book, *Strength to Love*, and seems to have been said originally in a 1957 sermon he gave on loving your enemies. Unlike the first quotation, it does sound like King, and it was easy to assume that the whole thing came from him.

So how did they get mixed together?

Thanks to Jessica Dovey, a Facebook user, that's how. And contrary to my initial assumption, it wasn't malicious. Ms. Dovey, a 24-year-old Penn State graduate who now teaches English to middle schoolers in Kobe, Japan, posted a very timely and moving thought on her Facebook status, and then followed it up with the Martin Luther King, Jr., quote.

> I will mourn the loss of thousands of precious lives, but I will not rejoice in the death of one, not even an enemy. "Returning hate for hate multiplies hate, adding deeper darkness to a night already devoid of stars. Darkness cannot drive out darkness; only light can do that. Hate cannot drive out hate, only love can do that." MLK Jr.

At some point, someone cut and pasted the quote, and—for reasons that I, appropriately chastened, will not speculate on—stripped out the quotation marks. Eventually, the mangled quotation somehow came to the attention of Penn Jillette, of Penn and Teller fame. He tweeted it to his 1.6 million Facebook followers, and the rest was internet history. Twenty-four hours later, the quote brought back over 9,000 hits on Google.

The quote also went viral on Twitter, and since the 140-character limit precluded quoting the whole thing, people stripped it down to the most timely and appropriate part: the fake quote. That's where I saw it.

The speed of dissemination is breathtaking: mangled to meme in less than two days. Also remarkable is how defensive people got about the quote—though admirably, not Penn Jillette, who posted an update as soon as it was called to his attention. The thread for my post now has over 600 comments, and by my rough estimate, at least a third of them are people posting that I need to print a retraction, because of the nonfake part of the quotation. But I didn't quote that part; I was only interested in the too-timely bit I'd seen twittered.

Even more bizarrely, several of these readers, who clearly hadn't read too closely, started claiming that I had retroactively edited the post to make them look like idiots, even going so far as to scrub all the versions in RSS readers so that they, too, showed that I was talking about the truncated version. Even if you think I am the sort of low scoundrel who would do such a thing, this seems like a lot of work for not much reward. I'm not sure whether it's even possible to completely scrub an RSS feed, but even if it were, I'd have had to notify my bosses, who tend to frown on retroactive editing.

Meanwhile, several other people began confabulating a provenance for it. *Obviously*, he was talking about Vietnam, and what sort of moral midget couldn't understand that? This even though the latest citation for the true part of the quote was a book published in 1967, which would have been written earlier than that, when U.S. casualties in Vietnam were still relatively low. Moreover, the ambiguity with which the antiwar movement viewed the North Vietnamese makes "enemy" a hard fit.

It is, of course, not strange that people might look for possible confirming facts. What's strange is that they were sure enough of themselves to make fun of anyone who disagreed. Yet several other people on the comment thread had linked to a version of the quotation from 1957. I am second to no one in my admiration for Dr. King. But I do not think that he prefigured Vietnam by seven years.

Which only illustrates why fake quotes are so widely dispersed. Though one commenter accused me of trying to make people feel stupid for having propagated the quote, that was hardly my intention—we've all probably repeated more fake quotations than real ones. Fake quotations are pithier, more dramatic, more on point, than the things people usually say in real life. It's not surprising that they are often the survivors of the evolutionary battle for mindshare. One person actually posted a passage which integrated the fake quotation into the larger section of the book from which the original MLK words were drawn.

We become invested in these quotes because they say something important about us—and they let us feel that those emotions were shared by great figures in history. We naturally search for reasons that they could have said it—that they could have felt like us—rather than looking for reasons to disbelieve. If we'd put the same moving words in Hitler's mouth, everyone would have been a lot more skeptical. But while this might be a lesson about the need to be skeptical, I don't think there's anything stupid about wanting to be more like Dr. King.

Ms. Dovey's status now reads: "has apparently gone back in time and put her words into one of MLK's sermons. I'm somewhere between nervous and embarrassed and honored . . . I really hope I haven't said anything he wouldn't agree with . . . Only what I feel in my heart."

A lot of us were feeling the same thing—and I think it's clear from his writings that MLK would have too. There's no reason to be embarrassed about that.

Activity 5.13 • Discuss "Anatomy of a Fake Quotation"

Collaborate

In your small group, discuss the following questions.

1. How was the fake quotation created? How did it spread on the internet?

2. Note the speed and the reach of the fake quote. What does Megan McArdle suggest the story of the fake quote says about why fake quotes can become so widely disbursed?

3. What is your reaction to this story of the fake quotation?

Image credit: "Pensacola Graffiti Bridge" by Judy Young

chapter 6

Writing Rhetorically

Praxis in Action

How I Write

Amy Brumfield
Instructor, Idaho State
University

Whether I have to write two pages or 200 pages, I break the writing process into steps so it never feels overwhelming. This is my personal approach to every assignment.

1. Make a mess. I read the assignment, and then grab a piece of paper. I write down every single thought I have about my topic until I have filled at least one whole page. I don't change or erase any idea, no matter how crazy, weird, or off topic it seems. In fact, I write until the ideas become really weird. My first thoughts are always boring, and boring essays are the hardest to write. At this point, I often do some basic background reading on my topic if I don't know the subject well.

2. Divide the ideas into basic categories, starting with the ideas that intrigue me most and which have the most avenues to explore.

3. Create a question about my topic that cannot possibly be answered with a simple yes or no. Ideally, it's a question that I can answer with a good guess but can't really explain from my current knowledge. I like the idea that the answer will teach me something or cause me to think differently by the time I finish researching the question.

4. Create a thesis that answers that question. I make sure the thesis has a topic, a viewpoint with an opposing side, and a reason for why it's right.

5. Reread the assignment to make sure that my thesis fits it.

6. Put the ideas into a logical order.

7. Write a pre-rough draft to make sure I have an argument of my own that isn't simply research material pasted together.

(continued on next page)

8. Start my main research by verifying the information I think I already know. I am often at least partly wrong about some of my conceptions.

9. Research wider. Because I have a thesis, I can classify each piece of evidence as "agrees with," "disagrees with," or "irrelevant to my argument." Because I have a basic draft, I can see where the evidence fits, and stick it in. Now I can revise and adjust until I have a real rough draft.

10. Reread the paper to see how my question and my thesis have changed. They always do.

11. Edit the paper with the new thesis in mind because I now know exactly what I want to argue.

12. Review and revise the introduction and the conclusion because they almost always can be improved.

13. Proofread, then have at least one other person give me feedback on my draft before I make final changes.

Enter the Conversation Through Writing

Cicero's famous work, *On the Ideal Orator*, is not a treatise or handbook about how to be an effective rhetorician. Instead, it is a dialogue, a conversation. The setting is a villa outside Rome belonging to Lucius Licinius Crassus, and the time is 91 CE, an era of dangerous unrest in the Roman Empire. Prominent and respected citizens gather with Crassus to escape, for a while, the political crisis developing in the city. Crassus and his guests settle at leisure under a wide, spreading plane tree, not only to enjoy its shade but also to pay homage to Plato's *Phaedrus*, which similarly took place under a plane tree, though in Greece. They take time this day to dialogue about the attributes of an ideal orator. The purpose of the arguments they present to each other is not to win out over the others but, conversing together, to come to knowledge. It is not a trivial pursuit. Cicero reveals what his characters do not know—soon they will all die horribly as part of the civil unrest in Rome, violence traceable to the failure of leaders to resolve their differences in nonviolent dialogue.

Throughout ancient times, dialogue appears alongside rhetoric. It was through dialogue that rhetoricians such as Aristotle, Isocrates, and Cicero taught their students rhetorical skills. Today, in the writing classroom, group discussion or pairs dialogue is also part of the teaching process. A rhetorical text, too, is a conversation with previous texts, responding to ideas they have presented. In addition, arguments include paraphrases and quotes from others' compositions, making them part of the conversation. Moreover, writers composing texts must anticipate their audiences' reactions—questions they might ask or objections they might raise—so responses to these questions and objections can be included in the argument. This process of responding to audiences in advance continues the conversation.

Academic Writing as Conversation

By Justin McCoy

Simply put, academic writing is a contribution to an ongoing conversation on a topic. When composing an academic paper, you join a preexisting conversation with the goal of elaborating, or furthering, the conversation on a given topic by offering a unique contribution. To produce an academic paper that effectively joins an ongoing conversation on a topic, you must build upon what other experts on the topic, or contributors to the conversation, have already established. This act requires that you know what others are saying about the topic.

Consider how academic writing functions like the following scenario on joining a conversation: imagine a party made up of various groups of people standing around having conversations. Upon entering the party, you do not recognize anyone but spot a group of people with whom you would like to meet and socialize. In order to join the group without being socially awkward, what do you do first? Listen. If the group is discussing the reality television show *Jersey Shore*, you would not approach the group and enter the conversation by saying "Hey, gardening is really great," especially if you want to make friends by presenting yourself as socially adept.

The act of listening in this example is the equivalent of researching in the production of academic writing. You must first conduct research on a topic before joining the ongoing conversation on the topic. This process is often referred to as a literature review, or synopsis of all the relevant research on the topic. Once you are familiar with the topic-specific body of research, then you will be prepared to finalize a thesis, or main point, in which you take a stance and prove it with your own unique reasons for why you hold your position.

Respond to the Rhetorical Situation

When you are faced with a familiar situation that compels writing, it triggers a response that demonstrates you know the unspoken rules in play. For example, if a friend sends you a text asking you to meet after class for coffee, you know how to respond using the shorthand language of texting. If you are ill, instead of calling in sick, you may send an email to your supervisor. You know how to do that. Laura Klocinski writes in her *Digital Age* post, "Can Social Media Make Us Better Writers?", that participating in diverse social media such as Facebook, Twitter, Blogger, and more, each with its own format, helps us as writers because writers learn to use a different tone and style with each site. She says,

You would not compose a blogger post in the same way you would write a short tweet. Facebook posts tend to be longer, with either personal or opinion topics. In contrast, LinkedIn is a professional network, which teaches you how to sell your work experience and skills. When switching from site to site, you are learning to communicate across different platforms. These changes in writing style help develop flexibility and rhetorical skills.

Though Klocinski does not use the term, she is talking about different rhetorical situations, a concept coined by Lloyd F. Bitzer. A rhetorical situation is the context in which speakers speak or writers write—a context created by the conversation that compels your response. The conversation may be immediate, as was your friend's text message asking you to meet for coffee, or it may be ongoing, as is your knowledge of how to tell your supervisor that you are taking the day off because you are ill. The conversation can be words, images, or actions, or some combination of the three.

If Twitter and Facebook had been around when Bitzer was writing in the 1960s, he would probably have used them as examples of different rhetorical situations. Rhetoric is pragmatic; we use it to perform tasks, not by physical action, but by words. A rhetor uses words to alter reality by engaging an audience and persuading the audience to change in some way. Sometimes the persuasive change is small, as when a friend's invitation causes you to meet for coffee. Other times rhetoric compels massive change, as when an enemy's surprise attack compels a declaration of war.

Bitzer and Klocinski would agree that, as critical thinkers, we innately search our brains for previous conversations that tell us the rules that are embedded in a rhetorical situation and guide us in how to respond. Bitzer writes,

> Cicero's speeches against Cataline were called forth by a specific union of persons, events, objects, and relations, and by an exigence which amounted to an imperative stimulus; the speeches in the Senate rotunda three days after the assassination of the President of the United States [John F. Kennedy] were actually required by the situation. So controlling is situation that we should consider it the very ground of rhetorical activity, whether that activity is primitive and productive of a simple utterance or artistic and productive of the Gettysburg Address.[1]

---

1. Bitzer, Lloyd F. "The Rhetorical Situation." *Philosophy & Rhetoric,* vol. 1, no. 1, Jan. 1968, pp. 1-14. *JSTOR* www.jstor.org/stable/i40008864.

Usually, our responses to a rhetorical situation are appropriate, fluid, and effective. Other times, our understanding of the context is flawed; in those cases, our writing is likely to be less than successful in eliciting the desired response from our audiences. One of the purposes of this textbook is to enable you to become more aware of rhetorical situations, so, if you are not sure how to respond, you can seek out sources of information that will guide you in writing optimal responses.

This chapter presents you with several writing situations: a blog post about writing, an op-ed editorial, and an argumentative research paper. The discussions, writing prompts, and activities are designed to highlight the rhetorical situation in each. As you work your way through the chapter, keep the concept of rhetorical situation in mind.

Laws Protecting Women From Upskirt Photo Assaults Fall Short

by Holly Kearl

[In March 2014], the Massachusetts Supreme Judicial Court made an alarming decision.

The op-ed "Laws Protecting Women From Upskirt Photo Assaults Fall Short" was published in the Daily Beast*. Holly Kearl, a facilitator with the OpEd Project, leads workshops empowering women to write op-ed editorials. Sadly, the laws protecting women from such invasions still vary from state to state.*

In 2010, Michael Robertson was caught by Massachusetts Bay Transit Authority police taking cellphone photos and videos up female riders' skirts and dresses. His case went to the Massachusetts Supreme Judicial Court where the judges ruled on March 5 that the upskirt photos were legal. They reached this decision, they said, because the women were fully clothed at the time.

Legislators in Massachusetts immediately drafted a new law making it illegal for someone to take secret photographs and recordings, even when someone is fully clothed, and Governor Deval Patrick signed it into law on March 7.

If you were surprised by this ruling and the way the Massachusetts law had been written, then you will be even more surprised to learn that the law is not so unusual. If you live in states like Hawaii, New York, Virginia, or Washington, non-consensual upskirt photos in public places are illegal. But if you live in states like Alabama, Nebraska, or Oregon, these photos are legal, just like it was in Massachusetts.

Another surprising fact is that only 15 years ago, it was legal for people to plant a recording device in someone's home. The first law against "video voyeurism" passed in 1999 in Louisiana after Susan Wilson discovered her neighbor had installed a video camera in her house. When she reported it to the police, they said that someone watching her in her home through a secret video camera was not a crime. Fortunately, the video voyeurism law she advocated for in Louisiana was quickly adopted in several other states, including California, Michigan, and Ohio.

Fifteen years later, it is standard for states to have a law against non-consensual photos and recordings when people are in places where they have a reasonable expectation of privacy, like their home, a hotel room, or a public restroom. At the national level, the Video Voyeurism Prevention Act of 2004 says it is illegal on federal property, such as a military base, national park, or prison, to capture an image of a private area of an individual without their consent, and to knowingly do so under circumstances in which the individual has a reasonable expectation of privacy. The narrow interpretation of the phrase "reasonable expectation of privacy" is why upskirt photos are still legal in so many places.

When I am waiting for a subway, in a store, or standing at a corner, waiting for the light to change, it seems reasonable to me, and probably to you, that I should expect privacy from this kind of violation. But many states do not interpret it this way. For example, in Nebraska, upskirt photos are legal because, as the law is written, lawmakers argue no one can have a reasonable expectation of privacy in a public place, including from someone photographing their intimate areas that are covered by clothing.

The concept of privacy in public spaces is much different today than even a few years ago when most of these laws were written. In 2013, 90 percent of American adults owned a cell phone and 58 percent owned a smartphone, according to the Pew Research Internet Project. This means that more people than ever have the ability to covertly take photos in public spaces, and social media and mobile phone apps mean it only takes a second to share them. The laws need to reflect this reality.

While having a law against upskirt photos doesn't mean an end to this problem, it can give more rights to victims who want to take action and it may act as a deterrent for would-be upskirt photographers. It is time for every state to update its law to make upskirt photos illegal.

Fortunately, just as in Massachusetts, a growing number of state legislators are working toward that goal. In Nebraska, Lincoln Senator Amanda

McGill introduced a bill last month to outlaw the act of taking pictures of people's private areas in public places. In January, lawmakers in Oregon said they are working to update the Invasion of Personal Privacy law after a 17-year-old girl reported a man who tried taking upskirt photos of her at a Christmas Bazaar.

For other states that need to update their laws and want guidance on the best language to use, I recommend they look to the laws in Hawaii and Washington.

Hawaii's law, Violation of Privacy in the Second Degree, says it is illegal if a person intentionally "covertly records or broadcasts an image of another person's intimate area underneath clothing, by use of any device, and that image is taken while that person is in a public place and without that person's consent."

Washington's Voyeurism law specifically states it is illegal for someone to take photos or videotape of the intimate areas of a non-consenting person's body under circumstances where the person has a reasonable expectation of privacy, including public places.

No one should have to worry about someone taking violating photos of them in public spaces, but should that happen, everyone deserves the right to legal recourse, no matter where they reside.

Activity 6.1 • Discuss "Laws Protecting Women From Upskirt Photo Assaults Fall Short"

Collaborate

In your small group, discuss the following questions.

1. What is Holly Kearl arguing in "Laws Protecting Women From Upskirt Photo Assaults Fall Short"?

2. What evidence does Kearl give to support her argument?

3. What is the counterargument?

4. Kearl draws parallels to the laws making it illegal to plant a recording device in someone's home. Why does she do that?

5. Do you agree or disagree with Kearl's argument? Why?

Collaborate

Activity 6.2 • A Logical Fallacy in Upskirt Laws?

In your small group, look at the list of logical fallacies in Chapter 3, and decide if Nebraska's position regarding upskirt photos is a logical fallacy. Upskirt photos in Nebraska, according to Holly Kearl, "are legal because, as the law is written, lawmakers argue no one can have a reasonable expectation of privacy in a public place, including from someone photographing their intimate areas that are covered by clothing." Which logical fallacy might it be and why? Hint: a premise or step in the logic may be missing.

Explore

Activity 6.3 • What Is the Rhetorical Situation of an Op-Ed?

What is the rhetorical situation that Holly Kearl is responding to in "Laws Protecting Women from Upskirt Photo Assaults Fall Short"? Remember the discussion from the beginning of this chapter about the rhetorical situation being the place where writers write, a site created by factors such as audience and ongoing conversations that compel a response.

Collaborate

Activity 6.4 • Write an Op-Ed Argument

The OpEd Project (www.theopedproject.org) is an online initiative to "expand the range of voices" submitting op-ed essays to media outlets. According to its statistics, 80 to 90 percent of op-ed pieces are currently written by men, which is something it endeavors to change by helping women and members of other underrepresented groups develop the skills to get published in top media markets. Whether you are male or female, you may belong to an underrepresented group that is not having its voice heard as part of the national conversation about issues.

An op-ed is an opinion piece printed in a newspaper, magazine, blog, or other media outlet. The name derives from earlier times in print journalism when these opinion pieces would be printed on a page opposite the editorial page. Op-eds are written by individuals not affiliated with the publication, as opposed to editorials that are written by the publication's staff.

This assignment asks you to write an op-ed piece suitable for submission to a major newspaper or other media outlet. It does not require you to submit your text. That is up to you.

(continued on next page)

For this assignment, you need to do the following.

- Read op-eds that appear in the major regional newspaper or other media outlet for your city, such as the *Chicago Tribune*, the *Washington Post*, or the *Arizona Republic*. The OpEd Project provides a list of the top 100 U.S. media outlets on its website. Read several op-eds to get a sense of the topics and style of the articles that the newspaper or other media outlet prints.

- Notice that op-eds are not academic writing. They must be well-researched, but they also generally are written in a more casual and engaging style than traditional academic writing. You must first attract your audience's attention in order to present your case. Analyze how each op-ed you read captures the reader's interest.

- Choose a topic that is timely and of interest to the readers of the publication that you choose. Research that topic using some of the basics in Chapter 4 of this textbook.

- The length and structure of your op-ed should follow the pattern of pieces recently published in your publication.

- Keep your audience in mind—the readers of the publication.

- Follow the basic op-ed structure recommended by the OpEd Project, reprinted below.

- Read the "Tips for Op-Ed Writing from the OpEd Project," in the sidebar.

(continued on next page)

Tips for Op-Ed Writing from the OpEd Project

1. **Own your expertise**
Know what you are an expert in and why—but don't limit yourself. Consider the metaphors that your experience and knowledge suggest.

2. **Stay current**
Follow the news—both general and specific to your areas of specialty. If you write about Haiti, read the Haitian press. If you write about pop culture, read the media that cover it.

3. **The perfect is the enemy of the good**
In other words: write fast. You may have only a few hours to get your piece in before the moment is gone. But also . . .

4. **Cultivate a flexible mind**
Remember that a good idea may have more than one news hook; indeed, if the idea is important enough, it can have many. So keep an eye out for surprising connections and new news hooks—the opportunity may come around again.

5. **Use plain language**
Jargon serves a purpose, but it is rarely useful in public debate, and can obfuscate—sorry, I mean cloud—your argument. Speak to your reader in straight talk.

6. **Respect your reader**
Never underestimate your reader's intelligence or overestimate his or her level of information. Recognize that your average reader is not an expert in your topic and that the onus is on you to capture her attention—and make a compelling argument.

(*Note*: A lede (or lead) is a journalism term that means the beginning of your article that catches your reader's attention and establishes your topic.)

Basic Op-Ed Structure from the OpEd Project

(*Note*: This is not a rule—just one way of approaching it.)

Lede (around a news hook)

Thesis (statement of argument—either explicit or implied)

Argument (based on evidence, such as stats, news, reports from credible organizations, expert quotes, scholarship, history, and first-hand experience)

- 1st Point
  - Evidence
  - Evidence
  - Conclusion
- 2nd Point
  - Evidence
  - Evidence
  - Conclusion
- 3rd Point
  - Evidence
  - Evidence
  - Conclusion

Note: In a simple, declarative op-ed ("policy X is bad; here's why"), this may be straightforward. In a more complex commentary, the 3rd point may expand on the bigger picture (historical context, global/geographic picture, mythological underpinnings, etc.) or may offer an explanation for a mystery that underpins the argument (e.g., why a bad policy continues, in spite of its failures).

"To Be Sure" paragraph (in which you preempt your potential critics by acknowledging any flaws in your argument, and address any obvious counterarguments)

Conclusion (often circling back to your lede)

Activity 6.5 • Freewrite about Your Op-Ed Essay

Compose

Freewrite for five minutes about your writing of an Op-Ed essay. Answer one or more of these questions or write about something else related to the topic.

1. Why did you choose your topic for an Op-Ed essay?

2. What evidence did you offer to support your position?

3. Did you have a counterargument?

As your instructor directs, revise your freewriting into a paragraph to turn in.

Writing Rhetorically in ENC 1101 & ENC 1102

by Bre Garrett

In ENC 1101 and ENC 1102, you learn to write and think rhetorically, meaning you learn to situate yourself in rhetorical situations as writers and researchers seeking action.

In ENC 1101, you write rhetorically for academic contexts, conducting research for academic audiences and learning academic genres. As a first-year College Composition course, the curriculum aims to introduce you to writing for the university. You predominantly write essays and other alphabetic-prose genres and modes such as analysis and reflection. ENC 1102, the second-semester College Composition course, takes a public turn and asks you to write rhetorically for audiences beyond the university and analyze a variety of texts and genres. In both courses, you learn to conduct research as a means of collecting meaningful data and entering conversations.

Let's explore how writing rhetorically works in ENC 1101 & 1102 using the Op-Ed section on the preceding pages. An op-ed exemplifies a type of writing that merges academic and public contexts. How so? How is an op-ed characteristic of academic writing? What makes an op-ed an example of public writing? What are the distinguishing factors?

Academic and public writing overlap in many ways; they differ, however, when it comes to audience and delivery. Published in a public news source venue, an op-ed is an opinion piece written for a public audience. Several conventions that we learn and associate with academic writing remain explicitly vivid—and necessary—in an op-ed as well as other public writing genres. Conventions are really just agreed upon audience expectations whether the audience is public or academic. For example, in Holly Kearl's op-ed, the writing remains succinct and clear; the writing is free of grammar errors; the writing is thesis-driven and presents a focused opinion with supporting evidence; and the writing sparks or engages an already existing conversation. Academic writing criteria are synonymous with professional ethos, or the credibility that a text and author embody. Kearl's op-ed also demonstrates research-based writing. Pause and consider, what types of research do you observe in Kearl's piece? How does Kearl, and how do you, use research to support your opinions?

In ENC 1101, you might read or write an op-ed to help you articulate, in a sophisticated way, your opinion about a selected topic. You can also make use of the op-ed structure to help you formulate a "lede" to open your essay or to develop evidence sections that support your argument. Writing an op-ed situates your topic in a cultural moment, presenting a public opinion about a timely topic. Reflect for a moment: what subjects or incidents would prompt you to write an op-ed? In response to what text, news story, or cultural event/ happening? When you feel an impetus to respond, to speak out, you have dis-covered a personal exigence, or motivation, for entering conversation. An op-ed format can help you invent essential parts of the rhetorical situation such as topic and argument, cultural context, and author purpose.

ENC 1102 extends writing and the rhetorical situation to public audiences and genres. Your study of the op-ed, in 1102, includes a more robust examination of the op-ed as a public genre, or a type of writing that engages public commentary. You might examine the delivery choices of the writer, the publication venue, and the target audience. Rather than use an op-ed structure to invent and develop an argument, in 1102, you might write an op-ed intended for publication.

In 1102, the standard assignment is a rhetorical analysis, a particular analytical method that examines textual context, author purpose, and audience to study how and why writers make particular choices and how those choices affect readers and move readers to action. In studying the op-ed as public writing, we critically explore the writing context. Where is the text published? The publica-tion venue matters, significantly, and informs expectations regarding the text's style, format, and tone as well as who has access to the text. In studying public audience(s), we have to anticipate a wide range of diversity and ability. An op-ed addresses kairotic topics. What is the timely, opportune moment for speak-ing about an issue/topic? In 1102, you might conduct a rhetorical analysis of an op-ed or series of op-eds that studies the cultural context and the timely moment for speaking.

The next several pages of this chapter devote instruction to the research-based argument essay, which you will write for ENC 1101. ENC 1101 immerses you in a semester-long research-based argument project. While the essay structure and topic differ across course sections, all 1101 students compose an academic research essay. In working on an academic essay, you engage in research in order to enter a conversation about your topic, to show and reference other voices and sources, and to learn ethical citation and source attribution practices.

Developing your academic research-based argument, you will engage in recursive a process that includes the following stages:

- Invention of a topic: selection, creation, and discovery of your topic (Re-read Chapter 4 "Inventing Rhetorically")

- Research: create a research plan, write an annotated bibliography, and conduct primary and secondary research

- Formulate a thesis and argument; academic writing is thesis-driven writing

- Writing process: draft, revise, and edit your work

- Peer response workshops: draft essays and share your work-in-progress with peers

- Delivery of an edited, final essay

The Research-Based Argument Essay

A research-based argument draws upon the skills you have been developing all semester. You've written persuasive arguments, and you have also incorporated different kinds of research. Now you put those skills together in a somewhat longer and more carefully documented version. Being able to write a well-thought-out research paper is a skill required in numerous college courses. Each time you are asked to write a research-based argument essay, the instructor will define the rhetorical situation, so pay close attention to the wording of the assignment.

Also, your argument essay is a response to an ongoing conversation on your topic carried on by your research sources. Some sources will agree with each other, and others may disagree. By paraphrasing or quoting your sources' stances on the issue you write about, you are including them in your conversation. Also, the sources' stances and evidence that you cite provide a context for your own thesis about the issue.

The goal of a research-based argument paper is persuasion, and it should begin with an introduction in which you clearly state your position on an issue. For example, "Understanding the Effects of Mass Media's Portrayals of Black Women and Adolescents on Self Image," the following research-based argument essay, takes the position that "Black-oriented media specifically tends to have a positive effect for Black women with strong ethnic identity, while Black women with weak ethnic identity were more at risk of the aversive effects of mainstream media."

Usually, an academic research-based argument relies upon *logos*—reasoning and evidence—as the primary appeal, though *pathos* and *ethos* have a place as well, if used appropriately. Cherish Green, the author of the essay offers evidence from articles published in academic journals including the *Annual Review of Psychology* and *Psychology of Women Quarterly* to support her argument. Thus, she is participating in the ongoing conversation about how mass media portraits of Black women affect the self-image of Black women.

Writing in High School Versus College

By Justin McCoy

For high school writing projects, you might recall writing with the aim of conveying information, demonstrating your comprehension of a text or your familiarity with a research topic. This type of writing may not have required you to take a stance and argue your point. When given opportunities to make an argument in your high school papers, you likely did so for a persuasive paper in which you expressed your opinion and then incorporated examples from your personal experience as support. Such writing projects are certainly important in your trajectory as a writer and thinker, as they likely helped you acquire foundational experience with composition.

Writing in college makes use of this past experience but goes beyond it by synthesizing research and opinion. In college-level, or "academic," writing assignments, you will often be prompted to express your opinion by making an argument that you support with credible research, regardless of your chosen major or discipline. You will certainly do so in first-year writing courses, which are designed to give you opportunities to practice employing writing strategies that will be useful not only in other classes but also in the workplace.

You may be wondering why discussions of argument are so prevalent in college writing classes. The primary reason is that argument is the distinguishing feature of college-level writing. But what does argument have to do with writing exactly? Well, the two are not mutually exclusive. In fact, they are one in the same because we make arguments all the time. Whether you are composing written, visual, or digital texts, you are either explicitly or implicitly selling an argument to an existing or imaginary audience. The strength and potential success of your argument depends on variables such as research: the expert opinions, data, facts, and sometimes anecdotal examples that support your reasons for why you hold a particular stance on a topic.

Write a Thesis Statement

A **thesis** may be a sentence or a series of sentences, or in a few cases it may be implied rather than stated explicitly, but a thesis is at the heart of any piece of writing. If a reader cannot identify your thesis, the meaning of your text is not clear. How do you develop a thesis? First, you determine your occasion for writing—who is your audience, what is your purpose, and what special circumstances are there (if any)? Then you write a working thesis that makes an assertion or claim about your topic, something that will be affected by your audience and purpose. For example, if you are writing a research paper about the advantages and disadvantages of biodiesel fuel, your claim may be stated differently depending on whether your audience is an English class or a chemistry class. In the latter, you might need to use technical language that would be unfamiliar to your English professor.

Working theses are statements that develop and change as essays are written; they are basic frameworks that provide a connection for the ideas you have decided to convey to your reader. Later, after you have completed a draft of your text, examine your working thesis. If needed, rewrite your thesis so that it states the main idea of your essay in a clear and engaging fashion. Consider the following examples of thesis statements.

> Example: The United States should implement a guest worker program as a way of reforming the illegal immigration problem.

> Example: Nuclear power should be considered as part of a program to reduce the United States's dependence on foreign oil.

Compose an Introduction

Experienced writers have different methods of creating a good introduction. One writer who tends to discover his paper as he goes along swears the best way to write an introduction is to write the entire paper and then move the conclusion to the beginning of the essay and rewrite it as the introduction. Another writer lets the paper sit around for a few days before she writes her introduction. A third always writes two or three different introductions and tries them out on friends before deciding which to use. However you choose to write the introduction, make sure it is interesting enough to make your reader want to read on.

The introduction to your essay is an invitation to your reader. If you invite readers to come along with you on a boring journey, they won't want to follow. In magazine and newspaper writing, the introduction is sometimes called a *hook* because it hooks the reader into reading the text. If a magazine writer does not capture the reader's attention right away, the reader is not likely to continue. After all, there are other and possibly more interesting articles in the magazine. Why should readers suffer through a boring introduction? Depending on the topic and pattern of your essay, you might employ different techniques to hook your readers and make them want to keep reading.

Essay Starters

If, after you have done extensive invention (prewriting and research), you still find it intimidating to face the blank computer screen, try one of the essay starters below. These are phrases to get the words flowing. Then, later, after you have written a rough draft, go back and revise the beginning. Delete the essay starter and, in its place, write a real introduction. As you probably know, you do not need to say, "In my opinion," because what you write in your essay, unless you attribute it to someone else, is your opinion. See the section in this chapter on writing introductions.

In my opinion . . .

I agree . . .

I disagree . . .

Studies show . . .

Experts say . . .

My paper is about . . .

I am writing this essay because . . .

In the beginning . . .

- An intriguing or provocative quotation

- A narrative or anecdote

- A question or series of questions

- A vivid sensory description

- A strongly stated opinion

Your introductory paragraph makes a commitment to your readers. This is where you identify the topic, state your thesis (implicitly or explicitly), and give your readers clues about the journey that will follow in the succeeding paragraphs. Be careful not to mislead the reader. Do not ask questions you will not answer in your paper (unless they are rhetorical questions). Do not introduce a topic in your introduction and then switch to another one in your paper.

Although the introduction is the first paragraph or so of the paper, it may not be the first paragraph the writer composes. If you have problems beginning your essay because you cannot immediately think of a good introduction, begin with the first point in your essay and come back to the introduction later.

Reading 6.2

The Truth about Writer's Block
by Judith Johnson

Judith Johnson suggests in this essay, first published in Huffington Post Books, *that there is no such thing as writer's block. She suggests what writers experience is the ebb and flow of the writing process.*

I don't choose to experience "writer's block" which I see as simply a matter of faulty perception. It is a mislabeling of a very natural part of the ebb and flow of the writing process. To say "I have writer's block" is to judge a temporary or permanent absence of writing momentum and productivity as wrong and therefore to see oneself as a failure in some way. The process of writing is an intricate interplay of conscious and unconscious dynamics and what actually lands on the page is a small part of it all. When we label and judge that process, we interfere with its natural flow and take a position of againstness with ourselves. It's all in how you look at it.

When a writer declares that he or she is experiencing writer's block, it is like grabbing hold of a fear (Fantasy Expectation Appearing Real) and fueling it with emotional distress. A way to reframe this is to simply trust that what appears to be a dry spell is a normal part of the process of being a writer and that either you need time to be away from the writing focus or that the process is largely unconscious at that time. Each writer has to make peace with this by finding their own particular rhythm and honoring that. For example, what works for me is not to have any rigid writing schedule, but rather to let the words come to me—and they always do—sooner or later. When working on a deadline, whether self-imposed or not, I never lose sight of the deadline, it is always there, but I don't beat myself up with it if time keeps passing and nothing is getting on paper. I'll notice that the topic is alive in me—turning this way and that finding its way to the paper. It takes a lot of trust to let this be. So far, it has never failed me.

I have lots of books and articles and projects on the back burner and no fear of running out of things to write about. I know that each piece of writing has a life of its own. For example, I have a poem that I started at the age of 16 that rumbles around in my head from time to time looking for its ending. I know it will end someday, but hasn't so far. That's not a problem to me—just a reality. I also keep what I call a "dump" file for each project and whether I am actively working on it or not, I capture ideas and information there.

In addition to building a strong bond of trust with yourself, here are some other keys to maintaining a good relationship with yourself as a writer:

Just Do It: There is a point at which every writer just has to sit down and write. Whether you write for five minutes or five hours straight doesn't matter, but if you are going to be a writer, you have to sit down and write.

Write with Freedom and Abandon, Then Edit Ruthlessly: It is important to give yourself permission to write whatever comes up without any judgment. Just focus on capturing your thoughts and ideas—forget about grammar, structure and eloquence. Just get a hold of whatever comes up. Then, just as Michelangelo described the sculpting process as discovering a statue inside every block of stone, each writer must ruthlessly revise and refine a piece of work until pleased with it.

Get Out of Your Own Way: If you get into a pattern of negativity and beating up on yourself when writing, find a way to be more loving with yourself and do not feed the negativity.

Patience: Writing takes enormous patience. As with any other art form, you are constantly revising and refining your work. For an artist the equation is never time is money, but rather "do I feel complete with this piece? Is it my best effort given the time I have available?"

Flexibility, Cooperation and Balance: There is always some level of agitation just under the surface that propels a writer forward giving momentum to the working process. But there are always other forces at work and writing is only one of many activities in an individual's life. Finding your own rhythm and being willing to cooperate with the other elements of life that often seem to intrude on the writer's solitary endeavor are like moving between shooting the rapids and gliding along on calm waters, never quite knowing which is going to present itself and when. Experience teaches us all to go with the flow and somehow that seems to yield maximum inner peace and outward productivity.

Keeping a Sense of Humor and Humility: I've learned never to take myself too seriously as a writer. I do my best and need to laugh at myself from time to time when I give too much importance to what I write. If people get value from what I write, that's great and positive feedback is extremely gratifying. However, while writing is ultimately about communication, I find it very funny that I don't write to communicate, but rather because I simply need to write—I am compelled to do so. If the end product of my endeavors is of value to others, that's great, but the solitary process of engaging in the art form itself is entirely for me and I think that is pretty funny.

Letting Go of the Illusion of Control: A really good writer is never in control of the writing process. You may find that having a rigid schedule works well for you or you might be someone who writes when the spirit moves you to do so. Either way, a good writer taps into the wellspring of human consciousness and like love, you can't make that happen on demand.

Is writing challenging? Absolutely! However, it is a great way to learn some profound lessons in life and to be of service to others.

Explore

Activity 6.6 • Discuss "The Truth about Writer's Block"

In your small group, discuss the following questions.

1. How does Judith Johnson choose to reframe the concept of writer's block?

2. Johnson makes recommendations to deal with the "absence of writing momentum." Which of her suggestions makes the most sense to you? Which makes the least sense to you?

3. What do you think? Is there such a thing as "writer's block?"

Support Your Ideas with Source Materials

A research paper, by definition, makes use of source materials to make an argument. It is important to remember, however, that it is *your* paper, *not* what some professors may call a "research dump," meaning that it is constructed by stringing together research information with a few transitions. Rather, you, as the author of the paper, carry the argument in your own words and use quotes and paraphrases from source materials to support your argument.

▌ After you think you have completed enough research to construct a working thesis and begin writing your paper, collect all your materials in front of you (photocopies of articles, printouts of electronic sources, and books) and spend a few hours reading through the materials and making notes. Then, put all the notes and materials to the side and freewrite for a few minutes about what you can remember from your research that is important. Take this freewriting and make a rough outline of the main points you want to cover in your essay. Then you can go back to your notes and source materials to flesh out your outline.

▌ Use quotes for the following three reasons:

1. You want to "borrow" the *ethos* or credibility of the source. For example, if you are writing about stem cell research, you may want to quote from an authority such as Dr. James A. Thomson, whose groundbreaking research led to the first use of stem cells for research. Alternatively, if your source materials include the *New England Journal of Medicine* or another prestigious publication, it may be worth crediting a quote to that source.

2. The material is so beautifully or succinctly written that it would lose its effectiveness if you reworded the material in your own words.

3. You want to create a point of emphasis by quoting rather than paraphrasing. Otherwise, you probably want to paraphrase material from your sources, as quotes should be used sparingly. Often, writers quote source material in a first draft and then rewrite some of the quotes into paraphrases during the revision process.

▌ Introduce quotes. You should never have a sentence or sentences in quotation marks just sitting in the middle of a paragraph, as it would puzzle a reader. If you quote, you should always introduce the quote by saying something like this: According to Dr. James A. Thomson, "Stem cell research. . . " Alternatively, you can make a short quote part of your sentence, as it is in this example: Dr. James A. Thomson found government regulations "restrictive and cumbersome."

▌ Avoid plagiarism by clearly indicating material that is quoted or paraphrased. See the appendix (at the end of the book) for more information about citing source material.

Incorporating Voices

By Laura Herbek

When writing an argumentative research paper, it's crucial that you differentiate between your ideas and the ideas of your sources. The focus of the paper must be on your argument, which should be supplemented, but not overwhelmed by, sourced material.

Remember that sources are actually just people. Let's imagine your sources as your guests at a dinner party. Just like any good host, you must announce your guests as they arrive to the party. You wouldn't just throw a guest into the mix without an introduction, so it follows that you shouldn't randomly insert a piece of evidence into your paper either. Avoid beginning or ending body paragraphs with quotes or paraphrases. Each quote or paraphrase needs an introduction to orient your reader. This introduction might sound like "According to Dr. Julia Lorenzo, . . ." or "Dr. Julia

Lorenzo adds: . . ." Following this piece of evidence and its in-text citation, you should include an explanation of the conclusions you expect the reader to draw from this quote/paraphrase. As an author, it's your job to help your audience digest the information you present. If your reader can't make sense of the paper's sourced material, it's unlikely that he or she will be able to follow your argument.

Back to the dinner party. How will you seat these guests so that the dinner conversation flows? If you envision your sources as people carrying on a discussion with one another, it's easy to see that some organizational strategies work better than others. Arrange evidence strategically to support your argument. Which sources seem like they should be grouped together to "talk" to one another? You may notice that one source doesn't seem to fit with the others. Don't be afraid to discard a source that isn't entirely relevant as your paper shapes up, even if that source contains interesting material. A guest that doesn't get along with others can throw the gathering into chaos!

Of course, this is your party, so you don't want to let any of your guests hijack the conversation. Avoid using sources back-to-back in your writing. This is overwhelming for your reader. It's also confusing, because *your* argument gets lost in the shuffle. Remember that research is only supposed to verify or illustrate your own ideas about a topic. This means that *you* are responsible for leading the argument by providing plenty of your own words between pieces of evidence. Guide the reader through your paper with clear topic sentences. Identify strong subclaims that support your thesis. Look for opportunities to explain how your ideas differ from those of your sources. Your goal is to highlight the contributions you are making to this ongoing conversation. After all, if your sources have already covered everything that needs to be said on this subject, why write the paper at all?

It's a tough job keeping all these chatty, opinionated guests in line. With some careful planning and attention to detail, you can stay in control and lead your reader to a compelling and persuasive conclusion.

Incorporating Voices: Group Wiki Autobiography

1. Break into groups of four. Identify a disappointing experience that all group members have in common. This shared experience will be the topic of your group autobiography. If you aren't familiar with the genre of the autobiography, spend a few minutes researching the genre and its conventions at the beginning of your conversation.

2. For this project, your group members will be the information base that you must research. You'll need to spend some time discussing your experiences in order to generate content for the paper. You may notice some differences in your shared experiences; as a group, you should negotiate the best ways to handle these differences and successfully integrate each group member's perspective. Through your discussions, work to determine *why* this experience is so disappointing. What expectations did you share, and where did those expectations originate? We can learn a great deal about ourselves and the culture we live in by examining shared assumptions and disappointments, so the goal is to situate your individual experiences within a larger narrative. As a group, take notes on these discussions and post them to the group wiki.

3. Begin planning the autobiography and its rhetorical strategy. Compile your research and decide what information to include. Design an organizational approach and an outline for the paper. Then, post this outline to the wiki. Divide sections among group members. Your job will be to access the notes and outline on the wiki and post your completed sections there before the group meets again. Remember to keep the project's rhetorical situation in mind as you write:

   a. This is a group autobiography, not a series of individual autobiographies. The value of the assignment lies in learning how to work together as one author.

   b. The medium for this project is not ink and paper, but a wiki. How will that change your audience? Think about how the choice of medium and prospective audience might impact your writing.

   c. How will your paper speak to the larger narrative from step 1? Remember that your purpose is not only to tell a collective story, but to explore how this shared experience might suggest something meaningful.

4. Once the group reconvenes, you will need to revisit the completed outline via the wiki. This is the first draft of your paper. Your next task will be to revise and edit this paper. Some students find it helpful to work together using Google Docs during this phase of the project. Look for ways to make the individual pieces work together as a cohesive whole. Correct choppy areas by improving their flow, and add transitions as needed. Search for information that hasn't been covered or has been covered more than once. After you've

revised the content of the paper, edit for clarity, consistency, and grammar. When you are finished, post your final draft to the wiki.

5. Browse other group wikis, posting comments as you read. Reading topics to reflect upon:

   a. Describe one group's writing process. How was it similar/dissimilar to your paper's development?

   b. How did the other groups incorporate their research? Did they manage to organize multiple perspectives under a unified purpose? Are the papers readable and orderly?

   c. Have you experienced any disappointing events covered by other groups? Did these groups relate said events in an accurate and purposeful way? Why or why not?

   d. Search for strengths in the other projects. Which group made a particularly impressive move? If you were to write another draft of your paper, how would you incorporate this strength?

   e. Generate an argument about the bigger picture. What do these autobiographies as a whole suggest about cultural expectations and disappointments? If you were to write a paper on the subject using these projects as your body of research, what might your thesis statement be?

Support Your Thesis

After you have attracted the interest of your audience, established your thesis, and given any background information and definitions, you will next begin to give reasons for your position, which further develops your argument. These reasons are, in turn, supported by statistics, analogies, anecdotes, and quotes from authorities which you have discovered in your research or know from personal knowledge. Ideally, arrange your reasons so that the strongest ones come either at the beginning or at the end of this portion of the paper (points of emphasis), and the weaker ones fall in the middle.

Answer Opposing Arguments

If you are aware of a contradicting statistic or other possible objection to your argument, it may be tempting to ignore that complication, hoping your audience will not notice. However, that is exactly the worst thing you can do. It is much better to anticipate your audience's possible questions or objections and address them in your discussion. Doing so prevents you from losing credibility by either appearing to deceive your audience or being unaware of all the facts. Also, acknowledging possible refutations of your position actually strengthens your position by making you seem knowledgeable and fair-minded.

Vary Your Strategies or Patterns of Development

When composing your essay, you have many different strategies or **patterns of development** available to you. You may write entire essays whose sole strategy is argumentation or comparison and contrast, but more often, you will combine many of these different modes while writing a single essay. Consider the following strategies or patterns of development.

- **Analysis** entails a close examination of an issue, book, film, or other object, separating it into elements and examining each of the elements separately through other writing modes such as classification or comparison and contrast.

- **Argumentation** involves taking a strong stand on an issue supported by logical reasons and evidence intended to change a reader's mind on an issue or open a reader's eyes to a problem.

- **Cause and effect** is an explanation of the cause and subsequent effects or consequences of a specific action.

- **Classification** entails dividing and grouping things into logical categories.

- **Comparison and contrast** examines the similarities and differences between two or more things.

- **Definition** employs an explanation of the specific meaning of a word, phrase, or idea.

- **Description** uses vivid sensory details to present a picture or an image to the reader.

- **Exemplification** makes use of specific examples to explain, define, or analyze something.

- **Narration** uses a story or vignette to illustrate a specific point or examine an issue.

Include Effective Transitions

Transitions take readers by the hand and lead them from one part of your argument to the next. The best transitions have a light touch, not a hard grasp, so readers hardly realize they are being led. Phrases like "for example," "thus," "as a result," "therefore," and "moreover" are all transitions, and it is fine to employ them, but do not overuse them. In other words, do not have three sentences in a paragraph with the word "therefore."

The best paragraph transition begins the following paragraph where the previous one left off. In the following example from a student essay about obesity, the last sentence of one paragraph is this:

> Policy makers in America must hold the food industry accountable by creating stringent guidelines that create boundaries on the marketing of the food being advertised—not only to children, but to all Americans suffering from this disease; these policies may be what help in lowering the dangerous percentages of obesity threatening the lives of millions.

The next paragraph follows logically, giving more specifics about how obesity "threatens the lives of millions."

> Obesity is a major risk factor for non-communicable diseases, such as diabetes, cardiovascular diseases, and cancers.

Moreover, the repetition of the word "obesity" also serves as a transition.

Sometimes, you need to add a transition word or phrase to strengthen the link between one paragraph and the next (see Table 6.1). This list is not exhaustive. If you need additional transitions, try searching on the internet for "writing transitions."

Don't worry too much about effective transitions in your first draft, but complete a revision pass through any text you write just to be sure your transitions are clear but not overworked.

Table 6.1 • Transition Words and Phrases

To emphasize	indeed, in fact, even, of course
To give an example	for example, namely, for instance, to illustrate, specifically
To prove	for, because, obviously, besides, in fact, in addition to
To show cause and effect	therefore, hence, accordingly, so
To provide additional support	additionally, again, as well, and, equally important

Write a Conclusion

After they have read the last paragraph of your essay,. your readers should feel satisfied that you have covered everything you needed to, and you have shared an insight. You may have heard the basic rules: A conclusion cannot address any new issues, and it should summarize the main points of the essay. Although these are valid and reliable rules, a summary is not always the best way to end an essay. The prohibition against new ideas in the final paragraph also might limit certain effective closures like a call to action or a question for the reader to ponder.

One effective technique for writing a conclusion is to refer back to your introduction. If you began with a narrative anecdote, a sensory description, or a question, you can tie a mention of it to your ending point. Or, if you are composing an argumentative essay, you might choose to summarize by using an expert quote to restate your thesis, giving the reader a final firm sense of *ethos* or credibility. You might also end with a single-sentence summary followed by a suggestion or a call to action for the reader. Another effective way to end an argument can be a paragraph that suggests further research.

A conclusion doesn't have to be long. As a matter of fact, it does not even need to be a separate paragraph, especially if your essay is short. If your closing comments are related to the final paragraph of the essay, one or two sentences can easily be added to the final body paragraph of the essay.

Consider Elements of Page Design

Professors now take it for granted that you word-process your paper using a professional looking typeface such as Times New Roman. However, producing your text on a computer with internet access gives you the option to do much more—including adding one or more images and other page design elements. Several of the assignments in this chapter offer you the opportunity to be creative with your project presentation. Even if you are required to submit your project in standard MLA or APA essay formats, however, you can still include one or more images, and it is important to consider where you place the images.

Some simple guidelines will help you design effective documents.

▪ Use space as a design element. Do not overcrowd your pages. Place material so that important parts are emphasized by the space around them.

▪ Rarely (if ever) use all capital letters. Words in all caps are hard to read, and on the internet all caps is considered shouting.

▪ Use headings to group your information and make your pages easy to skim. Readers often like to skim pages before deciding what to read. Indeed, many people will skim all the headlines, headings, and photo captions first, before reading the body text of any section.

▪ Put important elements in the top left and lower right parts of the screen. English readers are trained to read from left to right, so our eyes naturally start at the upper left-hand corner of the screen. Our eyes, when skimming, don't flow line by line, but move in a Z pattern, as illustrated in the following diagram (see Figure 6.1).

Figure 6.1 • Eye Movement When Skimming a Page

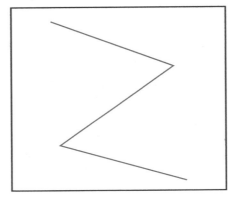

If you want to include a photo in your research paper, for example, you should put it either in the top left or the bottom right corner of the page, points of emphasis in the Z pattern. Today, with a sophisticated word processing program such as Microsoft Word, it is easy to import an image, size it, and move it to the desired place on a page. Once you have imported an image, you can click on it, hold your cursor at a corner, and enlarge or shrink the image by dragging the cursor. Also, by clicking on the image, you can activate the dialogue box that allows you to specify having the text run tightly around the image. Then you can easily move the image around on the page until you have placed it in a pleasing spot. Alternatively, Microsoft Word provides document templates that you can use for newsletters, brochures, and other types of projects.

If you look closely at Figure 6.2, you may notice that the text surrounding the image does not seem to make any sense (though it is actually Latin). That's because the text is Lorem ipsum text, sometimes called placeholder or dummy text, which designers use to create page layouts before they have the real text from writers. If you want to try using Lorem ipsum yourself, just do a search on the internet for that name, and you will find sites that provide paragraphs of the nonsense words that you can utilize as placeholder text.

Figure 6.2 • Lorem Ipsum Text

Solupta ventemporios Obiscium

Pa que minullupta voles eaquibus, sa viduciur, sitae eum,Luptiaes

Lenis ut voloresed eum intias aruptatatur? Quia nempos et prae. Pel et denihita est explita denis sitem. Nam, optaturiore et adi dit, qui as et aut liquistia di reperest aspelicime non consequi dolorat voluptatium re, si untionse plitate maio doluptas enda ium arunt.

Met volor si consequi ut perferferum quodit ut quid ut explabore nonsequ aspedicto moluptae. Itati nemporitas atem rehentotae. Nem incim ellabore occulparum, nam que prepre uptur? Quiam etum fuga. Ut fugit que enis inumqui volorep udant, sequid quidem quis vendit volesse quodit ullenda secearum que velestrum, cus cor se adi ra voloreptat fuga. Ut incim fugitas quid mos voleni sam quatur restiorro molorem hilluptiae idelloribus.

Pariatur aut is dolorum quias volupta venimpo ribusciistem in rem

Sequundae senis mossunti vent ium

Ovide perciaspid qui vel millabo rerferio. Nam que volupic ietur? Optatuscit es dolorib erumquodit, samendebita doluptatia veligendunt, ut ex ex exeria pla nes estin num et digent, et porerovit, auda ipsam harume voluptius nullis elest, quam quis cus mi, es nem voluptatius net.

Offic torere doles eaturit aut laboreheni volorumquid mi, tetur, que con perro bearum aliciur, quos volore, accatur, optatem ra nos audam as eos aborposam ad ullatem eatias dust, consequi rendic tet que eumqui omnimolore estrum ipsanima denimagnatem excerspit litiumqui consedis ea ditiaec uptaest, ommod ut ende vella voluptae veles iunt aliquid que atet idus, viduciden architiusae excepta ex estionet exceatiunt re essimol uptatqu asimost quatquiae dia ad magnihilla core volorro tempe nis

The image in this article has been effectively placed in the lower right corner, which is a point of emphasis.

Choose Evocative Photos to Illustrate Essays

The photo in Figure 6.3 of a demonstrator in Ferguson, Missouri, protesting the fatal police shooting of unarmed 18-year-old Michael Brown would be a good image to incorporate in an essay about police shootings of unarmed youths. The photo shows rhetorical gestures by both the protestor, with hands raised, and by the police in tactical gear, pointing their weapons toward the unarmed protestor. The photo was selected by both *Time* and *The New York Times* as one of the best photos of 2014.

Figure 6.3 • Evocative Photo Example

*Photo Credit: Whitney Curtis/*The New York Times*/Redux*

Activity 6.7 • Write a Research-Based Argument Paper

Compose

The Purpose of the Assignment

Writing a research paper gives you the opportunity to practice key academic writing skills, including locating and utilizing research materials, prewriting, drafting, and revision. It also requires you to take a position on a topic, create an argument, and support it with quotes and paraphrases from authoritative sources.

Purpose as a Writer

Your purpose as a writer is to convince readers to consider your argument carefully, and, if possible, to persuade them to agree with your point of view. To do this, include appropriate background material and definitions, as well as a consideration of opposing arguments.

Topic

Your topic should address a current issue about which you can take and support a position in the paper length your instructor specifies. Choose your topic carefully, as it should be one that engages your interest and enthusiasm.

Audience

Unless your instructor specifies otherwise, you can assume that your audience has general awareness of your issue but is unfamiliar with scholarly sources on the topic.

Sources

To do your research, you will need to utilize recent and credible sources that include a mix of recent books, scholarly articles, public speeches, and news articles. You may also use interviews, observation, and personal experience, if they are relevant to your topic. Sources will need to be cited in the text and in a works cited page or references page, according to MLA or APA style.

Information that you gather from your sources should support the argument you have created. A research paper is not an assignment in which you take information from sources and simply reorganize it into a paper. The expectation for this assignment is that you will use your sources to create an argument that is distinctly your own.

Thesis

Your essay should have a clear thesis that takes a position on an issue that can be supported within the word limitations of the assignment.

Rough Draft

As directed by your instructor, bring two copies of your rough draft essay to class for peer editing. The draft should have your sources credited in the text and should have a works cited or references page.

Final Draft

Submit your final draft in MLA or APA format in a folder with your rough draft and copies of all of your source materials with the location of quotes or paraphrased material highlighted. If you are using material from a book or books, copy enough of the text before and after your quotes or paraphrases so that your instructor can determine the context of the material being quoted.

Table 6.2 • Argument Formats: A Comparison

Ancient Roman	General Modern Format
Standard pattern the ancients modified to suit the argument.	Good all-purpose format that can be adapted for the needs of the argument.
Introduction—*Exordium* Attracts the interest of the audience and identifies the argument.	Introduction Attracts the interest of the audience through its opening strategy and states the thesis.
Background or narration—*Narratio* Details the history or facts of the issue.	First main point Supports the thesis.
Definition—Explication Defines terms and outlines issues.	Second main point Supports the thesis.
Thesis—*Partitio* States the particular issue that is to be argued.	Third main point Supports the thesis.
Proof—*Confirmatio* Develops the thesis and provides supporting evidence.	Counterargument Acknowledges the opposing argument or arguments.
Refutation or opposition—*Refutatio* Addresses the arguments opposing the thesis.	Rebuttal of counterargument Refutes the opposing argument or arguments.
Conclusion—*Peroratio* Reiterates the thesis and may urge the audience to action.	Conclusion Ties together the elements of the composition and gives the reader closure. May summarize the essay and include a call to action.

Toulmin Model	Rogerian Argument
Good for an argument that relies on empirical evidence such as scientific studies or data collection.	Good when the object is consensus or compromise, so that opponents can work together while retaining their positions.
Claim Presents the overall thesis the writer will argue.	**Introduction** States the problem to be solved or the question to be answered. Often opponents will also agree there is a problem.
Data Supports the claim with evidence.	**Summary of opposing views** Describes the opposing side's arguments in a neutral and fair manner.
Warrant (also known as a bridge) Explains why or how the data support the claim. Connects the data to the claim.	**Statement of understanding** Concedes occasions when the opposing position might be valid.
Counterclaim Presents a claim that negates or disagrees with the thesis/claim.	**Statement of position** Avoids emotionally charged language, and identifies position.
Rebuttal Presents evidence that negates or disagrees with the counterclaim.	**Statement of contexts** Describes the specific contexts in which the rhetor's position applies/works well.
Conclusion Ties together the elements of the composition (if not included with the rebuttal).	**Statement of benefits** Presents benefits that may appeal to the self-interest of readers who may not yet agree with you; shows how your position benefits them. Ends on a positive note.
	Conclusion Ties together the elements of the composition (if not included in the statement of benefits).

Write an Argumentative Essay

In ancient times, orators began a speech by attracting the audience's attention in what was called the *exordium,* which we would call the opening or introduction. Next, they provided background information in a *narratio* (narration), followed by an *explication* in which they defined terms and enumerated the issues. During the *partition* they would express the thesis or main issue to be discussed, and in the *confirmation* they would provide evidence to support the thesis. Opposition arguments would be addressed in the *refutatio,* and the composition would be wrapped up with a *peroratio* or conclusion. The order of these different elements was not rigid in ancient times, nor is it today. Sometimes one or more sections were eliminated if they were not needed, but then, as now, an effective text included most of these elements. For example, if your audience is very familiar with a particular subject, you may not need to define terms, as you would with an audience who was unfamiliar with the material.

As did the ancient Greeks and Romans, when you write an argument, you begin with an introduction that gains your audience's attention and presents your thesis; likewise, you end with a conclusion that ties together what you have said or presents a call to action. However, you have a choice of several formats for what happens between that introduction and conclusion. Following are three prominent alternatives; your choice of which to use depends on your purpose and the type of evidence you have.

Toulmin Model

Created by Stephen Toulmin, the Toulmin model for persuasion grew out of the twentieth-century emphasis upon empirical evidence and is most effective for arguments that rely on evidence from scientific studies, surveys, or other data. His model requires six elements.

1. Claim: Rhetors present a claim or statement that they want the audience to accept.

2. Data: Data back up the claim, what Aristotle would have called inartistic proofs.

3. Warrant (or bridge): A warrant links data and facts to the claim, explaining why the data make the claim valid.

4. Backing (or foundation): Backing provides additional support for the argument.

5. Counterclaim: A counterclaim acknowledges any objections or weaknesses in the argument.

6. Rebuttal: The rebuttal responds to any counterclaims, removing possible objections to the argument.

Toulmin Argumentation

By Rustian Phelps

In high school, you probably wrote five-paragraph essays: essays that started with a thesis statement followed by a brief list of the points you planned to make in support of the thesis, three body paragraphs containing supporting evidence (quotes or examples), and a conclusion in which you restated the thesis and the main points of the essay. In other words, you told them what you were going to say, you told them, and you told them what you said. Five-paragraph essays worked well if you were writing in "the modes," especially descriptive essays such as reports and narrative essays such as the infamous "What I Did Last Summer" essays.

For college writing, however, the five-paragraph essay may fall short of providing you with a rubric that allows you to write the more expansive and detailed papers many of your instructors expect. Notably, a five-paragraph essay tends to follow formal Aristotelian logic. Aristotelian arguments may be presented in the form of a syllogism: two premises (propositions or claims) that lead to an inevitable conclusion. Here is an example of a basic Aristotelian syllogism:

Premise 1: All cats are mammals.

Premise 2: Lunch-Box is a cat.

_____

Conclusion: Therefore, Lunch-Box is a mammal.

No one could reasonably argue against the logic of this syllogism. It is true that cats are, by definition, mammals, and if it is also true that Lunch-Box is indeed a cat, then Lunch-Box cannot be a fish or a bird; he must be a mammal. Whether we are conscious of formulating a syllogism or not, just such a syllogism is the basis for each of the body paragraphs of a typical five-paragraph essay. In outline, they look something like this:

> I. If Premise 1, Premise 2, and Premise 3 are correct, then my
> Conclusion is also correct.
>
> A. Premise 1 is true.
>
> B. Premise 2 is true.

Five-paragraph essays generally assume that the points the writer puts across as support for the thesis will be accepted by the reader as unquestionably true.

Now, consider the following:

> Premise 1: A complete meal includes at least one vegetable.
>
> Premise 2: Broccoli is a vegetable.
>
> _____
>
> Conclusion: Therefore, a meal that includes broccoli is a complete meal.

Some may object to such a simplistic definition of a complete meal. If we hold that, contrary to what Premise 1 suggests, more than having a vegetable on the plate is involved in defining a meal as complete, then we cannot conclude from Premise 2 alone that a meal that includes broccoli is necessarily complete.

If, on the other hand, we decide to accept that both Premise 1 and Premise 2 are true, we still have a problem, as we can see in the next syllogism:

> Premise1: A meal that includes broccoli is a complete meal.
>
> Premise 2: All healthy people eat complete meals.
>
> _____
>
> Conclusion: Therefore, all healthy people eat meals that include broccoli.

We have already accepted Premise 1 as true. Moreover, while it is not necessarily the case that all people who eat complete meals are healthy—there are certainly other factors that go into good health—it is certainly true that complete meals are an important component of a healthy lifestyle; all things considered, one cannot be healthy without a healthy diet. Thus Premise 2 is also true. Yet, few would agree that eating broccoli is necessary for good health. The rigid, syllogistic nature of the five-paragraph essay, however, demands that we accept just that—if Premises 1 and 2 are both true, then the conclusion is inescapable.

A five-paragraph essay might not offer us the flexibility to address this conflict, but the Toulmin model of argumentation does. Toulmin argumentation allows for emotional responses, such as the vehement objection of those who dislike broccoli to defining healthy people as broccoli eaters. It also allows us to acknowledge logical or fact-based objections from other sources, such as a critical comparison of the vitamin and mineral content of broccoli to those of other vegetables such as cauliflower. Rather than forcing conclusions on both writer and reader, Toulmin offers us a rubric through which to seek solutions that are satisfactory for everyone.

An easy way to develop a basic Toulmin argument is to start with a paragraph outline and expand that paragraph into a complete paper. The following is a simple paragraph outline.

The Battle of the Crucifers: Broccoli vs. Cauliflower

In my family, there is an ongoing debate over which vegetable we should serve at family gatherings: broccoli or cauliflower. Each member of the family has a different strongly-held opinion on the matter. Broccoli is a better overall choice than cauliflower because broccoli has just as many of the most important vitamins and minerals as cauliflower does; broccoli has a bolder flavor than cauliflower has; and broccoli's beautiful, bright green color makes it appear more appetizing on the plate than cauliflower. Some might argue that cauliflower's milder flavor and less vegetable-like color make it a more suitable choice for the young children who attend our gatherings, but even the most finicky children can often be induced to eat broccoli if cheese is melted over it. Therefore, I propose that broccoli with cheese become the vegetable of choice for all our family gatherings from now on.

Note that this paragraph outline has eight parts:

- a **Title**, not the title of any of the sources,

- a sentence briefly describing the history of the argument or the context in which it occurs (**Exigence**),

- a brief statement of the problem the argument hopes to solve (**Problematization**),

- an arguable claim (**Thesis**) that tells your reader what you hope to convince him or her of,

- several (not necessarily three) distinct **Reasons** that support the main claim,

- a brief acknowledgement of possible objection(s) to the argument (**Reservation(s)**),

- a counterargument in **Response** to the reservation(s), and

- a **Qualified Conclusion** that acknowledges the legitimacy of the reservations and seeks to offer a solution that will satisfy both sides.

The eight parts are labeled in the following paragraph:

[Your Own Title:] The Battle of the Crucifers: Broccoli vs. Cauliflower

[Context or Exigence:] In my family, there is an ongoing debate over which vegetable we should serve at family gatherings: broccoli or cauliflower. [Problematization:] Each member of the family has a different strongly-held opinion on the matter. [Thesis:] Broccoli is a better overall choice than cauliflower because [Reason I:] broccoli has just as many of the most important vitamins and minerals as cauliflower does; [Reason II:] broccoli has a bolder flavor than cauliflower has; and [Reason III:] broccoli's beautiful, bright green color makes it appear more appetizing on the plate than cauliflower. [Reservation(s):] Some might argue that cauliflower's milder flavor and less vegetable-like color make it a more suitable choice for the young children who attend our gatherings, [Response(s):] but even the most finicky children can often be induced to eat broccoli if cheese is melted over it. Therefore, [Qualified Conclusion:] I propose that broccoli with cheese become the vegetable of choice for all our family gatherings from now on.

With the basic outline of our Toulmin argument in place, we can now prepare to flesh our paper out. We will start by placing our curser immediately behind the thesis and hitting Enter. Then, we'll go to the end of each Reason, Reservation, and Response and do the same. Once we clean the resulting sentences up, we are left with a series of topic sentences that we can expand into new paragraphs.

We can fill out the first paragraph by explaining the exigence and the problematization of the argument in greater detail. For exigence, we might describe how the debate got started or how it has evolved over time. For the problematization, we might offer details on the two (or more) sides of the debate or introduce an element of the debate that has been largely ignored, or we might explain why we think the conversation around the topic has been one-sided or simply wrong. The thesis is our proposed resolution to the problem.

The Battle of the Crucifers: Broccoli vs. Cauliflower

In my family, there is an ongoing debate over which vegetable we should serve at family gatherings: broccoli or cauliflower. Each member of the family has a different strongly-held opinion on the matter. Broccoli is a better overall choice than cauliflower.

Broccoli has just as many of the most important vitamins and minerals as cauliflower does.

Broccoli has a bolder flavor than cauliflower has.

Broccoli's beautiful, bright green color makes it appear more appetizing on the plate than cauliflower.

Some might argue that cauliflower's milder flavor and less vegetable-like color make it a more suitable choice for the young children who attend our gatherings.

Even the most finicky children can often be induced to eat broccoli if cheese is melted over it.

Therefore, I propose that broccoli with cheese become the vegetable of choice for all our family gatherings from now on.

With the first paragraph done, we can move on to the Reasons, Reservation(s), and Response(s). Each of these topic sentences requires

- at least one piece of **Data**, which might include quotations from or summary of scholarly sources, logical proofs, anecdotal examples, and in some cases, even appeals to emotion to support the topic sentence,

- **Warrant(s)**: an analysis of the Data that shows what assumptions we are making in choosing the data that we use, thereby legitimizing our use of data by showing how it relates to our thesis.

Finally, some of our warrants need **Backing**. Backing is additional data used to defend warrants that might not be easily understood or well received by the reader. For example:

[Topic Sentence] Broccoli's beautiful, bright green color makes it appear more appetizing on the plate than cauliflower. [Data] **According to** C. M. Christensen in an article entitled "Effects of color on aroma, flavor and texture judgments of food," trials show that foods are judged to smell better and to taste both stronger and better when they have color compared to foods with no color. [Warrant] While the flavor of food is certainly important—after all, no one wants to eat food that is flavorless or that tastes bad—the food must first make it onto the plate before anyone will know how it tastes. Colorful food is more appetizing than colorless food, and if food does not look appetizing, it will not be eaten, no matter how good it tastes. **If our intent is to provide food that will be appetizing to the greatest number of people who attend our family gatherings,** we can start by serving food that is colorful. [Backing] **Many experienced cooks** instinctively understand the importance of color in food. My grandmother, for example, never set a table with food that was all brown and white; she made sure that every meal included something green, yellow, or red because "it's just how you make a nice dinner." Grandma recognized, even without scientific trials to back her up, that a good meal is a colorful meal. Color should always be taken into account when planning any meal.

Qualifiers are words and phrases that allow us to concede that our argument may have some weak spots. *Usually, sometimes, often, most, virtually,* and *unless* are qualifiers, but there are many more. Rather than granting that eating broccoli is necessary for good health, we can use qualifiers to allow for important contingencies:

Premise 1: Broccoli is **one kind of** vegetable.

Premise 2: A complete meal **may be defined in part** as one that includes at least one vegetable.

Conclusion: Therefore, a meal that includes broccoli **could be considered one example of** a complete meal.

Qualifiers such as the ones above may be used to mitigate the claim to absolute truth in any part of a Toulmin essay, including the Exigence, the Problematization, the Reasons, Data, Warrants, and Backing. Another very important function of qualifiers is to help you the writer broker a compromise with those whose objections to your argument you have anticipated and explicitly stated in the Reservations section. Note the solution to the Reservation expressed below. By proposing that broccoli be served with cheese, we recognize the legitimacy of the Reservation and negotiate a means by which both broccoli lovers and young broccoli haters might be satisfied:

Some might argue that cauliflower's milder flavor and less vegetable-like color make it a more suitable choice for the young children who attend our gatherings, but even the most finicky children can **often** be induced to eat broccoli **if cheese is melted over it**. Therefore, I propose that broccoli **with cheese** become the vegetable of choice for all our family gatherings from now on.

Although **Transitions** are not specifically included in our list of elements essential to argument, they are nonetheless vital to a coherent essay. The individual paragraphs in an argument are not intended to be discrete units; rather, they should reference one another and work together to explicate the thesis. Transitions carry the reader smoothly from one paragraph to another, pointing both backward to the previous paragraph and forward to the idea being presented next. Try to avoid generic transitions. Instead, create transitions that refer back to the previous paragraphs and locate the paragraph at hand within the larger argument. For example, rather than saying,

> **Another reason** to choose broccoli over cauliflower is that broccoli's beautiful, bright green color makes it appear more appetizing on the plate than cauliflower.

Try saying something like,

> **While flavor is an important consideration in our choice of broccoli over cauliflower, taste is of no consequence if the food does not look enticing in the first place.** Broccoli's beautiful, bright green color makes it appear more appetizing on the plate than cauliflower.

By referring back to our discussion of the importance of bold flavor in the previous paragraph, we rise above the plodding "Reason I, Reason II, Reason III" logic of the five-paragraph essay to situate our paragraph on color within the larger pattern of interrelated claims that make up a cohesive argument in favor of broccoli over cauliflower for family gatherings.

Finally, unlike a five-paragraph essay, a college-level essay needs a **Conclusion** that does more than simply reiterate the thesis. In most cases, your conclusion will incorporate the qualifier; thus the **Qualified Conclusion** in our broccoli argument. Additionally, your conclusion should answer several questions:

- **What?** What is the most important thing you want your reader to take away from your essay? What do you want to leave your reader to think about?

- **So what?** Why does this issue matter to the reader? Why should your reader care about your position?

- **What now?** Can the information gleaned from your essay be taken as-is and used for some immediate purpose? Is further research necessary to make a convincing case for your argument? Does your argument suggest other questions that merit investigation?

The model of Toulmin argumentation shown above is a good all-purpose system for organizing ideas and information into a cohesive, readable essay. However, there are other ways of organizing an argument. The one you choose will depend largely on your audience and what you hope to achieve through the argument you present. If you know you already have common ground with your audience and simply want to inform them about something you think they will have little trouble believing once they have the facts, the argument above may suffice. In outline form, that argument looks like this:

Sample Argument #1
I.   Introduction
       A.Exigence
       B.Problematization
       C.Thesis
II.   Reason One (Topic Sentence)
       A.Data
       B.Warrant(s)
       C.(Backing)
III.   Reason Two (Transition and Topic Sentence)
       A.Data
       B.Warrant(s)
       C.(Backing)
IV.   Reason Three (Transition and Topic Sentence)
       A.Data
       B.Warrant(s)
       C.(Backing)
V.   Reservation(s) (Transition and Topic Sentence)
       A.Data
       B.Warrant(s)
       C.(Backing)
VI.   Response(s) (Transition and Topic Sentence)
       A.Data
       B.Warrant(s)
       C.(Backing)

VII.   Qualified Conclusion (What?)

     A. So what?

     B. What now?

If, on the other hand, you have some common ground with your audience but expect resistance to certain parts of your argument, particularly specific pieces of data or the warrants associated with specific data, then outline #2 might work better for you:

Sample Argument #2

I.   Introduction

     A. Exigence

     B. Problematization

     C. Thesis

II.   Reason One

     A. Topic Sentence

          1. Data to support Reason

          2. Warrant(s)

          3. (Backing)

     B. Reservation(s)

          1. Data to explicate Reservation

          2. Warrant(s)

          3. (Backing)

     C. Response(s)

          1. Data to support Response

          2. Warrant(s)

          3. (Backing)

III.   Reason Two

     A. Transition and Topic Sentence

          1. Data to support Reason

          2. Warrant(s)

          3. (Backing)

     B. Reservation(s)

          1. Data to explicate Reservation

          2. Warrant(s)

          3. (Backing)

     C. Response(s)

          1. Data to support Response

          2. Warrant(s)

          3. (Backing)

IV.   Reason Three
    A.Transition and Topic Sentence
        1. Data to support Reason
        2. Warrant(s)
        3. (Backing)
    B.Reservation(s)
        1. Data to explicate Reservation
        2. Warrant(s)
        3. (Backing)
    C.Response(s)
        1. Data to support Response
        2. Warrant(s)
        3. (Backing)
V.   Qualified Conclusion (What?)
    A.So what?
    B.What now?

Finally, you might want to consider sample #3 if you have little or no common ground with your audience and feel that they may be resistant to the argument as a whole. In this model, you put your audience's potential objections on the table from the beginning so that it is immediately clear that you are responding to a contentious, ongoing debate. Sample #3 requires considerable audience interaction with the text and may be most useful for arguments in which you would be satisfied with a compromise or in which you are simply throwing your hat into the ring on a very controversial issue:

Sample Argument #3
I.   Introduction
    A.Exigence
    B.Problematization
    C.Thesis
II.   Reservation(s) One
    A.Topic Sentence
        1. Data to explicate Reservation
        2. Warrant(s)
        3. (Backing)
    B.Response(s) act(s) as Reason
        1. Data to support Response/Reason
        2. Warrant(s)
        3. (Backing)

        4. Qualification(s) of Reason

III.   Reservation(s) Two

    A.Transition and Topic Sentence

        1. Data to explicate Reservation

        2. Warrant(s)

        3. (Backing)

    B.Response(s) act(s) as Reason

        1. Data to support Response/Reason

        2. Warrant(s)

        3. (Backing)

        4. Qualification(s) of Reason

IV.   Reservation(s) Three

    A.Transition and Topic Sentence

        1. Data to explicate Reservation

        2. Warrant(s)

        3. (Backing)

    B.Response(s) act(s) as Reason

        1. Data to support Response/Reason

        2. Warrant(s)

        3. (Backing)

        4. Qualification(s) of Reason

V.   Conclusion (What?)

    A.So what?

    B.What now?

Works Cited

Christensen, C. M. "Effects of color on aroma, flavor and texture judgments of food." *Journal of Food Science* 48 (1983): 787-790. Web. May 2011.

Toulmin, Stephen. *The Uses of Argument*. 1958. Updated ed. Cambridge: Cambridge UP, 2003.

T.R.A.C.E.: Examining the Rhetorical Situation

By Rustian Phelps

Argument, points out Nancy Wood, "does not occur in a vacuum."[1] Indeed, before argument can take place, there must be some reason to construct the argument in the first place—some event or state of affairs that gives rise to the need for the argument. Such an event must necessarily involve controversy; after all, if everyone agrees about what happened, why it happened, and what to do about it, there is nothing to talk about and we can just skip the argument altogether. Moreover, in a written argument, the people concerned with that controversy are as much a part of the argument as the thesis and the data that make up the text. The shape of the argument depends on a set of relationships. One important relationship is the one that exists between the author of the text and his or her intended reader—how they are alike and how they are different. Another relationship exists between those participants (the author and the reader) and the precipitating event or state of affairs. This set of relationships is called the *rhetorical* situation.[2]

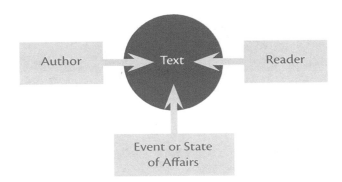

---

1. Wood, Nancy. "The Rhetorical Situation: Understanding Audience and Context." *The Essentials of Argument.* 2nd ed. Upper Saddle River, NJ, USA: Pearson, 2009.

2. For further reading on the rhetorical situation, see Young, Marilyn J. "Lloyd F. Bitzer: Rhetorical Situation, Public Knowledge, and Audience Dynamics." *Twentieth-Century Roots of Rhetorical Studies.* Ed. Jim A. Kuypers and Andrew King. Westport, CT, USA: Greenwood Press, 2001. 275-301. Web. 26 Jan. 2012.

The Rhetorical Situation

To make it easier to understand all that goes into an argument, we organize the five elements of the rhetorical situation according to the acronym TRACE: Text, Reader, Author, Constraints, and Exigence. Each of these elements comes with a set of questions to ask yourself about the argument.

Text:

- What type of text is it? Is it a book? A speech? An article in an academic journal? A film or television program? Is it a cartoon or photograph?

- What is the author's main argument? Is this thesis explicitly stated, or does the reader have to infer the argument from the supporting data or other verbal or visual cues the author provides?

- What is the style of the text? Is it casual, or is it formal? Is it funny? Is it friendly, or is it belligerent? Does the author seem to respect the reader, or is the language patronizing or arrogant? Does the author use academic language? Is the language accessible, or is it difficult to understand?

- What does the style and language of the text say about its credibility? Is it well organized, or is it incoherent? Is it well edited, or is it fraught with grammar and punctuation errors? Is the language ingratiating, inflammatory, or hateful?

- Is the main argument supported with data from reliable sources? Does the author use statistics without revealing where they came from? Does the author jump to conclusions or oversimplify complex issues? Is the evidence provided purely anecdotal?

Reader:

- Who is the author's intended audience? Is the text meant to appeal to young college students? Experts in a particular field? Members of the general public who have special interests? There is no homogenous audience; the world is made up of many small audiences. Remember that audiences with similar interests can still have different expectations of a text based on their experiences, their education levels, and the degree of commitment they have to the issue; readers of *Birds and Blooms* and *The Journal of the American Society for Horticultural Science* are both interested in plants, but the *Birds and Blooms* reader is a hobbyist, while the *The Journal of the American Society for Horticultural Science* is intended for researchers.

- How does the intended audience affect the way the text is presented? Are there lots of pictures for children? Is it short and to-the-point for casual, on-the-go readers? Is it a detailed analysis intended for an academic or professional audience?

- What does the author assume is the position of the audience in regard to the argument? Is the author writing for an audience he or she expects to be receptive? Does he or she expect the audience to be noncommittal, requiring a good deal of effort to get them excited about the topic? Perhaps the intended audience knows little or nothing about the topic and requires education. The author may even be writing for a hostile audience.

- How does the intended audience's position affect the way the author presents the argument? Does the author provide lots of data in the form of charts and graphs? Are there photos or diagrams? Does the author provide copious detail, or does he or she assume the reader is already somewhat informed about the topic?

Author:

- What is the author's area of concentration? Is the author an expert in a particular field, an interested layperson, or someone who has had an interesting experience to tell about?

- How does the author's area of concentration affect his or her point of view? It goes without saying that a college theater major, a psychologist interested in gender studies, and a fundamentalist Christian pastor are going to have very different reasons to write about *The Rocky Horror Picture Show*.

- How reliable is the author? Does the author belong to a nationally recognized organization in the field? Does he or she work for a public or accredited private university? Is the text peer-reviewed? Does the text come from a nationally respected print publication or is the author a well-respected journalist? Does the author have some personal experience that might qualify him or her to weigh in on the subject? Keep in mind that circumstances that seem to you to confer credibility on an author do not necessarily suggest to someone else that the author is reliable. Always consider how others might view the credibility of the author, especially if the author is a controversial figure.

- Does the author seem to respect other points of view, or is he or she clearly biased? Might the author's views be construed as extremist?

Constraints:

- What might cause the author to fail to get his or her message across? Is the text difficult to read or understand? Are there problems with the means of delivery: poor print, video, or sound quality or undue distractions during a public showing or performance? Is there a language barrier or cultural differences that hinder comprehension?

- What might limit the text's readership? Is the text out of date or otherwise irrelevant to many readers? Might the reader consider it offensive? Does the author or one or more of the author's source materials lack credibility? Is the text obscure or hard to locate?

- Does the author have common ground with the audience? Are the author and the audience united by common beliefs, cultural backgrounds, interests, or desires? Without common ground, the author and the reader might as well be speaking different languages. In regard to beliefs, for instance, Garry will not persuade Alice that any tenant of his religion is correct simply by citing his own religious texts because those texts are irrelevant in the decision-making processes of anyone who does not subscribe to Garry's religion. In regard to interests, Nettie will not convince her father that the latest designer shoes are worth $800.00 on the basis that a character on her favorite TV show wears them; Nettie's father does not watch that program and does not care what the characters on that program are wearing.

- Does the argument ask too much of the reader? A very polarizing subject may make it impossible for the reader to accept the truth of the argument. For example, no matter which side Jane takes in the abortion argument, she would have to convince someone on the opposing side that he or she has been, by his or her own definition, a "bad person" before he or she can come round to Jane's point of view. Such an argument might be construed as disrespectful by readers who are morally or ethically bound to their positions on the topic.

Exigence:

- What events or situations occurred to make the author want to write about this topic?

- So what? Why is this argument important?

- What problem might be solved by presenting this argument?

- What is the purpose of the text? Does the author simply want to inform the reader? Confirm the reader's preexisting beliefs? Change the reader's mind about something?

- What reasons does the author offer the reader for considering the text? What ideals or desires does the author hope will motivate the audience? Should the reader expect to be entertained or inspired? Can the reader use the text for educational or self-improvement purposes? Can the reader expect to gain some new understanding about a topic that has heretofore been confusing or worrisome?

- How does the exigence of the text suggest who the intended audience might be and what the constraints of the text might be? Is the topic equally important to both the author and the reader, or must the author convince the reader that the topic is important? Do author and reader share some common experience, such as the shock of 9/11, that inspires both the author to write about it and the reader to read about it?

Close Reading with T.R.A.C.E.

One way to use T.R.A.C.E. is to create a bulleted list to get a clearer sense of what message an author is attempting to convey. T.R.A.C.E. is an invaluable tool for close reading. The following is the text of Abraham Lincoln's Gettysburg Address followed by an example of reading notes in the form of a T.R.A.C.E. analysis.

Gettysburg Address

Fourscore and seven years ago our fathers brought forth on this continent a new nation, conceived in liberty and dedicated to the proposition that all men are created equal.

Now we are engaged in a great civil war, testing whether that nation or any nation so conceived and so dedicated can long endure. We are met on a great battlefield of that war. We have come to dedicate a portion of that field as a final resting-place for those who here gave their lives that that nation might live. It is altogether fitting and proper that we should do this.

But in a larger sense, we cannot dedicate, we cannot consecrate, we cannot hallow this ground. The brave men, living and dead who struggled here have consecrated it far above our poor power to add or detract. The world will little note nor long remember what we say here, but it can never forget what they did here. It is for us the living rather to be dedicated here to the unfinished work which they who fought here have thus far so nobly advanced. It is rather for us to be here dedicated to the great task remaining before us—that from these honored dead we take increased devotion to that cause for which they gave the last full measure of devotion—that we here highly resolve that these dead shall not have died in vain, that this nation under God shall have a new birth of freedom, and that government of the people, by the people, for the people shall not perish from the earth.

TRACE: Gettysburg Address

Text:

- Text is a speech

- Language is formal and a bit old-fashioned

- Tone is reverent and patriotic

- Country founded on the premise that "all men are created equal"

- Civil War a test of the strength of that premise

- "Fitting and proper" to dedicate part of battlefield as a place of rest and remembrance of those who fought and died for that founding ideal

- The sacrifice of the dead, not survivors' feelings, makes that ground sacred

- Work of the living is to continue the struggle for liberty for all

Reader:

- Specifically, those who went to the battlefield for the dedication

- Additionally, locals who went to the battlefield out of curiosity because the President was going to be there

- More broadly, the whole country, still embroiled in the Civil War

- Even more broadly, readers over the last century and a half who have come to see Lincoln's words as a concise definition of the American political and social project

Author:

- Abraham Lincoln, sixteenth President of the United States, during whose administration the American Civil War took place

- Defender of the union and of civic nationalism, denied a moral basis for popular sovereignty and advocated limitations on states' rights

Constraints:

- By many accounts, Lincoln himself may not have considered the speech one of his best efforts. The speech was only ten lines long and took just over two minutes to perform.

- Authenticity of the text: There are at least five different manuscripts of the speech in existence, and several points, especially whether Lincoln included the words "under God," are still disputed.

- Politics: Well into the twenty-first century, the notion of states' rights continues to be a source of contention in American politics.

Exigence:

- Dedication of the Soldiers' National Cemetery at the Civil War battlefield at Gettysburg, Pennsylvania, 1863

- Lincoln was motivated by a desire for national reconciliation

Annotated Bibliographies

T.R.A.C.E. also provides a useful outline for annotated bibliographies. An annotated bibliography is a list of citations for primary texts and other sources of information such as academic journal articles or statistical publications. Each citation (bibliographical entry) is followed by an annotation, a short description of the text, usually just one 150-250 word paragraph. The point of the annotation is to preview the content of the source and to give an assessment of its quality and relevance. The elements of T.R.A.C.E. align well with this purpose. *Text* provides a preview of the content, *Reader* and *Exigence* point to its relevance, and *Author* and *Constraint* speak to the quality of the text. The following is an example of the same T.R.A.C.E analysis you just read used in an annotated bibliography entry. Note that the elements of T.R.A.C.E. have been reordered to make the writing flow better. Note also that only selected points are included for the sake of brevity.

Lincoln, Abraham. "The Gettysburg Address." 19 Nov. 1863. *The Avalon Project*. Yale Law School. Web. 10 Feb. 2012.

(Exigence) President Abraham Lincoln delivered his iconic Gettysburg address at the dedication of the Soldiers' National Cemetery at the Civil War battlefield at Gettysburg, Pennsylvania in 1863. (Text) Lincoln believes that it is "fitting and proper" to dedicate part of the battlefield as a place of rest and remembrance of those who fought and died for the founding ideal that all men are created equal. Lincoln goes on to assert that the work of the living is to continue the struggle for liberty for all. (Reader) Though Lincoln's words at Gettysburg were directed toward Americans still embroiled in the Civil War, current readers continue to see Lincoln's words as a concise definition of the American political and social project. This text is one of the most memorable speeches in American history. (Author) Abraham Lincoln, during whose administration the American Civil War took place, is remembered as a defender of the union and of civic nationalism. His denial of a moral basis for popular sovereignty and his belief in limitations on states' rights still hold weight today. (Constraints) Nonetheless, well into the twenty-first century, the notion of states' rights continues to be a source of contention in American politics.

Sample Toulmin Essay

Teacher's Note

By Justin McCoy

Catherine Lambert's "To Test or Not to Test—That Is the Question" is a final researched position paper for English Composition I. The primary aim of this assignment is to produce an argument-driven essay that not only incorporates credible research for support but also utilizes the Toulmin model of argument as a rhetorical tool for content invention. Lambert's main argument takes a stance on a controversial topic in American culture: standardized testing in public schools. Lambert makes the case that standardized tests are more detrimental than beneficial to student success for three key reasons:

- The time commitment imposed by standardized testing robs students of learning opportunities.
- Standardized tests are not an accurate measure of students' abilities.
- Standardized-test preparation does not translate to college readiness.

Additionally, Lambert objectively characterizes the opposition's side in a rebuttal section that both gives the opposing voices fair treatment and demonstrates that she understands the arguments made across the aisle. This rhetorical move reflects the practices of careful writers intent on crafting convincing arguments for both academic and public projects. Addressing the opposition's arguments objectively before engaging them is a style of civic discourse that will optimize favor with readers who are undecided on the issue.

Ultimately, Lambert concludes that her argument is stronger than the arguments put forth by proponents of standardized testing, pointing to several proposed solutions for measuring student performance that function to weaken her opponents' position. Lambert's essay functions as a contribution to the ongoing conversation linked to standardized testing in public schools and prompts readers to consider the following questions: What is the value of standardized testing? What are its benefits and drawbacks? Where do I, as a reader, stand on the issue? Which path will result in progress for our educational system?

To Test or Not to Test—That Is the Question

Catherine Lambert

Standardized testing has been used in the United States for generations. Through the decades, these tests have been used to gauge students' mastery of school subjects, place students in classes, judge the adequacy of teachers, and determine what types of schools a student can attend. However, in more recent times, the authority of standardized testing has been questioned. The amount of time spent preparing for these tests takes time away from real learning in classrooms. While standardized testing is supposed to be used as a way to recognize students' intelligence, these tests lack in this area in a multitude of ways that could heavily affect America's students. Additionally, colleges and higher education institutes can be selective with their admission without the use of standardized testing. By cutting standardized testing from the curriculum, America can take a large leap toward a better education system.

One of the most detrimental issues of standardized testing is that these tests take valuable classroom time away from students. According to a recent survey, the average student in the United States takes approximately 112 standardized tests between preschool and high school graduation; this amount is equivalent to twenty-five hours of testing per year ("Obama Wants Students to Stop Taking Unnecessary Tests"). Considering the fact that students in the U.S. spend, on average, 6.5 hours per day at school, the prior statistic shows that students spend approximately four days of school merely taking these tests (Nisen). While this amount may not seem lengthy, it does not even account for the myriad of days students spend learning how to take the test by learning how to fill out grids and bubble sheets accurately. When there are only about 180 days of school per school year, this time adds up (Nisen). Schools do not have time to spare, yet they still dedicate so much time to filling in mountains of bubble sheets. This wasted time could be much better spent on actual learning. The real purpose of school is to learn math, science, English, and history, not how to make "educated guesses" and fill in circles. By ridding schools of standardized tests, schools will have more time to teach more valuable skills and students can get the opportunity to learn more.

Standardized testing not only deprives America's students of class time, but the tests also fail to adequately demonstrate students' abilities. According to Richard Delgado, paper-and-pencil tests can demonstrate only a small scale on the broad range of abilities students possess (Delgado 103). While schools directly teach skills like arithmetic and spelling, schools also indirectly teach skills like sociability and problem solving, both of which are just as crucial for surviving in the world as reading and geography. By depending so heavily on standardized testing to gauge students' abilities, many talents are left unseen. This issue could cause a problem in several work fields (Delgado 104). For example, despite being highly intelligent, a political leader without moral sense would prove to be dangerous (Delgado 104). Using standardized tests provides only a demonstration of a fraction of students' abilities. According to Richard Delgado, "[r]ewarding one skill exclusively may not be like having half a loaf of bread, better than none at all" (104). In other words, merely judging a certain skill and not looking at the individual as a whole could lead to major problems because having just one certain skill but lacking another may lead to several problems in the future. If schools cease to depend on standardized testing to determine the intelligence of their students, several problems in the work field can be more easily avoided.

Across the nation, tests such as the ACT and SAT are given to students to determine college readiness and used by colleges as a guide for selective admittance. According to Dana Goldstein, several studies have found that high school grades are much more effective in predicting the performance a student will have in college than SAT scores (Goldstein 11). Additionally, the prep for such tests falls short in teaching students skills important for college success, such as how to research and critical thinking (Goldstein 11). Since standardized tests do not adequately predict the performance of a student in college, their role is obviously unnecessary. A college wants to be selective in who it admits in order to maintain its image. That notion is perfectly understandable, but what is not understandable is why colleges are using such an ineffective method to accomplish this task. By focusing more on how well a student did in high school, demonstrated by his or her grades, colleges can still be selective but also pick their student body more effectively. Doing away with standardized tests would not heed the college admittance process and would better help determine whether students are ready for certain universities.

Of course, there are many who feel standardized testing is a must for success in schools. People such as Dr. Gail Gross believes that standardized testing is a way of efficiently transferring information about students (Gross). Gross argues that "[s]uch testing gives the teacher important diagnostic information about what each child is learning in relation to what he has been taught" (Gross). This argument is supported with the claim that standardized testing is the only effective way of determining whether or not a student needs remediation or if the curriculum matches the course requirements (Gross). Along with diagnostic information, Gross also believes that "[t]he standardized test is an objective and critical measure of achievement in skills, knowledge, and abilities" (Gross). In other words, she feels standardized testing takes any subjective undertones away from the evaluation of a student.

While the opposing party seems to believe standardized testing is how the education system should be run, there are a multitude of more efficient ways of determining what a student has learned during his or her year of school. Major textbook publishers and companies such as Scholastic, Dreambox, and Khan Academy have software that registers every answer a student inputs ("What Schools Could Use Instead Of Standardized Tests"). These "stealth assessments" not only show that mastery students have certain skills, but also demonstrate how quickly students learn and how diligently they work ("What Schools Could Use Instead Of Standardized Tests"). To judge higher-order thinking skills, such as systems thinking or how well a student takes feedback, video-game-like assessments can measure some of the skills that traditional, paper-and-pencil tests cannot measure ("What Schools Could Use Instead Of Standardized Tests"). According to Haley Edwards, Matthew Tosiello used a similar way of testing as the final exam in his science classroom (Edwards 28). The eight and nine-year-old students in his class were asked to design an experiment that would see which of two natural adaptations would help frogs get flies better (Edwards 28). The students used origami frogs and left-over paper from a three-hole punch to simulate frogs and flies. Mathematical concepts in the students such as symmetry and measurement were determined via frog construction because every frog had to be folded precisely and have the same-length tongue (Edwards 28). This experiment also involved students' abilities to form and test a hypothesis, skills that are critical to understanding science. These students were able to be tested in a way that effectively demonstrated their abilities and did not involve the stress of a paper-and-pencil test. While using these alternative methods may seem a bit more precarious in practice, the cons of keeping standardized testing heavily out-weigh the pros of keeping it. School is about cultivating knowledge in students. If schools feel they have to take time away for this cultivating of knowledge and feed it to multiple-choice monsters that fail to test the wide range of knowledge the students have gained in their schooling career when there are a plethora of more effective test routes, it is obvious this system is broken. The education system is what teaches the next generation's youth the knowledge necessary for future success; however, in order to ensure that students retain the information, America needs to take a step away from the traditional paper-and-pencil standardized test. If schools continue to mandate standardized testing, America will continue to inhibit its students from meeting their academic potential. By incorporating alternative test methods into the classroom, a better understanding of what students have learned will lead America down the path of progress, down the path of a better education system for future generations. To test, or not to test—that is the question America faces today.

Works Cited

Delgado, Richard. "Standardized Testing as Discrimination: A Reply to Dan Subotnik." *UMass Law Review* 9.1 (2014): 98-107. *Opposing Viewpoints in Context.* Web. 2 Nov. 2015.

Edwards, Haley S. "Leaving Tests Behind." *Time* 185.5 (2015): 28-31. *Academic Search Complete.* Web. 15 Nov. 2015.

Goldstein, Dana. "Testing testing." *The American Prospect* 20.6 (2009): 11. *Opposing Viewpoints in Context.* Web. 16 Nov. 2015.

Gross, Gail. "The Values of Standardized Testing." *Huff Post Politics.* N.p. 31 July 2013. Web. 7 Dec. 2015.

Kamenetz, Anya. "Obama Wants Students to Stop Taking Unnecessary Tests." *nprEd.* N.p. 24 Oct. 2015. Web. 15 Nov. 2015.

Kamenetz, Anya. "What Schools Could Use Instead Of Standardized Tests." *nprEd.* N.p. 6 Jan. 2015. Web. 15 Nov. 2015.

Nisen, Max. "America Needs to Suck it Up and Make School Days Longer." *Business Insider.* N.p. 1 Oct. 2013. Web. 15 Nov. 2015.

Rogerian Argument

The Rogerian (or common ground) argument is named for psychologist Carl Rogers. It is most effective for arguments that attempt to establish common ground between opponents on an issue. Rogerian arguments exhibit these characteristics:

1. Includes an introduction: An introduction states the problem to be considered, explaining how it affects the people involved.

2. Presents common ground and common arguments: In a much different move than the Toulmin model, the rhetor voices the common ground between the two sides of the issue, as well as the arguments of the two sides, stated in neutral language.

3. Takes a position: The rhetor reveals his or her position, asking that the audience consider it but without saying it is better.

4. Ends with a positive: The Rogerian argument ends on a positive note, describing how the rhetor's position could, at least in some instances, benefit the opposition.

Teacher's Note by Jasara Norton

Tabitha Read-Cayton's "Should the UK Accept More Refugees?" addresses a highly controversial topic: the Syrian refugee crisis. Read-Cayton chose to write about this topic using the Rogerian argument, a model that emphasizes common ground between opponents as opposed to elimination of opponents' objections. By using this model, Read-Cayton explores rather than asserts, providing a guide for meaningful dialogue about a topic that is naturally provocative. If we think of rhetoric as acts of communication designed to bring together rather than divide audiences, the invitational tone of this essay becomes particularly significant. Can you identify the varying positions Read-Cayton explores? Where does she place these points, and how does that placement lead to her conclusion? What is her conclusion?

Sample Rogerian Essay
ENC 1101 Essay Award

Should the UK Accept More Refugees?

Tabitha Read-Cayton

Experts have called it the worst refugee crisis since World War II. The ever-growing refugee crisis is causing chaos in Europe as millions of refugees flee war-ridden countries like Syria and Iraq. They hope to seek refuge in peaceful Europe, but with more refugees arriving than given asylum, many are left stranded in makeshift camps on the borders. These camps are squalid conditions and are not at all what these troubled people imagined their new lives in Europe would be like. Adding to the problem is the fact that the refugee crisis is not slowing down, with more and more refugees fleeing Syria every day. E. Tendayi Achiume's recent peer-reviewed scholarly article "Syria, Cost-sharing, and the Responsibility to Protect Refugees" states that "in March 2013, the number of refugees fleeing Syria hit the one million mark and as of August 2015 this number had more than quadrupled" (697). These figures indicate that more refugees will continue to flee and suggests the situation will only deteriorate if no action is taken. The situation will continue to worsen due to the violent and on-going civil war in Syria that was triggered by protests against President Assad. The unforgiving war is leaving innocent Syrian people feeling unsafe in their own country, and they have naturally responded by escaping the danger and fleeing the country, leaving us with the debate of whether the UK should accept more refugees.

Some people believe that the UK should not accept more refugees because they believe it will damage the culture, cost too much, and result in economic migrants rather than refugees. Yet with Great Britain already such a multicultural population, I do not expect that accepting more refugees will make any difference to our culture. According to the "2011 Census Analysis" by the Office for National Statistics, "the multicultural population in the whole UK is 7.5 million" (2). Accepting a few thousand more refugees is unlikely to endanger our cultural stability. In her speech to the Centre of European Reform, Shadow home secretary Yvette Cooper claimed that, "If every area in the UK took just 10 families, we could offer sanctuary to 10,000 refugees." This statistic demonstrates what a hardly noticeable impact these refugees would have on the lives of British people and the existing culture of the UK while also helping those in need. Many people also worry about the cost of accepting more refugees, which is understandable considering the significant funds required for housing and healthcare for each refugee as well as support needed for adjusting to their new lives. Some are also concerned about how we will tell who is a genuine refugee and who is an economic migrant just looking for a better job. This concern is a genuine issue because many of these refugees arrive in Europe without any form of identification, making it difficult to tell if they are who they claim to be. However, Pinar Yazgan, et al suggest in the scholarly journal "Syrian Crisis and Migration," that the difference between refugees and economic migrants is in fact "imagined" (182). Yazgan, et al explain that "most economic migrants have some story of difficulty driving them to other countries whilst all refugees have an obvious economic cause along with the immediate threat they are escaping from" (182). It seems that all refugees have an economic reason pushing them away, and after everything they have been through to get to Europe, we should do anything we can to help them.

Those who oppose Great Britain accepting more refugees have raised concerns that accepting more refugees will not only fail to solve the crisis, but may actually worsen it. These concerns are very plausible because, just as the previous Prime Minister David Cameron spoke about in a video clip with *The Guardian* in September 2015, the whole crisis cannot be solved simply by accepting more refugees because, no matter how many refugees we accept, if the war continues, people will continue to flee. Instead, Cameron suggests that our focus should be to "try to bring peace and stability to that part of the world." Although stopping a large civil war is easier said than done, I agree with Cameron's sentiment: ending war is the only way the crisis will ever truly end because the war is the trigger and cause of the whole refugee crisis. It is also possible that accepting more refugees will worsen the problem because it will encourage more people to make the same dangerous journey to Europe. Yazgan, et al suggest that "people make decisions to move based on hearsay—often good stories relayed by past movers" (184). This account indicates that we may worsen the situation further by accepting more refugees because they may contact their friends and relatives in their home country and encourage them to make the life-threatening journey too. Despite these extremely valid concerns, it is hard to see how the crisis will ever improve without the already large and displaced population of refugees being rehomed.

Ultimately, we have a moral responsibility and obligation to help others who are in danger, especially since our nation is stable and developed. Achiume speaks about this responsibility to protect (RtoP) in his article "Syria, Cost-sharing and the Responsibility to Protect Refugees." Achiume affirms our responsibility to protect refugees by stating that, "RtoP conceives of sovereignty as entailing a responsibility on each state to protect its territorial population from genocide, crimes against humanity, ethnic cleansing, and war crimes (RtoP crimes)" (691). Achiume goes further by extending this responsibility to protect to the international community (691). It would be inhumane to allow any of the RtoP crimes to happen, no matter what our financial or political situation were. The United Kingdom is a wealthy country that can afford to help others, which gives even more reason that the UK should accept more refugees alongside searching for other solutions to the refugee crisis.

There are many possible benefits available to us if we accept more refugees. Offering refuge would not only improve the lives of thousands of innocent victims of war and improve the European refugee crisis, but it also would provide a number of highly-valued and professionally-qualified workers and would further enrich our culture. A recent online article in the *International Business Times* by Jess McHugh explains how the stereotype that refugees are useless to society and live off the state is highly inaccurate. McHugh gives evidence from the United Nations and other aid organizations that have shown that "the majority of people [refugees] arriving in Europe often come from upper middle class, well-educated backgrounds." These findings are most likely because only those wealthy enough to afford education could afford to make the lengthy and expensive journey to Europe. The United Nation's data also indicates that many refugees are highly-qualified professionals, such as doctors and bankers who could help to fill some of the gaps in the British job market. Moreover, accepting more refugees will provide a safe, new start for troubled refugees and will reduce the number of refugees held in squalid camps; therefore, easing the crisis. Furthermore, accepting more refugees will help to further enrich our already culturally diverse country.

There are numerous examples of when accepting refugees has been achieved successfully, including several other European countries that have already made promising steps towards accepting more refugees and the UK itself. Germany's open-door policy and welcoming attitude towards refugees provides a positive example for Great Britain. The German Chancellor recently announced that they will accept many more refugees. These encouraging signs show that if each European country, including the UK, did its part, we would be much closer to solving the crisis. Further examples include the UK's, which has a long history of accepting refugees, providing evidence that they will not harm or change our culture and values. All these examples illustrate that if the refugees are well-integrated, accepting more refugees can be a successful and smooth process.

Being a British citizen myself, I am deeply affected by the refugee crisis and have been particularly moved by the awful things that have been happening so close to the country I call home. I have heard of too many tragedies involving desperate refugee families trying to reach Europe. I believe that, for the time being, the best solution for the UK is to take in more refugees because, above anything else, we have a moral responsibility to help and protect innocent civilians fleeing war. I accept that taking in more refugees is not going to completely resolve the problem, so the UK should continue to search for other solutions for the refugee crisis. This problem will not be going away in the near future unless we stop overlooking the severity of the crisis and address the issue accordingly. For now, all we can do is accept our fair share of refugees, encourage other countries to do the same where possible, and search for solutions to end the crisis completely. Ending the crisis entirely would involve stopping the cause of the crisis: the war.

Works Cited

Achiume, Tendayi. "Syria, Cost-sharing, and the Responsibility to Protect Refugees." *Minnesota Law Review*, Vol. 100, Issue 2, 2015, pp. 687–762. *EBSCO* ezproxy.lib.uwf.edu/login?url=http://search.ebscohost.com/login.aspx?direct=true&db=lft&AN=112011554&site=eds-live.

Cameron, David. *The Guardian Newspaper*, 2 September 2015, Northamptonshire. www.theguardian.com/world/2015/sep/02/david-cameron-migration-crisis-will-not-be-solved-by-uk-taking-in-more-refugees.

Cooper, Yvette. "The Growing Refugee Crisis." The Centre for European Reform, 1 September 2015, London.

McHugh, Jess. "Europe Refugee Crisis Facts: Wealthy, Educated Syrians Risking Lives to Leave War." *International Business Times.* 9 September 2015, www.ibtimes.com/europe-refugee-crisis-facts-wealthy-educated-syrians-risking-lives-leave-war-2089018.

2011 Census analysis: Ethnicity and religion of the non-UK born population in England and Wales. Office for National Statistics. 18 June 2015, www.ons.gov.uk/peoplepopulationandcommunity/culturalidentity/ethnicity/articles/2011censusanalysisethnicityand relegionof henukbornpopulationinenglandandwales/2015-06-18

Yazgan, Pinar, et al. "Syrian Crisis and Migration." *Migration Letters*, Vol. 12, Issue 3, 2015, pp. 181-192. EBSCO. ezproxy.lib.uwf.edu/login?url=http://search.ebscohost.com/login.aspx?direct=true&db=a9h&AN=110010898&site=eds-live.

General Modern Format

The general modern format for argument is one that will probably be familiar to you from previous English classes. It is a format that you can use when your argument does not fit neatly into either the Toulmin or Rogerian patterns. Moreover, you can adapt it to serve the needs of your argument. Organize your text similarly to the five-paragraph essay.

1. Introduction: State your thesis in an introductory section that provides background, an anecdote, quote, or other information that gets the attention of your audience and provides a context for your thesis.

2. Main points: Two or three sections each present a major point that supports your thesis.

3. Counterargument: The next section presents a counterargument, which anticipates audience questions or objections and is followed by a rebuttal of the counterargument.

4. Conclusion: A conclusion ties the argument together, perhaps by reflecting back to the introduction or issuing a call for action.

First-Person Exigence: You Mean I Can Use First Person in My Paper?

By Jasara Norton

Most of us have been told, at one time or another, not to use first person in academic writing. Teachers establish this rule for good reason: academic writing requires a level of discipline and self-restraint. Writers build credibility through rigorous research and careful presentation of that research. They qualify their language and strive to establish common ground to better reach their audience. All of these decisions result in a tone that some interpret as objective.

As you can see, what objective really means is deliberate restraint designed to persuasively connect with an audience. Based on this clarification of perceived objectivity, we begin to understand that it is possible to be "objective" and personal at the same time. In fact, personal context can be an effective means of creating a reason and an appeal for your argument.

Earlier in this chapter, you learned that this reason for an argument is called **exigence**. To determine the exigence for an argument, we ask, "Why is the author writing this?" Every argument comes with context, and strong writers purposefully acknowledge and communicate that context in their writing. Oftentimes, that context either stems from or is reflective of your own experiences in some way. We call this **first-person exigence**. Writers who use first-person exigence identify and explore their personal interest in and motivation for a selected topic or research question. This type of exigence acknowledges that meaningful research requires curiosity and genuine inquiry. In other words, on some level, meaningful research starts with the self.

The idea of a research process based on genuine inquiry is a significant aspect of writing rhetorically. One prominent rhetorician, Lloyd F. Bitzer, writes in "The Rhetorical Situation" that exigence "strongly invites utterance."[1] He explains how "this invited utterance participates naturally in the situation, is in many instances necessary to the completion of situational activity." Essentially, exigence isn't borrowed. It isn't inherited or a hand-me-down. It is functional in that it is embedded in the particular human behavior of a particular situation.

Your job, then, is to investigate your own situations. Perhaps, the first step is to simply realize that you have situations. Whatever interests you, excites you, confuses you, worries you, or inspires you—these are the moments when your essay begins. Your experiences, perceptions, and concerns shape the direction of your research and writing. Without these real situations, our classroom acts are empty exercises, but when you intentionally engage with first-person exigence, you will be well on your way to making meaning rather than simply performing an assignment.

So, let us suspend the well-intentioned but perhaps oversimplified rule to avoid first person and take the opportunity to recognize that first-person exigence can be a powerful, even integral, part of academic writing.[1]

How to Use First Person in Academic Writing

Simply incorporating the word *I* into your essay does not mean that you necessarily have provided personal context for your argument. Consider the common phrase, "I believe." You might be tempted to begin your thesis statement with this phrase as a way of providing personal context for your argument. However, because the thesis statement for an argument is a personal statement of belief or opinion whether or not you use first person, an "I believe" phrase is redundant.

Instead, think of first-person exigence as a substantive process rather than a last-minute edit. Below are a few activities to help you engage with first-person exigence:

1) Narrate your research and writing process.

    a. One way to do this is to keep a research journal that begins at the beginning. How did you develop your research question or research topic? What were you doing when you thought of the topic? Why is that topic important to you personally? How does it relate to your life, past, or present?

---

1 See pages 4-5 of the *Philosophy & Rhetoric*'s 1992 supplementary issue, available at jstor.org/stable/40237697.

b. Once you begin researching your topic, incorporate first-person narration into your annotations. How does the research change the way you feel about your topic? Does it inspire you? Worry you? Confuse you? Does it change your opinion?

2) When you begin composing a draft, purposefully incorporate pieces of this narrative into your essay. This genuine reflection is sometimes the most compelling part of an argument. For example, don't be afraid that expressing confusion will undermine your position. Rather, it might just be the moment that, because of its honest investigation, is most persuasive to your reader.

3) Incorporate first-person explanation *after* writing a draft. The best way to accomplish this task is to look for two things in the draft: a) an under-developed introduction/conclusion and b) under-supported borrowed material.

a. Under-developed introductions and conclusions are often short and repetitive. This kind of introduction is one that skips steps. It might begin with a sweeping generalization and then jump to an opinion about a topic without sufficient explanation. An under-developed conclusion is one that is usually merely summary and, therefore, unimaginative; however, a conclusion should both summarize *and* persuade. Using the personal to further contextualize your argument can help solve this issue of under-developed introductions and conclusions.

b. Any idea that is not your own must be contextualized, a concept most often referred to as "avoiding plagiarism." For example, you learned to avoid plagiarism by citing paraphrases and quotes. But distinguishing between your voice and someone else's is more complex than simply providing a page number. What is your response to the quote or paraphrase? How does it impact your opinion on the topic? How do you interpret the material, and how is that interpretation specific to your personal experience and concerns? This first-person response to other voices is an important part of making your argument as full and persuasive as possible.

i. Additionally, sometimes you provide material that is common knowledge for you but not your audience. These moments are further opportunity for you to provide relevant first-person context. Tell your reader why and how you know that material, a writing practice that not only helps demonstrate exigence but also helps establish credibility.

4) Read the sample student essay "Buying Bisexuality." What is the exigence for this student's argument? Does the student's use of first person enhance the essay's persuasiveness? Why or why not? What other first-person context might make the essay more compelling? What assumptions does the first-person context make? Do you agree with those assumptions? Why or why not?

ENC 1101 Student Essay with First-Person Exigence

Teacher's Note by Jasara Norton

Mollie Lynch's "Buying Bisexuality" is a final research essay written in an English Composition 1101 course. Her topic selection reflects the theme of the course, titled, Critical Perspectives of Advertising. In the essay, Lynch examines the ubiquity of advertising appeals and the difficulty in separating consumerism from identity. More specifically, Lynch's essay reflects a personal exploration of the intersection between bisexuality and advertising. Lynch's implied research question is not the dispassionate inquiry we often think of when we hear the phrase research question, such as, how does advertising affect bisexuality? Rather, she asks the much more intimate question: am I truly bisexual? At the center of this question is a rhetorical awareness of exigence. How does this awareness inform other writing choices? What is the impact of first-person usage on author credibility? Also, how can we incorporate personal inquiry without losing the rigors of the research essay genre?

ENC 1101 Essay Award

Mollie Nichole Lynch

Buying Bisexuality

I am a bisexual adolescent female. How do I "come out" when bisexuality is so often confused with being a slut? Many people believe that bisexuality is a phase, saying it is the confusion of physical gratification for sexual and emotional attraction. In many cases this definition is true; sexualized imagery in advertising impacts gender identity in adolescent females unethically and significantly, particularly in regards to bisexuality. These advertisements prey on the vulnerability of adolescents throughout a crucial developmental period, altering our perception of conventional sexual partnering, and using subliminal gender roles in product advertisements.

As previously mentioned, one common misconception about bisexuality is that those who claim a bisexual identity do not have a heightened sexual attraction to both sexes, but instead have heightened sexual urges which they are willing to allow either sex to fulfill. In order to understand the true nature of bisexuality, one must analyze the continuum of sexuality and its components. In "Identity Development and Exploration among Sexual Minority Adolescents: Examination of a Multidimensional Model," the authors define sexual orientation, stating that it includes identity, attraction, and behaviors. This article explores the Storm Model and concludes that within each of these sub-categories of sexual orientation ranges a dimension between heterosexual and homosexual with variations of asexuality and homosexuality in between. Therefore, sexual orientation is a continuum, and each individual can find his or her identity somewhere on the continuum of sexuality. Bisexuality is often thought to be a median of homosexual and heterosexual attraction; it is, rather, a heightened attraction in both respects. To identify as asexual, however, is to have low levels of attraction to both sexes according to the model Storm presents. On the continuum of sexuality, psychologists accept asexuality as being on the left side of the spectrum, while bisexuality falls into place on the right.

The idea of sexual identity in adolescents is complex because this time is a crucial developmental period during which sexual identity is fully developed. There are several different interpretations of what age ranges encompass adolescence, however, in this essay the focus is on ages ten to nineteen. Identity, attraction, and behavior are components which adolescents explore throughout this developmental period in order to develop a more cohesive identity, a concept which is commonly discussed in many self-help books. The cohesive identity is fully formed when one recognizes different aspects of self, including but not limited to sexual orientation, moral standards, belief systems, values, and personality types (Priebe, 730). During this developmental period, adolescents form their own cohesive identities while also striving to maintain a sense of belonging, feeling both independent and supported.

Today in the media, parents and adults are portrayed through certain stereotypes. Television shows commonly depict fathers as being incompetent or distant, mothers as being dedicated to work or the family unit, and siblings as individuals who battle for attention. Examples of this formula are found in shows such as *Modern Family, Wizards of Waverly Place, Family Guy, Pretty Little Liars, Awkward,* and *That's So Raven*. The primary focus of these shows and many others is the dysfunction of the family unit, and a byproduct of most of these shows is a secondary focus on the importance of strong friendships outside the family unit. From a young age, children learn to identify friends and peers as those to surround themselves with. This behavior is learned by adolescence, where each individual yearns for a group and social acceptance. Because of the "hipster" culture, a culture which celebrates the idea of being the first to start a fashion, music fixation, belief, idea, or movement, bisexuality is becoming increasingly trendy. Bisexuality is an idea which advertisers sell along with the other trends. Because of hipster culture's demand to stay up to date with trends, many adolescents are influenced to identify with the bisexuality these advertisements promote.

Although the majority of those who identify as homosexual or bisexual will remain consistent in that identity over time, one still must question the effect that the eroticization of images in advertising and the exaltation of the hipster fad plays on the development of gender identity throughout the period of adolescence. Keeping up on the latest trends is a behavior which allows adolescents to establish a sense of belonging with their peers, a behavior which is important because it is the learned support system for the millennial generation. During adolescence, the understanding of an individual's sexuality becomes a priority, quest-like in nature, as does the need for acceptance. When girls see advertisements which glorify bisexuality, they are likely to equate bisexual identity with social acceptance.

The eroticization of advertisements unethically encourages both sexual exploration and immediate gratification throughout the crucial developmental period of adolescence, leading to an increase in sexual experimentation at increasingly younger ages and in turn resulting in potential mental, emotional, and physical health risks. These risks are prevalent in females within primary and secondary schooling environments. Increased sexual experimentation throughout adolescence has the potential to lead to multiple partners and consequently sexually transmitted infections, as well as pregnancy. Other possible results of early and excessive experimentation are low self-esteem, self-image disorders, and heightened uncertainty or confusion regarding sexual identity.

Previously, advocacy groups said 10% of the American population did not identify as heterosexual. 10% was not an actual statistic; however, it was a number large enough to warrant equal rights for the 10%, and small enough so as not to raise concern for those against a non-heterosexual lifestyle. In 2011, nine million Americans, or 4% of the population, identified as homosexual or bisexual. From those 4%, 1.8% identified as bisexual, and an additional 3.5% are estimated to be "closeted" bisexuals. A total estimate of 5.2% of the American population identified as bisexual, 2.2% identified as homosexual, and an insignificant amount of those who were homosexual and remained "closeted" throughout their entire lifetime (Donaldson-James). These statistics support my warrant that as advertising becomes more predominant, so too does the development of a bisexual identity. Though the correlation between increased advertising and increased bisexuality does not necessarily relate directly, much evidence supports that these issues are related.

Images of women of all ages are sexualized in magazines. Images illustrate a heightened reality of sexuality by portraying women posed erotically and wearing little or no clothing. Women are posed embracing one another, close in contact, touching or looking at the other in a way that is uncommon in everyday life. The men paired with women in magazines such as *Seventeen*, *Teen Vogue*, and *CoverGirl*, publications which target adolescent female consumers, often have feminine features. This portrayal constitutes as subliminal messaging. Often magazine readers may have difficulty differentiating whether pairs advertised in these magazines are a man and a woman, a man and a man, or a woman and a woman. The lines between friendship and sexuality are also often blurred as couples are presented doing everyday activities yet are posed in ways which increase the sexuality of an everyday interaction. The sexualized images in these magazines evoke an emotional response from adolescent females who already question their acceptance, identity, and independence within their support systems. The vagueness in interactions between different sexes is likely an attempt to alter perceptions of conventional partnering and allow adolescents to make their own decisions and explore more fully their sexual identity.

It seems this attempt by advertisers to alter perceptions of conventional partnering has rather added to the confusion adolescents experience when developing a sexual identity. Girls emulate the models they see in hopes of being sexy, beautiful, and ultimately, accepted. When girls are frequently exposed to models posed together in a heightened sexual reality they consider this both common and trendy. Adolescents then experiment with their sexuality, engaging in sexual activities with both men and women. As the formation of a cohesive identity is not yet developed, adolescents are primarily reliant on the approval of their peers. The affirmation from male peers upon hearing about same sex encounters validates these girls, as does the admiration of other female peers who have yet to be bold enough to engage in such activities. Also, the physical gratification of same sex interactions paired with the validation from peers is easily confused with having an actual emotional and physical attraction to the same sex. Adolescents often claim they are bisexual, however an increasing amount of adolescents are misidentifying their sexual orientation, largely because of the influence of trendy teen magazine advertisements. As seen in the hipster culture, the first girls to catch on to a popular trend gain the most recognition, acclaim, and admiration. The millennial generation is beginning to stray away from a slow learned development of their sexual orientation to a rapid and urgent approach to discovering sexuality. "First is the worst, second is the best," is no more due to the hipster epidemic.

Another approach advertisers are taking emphasizes a change in direction in the portrayal of men and women and is common in male-focused advertisements. In "Beyond the 'Sexualization of Culture' Thesis: An Intersectional Analysis of 'Six packs,' 'Midriffs,' and 'Hot Lesbians' in Advertising," Rosalind Gill asserts that advertisers are shifting from the objectification of women in male focused advertisements to a new concept of "subjectification." Consequently, there is a shift from male subjectification in advertising to male objectification. The male body is now toned and eroticized, much like female advertisements have been for decades; however, women are now portrayed as sexual subjects (Gill, 143). This means that women are displayed in advertisements owning their sexuality and using it to their advantage rather than men taking advantage of feminine sexuality. This shift is also occurring in pornography, a new emphasis on female domination in sexual encounters. Not only are men being dominated by women in pornography, but lesbian pornography is becoming more predominant, and it is not uncommon that men utilize lesbian pornography. These subliminal gender roles in product advertisements, as well as within the subculture of pornography alter both the male and female perceptions on feminine sexuality. Adolescent males, when exposed frequently to these advertisements, are likely to perceive females as being confident sexual firecrackers, willing to engage in sexual activity with anyone of any gender at any place and time. Adolescent females are again exposed to the idea that a heightened sexuality is necessary in order to gain acceptance from their peers and feel more confident in their development of a cohesive identity.

Perhaps advertisers are making these changes in order to follow suit with the Hollywood movement to legalize non-heterosexual marriages in the United States by targeting adolescents with these new advertising styles as they will soon be voters. By making bisexuality appealing to both adolescent males and females, advertisers are more likely to gain momentum in legalizing same sex marriages. Rather than solely enforcing equal rights, the actions taken by the advertisement industry simply adds to the confusion adolescents already experience in regards to their sexuality. It is evident that advertisers do indeed prey on the vulnerability of adolescent females throughout a crucial developmental period, and there is no doubt that these advertisements alter perceptions of conventional partnering, and utilize subliminal gender roles in product advertisements to suit their own agenda. The consequences adolescents face because of this new approach to advertising can be life changing. I have done my research and am aware on where I stand in regards to my emotional and physical attractions: on the far right of the continuum; yet as I write this, part of me wonders if I am truly bisexual, or if I am simply buying bisexuality. How much of my sexuality has been influenced because of messages received from advertising and the media? Advertisers are not doing adolescents any favors, and I would propose that they leave sexuality out of this new Hollywood hipster culture.

Works Cited

Donaldson-James, Susan. "Gay Americans Make up Four Percent of Population." *World News.* ABC News, 8 April 2011. Web. 29 Oct 2013. <http://abcnews.go.com/Health/williams-institute-report-reveals-million-gay-bisexual-transgender/story?id=13320565>. Search Path: Google.

Galliher, Renee V., Jenna A. Glover, and Trenton G. Lamere. "Identity Development and Exploration among Sexual Minority Adolescents: Examination of a Multidimensional Model." *Journal of Homosexuality* 56.1 (2009): 77-101. *Academic Search Complete.* Web. 28 Oct 2013.

Gill, Rosland. "Beyond the 'Sexualization of Culture' Thesis: An Intersectional Analysis of 'Six packs,' 'Midriffs,' and 'Hot Lesbians' in Advertising." *Sexualities* 12.2 (2009): 137-60. *Academic Search Complete.* 29 Oct 2013.

Gill, Rosland, Sue Jackson, and Tina Vares. "Preteen Girls Read 'Tween' Popular Culture: Diversity, Complexity, and Contradiction." *International Journal of Media & Cultural Politics* 7.2 (2011): 139-54. *Academic Source Complete.* Web. 30 Oct 2013.

Priebe, Gisela, and Carl Göran Sveden. "Operationalization of Three Dimensions of Sexual Orientation in a National Survey of Late Adolescents." *Journal of Sex Research.* 50.8 (2013): 727-38 *Academic Search Complete.* Web. 28 Oct 2013.

Teacher's Note by Karen Manning

In her ENC 1101 research essay, "The Abusive Effects Left on a Child," Elexus Toque explores her memories, develops critical thinking regarding her lived experiences, and invents from the source of these memories. She therefore demonstrates an ability to move into the greater cultural conversation by analyzing her past. She reconstructs and regenerates her story to address the current, pressing cultural issue of domestic violence and the effects it has on children. Toque invites her readers to explore with her questions regarding how children of domestic violence perceive love. How does domestic violence affect relationships between children and victim-parents? What kinds of relationships do children of domestic violence seek later in life? She places her most powerful prose at the beginning of her piece, establishing upfront her profound *ethos* and utilizing *pathos* to signify to her readers the importance of these questions. She also establishes *logos*, using secondary sources to delineate the physical and psychological trauma that children of domestic violence endure and then comparing this research with her own experiences. Toque successfully constructs a research essay that is unique, because it is informed by her distinct perspectives, and yet the essay speaks to others because she allows her personal narrative to be published and studied.

ENC 1101 Essay Award

The Abusive Effects Left on a Child

Elexus Toque

Standing in the hallway, I see my mother hit her face on the door frame and fall to the ground as my stepdad stands over her, ready to leave the marks that show he is in control. His red, heartless eyes stare at my fearful face. Sadly, millions of children witness similar abuse between parents and see the same heartless eyes that once stared at me. Parents allow a child to see, hear, and sometimes be a part of the abuse. An ongoing controversial debate exists regarding whether children should stay with their parents even if one may be abusive. This situation is important according to Ramona Alaggia because domestic abuse poses a higher risk compared to other child maltreatment cases. Out of 785 cases that she evaluated, twenty-six percent were domestic cases (1). A parent's responsibility is to ensure the child's safety even if the job includes being a single parent. Children need to be removed from these abusive situations because as witnesses, children end up having the wrong idea of what love really is. Also, domestic violence can cause psychological and physical problems for the children, which can drastically affect their views on life.

When children witness abuse between parents, physically or verbally, their views on what love should look like change. While children are growing up, they are taught life lessons by their parents. Fighting between the two parents can impact a child emotionally; an example of this type of impact is evident in a video by Dr. Phil, in which an eighteen-year-old girl believes that her boyfriend loves her because he is willing to go to jail for abuse if she calls the police. Dr. Phil advises the woman that she should not say things such as "love is abuse," especially on social media, because younger girls might see her situation and stay in abusive relationships thinking that it is love (McGraw). According to Unicef, many girls and boys that witness abuse toward their mother actually follow in their parents' footsteps. A son might feel as if abuse is acceptable because it was the only relationship he saw between his father and mother. A daughter might be fine with being abused because that is the only type of "love" she saw growing up (Unicef 7). This feeling is familiar to me because I ended up in an abusive relationship since it was something to which I was exposed. I felt that it was not bad since my parents did not leave their abusive relationships because they were "in love." I thought that if I was strong, then my boyfriend's abuse toward me, emotionally and sometimes physically, would pass and get better. Girls need to be shown that love occurs when a man does not put his hand on them or break them down in order to keep them by his side. However, if a mother does not dispel the idea that abuse is love, her children will continue their own relationships following their parents' example.

After years of abuse, a victim may have psychological problems that take a lifetime to heal, if the problems can heal, yet what people do not see is that children who witness abuse become victims as well. Children who witness abuse can have mental health issues such as depression, anxiety, and post-traumatic stress disorder, just like their mothers (Culp-Ressler). Unfortunately, people do not understand that seeing abuse can ruin relationships between family members. When a child witnesses his or her caretaker being abused, the relationship between the two is broken. Children may feel betrayed because the person who is supposed to protect them cannot. Diane Tatum, from Child Protection Services, uses the term "failure to protect" for cases similar to this because the adult victim cannot take care of the child when being abused (288). The abuse not only psychologically breaks the bond between mother and child, but also physically causes a child to lose all hope and have serious mental issues as a result of his or her loss. I experienced these mental issues when I felt that my mother cared for men more than her own children. I blamed my mother for staying in an abusive relationship, causing me to neglect her as a person, let alone as a mother, because I no longer felt safe in the place I called home. One thing I learned is that children should not have to worry about whether they should stay up at night because their parents might start fighting again.

While the psychological effects cause problems internally, there are multiple effects on a child physically when witnessing abuse.

The organization, Bethesda House, states that children from infants to teenagers suffer different effects and symptoms based on their age. Bethesda House states the following:

> Kids from ages 0-5 years old usually have symptoms like stomach aches, fear of the dark, sleep disturbances, bed wetting, whining, clinging, anxiety, and failure to thrive. While kids ranging from 6-12 years of age commonly have symptoms like seductive or manipulative behavior, eating disturbances, distrustful of people, fear of being abandoned, difficulty concentrating in school, girls may become passive while boys may become aggressive.

Many children in my family suffer from these symptoms; for example, a three-year-old child that I would watch occasionally grew up seeing abuse between his mother and father. Over the years, he has become scared of the dark and has a hard time sleeping through the night. If he wakes up, he cries, unsure of what is going on around him, and he occasionally wets the bed. Even though these effects are bad, there are other effects including depression, antisocial behavior, low self-esteem, the presence of pervasive fear, loneliness, school difficulties, peer conflict, impaired cognitive functioning, suicide attempts, and increases in the likelihood of substance abuse (Metcalfe). The three-year-old was living a child's worst nightmare, including heartbreaking moments when his parents were abusive in front of him, as he sat on the floor playing with a toy, acting as if the abuse was not happening. Being in an abusive home creates stress and depression in children while growing up, even if the children are not being abused. Unfortunately, many kids that leave an abusive home tend to still have these symptoms as adults, leading to more severe and dangerous illnesses over time when they do not receive proper help and treatment.

Even though a child's safety is at risk, many people will disagree with my statement promoting the removal of a child from an abusive home because of three main ideas. First, some believe that children should stay with both parents as long as the child is not being physically harmed. Since a child is not put in imminent danger, people see this as proof that an abuser can still love and care for his or her child. Second, many people believe that a woman might not leave because she lacks resources and education to take care of the child alone. As described above, the term "failure to protect" describes circumstances in which a victim of spousal abuse may not be able to care for the child the way the child needs (Tatum 288). Third, researcher Faye Blair states that children who witness domestic violence still tend to be "normative" overall even after years of watching the abuse between parents (26). Certainly, being with both parents is important because growing up in a single-parent household is not an easy task; when people have children, both parents should share the responsibility of caring for the child. However, a child who witnesses abuse is also being abused emotionally and mentally, and additionally may suffer the physical effects, discussed above. Children are also victims in the fights during and after the battles.

As important as it is for children to be with their parents, the physical and psychological effects cannot be ignored; these effects are why a child needs to be removed from the abusive home. Furthermore, when a victim leaves the relationship, his or her connections with the abuser do not end. Ramona Alaggia talks about how many cases stay open for months, even years, because mothers try to allow the father to be a part of the child's life (90). Programs should be set up so that fathers are able to have supervised visitation with the child but not custody in order to lower the risk of danger to the mother and child. Furthermore, funds should be set aside so spousal abuse victims and their children can receive proper professional help. Funding can help set up more treatments to have the children talk about the problems of the abuse before they continue on the same path and experience serious effects. Unfortunately, many people believe that women who are abused cannot care for a child because they lack resources and education. In fact, Blair's study shows that over one-half of the women questioned received one-to-three years of college education (25). With a new chance, children can end the cycle they had to witness, and women will be able to get work and care for their children while knowing they are safe; but, help is needed to start new.

If domestic spousal abuse continues, the children who witness the abuse will continue the cruel cycle because they saw abuse as love between their parents (Unicef 7). With society's help, children can learn the real meaning of love and how to show it to others. Furthermore, the most important thing is to remove the child from the abusive situation. Equally important is providing treatment to the children and parents for the physical and psychological problems that result from the domestic abuse. When treatment is provided, the children's view of life could drastically change compared to what they used to know while growing up.

Works Cited

Alaggia, Ramona, Tahany M. Gadalla, Aron Shlonsky, Angelique Jenney, and Joanne Daciuk. "Does Differential Response Make a Difference: Examining Domestic Violence Cases in Child Protection Services." *Child & Family Social Work 20.1 (2015):* 83-95 CINAHL Complete. Web. 24 Feb. 2016.

Blair, Faye, Judith McFarlane, Angeles Nava, Heidi Gilroy, and John Maddoux. "Child Witness to Domestic Abuse: Baseline Data Analysis for A Seven-Year Prospective Study." *Pediatric Nursing 41.1 (2015):* 23-29 CINAHL Complete. Web. 23 Feb. 2016.

Culp-Ressler, Tara. "The Hidden Consequences Of Domestic Violence Linger For Decades." ThinkProgress RSS. *Center for American Progress Action Fund*, 26 Sept. 2014. Web. 23 Feb. 2016.

Metcalfe, Susan. "It's the Kids Who Are Hurt When Mum and Dad Hit Each Other." *The Age (2011);* 13. *LexisNexis Academic*. Web. 7 Mar. 2016.

McGraw, Phillip Calvin. "18-Year-Old: 'If Your Boyfriend Hits You, It's A Sign of Love'—Dr. Phil." *YouTube.com*. YouTube, 28 Jan. 2015. Web. 23 Feb. 2016.

Tatum, Diane. "Why The Label Child Abuse Puts Children Who Witness Domestic Violence At Risk." *Trauma, Violence & Abuse 1.3 (2000):* 288. Web. 7 Mar. 2016.

"The Effects of Relationship Abuse on Children." My CMS. Bethesda House, n.d. Web. 23 Feb. 2016.

Unicef. "Behind Closed Doors." *Human Rights Documents Online* (n.d.): 1-14. Unicef, 2006. Web. 21 Feb. 2016.

Case Study ENC 1101: Use of Personal Experience in Argumentative Writing

Listening to Memory as a Means of Inventing and Writing Rhetorically

By Karen Manning

Engaging in academic writing necessarily involves critically thinking about a topic, not only by researching and understanding the views of other writers, but also by engaging these writers' arguments and adding one's own voice to the conversation. This particular aspect of academic writing—bringing something new to the conversation—often presents a dilemma for student writers: "What unique perspective can I possibly bring to an issue that already has been debated thoroughly in the public square?" A writer's use of first-person exigence provides an effective answer to this quandary. According to Octavia Davis and Bill Marsh, "[T]elling our stories can create the conditions for social change, but only if those stories are circulated and studied" (183).[1] Indeed, as Robert Nash points out, students who learn to narrate their stories well provide readers with "delicious aha! moments of self and social insight that are all too rare in more conventional forms of research" (24).[2] By focusing on their own lived experiences and evaluating the impact of these events, students are able to move into the greater cultural conversations, deliberately reconstructing and regenerating their stories to address current, pressing cultural issues. Jasara Norton's essay in this chapter regarding first-person exigence (page 333) provides excellent methods by which student writers are able to listen to their personal histories with critical distance from their own perspectives, helping them to develop critical thinking regarding their life stories.

Here, we provide an example of the semester-long process by which one student in English Composition I utilizes first-person exigence to develop her researched position paper entitled, "Elite Adjustments: A Nation's Inadvertent Pitfall." By examining her own history in the military, Taylor Anliker provides insightful primary research that uniquely informs the controversial issue regarding the integration of women into the United States Armed Forces' special forces units. Anliker took to heart class instructions to delve into her personal experiences when deciding on a research topic. Her first

---

1 Octavia Davis and Bill Marsh, "Networking, Storytelling and Knowledge Production in First-Year Writing," *Computers and Composition*, vol. 29, 01 June 2012, pp. 175-184. *EBSCOHost*, https://doi.org/10.1016/j.compcom.2012.03.002.

2 Robert J. Nash, *Liberating Scholarly Writing: The Power of Personal Narrative*, Teachers College Press, 2004.

assignment, "Research Paper Proposal," reflects her movement toward using her personal experiences as primary source material.

Research Paper Proposal

The topic I have selected for my research paper is women in special forces and the negative impact it will have on the capability of these specialized units. On January 1, 2016, Ashton Carter, the Secretary of Defense, officially lifted the ban on women to serve in special forces units in all branches of the United States military. The only exception to this admittance is if a branch elects to keep the ban, which up to this point, the Marine Corps is the only branch of service to do so. Although equal rights in the military is an important issue, the more important question that needs to be asked is, "Will this make our military a stronger warfighting force?"

Having served in the United States Air Force for six years on active duty and continuing as a reservist, I have experienced firsthand the effects gender can have on the interaction between fellow soldiers. While participating in prisoner of war (POW) training, I witnessed the influence my gender had on the males who were also participating in the same training. I have served with U.S. Air Force pararescuemen who believe that they will treat a woman in their close-knit unit differently than another man in the same unit. My opinion is backed by the Marine Corps and the RAND corporation, a think tank, that conducted research on the issues stated above. I intend to continue researching not only the psychological issues this service authorization reveals, but also the logistical and physical issues.

Note Anliker's comment that she witnessed firsthand how her gender influenced her male comrades who participated in POW training alongside her. We see, early in her drafting process, a specific memory that guides her choice of topic and influences the position she will take regarding military integration. Later in the writing process, Anliker effectively uses this memory to persuade her readers regarding her stance on integration.

As Anliker delves into research regarding her topic, she keeps a journal as part of a class assignment. In the following excerpt, she inserts her personal responses into the annotations (see Norton 334), responding with first-person narration to data that she finds.

Citation:

"A Quick-Look Analysis of the GCEITF Baseline Climate Survey." CNA Analysis
and Solutions, January, 2015.

Quote: *"Female volunteers tended to be unconcerned about being the only
woman in a unit, fitting in generally, and having to suppress their femininity"*
(7).

My Voice: *Having experienced the position of a combat role in the military,
I agree that my own personal concern for risks was not any greater than a
male's concern for himself. However, I did experience expressed concerns from
males within my unit about my safety, which I quickly disregarded. Those
males most likely worried about my safety over the safety of their fellow men,
which is not putting the mission first.*

Anliker's research journal demonstrates that information from reliable secondary sources confirms her own experiences: women are not concerned with
the gender differences in military roles, but the men are. These differences in
perspective become the theme for Anliker's research paper. The problem with
integrating small special operations units is the attitude of men toward their
female counterparts. Supported by solid research, Anliker argues that men's
attitudes hinder the unit performance necessary in the often intense missions
that small units face.

Anliker's next assignment is to complete a Toulmin outline of her paper. Rustian
Phelps' essay in this chapter regarding "Toulmin Argumentation" (page 300) describes the process of outlining according to the Toulmin method and sets forth
its benefits. By means of the outline, Anliker is able to "acknowledge logical or
fact-based objections" to her position and to find solutions to the issue of military integration that account for these objections (Phelps 303). The following
excerpts from Anliker's outline evidence both the development of nuance in her
argument and the engagement in deeper critical thinking about her topic.

TOULMIN OUTLINE

I. Introduction

    A. Exigence—   *(Why are you writing this paper?)*

                                     My personal treatment at POW training.

    B. Problematization— *(What problem am I trying to solve with this
                                    paper?)*

                                     *A policy issue: Would it make the military
                                     stronger if we allow women to serve in combat?*

C. Thesis—   (How do you propose to solve this problem?)
                              Changing standards equals weaker military
                              due to psychological issues, higher recruiting
                              levels to maintain numbers, medical issues, and
                              funding issues.

D. Reservation—   (Acknowledge opposing arguments and respond
                              to these arguments.)
                              As a woman, I acknowledge and personally
                              understand the equality rights that are
                              being dampened with a policy [that does not
                              promote integration]. Unit cohesion is proven
                              to be stronger when both males and females
                              are present in a unit, despite the differences
                              between the genders. Also, changes begin in the
                              military first (i.e. multi-racial inclusion, women
                              in service, gay rights, etc.)

E. Nuanced Thesis— (Thesis now accounts for the reservation.)
                              A compromise—allow women to serve in
                              large special operations units rather than
                              small teams. Unit cohesion is important;
                              however, unit performance is the priority of
                              the US military.

Nuanced Thesis Statement: Allowing women to serve in small special operations units will hinder the overall performance of the United
States military due to psychological issues between genders, funding,
and the standards changing due to the policy change. To continue promoting gender equality while maintaining the strongest military in the
world, I recommend we allow women to serve in large special operations units where women will not be isolated and unit cohesion will be
more effective.

Anliker's Toulmin outline reflects the results of her research: unit cohesion and unit performance are different matters. Data shows that
unit *cohesion* may be enhanced by the integration of women in combat roles; however, Anliker argues that unit *performance* is hindered by
integration because men instinctively act differently when women are
present, particularly in intense situations. She proposes a compromise:
integration should take place in large special operations units, but for
small special forces units, teams should be all male or all female in order to maintain superior unit performance.

Anliker's final researched position paper reflects her nuanced position. She combines her solid secondary research with poignant descriptions of her military experiences to avidly support integration of women into large special operations units and combat positions but to simultaneously argue that small special forces units should not be integrated. Her strong advocacy for herself and other women in the military, coupled with her personal experiences, give credence to her position, establishing her *ethos*. She is bringing something new to the conversation, establishing first-person exigence in her academic writing. Readers consider whether, as Anliker writes, "the performance of the US military is the number one priority." How should gender equality be actively promoted while maintaining the strongest military in the world? Based on her personal experience and secondary sources, Anliker confidently pinpoints the problem, not in how women perform physically or in how they perceive themselves as soldiers, but in the ways that men perceive them. How then should men be trained to overcome these perceptions, and is funding available for such training? Anliker establishes exigence, born from personal experience, that effectively ushers her readers into these areas of inquiry.

In her first class assignment, the "Research Paper Proposal," Anliker writes, "While participating in prisoner of war (POW) training, I witnessed the influence my gender had on the males who were also participating in the same training." Now, by focusing on her lived experience in the POW training camp and analyzing this event, she moves into the greater cultural conversation. By sharing her personal memory at the outset of her paper, she accomplishes the "aha! moment of self and social insight" that Nash argues is possible when students effectively narrate their stories. The result is the deliberate reconstruction and regeneration of her story to address the current, pressing cultural issue of military integration, and she accomplishes this regeneration with great effect.

Elite Adjustments: A Nation's Inadvertent Pitfall

Taylor Anliker

I cringe in anticipation awaiting another backhand to strike my cheek, still tasting the blood in my mouth from the last one. My attacker stands four feet taller than I as I stare up at him from my knees. The room I am being held in is completely concrete with no windows for sunlight to creep in, and the silent noise is unbearable. Thirteen other prisoners are lined along the walls, watching the bloody exchange take place in the middle of the room, not able to take their eyes off my swelling face. For a moment in time, the fourteen of us forget where we are and completely cave to the pressures of being prisoners of war. It is the next moment, when I make eye contact with the man striking me, that I remember to stay calm; this was all just a training exercise.

Women officially integrated into the military in 1948 (Alfonso 53). The contributions women have made to the service have far exceeded any expectations placed on them. From training, such as the survival, evasion, and resistance (SERE) training mentioned above, to real-world combat, women have proven themselves to handle military standards and pressures. Being a woman in the service, I am proud of the accomplishments that I and my fellow servicewomen have made, which are leading to more opportunities for us in the military. On January 1, 2016, all special forces and combat jobs officially opened to women, with only the Marines requesting an exemption for a few infantry positions (Women in Service). Although I believe in the capabilities of my gender, allowing women to serve in small special forces units will hinder the overall performance of the United States military as a result of psychological issues between genders, funding, and the prestigious standards being altered because of the policy change. To continue promoting gender equality while maintaining the strongest military in the world, I instead recommend we allow women to serve in large special operations units and combat positions where women will not be isolated and unit cohesion will be stronger.

During the week-long SERE training that I participated in, I realized the psychological effects that my being beaten in front of my male counterparts had on them. Speaking with them after the training, they explained how their instincts threatened to take over, exposing a weakness during a crucial time when strength was most needed. This situation led me to consider the much more danger-ous, real-world, high-stakes situations taking place in small special forces units who are conducting missions in remote, isolated parts of the world. The unit cohesion between the members of these units directly correlates to the unit's performance, which is the tip of the spear the United States wields to make the United States military one of the most respected in the world. During a special hearing in Con-gress reviewing the January 1, 2016 policy change, General Sacolick stated, "I don't want to do anything that affects that dynamic [unit cohesion]. That is why unit cohesion has been and continues to be so important" (Women in Service). Sacolick emphasizes the differences between genders as a possible flaw in the policy change of allowing women in all combat roles because it will affect the dynamic of the units. Although physical differences are most likely the first issue brought to the table, psychological variations between genders will be the Achilles heel of a small integrated special forces unit. Beyond a member's conscious thought, the mental perception the two gen-ders have of each other will change their actions in situations where instincts are heavily relied upon. Most individuals reviewing this policy change focus on the differences women have from the men physically; however, we should be more focused on the differences between how women view themselves versus how they are perceived by men.

The underlying issue is not how women view themselves as sol-diers, but instead on how men view women as soldiers. CNA Analy-sis focused on a study conducted by the Marine Corps called the

Ground Combat Element Integrated Task Force Study (GCEITF). CNA Analysis emphasized the fact that female volunteers tended to be unconcerned about being the only woman in a unit and having to suppress their femininity (A Quick Look). This GCEITF study observed the benefits and difficulties of an integrated military unit versus an all-male unit. Aside from finding physical differences in the performances of the two units, the study also identified psychological differences in how women viewed themselves versus how men viewed the women. Women have no problem adapting to situations they are put in, such as special operations training. Women today are making history and graduating from special operations schools with no issues. However, when men are asked if they felt the females aided or hindered unit cohesion, many agreed with this statement: "This gives us something else to worry about, in the back of our minds, which distracts from the mission" (A Quick-Look). Although this obstacle can be overcome in large combat units, small special operations units have the hardest missions physically and psychologically; unit cohesion is extremely important here. If we are going to effectively integrate women into special operations units, we will need to implement training for a smooth transition.

Additional trainings for military men and women during this integration will require additional funding, which is something the United States government cannot afford right now. As of November 16, 2016, the US government is $19 trillion in debt (The Debt). Military spending has already been cut by 15% in the past five years (Jacobson). These additional trainings will add to an already growing government spending deficit for a shrinking military. Not only will these trainings require more funding, but a female solider also costs more than a male soldier does. After conducting a private study on the effects of integrating women into combat positions, the RAND Cooperation, a think-tank, stated: "A main driver of recurring costs will be differences in attrition or retention rates. To the extent that women complete training at a lower rate, or spend fewer months on average in the infantry, substituting women for men will eventually result in fewer personnel serving in the infantry. Therefore, the Marine Corps will need to recruit or retain additional personnel to maintain the size of the infantry" (Schaefer et al. 101). In an all-volunteer force (AVF), recruiting men and women into the service has not been a difficult task because of the state of the US economy. The area where military spending will grow is the maintenance of the size of our military because of the differences in retention rates between male and female soldiers. Keeping a female in the service costs more money than it does a male soldier because she will not stay in the service as long as a male does. This is mainly due to a female's duty to her family coming before her military career; for example, women have the option to automatically separate from the service if they become pregnant, an option men do not have. If more women are continuing to enter the service, recruiting will need to increase to maintain the military's current size. This uptick in recruiting will undoubtedly increase military spending. Not only will the funding change with the integration, but also the standards of the special operations units.

Special operations units have the most supreme standards in the world, which makes the United States one of the best militaries. During the Review of Women in Services Hearing conducted before the Subcommittee on Military Personnel in the House of Representatives, 113th Congress, Ms. Beyler, the Director for Officer and Enlisted Personnel Management, was asked about the changing standards of the positions being opened to females. Beyler responded, "The Services will probably speak to that individually, but what I would say across the Department is exactly, we are not going to lower standards, but it is not a matter of lowering or raising the standard. . . . The key is to validate the standard to make sure that it is the right standard for the occupation" (Women in Service). If the Department of Defense (DOD) is in truth reviewing and changing the standards for occupational reasons and not because of the policy change, they are choosing a terrible time to do so. Although the DOD may continue to insist the changing standards are due to technology and adaptation reasons, the general public, along with the military servicemen and women, will relate the change to the recent integration policy change, which in turn will been seen as a weakness in these units. One issue that most people who support the policy change agree on is the physical standards not changing in order for women to be in a special operations or infantry position. The statement by Beyler only proves those changes will still be made, just under the name of "changing times." Insisting standards should remain unchanged is one area policy supporters and I can agree on; however, there are numerous other areas where our views do not align.

Supporters of the policy change allowing women in all combat positions point out several valid arguments during this debate. Our society and culture have changed even since the Cold War, and women now have a different role in society. Women are increasingly moving their way up to the top of not only military organizations, but also civilian sectors. These changes are contributing positively to both military and civilian organizations, and arguers will point out that these changes should start with policy changes. A female Lieutenant Colonel in the Air Force reinforces the positive contributions integration has brought to our military: "Over the three decades since women integrated into the armed forces, organizational decisions, cultural shifts and evolutions, and the performance of women have contributed to an organizational schema, a thought process that pervades the current US military" (Alfonso 98). I agree with her. The evidence presented day after day of successful missions completed by women prove that the Integration Act of 1948 was essential to the survival of our military. However, when considering my personal experience and evidence of the effect that gender can have on a mission, I strongly stand by my recommendation to not allow integrated small special operations units, for example, Sea, Air, Land (SEAL) teams. Women will be effective in combat positions, and possibly in an all-female special operations unit where integration will not be a factor, and they will excel at these positions. However, the performance of the US military is the number one priority, not our social opinions.

Although I agree with the January 1, 2016, policy change allowing women to serve in combat positions, I believe the military should refrain from integrating small special operations units. "Military units, not individual soldiers, win wars, and the military must diminish the rights of the individuals who serve in it in order to create effective units" (Field 34). A proposal made by two former Army officers, one of each gender, highlights the importance of the statement above. Standing up for an entire country's freedom means you must put down some of your own in order to serve the greater good. This statement is true even in a democratic society where equal rights are the foundation of our government because the military is held to a different standard than that of those they are protecting. I am not proposing that we ignore the rights given to us by our forefathers; I am proposing that we continue to be the best military in the world by recognizing our celebrated diversity and prestigious standards.

Works Cited

"A Quick-Look Analysis of the GCEITF Baseline Climate Survey." CNA Analysis and Solutions, January, 2015, http://www.defense. gov/Portals/1/Documents/wisr-studies/USMC%20%20A%20 QuickLook%20Analysis%20of%20the%20GCEITF%20Baseline%20 Climate%20Survey.pdf

Alfonso, Kristal L. "Femme fatale 2010" *Air & Space Power Journal - Africa and Francophonie*, Spring 2011, *Military and Intelligence Database Collection*, go.galegroup.com/ps/i.do?p=PPMI&sw=w&u=pens4986 6&v=2.1&id=GALE%7CA369062708&it=r&asid=6032917df7b3d1 c7ffdf4002f3ab9441.

Field, Kim, and John Nagel. "Combat Roles for Women: A Modest Proposal" *Parameters*, Summer 2001, p. 74, *Military and Intelligence Database Collection,* go.galegroup.com/ps/i.do?p=PPMI &sw=w&u=pens49866&v=2.1&id=GALE%7CA76496210&it=r&asi d=2793f0391bffacbd99043270fc0e8c3c.

Jacobson, Louis, and Amy Sherman. "PolitiFact Sheet: Military spending under Obama and Congress." *Politifact,* December 14, 2015, http://

www.politifact.com/truth-o-meter/article/2015/dec/14/politifact-
sheet-our-guide-to-military-spending-/

Schaefer, Agnes Gereben, et al. "Implications of Integrating Women into
the Marine Corps Infantry." RAND Corporation, 2015, http://www.
rand.org/pubs/research_reports/RR1103.html

"The Debt to the Penny and Who Holds It" *Treasury Direct,* US
Department of Treasury, Bureau of the Fiscal Service, 16 November,
2016, http://www.treasurydirect.gov/NP/debt/current

"Women in Service Reviews." *Hearing before the Subcommittee on
Military Personnel of the Committee on Armed Services House of
Representatives One Hundred Thirteenth Congress.* US Government
Printing Office, July 24, 2013, https://www.gpo.gov/fdsys/pkg/
CHRG-113hhrg82465/pdf/CHRG-113hhrg82465.pdf.

Activity 6.8 • Presenting in English Composition I

Explore

As you know, English Composition I is an introduction to academic writing and re-search. When you signed up for this course, you might have assumed, and correctly so, that you would be developing topics, researching those topics, and writing about your conclusions. What might be new is the idea of presenting your findings. In fact, presentations of academic writing and research are quite common. The question is, what does a presentation look like in the academic genre, and what is its purpose?

Writers and researchers have been attending conferences to read or summarize their papers for many years. More recently, writers and researchers are respond-ing to our multimodal culture by presenting their ideas through **poster presenta-tions**. A poster presentation provides your audience with a visual version of your argument. This kind of poster should be immediately compelling with an attention to best design practices. To accomplish this goal, you will want to determine the purpose of your poster presentation, make rhetorically purposeful content selec-tions, pay careful attention to design and format, and revise meticulously for a wide viewing.

Create a poster of your researched argument to present to your classmates. Here are some guidelines:

1. Depending on where you are in your writing and research process, determine the purpose of your poster presentation. Your purpose might be to invent, to inform, to persuade, or to get feedback.
2. Based on your purpose, selectively choose ideas from your research project to present. Because of space limitations and context, not all of your ideas will make it onto your poster. Also, the way you present those ideas will be different than the way you present them in an essay. You want the information on the poster to be easily understood, inviting, and memorable.
3. Once you decide which information to include, consider the design and format. Whole professions are devoted to innovative and appealing design techniques, so don't get overwhelmed by all the rules and options. Rather, follow a few basic principles:
    a. **Less is more.** A cluttered space is difficult to digest and undermines your ability to grab your audience's attention. Strategic negative space is your friend.
    b. **Be consistent.** Consistency in terms of font and color creates a sense of structure and cohesiveness.
    c. **Know your genre.** The poster presentation is its own genre and requires professionalism. Avoid being cutesy, crafty, or campy both in terms of vi-suals and content. Another essential element of professionalism is citing your sources.
    d. **Organize the content.** Use headings, subheadings, bullet points, and oth-er organizational tools to help your audience move seamlessly through the poster.
4. Because poster presentations often have a larger audience than a paper, revision is imperative. With less written material to read, viewers will notice errors more easily in a poster than in a longer essay. Also, because you are working with less material, your audience will be less forgiving of those mistakes.

ENC 1102 Public Writing

ENC 1102 emphasizes public writing. What is public writing, and for what situations do you find yourself composing as a public writer for public audiences? Email? Social Media? Professional, work-place writings? Everyday cases of persuasion and making arguments? Public writing, similar to academic writing, stages a context that consists of actors, texts, and communication channels—or material paths that deliver text from author to audience.

Public writing covers a wide possibility of communication that includes multiple genres, modes, media, technologies, and audiences. Similar to academic writing, public writing asks a writer to situate oneself in a rhetorical situation. Think of all the ways you communicate online; think of the numerous messages you encounter each day; think of all the texts that you read or view. Think of all the occurrences in which you respond, sending out posts, text, and messages to a reading, receiving public. When you send an email, that is an example of public writing. When you post an image to Instagram, that is public writing. When you comment on a thread or forum, that is public writing. When you attend a march, that is public writing. When you compose a consumer review, that is public writing. When you craft an argument and post or publish the text for public consumption—that is public writing.

- Public writing is communication intended for a public audience.

- Public writing consists of multiple genres and makes use of multiple media and modes.

- Public writing is purpose-driven and anticipates action

ENC 1102 creates writing situations that ask you to transfer and apply what you know about academic writing to public writing contexts. In ENC 1102, you analyze and write in multiple genres, and you might find yourself composing with multimedia in ways that are completely new to you. For example, using audio recording and editing software in conjunction with written transcripts, in 1102, you might be asked to create a podcast.

In today's 21st-century, digital world, we communicate through a range of styles, technologies, modes, and genres and for several different purposes. To prepare you to write rhetorically for a vast public arena, the standard assignment in ENC 1102 is a rhetorical analysis essay. Rhetorical analysis is a *methodology*, meaning it is both a theory and a method, of effective communication. When you write a rhetorical analysis, you employ critical analysis that helps you closely-read and unpack textual situations. In writing a rhetorical

analysis, you learn to apply this methodology to your own writings. The remaining pages of this chapter include instruction on writing a rhetorical analysis and other public genres.

Case Study: What Is Public Writing?

By N. Fox Edele

> We know of no people without names, no languages or cultures in which
> some manner of distinctions between self and other, we and they, are not
> made.... Self-knowledge—always a construction no matter how much it
> feels like a discovery—is never altogether separable from claims to be
> known in specific ways by others.

"*We know of no people without names ...*" With these arresting words the California social scientist Craig Calhoun describes the ways we create our identities and want to be known for who we are uniquely. What began over 2500
years ago as oral composition, supported by writing, moved to the letters, reports, narratives, and some diaries intended as public docs, and to our robust
literature now—on paper, on the screen, on the street. As illustrated by this
photograph of a busy intersection in downtown Atlanta, we use many different
kinds of language to shape and express our identities, to form and sustain our
relationships, to design and de-
scribe our communities. In the act
of **public writing** we inform one
another, we tell our stories, we
analyze our experiences, and we
argue our positions.

Peachtree and John Portman, Atlanta. Photo by
Giovanni

The American poet Lisel Mueller,
who emigrated from Germany as a teenager, describes the intrinsic connection
between our private selves and our public language in "Why We Tell Stories":
"Because we awakened and learned to speak ... Because the story of our life
becomes our life / Because each of us tells the same story / but tells it differently / and none of us tells it the same way twice."

Our work in ENC 1102 Public Writing explores the ways we use language to
communicate—verbally, visually, electronically—in the everyday settings of our
lives as individuals and members of communities. In Public Writing we speak
about who we are through the issues and ideas we choose to show and teach
our compatriots: What issues do we care most about? What changes would we

like to see in our world? How can we as a "public" make those changes happen? In the process our language reveals how power works in our communications as citizens, colleagues, family members, friends, students, and witnesses to this historical and cultural moment.

"Young adults know how to complain," notes Robin, a student in 1102 whose urgent concern is the environment, "but we do not know how to word our complaints the right way. Through this course, I have learned how to make an argument, how to make people feel what I feel, and how to reach the audience. I am an environmental studies major ready to make a change in this world, I do not like what is happening to our beautiful home so I wish to take action. When I make a high-stakes argument and change the outlook of people's minds, I will have this class to thank for helping me make a difference."

As Robin's testimony shows, an important part of your university experience is vigorous, intelligent debate—and a university class in public writing is the place to learn how to understand and discuss our differences while respecting one another for who we are, and what we think and value. The best kind of public conversation for over 2500 years has faced and resolved differences to create a better world. ENC 1102 is where YOU join that conversation.

"Every Single Thing Put Out Into the World": Public Writing and Rhetoric

"This course has reshaped my thinking," writes Olivia about 1102. "I now realize that every single thing put out into the world (texts, movies, songs, the way we carry ourselves, even a place) has a specific purpose and that it can tell you more than what you see at face value."

As you discovered in Chapter One, you've been using **rhetoric** all your life. You've been reading and analyzing people, places, things—i.e., texts—all your life, and speaking up, talking back. Rhetoric gives you the knowledges and understandings to put you in control. And your *voice* arises from your ability to make a *choice*, the key point in Chapter One, "Stop! In the Name of Rhetoric." In Public Writing you learn how to recognize and practice the **rhetoricity** of language, i.e., the ways we design our verbal and visual communications with purpose, an awareness of our audiences, and the influence of our context, or cultural and temporal situations.

As you know, **rhetoric** is the practice, and theory, of deciding how best we can reach out and communicate with one another. In our history as human beings we find these practices as the reasons for our first schools—and subjects of our first textbooks: how do we create ways of using language to have an effect or impact? Our purposes might be to explain or express an idea or feeling—to make an argument and persuade one another—to teach—or praise—(or not): rhetoric always has a purpose, a listener or audience, and a design. It is the way we use and demonstrate our intelligence.

Here again is the definition of rhetoric from one of our first teachers, Isocrates, now expanded from our earlier section, "Rhetoric and Democracy":

> *Rhetoric, or* logos, *is that power which of all the faculties that belong to the nature of man is the source of most of our blessings. ...Because there has been implanted in us the power to persuade each other and to make clear to each other whatever we desire, not only have we escaped the life of wild beasts, but we have come together and founded cities and made laws and invented arts; and, generally speaking, there is no institution devised by man which the power of speech has not helped us to establish.*

> *For this it is which has laid down laws concerning things just and unjust, and things base and honorable; and if it were not for these ordinances we should not be able to live with one another.*

Right there is the direct connection between our rhetorical tradition as thinking human beings and the "public writing" we are talking about here in 1102: without this "source of most of our blessings ... we should not be able to live with one another."

In "Rhetoric and Democracy" you also took a look at the collage, "Leave Only Your Footprints" (reprinted here) created by your colleague in 1102, Jessica. Like Robin, Jessica is deeply concerned with the health and well-being of our environment. And—perhaps like your developing commitment to issues and situations that matter to you—Jessica's focus on our physical world was sharpened by her own experiences and values.

Jessica is a child of the Mississippi delta, born too late, she tells us, to travel that iconic river blithely

Jessica's collage, "Leave Only Your Footprints."

unaware of algal blooms and the Dead Zone where nothing breathes. As she presents her collage in our 1102 class, she draws for us, her rapt audience, the map of her journey here to Florida's Gulf Coast, called to repair the living laboratory where "sea turtles or dolphins or shore birds (are) in distress or dead from garbage in the ocean," she states. She shows us her pictures of plastic beer cups tossed on the sand beside recycling bins; a truck tire—"these don't biodegrade," she notes—in an inlet where the elegant blue herons fish.

Nor is the problem local or specifically American, she tells us, pointing to maps of circular "gyres" where islands of plastic congeal in every ocean on the planet. It is her love of nature and outdoors that leads her now to study Marine Biology, support the International Coastal Cleanup, adjure an audience like us, her public writing class, to "go green, recycle, and volunteer": "Without Earth," she argues, "we wouldn't have existence. We can make a difference."

Jessica's composition and content—the visual slides saturated with blues of sea and sky; the charts and graphs that indicate toxic threats to those elements; the printed or spoken words that convey her backstory, knowledge of science, experience, concern, and admonitions to us, her audience— demonstrate the rhetorical power of public writing.

Public Rhetoric and Democracy

Jessica's colleague in 1102, Trevor, tells us that "rhetoric is about organizing and voicing one's beliefs for the means of persuasion," and he states: "ENC 1102 has aided me in the ways that I will use rhetoric for years to come." Trevor describes a class experience in which we come together, from many different backgrounds and experiences, and we learn to create a community where our different viewpoints are delivered to one another and discussed. The course in Public Writing is based on the understanding

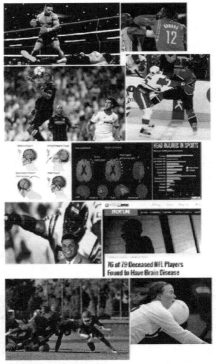

ALL head injuries are serious doesn't matter what sport it is.

Public rhetoric created by Dylan in ENC 1102 at UWF.

that our arguments are often entirely different. That practice—of "listening to different views," as Trevor's friend Victoria explains, and being open-minded" (which she fears is "a skill that is going extinct")—reflects the nature of American democracy: "*E pluribus unum*"—"out of the many, one."

This ideal of unity is not achieved without struggle, a clash of many different "publics," each with its own *ethos*, and politics, and ideology. But at the heart of public rhetoric is, as Trevor notes, "persuasion"—and the practice of rhetoric is integral to our mature thinking and need to express ourselves and understand how the world—with its tensions and connections—communicates itself to us.

Marianna, who has preceded you in this class, describes the ways that students in 1102 deliver and negotiate their diverse and often conflicting points of view: "Each of us as a member of a society needs to make our opinions and existence matter and take the opportunity we are given to have a say. Each of us has the responsibility to not let ourselves be reduced to the mediocrity of public opinion and to start expressing our opinion."

By experiencing, as Jamal notes in his 1102 reflection, "how many different issues there are and how many of them don't have solid solutions on how to fix them," we exercise the first crucial goals of the Composition Program, that "democracy is best sustained by an educated and informed public versed in the practices of critical perception and expression." Jamal continues: "The ideas and group practices in this course affect my life because going forward I'll be more concerned about what's going on in the world; the course has made me more open to listening to people's points of view"—and in this way 1102 uniquely prepares its student communities for "dealing with the world at large" and "become contributing members not only of the academy, but also of the democratic public."

In Public Writing at UWF we engage in activities and practices that encourage civic learning. We experience values of community, commitment, and the creation of arguments and discussions that teach, inspire, promote understanding, and potentially persuade, in the public forum. Certainly the intent of an education in public writing—i.e., community partnerships and involvement in local government, among other endeavors—are integral to this dimension of university life, a value on which the first schools were founded in Athens over 2500 years ago. Students in 1102 define and research issues that matter to them, such as voting rights, college tuition, saving the coral reef, saving the oceans, same-sex marriage, preventing abuse in families and neighborhoods, and present their arguments to a class of active, questioning, often changed but always challenged listeners. In this way we learn to mediate our differences through education, discussion, and mutual respect.

As former President Barack Obama has said to all of us on behalf of the the people of Flint, Michigan, experiencing an extreme crisis because of toxic lead in the water, "By investing in the common good, we invest in ourselves."

Project in Public Writing:

Following this chapter, you'll find a class project that can be adapted to your own ideas and interests—"The Documentary Profile: The Critical 'I' in Public Writing"—which expands our ideas of "public writing" to include graphics, videotexts, and writing forms we deliver on a PC, projector, email, flash disk, and posts on a website. In this project we consider how our ideas of writing and its potential have changed, and what we are able to say and show that traditional print culture might not be able to convey as well and directly.

PROJECT: DOCUMENTARY PROFILE: The Critical "I" in Public Writing

Length: 1 Videotext (PowerPoint, Prezi, etc.) + 3-4 single-spaced pages (analysis of rhetorical context)

In this project you will describe and present *YOUR connection to a social issue.* **You may design this text for delivery to any audience. But you should know (see questions that follow) who that audience is, specifically.** Your material can be targeted to a class, the editor of a publication, an organization or politician, a friend or relative, an opinion editor for an online magazine, a weblog, and another audience engaged in this contemporary issue. Your purpose is to show us why you advocate change or hope to persuade the particular audience.

The Yes and the No:

Yes: Your argument must be based on verifiable evidence—it must *arise* from evidence that is, itself, precise data and not someone else's opinion. You must use the databases introduced in the library orientation for this class. *A prospectus for this argument is due for approval before you may present it, which will outline your position and the data you are using to support it.*

No: Arguments that directly insult or disrespect people based on sexual preference; political opinion; gender ID; ethnicity; religious faith; economic status. *You must play fair:* no fallacies (i.e., attacking a person rather than a policy; hiding or distorting facts you don't like; making claims you can't substantiate). No propaganda or political campaigning.

Part 1. The Videotext

Here you will create a documentary—a combination of written, verbal, digital material, and sound—in which *you communicate your interest in this important topic.* The documentary should tell the story of your interest or involvement in this issue. You may use a program like PowerPoint or Prezi for this videotext, or create a poster or brochure that you show the class, or use a collection of objects you design (not pre-existing). **You have no more than 15 minutes for your presentation/discussion.**

The text you create can include photographs, clip art, collage, an interview with someone engaged with this topic, your observations of yourself as you made this commitment or encountered this issue, lines from songs—whatever is available. (From Aristotle: "the available means of persuasion"). Persuade us about the importance of this information—and its grounding in data, not only emotion.

Part 2. The Short Paper (APA or MLA citation)

A short paper (3-4 pages, no more, no fewer—and a final page of sources in APA or MLA) should accompany your text in which you explain the following decisions:

• **Invention:** Why did you choose to focus on this particular experience or issue? What method did you use to make this decision? What did you need to research to tell this story? What sources did you use and how did they lead you to take this position? *(Remember—the sources predate the position; you don't use sources to support a position you already hold.)*

• **Arrangement & Style:** How did you design your documentary text for this particular audience, at this particular time and place—let's start by writing a definition of the audience as you imagined them to be—what did you consciously use to communicate your message to that audience? (Arrangement)

• **Delivery:** What governed your selection of the media you used to deliver this documentary—and what were the benefits and constraints (limitations) of that media (if any)? Do you think the media fits the particular audience? Talk about that.

- **Argument:** How would YOU state your argument in this text, if you were being interviewed about it on CNN or MSNBC or NPR? What is your message and what are the stakes of this issue?

Writing in Digital Spaces

These days, for most of us, writing happens in digital spaces more than on paper. Emails, text messages, tweets, Word or Google Docs, submission forms, notes, and calendar apps on our phones: the daily writing experiences in which we participate largely happen in digital spaces. And that matters.

For one, what we can say in a space is limited by what that space can do, its affordances and constraints. Consider a PowerPoint slide. Generally it is designed as a series of static, rectangular digital "slide" spaces unified visually by a central theme and color scheme, and unless we are graphic designers composing our own themes, we tend to fit what we want to say into prefabricated boxes and arrangements within those slides. The progression of slides is decidedly linear; we click a button and move forward or backward through the series to the presentation's end. That is the only motion. What if what we want to say involves a complex, non-linear relationship between ideas? This will be hard to enact or work out via a PowerPoint presentation.

A Prezi, however, although also decisively linear in progression, enables writers to design more motion into their arguments, and offers the opportunity for visually representing relationships between ideas with the impression of dimensionality in ways PowerPoint cannot. This motion and perhaps-more-shapely "slides" meant to receive a writer's message are predesigned, too, usually. Although it isn't necessarily difficult to alter the arrangements and predesigned features in PowerPoint or Prezi, if we know how to do it, the spaces themselves are packaged and promoted to us for simply plugging in messages that we've already formulated. As if the graphic art of the PowerPoint or Prezi itself was enough to make someone's message interesting. However, we all know generally it's not. In fact, media platforms like PowerPoint and Prezi can be downright distracting.

Furthermore what we can say in a space is limited by what *we* can do with the space itself, our **digital literacy**. If you're playing the video game *Assassin's Creed* and have very little idea on how to move your character through the landscape, fight, steal, spy, or communicate with your sidekick, you're not likely to get very far in the game. This is true of any video game experience; knowing how to use the tools and affordances of the game itself leads to greater success in the digital space of the game, and a greater sense of control of the experience itself (our "video game literacy").

Writing spaces are not scripted like most video games are, but they come with pre-designed frameworks that enable us the same potential for success in communicating our messages to our intended audiences, the same potential sense of control. To what extent do I know how to manipulate images in a digital environment? Or utilize the headers in Word to organize my longer arguments? Or embed a video directly into my Prezi presentation? Or edit a podcast? These are the kinds of questions that illuminate the state of our digital literacies and greatly affect our writing.

Many writing and communication scholars argue for the importance of expanding our digital literacies so that we can participate more fully in our culture, as our culture plays out in online, digital spaces more and more. This chapter will address how our digital literacies affect the choices we make when we write in digital spaces in the classroom and in our professional lives, particularly as these choices position us as consumers and producers of digital media in the composition classroom and in all college classrooms.

Audience

In the authoring of a successful composition—one that inspires its readers to feel, believe, and act—considering audience is of prime importance. Maybe not at first, when you're working out an idea through early drafting. But later, when you feel confident about what you want to say, in order to make clear decisions about how to craft your message, it's imperative to consider audience. To whom do you write this...letter, email, song, poem, blog post, article, essay, chat message? Why? What is it you want the writing to accomplish in the world? To whom do you need to address this work in order to accomplish it?

In school the answer to the question of audience might seem easy. To whom do you write the essay? To your instructor, of course. Why? In order to pass the class, or get an "A." The early chapters of this book speak often of crafting messages to particular audiences, particularly instructors. Often it's useful to think of the writing's potential beyond the classroom, to imagine an audience and a purpose beyond the classroom. In this sense, classroom writing becomes a workshop space for "real world" writing.

Of course the composition classroom is a real world space, with it's own audience, purpose, and kairotic moment. But it's also a cyberspace. Writing in online spaces means writing for potential audiences beyond the instructor in no imaginary sense. When you publish a blog post, anyone might happen upon that blog post. That reader will likely form an idea about you and your work upon reading that blog post, or skimming it. That reader has a certain power, the power to listen to you (read your work) or not, the power to pay you some *attention*, etc. Crafting your writing to encourage readership is an important aspect of writing successfully online. In order to make important decisions about how to craft for readership, it helps to decide what kind of audience you're hoping to reach and what that audience is like.

Audience: Medium

Medium: "an instrument by which something is conveyed"

Plural, media

Most of the time our instructors will dictate to us which medium we must use to communicate our message. "The assignment," they say, "is to write an essay... It must be a Word document using 12 pt font...,: etc." Word processing documents are media. Video, podcast, Prezi, PowerPoint, website, blog post... These are all media. And though currently your instructors are likely to have arisen in a system that still privileges "papers," and thus the media of the word processor, more and more instruction is happening in digital spaces and final products are slowly beginning to reflect our multi-media age. During the course of your academic career you will likely be asked to produce a multimedia presentation. Here are some tips for approaching this task:

1. When given the option to choose which medium to use in the conveyance of your ideas, consider your audience: What kind of technology is likely to appeal to them? Why? What media are they used to? Comfortable with? Expecting?

2. When choosing a medium consider your message: What technology is likely to *enhance* your message? Why? What technology might detract from your message? Why? (Think about the affordances and constraints of the medium.)

3. When you've chosen your medium, go online and briefly search for tutorials on how to use the technology of the medium (even Word documents!);

you'll likely learn how to use the technology in ways you'd never known before, augmenting your digital literacy and expanding the possibilities of your creativity and your ideas as they are formed by the medium itself.

4. When you've chosen your medium, begin composing *within the medium* instead of writing in a Word document and cutting and pasting into your other medium. It is easy to tell when someone has cut and pasted into a PowerPoint slide, for instance, as the slide is usually packed with words, a whole paragraph or two of words that are difficult to read from the distance of an audience. It is likely no one will read the words, leaving the audience wondering what the purpose of the slide is in the first place. Compose in the medium, a medium chosen with audience in mind, and you'll likely come closer to designing a successful composition.

Multimodality: Audience and Writer

In 1996, a group of scholars, "The New London Group," convened to discuss the implications of new media, globalization, and diversity on contemporary literacy teaching and practice (http://www.newliteracies.com.au). The result was a significant shift in the way we think about communication and writing, one that situates the composing of words in the context of all the other ways people compose to communicate.

Think about it. The last time you browsed a website, to what were you immediately drawn? The words? The images? The soundtrack? Most likely your first response wasn't, "The words...in fact I read every word on the digital page! I didn't even notice the images." Our current reality is one in which readers' eyes or ears browse digital pages, and sometimes paper ones. Perhaps they're more likely to read words on pages more completely, but digital pages promote the habit of skimming. We skim for information we want or need; there is simply too much "out there" to invest our attention in slowly consuming the entirety of one web page experience...unless, perhaps, you're a writing instructor, or unless the writing on the page is so compelling one can't tear away from it, or the writing is information that we very much need. And by "writing" we mean... what exactly?

The New London Group's work emphasized the varied ways people communicate. We don't just write letters, of course, we use gestures to communicate. We use sounds and space and images to communicate. And each of these "modes" of communication...

- Visual
- Gestural
- Audio
- Linguistic
- Spatial

...brings with it unique elements for meaning-making and communication.

This is always the case. An essay composed in a word processing program and printed on white paper communicates not only via the linguistic mode—the words written on the page—but also through the spatial mode. Have you ever written a three-page essay that is only one paragraph long? Why not? A paragraph is a unit of meaning created via space (sometimes indentation, sometimes a line of space before and after). If you stand back from your paper and look at it from across the room, you'll see the paper is a visual phenomenon as well. It has a "look," a look that, likely, adheres to certain genre conventions of a university paper. Have you ever adjusted the margins of a Word document so that your words get squeezed through a narrower tunnel of text in order to meet page requirements for an assignment? (If so, you're using the affordances of the medium to produce a desired effect. Good for you, kind of.) The vast majority of writing instructors can immediately spot this trick. And what does it communicate, visually, this added space to the margins of a course paper? How does it affect the author's *ethos?*

Writing in digital spaces privileges the visual and the spatial over the linguistic, although written words take on a different and important focus in these spaces. Writing in a Word document and cutting/pasting that work into a blog post, for instance, just doesn't work. What audience wants to read big blocks of text online? Few people do. So one of the big shifts when it comes to writing in digital spaces is thinking about what the visual images and spaces, what the sounds and motions of a digital space *communicate.* How does an image enhance a message? Detract from it? Or a sound, or a motion, or a space? These are the kinds of questions we must begin to ask as composers and designers in digital spaces. We must grow our awareness of the multimodal nature of communication.

There is a social justice aspect of the New London Group's concept of multiliteracies as well. Some of us learn and communicate with greater facility in images or sounds than we do in linguistic writing. Does that make our messages somehow lesser? Is a thesis, for instance, less interesting or important or potentially true if it's spoken out loud than it is if it's written down in words? Is an idea less valuable if it's expressed gesturally, via sign language, than if it's written down in words? The New London Group's contextualizing of linguistic writing creates the potential for greater access to messages best communicated through sound, images, gestures, spaces, and combinations of these, depending on the preferences and abilities of composers, and the preferences, abilities, and expectations of their audiences.

Essentially what this means is that becoming more effective writers, particularly in digital spaces, requires broadening our perceptions of what writing is beyond the written word. Writing involves images, sounds, spaces, gestures, *and* words, together. And in digital spaces, the linguistic must be situated in the context of all these other modes of communication. So the power we have as writers in digital spaces rests heavily on the knowledge we have of the affordances and constraints of the medium we're using, and in our abilities to manipulate technological tools towards crafting messages in multimodal ways.

For Thought and Discussion

Can you recall a time when a message was communicated to you gesturally, or via sound, without words? What was the message? Was it clear?

How does the New London Group's notion of the multimodality of communication and the dethroning of the written word change the way you think about writing? Do you think it's useful or not in terms of writing for school? Why?

Activity 6.9 • **Multimodal Communication**

Explore

Part I:

Take a thesis from an old paper and communicate it using, primarily, a different mode of communication. For instance, perhaps you wrote a paper critiquing how texting while driving issues manifest in local laws. Create an infographic promoting your thesis. Remember: an infographic requires a privileging of the visual and spatial over the written word.

When you're finished, share your work with your colleagues. Can they discern your argument? Why or why not? What was challenging about this activity? What was surprisingly easy, if anything?

Part II:

Find an image or song that you really feel strongly about, then translate that image or song into an essay. If the song were an essay, what would that essay say? ***Important: do not write *about* the image or song. Instead, put yourself in the place of the artist; use the artist's voice. Alternatively you might translate a song into an image or an image into a song. Do you think this would be easier than translating into a written essay? Why or why not?

Reading 6.3

Jason Tham says the first step in creating a multimedia presentation is to consider your deliverables. He is a Ph.D. student and instructor in rhetoric and scientific and technical communication at the University of Minnesota.

Student Essay, "How I Create a Multimedia Presentation"

by Jason Tham

It is not uncommon for an instructor to require students to present their papers or arguments using a combination of texts, visuals, audios, and videos. A multimedia presentation, as I explain

further below, is one that challenges you to consider communicating your ideas using more than one (hence "multi") form of composing technology. A typical multimedia presentation is the slideshow (like PowerPoint, Prezi, or Keynote) presentation, where you enhance your arguments using relevant images, sounds, and video clips in addition to text and your spoken words.

Moreover, a presentation can be interactive, requiring the audience to participate by making choices that affect the outcome of the experience. For example, audience members may choose between divergent endings to the experience or may contribute comments, images, or other content.

While multimedia or interactive presentation can be very effective for demonstrating ideas, I have seen how some presenters' insensitivity toward the rhetorical functions of different media results in boring presentations. Proper planning, however, increases the likelihood that a presentation will be both pleasant and persuasive.

So, whenever I am creating a multimedia presentation, my first step is to consider my deliverables, that is, what I wish to accomplish through this particular presentation. Sometimes my goal is to invoke urgency, other times I am more interested in creating a sense of community. First, I choose media that best serve my intentions. My intentions help determine the kind of media I employ. For example, when I intend to showcase an overview of content—instead of the details of this content—I make a collage of images on a PowerPoint slide to give my audience a bird's-eye view of my scope of presentation. This also simulates a family photo album or a yearbook viewing experience. However, when my intention is to "dive" deep into a certain topic, I use the Prezi canvas to create a sense of depth using the exciting zoom-in transition feature afforded by the slideware. While, if you intend to highlight synergy, collaborative editing apps like Google Slides and Zoho Show are great for demonstrating participatory effort.

Then, I proceed to evaluate my options. I usually look at what limits my options, i.e., time limit on the presentation, the physical environment in which I will deliver my presentation (e.g., classroom, lecture hall, roundtable, etc.), as well as my access to specific media (e.g., can I download an audio file for free, or do I need to purchase it?). These constraints are crucial as they inform my next step in exploring my media options—examining their rhetorical capabilities. For instance, a graph or statistical chart not only makes numbers more comprehensible but also conveys *logos* and tends to garner credibility for the presenter, or *ethos*. Photographs and videos are usually great for arousing emotions—*pathos*—because the audience can easily comprehend or make sense of their messages, which renders them rhetorically strong. The use of certain products and brand names as representations of a subject matter (e.g., using an Apple iPhone as a symbol for smartphone, or Facebook and Twitter as symbols of social media) is not uncommon in presentations as they carry the rhetorical capacity of referencing or reinforcing collectively assured characteristics—and, therefore build *ethos* and inspire *pathos*—especially when the representative object is a household name or item.

Colors are another important element that requires careful deliberation in creating a multimedia presentation. When choosing which color combination to employ, I always remind myself of the cultural meanings behind the colors and the rhetorical power they have over the audience (e.g., red tends to be an attention-getter, blue tends to suggest calmness or establishment, while green signifies nature and freshness). (By the way, red, blue, and green together would make a poor color combination according to color theory.)

Finally, when I consider my audience I think of much more than just its size. I try to find out as much as I can about my potential audience, such as their ages, socio-economic backgrounds, education levels, cultural affinities, professions, etc. Such sociographic information helps me to tailor the content of the presentation to be effective for my particular audience.

Following these steps, I am now able to select the most appropriate media, including images, text fonts, colors, videos and audio (if I choose to use them), animations, and transitions. Also important is the tone and manner of my presentation (e.g., humorous, authoritative, etc.). Of course, creating is just the beginning. After composing a presentation, I always polish it by practicing it and trying it out on colleagues to get a better feel for my presentation as well as feedback for revision. These steps have helped me to be a better presenter, not just someone who merely recites words on a PowerPoint slide without acknowledging the goals, options, and rhetoric of multimedia presentation.

Including Images in Your Projects: Copyright Implications

United States copyright law includes a provision called "fair use" that allows copyrighted images to be used for educational projects. However, copyright laws are complicated, and the implications of using digital images are still being determined in the courts. Clearly, if you take the photo yourself, you own the copyright. Many photographers post photos on websites such as Flikr.com and give permission for "fair use" of the images on the internet, so long as their work is credited. Others, however, post their work for viewers to enjoy but do not allow it to be copied. Scanning a photo from a published work and using it once for a class project falls more clearly under the spirit of the "fair use" law than does putting such an image up on the internet. If you are doing a web page or blog project that includes images, be sure to contact the copyright owner to obtain permission.

Rhetorical Analysis in ENC 1101 & ENC 1102

By Bre Garrett

Media and popular culture references tend to malign rhetoric as empty speech, as propaganda, and as unethical, political spin. While speakers can certainly employ rhetoric in this way—to enforce "commerce-driven" consumerism, as Wayne Booth argues in *The Rhetoric of Rhetoric* (8), rhetoric maintains a much more capacious history and use that encompasses the aims of persuasion and remedy. To persuade effectively and ethically falls upon the responsibility of the rhetor (author/speaker): he or she must vow to do no harm with language and other communication symbols and modes that, together, package and deliver messages for audience reception. But, what is rhetoric according to classical and modern definitions?

Classical definitions of rhetoric:

Figure 1. Image of classical Rhetorica portrayed as reigning over the other subject areas. In classical Greek education, primary education consisted of the trivium (Logica, Rhetorica and Grammatica), in the middle, and to the right, the quadrivium (Arithmetica, Musica, Geometrica and Astronomica). Image available on Google.

- "the available means of persuasion" (Aristotle)

- "The power of eloquence" (Cicero)

- "The science of speaking well" (Quintilian)

- "the art of expressing clearly, ornately (where necessary), persuasively, and fully the truths which thought has discovered accurately (St. Augustine)

Modern additions and adaptions:

- "Study of misunderstandings and their remedies" (I.A. Richards, 1936)

- "an epistemic art; the study and practice of shaping content" (William A. Covino & David A. Jolliffe, 1995)

- "the art, practice, and study of all human communication (Andrea Lunsford, 1995)

- "The ability to bend belief and motivate action" (Bre Garrett, 2012)

While definitions of rhetoric shift depending on the context, rhetorical analysis, as a method for analyzing and crafting textual situations remains fairly consistent. In *Writer/Designer*, Kristin Arola, Jennifer Sheppard, and Cheryl Ball define **rhetorical analysis** as "a method of describing the context in which an author wants to communicate his or her purpose or call for action to the intended audience in a genre" (22). As a method of interpretation and critical reading, rhetorical analysis is useful for both writers and readers. Rhetorical analysis is a method of deeply listening to a text, understanding a text's meaning and purpose and message(s), as well as producing or creating a text.

Rhetorical Analysis: Writer Roles/Reader & Audience Roles

Rhetoric is both theory and practice. In everyday communication endeavors, one theorizes, or critically examines and unpacks textual situations from a rhetorical standpoint. With more trained skill and explicit knowledge of theories, one becomes more adept at applying rhetoric as a means to access and create textual situations. By studying the rhetorical triangle as a visual framework for how to enter a text, readers can begin the process of textual interpretation and analysis. Writers can begin the process of textual production and invention. Writers create textual situations, using the rhetorical triangle to determine their own motivation and purpose, to identify audiences and create appeals that speak to particular audiences, and to invent or discover subjects that they will deliver in appropriate genres.

Readers go through the same angles of the triangle not for production and creation processes, but rather, readers analyze rhetorical situations to discover the textual context. Examine the two triangles here to see how when we read a text, that is one rhetorical situation, and then we reposition ourselves as writers of or about a text, another triangle emerges. In the first triangle, on the left side of the page, think of you as in the author or designer positionality, writing a text. In the second triangle, on the right side of the page, you are an audience, reading and interpreting a text. Both methods are useful depending on your role as either writer of a text or reader of a text.

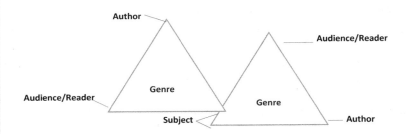

Learning new concepts associated with rhetorical analysis enables writers and readers to theorize communication events and exchanges as part of more significant contexts than mere utterances. Rhetorical analysis foregrounds the interaction between authors and audiences. The terms author, audience, subject, genre, exigence, *Kairos*, context, as well as the rhetorical appeals, *ethos*, *logos*, and *pathos*, provide key elements that readers and writers can study to examine the production, construction, and analysis of a text. When analyzing a rhetorical situation, consider the following questions:

- What is the motivation and purpose for why an author composes a text? Why do you think so?

- How does an author establish credibility/*ethos*?

- What is the historical context and cultural timing in which a text emerges and provokes particular messages? What else is happening in the cultural and historical moment?

- How does a writer discover and create topics or subjects for communication?

- Who is the target audience or composite audience for a particular text? Who are secondary audiences? How do speakers/writers reach particular audiences?

- How do authors appeal to the values and opinions of different audiences? What appeals does a writer employ in order to persuade audiences in particular ways?

- What is the medium of a text? How does medium relate to audience expectations or textual conventions?

- Where is the text published? Where, literally, do audiences encounter the text?

- In what discourse community is a text delivered? How do you know?

- How do audiences interact with the text? What are the textual materials and modes, and how does genre/medium invite particular modes?

Writing and Conducting a Rhetorical Analysis in ENC 1101 & ENC 1102

So far, this discussion has presented definitions, heuristics (or tools), and questions to guide you to conduct and engage in the method of rhetorical analysis. ENC 1101 introduces rhetoric and the rhetorical situation so writers can effectively position themselves as writers in university contexts, writing for academic audiences. In ENC 1101, authors compose academic research essays, developing and proposing arguments and focused conversations about self-selected topics. Writers may conduct rhetorical analyses of peer papers, learning to become critical readers of peers', as well as their own, papers; writers also spend an immense amount of time working through the rhetorical canons of **invention, style, memory, arrangement,** and **delivery** as they draft, revise, and produce their academic research essays.

ENC 1102 extends the study of rhetoric to a more sophisticated production activity in which writers compose a rhetorical analysis essay. Rhetorical analysis is the standard assignment sequence for all sections of ENC 1102. The rhetorical analysis essay is similar to other traditional academic analytical essays in that writers develop and select a topic, the essay arrangement consists of an introduction section, body, supporting paragraphs that contain evidence, claims, and analysis, and a conclusion section. Rhetorical analysis essays have clearly identified thesis statements, or argument stances, in which authors name for readers the focus of their analysis that will proceed in the remainder of the essay. In rhetorical analysis, a writer makes an argument about how a text functions according to the rhetorical triangle, the persuasive elements at play that impact audiences such as *pathos, logos,* and *ethos.* A thesis argument may also focus on *Kairos* or exigence or context. Using rhetorical concepts in the thesis helps mark the essay as the genre and mode of rhetorical analysis as opposed to say another type of analysis.

Examine the introduction paragraphs from two ENC 1102 student rhetorical analysis essays (full essays are included in this textbook chapter). Consider how the writers set up their topics and pose thesis statements, or statements of focus, in the first paragraphs of their essays. Also, notice how the topics speak to kairotic moments for the historical and cultural contexts in which they were written.

In James Austin Benfell Williams' rhetorical analysis essay "Using Aristotle's Appeals with Attitude," observe how the introduction sets up his topic and argument:

> Higher education is not getting any cheaper. The more expenditures a university has, the more it has to cut funding and raise tuition to meet current demands. Football, for example, is one of America's favorite sports, and it manifests in college where the high school stars are separated from future NFL material; however, not every college has the means to support such a financially-draining program. Josh Hart, a staff writer for the University of West Florida's

publication *The Voyager*, decided to speak out about this dilemma. **Hart effectively exposes the hidden potential drawbacks of developing a Division II team by utilizing pathos to gain sympathy and understanding for student sacrifice and by using logos to reveal the negative financial impacts that the University of West Florida (UWF) is likely to endure.**

The bold portion of Williams' first paragraph identifies a thesis statement. Why? How do you know? What makes this sentence a thesis? What function does the sentence play, and what do readers anticipate to locate in the proceeding pages of the essay?

Teacher's Note

By Jasara Norton

The following student essay is an example of rhetorical analysis. Rhetorical analysis comes in many forms. Some explicitly address Aristotle's appeals: *logos*, *pathos*, *ethos*, and *kairos*. Others draw on these concepts without naming them.

The purpose of the assignment was to notice and select a local text. Students were asked to study it closely to better understand others' rhetorical choices as well as their own. The students then presented an argument about the persuasiveness of that text and based that argument on no more than two appeals.

James Williams' "Using Aristotle's Appeals with Attitude," is an example of a reader who was wholly persuaded by an argument regarding UWF's newly formed football program. Part of the reason the text was persuasive to Williams, as he describes, is because he used business industry knowledge from his major to fact-check the article's *logos*. Williams' ability to articulate the conversation he shared with the text is part of what makes his argument compelling.

Sample Student Essay: Rhetorical Analysis

Using Aristotle's Appeals with Attitude

by James Austin Benfell Williams

Higher education is not getting any cheaper. The more expenditures a university has, the more it has to cut funding and raise tuition to meet current demands. Football, for example, is one of America's favorite sports, and it manifests in college where the high school stars are separated from future NFL material; however, not every college has the means to support such a financially-draining program. Josh Hart, a staff writer for the University of West Florida's publication *The Voyager*, decided to speak out about this dilemma. Hart effectively exposes the hidden potential drawbacks of developing a Division II team by utilizing pathos to gain sympathy and understanding for student sacrifice and by using logos to reveal the negative financial impacts that the University of West Florida (UWF) is likely to endure.

In August of 2015, Hart wrote an opinion article outlining the negative impacts of creating a Division II football team at UWF. Hart's main focus seems to be Aristotle's appeal to pathos, to draw in the reader, and logos, by utilizing accurate statistics directly from studies conducted by the National Collegiate Athletic Association (NCAA). Hart simplifies the mathematics so that just about anyone can easily see the detriment that many collegiate institutions face financially. Additionally, Hart relies on pathos to connect with students about benefits, both monetary and natural, that are being taken away, posing the question as to what exactly the student body will get out of the deal. It is clear that the article is directed towards both current and future students, for his tone is nothing less than critical and incredulous, beginning with the title "Excitement for UWF Football Overshadows Pattern of Failure."

Initially, Hart uses pathos to draw in the reader by gaining interest through his title, provoking an element of curiosity from his audience. The portion that reads "Overshadows Pattern of Failure" is enough to grab nearly any reader's attention. Given that the intended audience is students and faculty who frequently read *The Voyager,* Hart takes a chance by utilizing a heavy choice of diction that may evoke strong feelings, potentially offending a portion of the audience that supports the growth of UWF's football program. Nevertheless, that spark draws the reader into Hart's argument about a faulty program that is currently portrayed as a grand opportunity for the university. The momentum of Hart's words is carried even more, albeit in a more satirical tone, with the line, "UWF football is kind of a big deal, so we've been led to believe." This statement reinforces the curiosity established through Hart's article. Typically, these bold statements would be difficult to work with, but the logos mentioned later builds Hart's persuasive momentum as he emphasizes the "practical realities" that the university will have to face.

Moving forward, Hart continues his appeal to pathos by relating to students in two ways. Hart mentions that the Oak Grove was demolished to clear a space for the stadium (See figure 1). Losing a large part of UWF's natural beauty resonates with students, and also faculty, who enjoy the peaceful areas of the campus. I was personally drawn into this example because I used to play disk golf in the Oak Grove. Massive trees towering over a park-like field seemed to be a wonderful place to have lunch, take a walk, or in my case, play disk golf. UWF prides itself on all of the "little things" that make it stand out to potential students, and its large campus filled with peaceful elements of nature is one of them. Another, was the free WEPA services that were offered to students. Hart brings up the point that "cash-strapped students" no longer have access to this service that offered ten free pages per week. This appeal is strong because everyone can relate to the expenses incurred through printing various assignments regularly. Most professors I have encountered expect you to have a printed copy of their syllabus ready to go. That can equate to about 40 pages for a full-time student. Appealing to personal financial strain will almost always be an effective way to gain your audience's attention and make them think about the topic at hand. Understanding that resources, such as WEPA, are being sacrificed to help fund the football team will motivate people to think critically about future negative effects that could be generated by sponsoring a football team.

Figure 1. What used to be the Oak Grove park has been cleared for the UWF football field.
—Dustin (Top Left), Graner (Top Right, Bottom).

The momentum that Hart has gained thus far would not be nearly as effective without the following sentence: "All of this would be a nuisance, but an acceptable one, if what we've been told about the benefits of increased alumni support and the money UWF will make is guaranteed, or even likely." Hart thus far seemed to be ranting and complaining about menial things that may not even affect UWF's long-term financial situation. That is why, without his detailed attention to logos, this article could be easily dismissed. "Unfortunately, Division II football is steadily making less and less money" (Hart). That hurts. The pride that UWF has for its up-and-coming football team is tremendous, but the team is supposed to grow support and generate revenue for the University. Beginning with this word selection is extremely effective because it solidifies the transition from pathos to logos. Hart did not generate inaccurate facts. His research through the NCAA proved to be a valuable asset to his purpose and rhetoric. Hart cites the fact that universities with Division II teams spend roughly 4.8 million dollars a year on their athletic departments. That figure is a lot of money that could be soaking up some of the rising tuition prices and technology fees, or even money that could be spent in the colleges for improvements and teacher bonuses. This statistic alone begins the devolution of excitement for a football team.

Though, a single statistic would never be sufficient evidence for a reputable study. Before Hart delves into more details, he asks an effective rhetorical question that tackles a point that many may try to use. Using Albany State University as an example, Hart further complicates the issue, expressing that "[a] dedicated football town...can't recoup the money they spent on athletics. What chance does UWF have?" At this point, I believe that Hart feels as though his argument has been won, yet he still includes more statistics to solidify his stance. Rather than utilizing a plethora of numbers and figures, Hart simply states that "[o]nly 20 of 123 Division I teams... made any money at all in 2013." Yes, even Division I schools are losing massive amounts of money each year. If that statistic isn't bad enough, he goes on to say that, on average, the amount lost was 2.9 million dollars. This number shows that even the top teams in the nation struggle to recoup expenses, and UWF is nowhere near the top. As we say in the College of Business, this seems like a very bad business deal.

According to my own research, Hart did an exceptional job of interpreting the facts that were given about Division II football. Having studied financial statements at UWF's College of Business, I was able to find a few reasonable misinterpretations about the numbers provided. In actuality, they are much worse than previously stated. Dr. Daniel Fulks generated a new report in September of 2015, showing that the average university that sponsored a Division II football team in 2014 lost 5.6 million dollars, and in 2013 the overall revenue was negative 4.8 million dollars, not just the cost. To make matters worse, Dr. Judith Bense included information in her "State of the University" address last fall that UWF was in danger of losing 10-15 million dollars for not scoring well on the new Board of Governors Metrics. Can UWF really expect to reasonably deal with all of these potential losses without gouging funding from other departments or placing the burden on students?

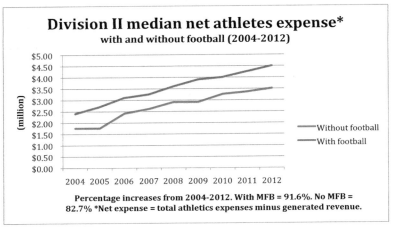

Figure 2. The NCAA shows an increasing gap between schools with Division II football teams, and those without is illustrated above. Division II Athletic Expenses, NCAA. Web.

Finalizing his argument, Hart shifts to a dismal tone in his next paragraph. He expresses that UWF has "[c]ast its die in a dead game," and he portrays his thoughts in a defeated-like tone. This moment is kairotic. After drawing readers in emotionally, he then maintains their attention with numbers that are both easy to understand and frightening to think about. At this point, any text that is portrayed as hopeful or ambitious would fire up the audience once again. Hart asks a series of questions about the state that the student body will be left in and why students should be suffering for what seems to be a bad deal. These questions are especially significant after the emotional and logical strain that he has imposed throughout his article. Hart clearly wants others to be fired up about this issue. Even if no one is protesting or reacting loudly, there is much more incentive for any person acquainted with UWF to ask more questions. "It's not only the University's own future they are playing with, it's ours"—a very bold, direct, and moving statement on Hart's behalf.

Josh Hart utilizes pathos and logos to effectively captivate his audience at the University of West Florida. He draws in his audience with an element of curiosity and uses sarcasm to further provoke his readers; but, rather than solely relying on emotional appeal, he uses strong research and simple figures to solidify his argument. At the end, the dismal tone, coupled with a series of questions followed by a bold statement, is especially power-ful. This persuasive strategy seems to be exceptional because every person at UWF could be adversely affected. Hart reveals questions that many may not even stop to consider until they are pointed out. I know that, as a stu-dent, I can directly relate to all of his sub points, and I am also very curious to see how the university handles its new financial endeavor. Overall, this article begins a crucial conversation that will have significant effects on stu-dents now and in the future.

Works Cited

Bense, Judith. "The State of the University." *Office of the President*. 24 Sep. 2015. PDF File. <http://uwf.edu/media/university-of-west-florida/of-fices/presidentsoffice/communications/SOU-2015-speech.pdf>

"Division II Athletic Expenses." *National Collegiate Athletic Association*. 2013. 25 Feb. 2016. <http://www.ncaa.org/about/resources/research/division-ii-athletics-expenses>

Dustin, Jason. "Excitement for UWF Football Overshadows Pattern of Fail-ure." *The Voyager*. 30 Aug. 2015. JPG File. http://uwfvoyager.com/wp-content/uploads/2015/08/footballopinion.jpg

Fulks, Daniel L. "Revenues & Expenses: NCAA Division II Intercollegiate Athletics Programs Report." *National Collegiate Athletic Association*. Sep. 2015. PDF File. <http://www.ncaa.org/ sites/default/files/2015%20 Division%20II%20RE%20report.pdf>

Graner, Bruce. "UWF Oak Grove Area on Campus." *Pensacola News Journal*. 27 Feb. 2015. Web. JPG Gallery. <http://www.pnj.com/picture-gallery/news/2015/02/27/uwf-oak-grove-area-on-campus/24142563/>

Hart, Josh. "Excitement for UWF Football Overshadows Pattern of Failure." *The Voyager*. 30 Aug. 2015. Web. 19 Feb. 2016. <http://uwfvoyager.com/2015/08/excitement-for-uwf-football-overshadows-pattern-of-failure/>

Making Zines

By Scott Satterwhite

Probably, the first question you have is simple: What is a zine?

A zine (pronounced "zeen", like bean) is a small, independently published magazine. Actually, giving a good definition for a zine is difficult because this definition could apply to many things, so everything that goes into defining a zine should be qualified. A zine (usually) has a small print run. A zine (usually) is in print form. A zine (often) comes from the punk community. A zine (sometimes) is very good reading. A zine (magically) can save your life. I hate to rely on dictionary definitions, but essentially a zine is a small magazine, created with human hands, and brought to fruition with a lot of energy and heart. I know this definition is inadequate, and it's not enough to say "you'll know it when you see it," but maybe when you understand a bit of the history, zines will become more clear—and hopefully you'll be so inspired you will make one yourself!

A Brief and Incomplete History of Zines

Some argue that the first zines were political pamphlets, similar to Thomas Paine's Common Sense, yet others look at zines as something different. While the format may be similar to a political pamphlet, and the edgy political nature might also be similar to a modern zine, neither actually makes a zine. The term itself came into existence with the advent of Science Fiction magazines of the 1930s. Fans of the genre made their own do-it-yourself (DIY) magazines to reflect specific content the writers felt was unaddressed by the major publishers of the day. These DIY magazines, written by fans, were called "fanzines," or zines.

In the 1960s, another movement of writers and activists decided to take the media into their own hands and started what historians now call the Underground Press Revolution. In 1965, five underground newspapers existed. By the end of the decade, hundreds existed from New York to Pensacola, Florida. The content was usually political, but many also focused on gender, race, sexuality, and music. A few of these "undergrounds" still exist, most notably *Rolling Stone*. Few, however, would confuse the modern *Rolling Stone* with an underground paper, even though the content is roughly the same. The main difference is production, which goes back to what makes a zine a zine.

When modern zines truly exploded was in the early punk era. The reasons punks produced self-published media were similar to why Thomas Paine produced his revolutionary diatribe against the monarchy, why sci-fi fans decided to hand-illustrate their own cheesy stories about space ships, and why activists from the '60s decided to tell their own stories in their own newspapers—few publishers took them seriously and no one else would do it.

When punk exploded, few in the music industry paid much attention. To critics, the antics and haircuts were interesting, but the music was very rough. Many professionals dismissed punk as sloppy and immature, compared to popular rock bands of the era. Nevertheless, those in the midst of this movement knew they were witnessing a revolution in the making, and they took the revolutionary act of recording what they heard and saw. They took pictures, interviewed bands, wrote reviews, and put these often-handwritten pages under a photocopier, collated the pages, and stapled the finished project.

From there, a movement began.

Between the Covers

"So what are zines about?" you might ask. Zines can literally be about anything. Whereas most zines are rooted in the punk community, many are not about music. Some focus on a single subject, such as Prince or freak accidents at amusement parks. Others focus on feminist politics and others are travel journals. The most famous zine, *Cometbus*, has a different focus each issue. Some issues of *Cometbus* are novels, others are historical and anthropological studies of various cultures within his world. For whatever topic is of interest to you, most likely there is a zine about that topic. If not, and you're up for the challenge, the world awaits your contribution.

How to make a zine

There are several videos on YouTube which might give you good formatting ideas. Since there are several different formats, I'd suggest you look at those videos for some idea first. Simply search for "How to Make a Zine" and you'll find several. Learning how to fold paper is easy enough, but making a zine someone wants to read is the challenge.

To begin, first thing you should have is an idea of what you want to write. Your zine doesn't have to focus on one single issue. Many, if not most, are written like little magazines. Some pages are personal stories, others are music reviews or musings on travel. One famous zine, *Dishwasher*, was all about washing dishes. That might not sound interesting at face value, but a good writer with a solid idea can make any subject interesting. Another famous zine, *Doris*, is mostly diary-type reflections on various topics ranging from sexual violence and war to baking cakes and reviewing other zines (and hundreds of topics in-between). There's no limit.

Once you have an idea of what you want to write about, building an outline is helpful. What I often do is create a rough table of contents, including the covers (front and back). Here's a sample that might work for you:

Page 1. Cover

Page 2. Introduction

Page 3. Introduction (continued)

Page 4. Memoir (My hometown)

Page 5. Memoir (My hometown-continued).

Page 6. Memoir (My hometown)

Page 7. Memoir (My hometown-continued).

Page 8. Interview with my roommate

Page 9. Interview with my roommate (continued)

Page 10. Interview with random band I saw

Page 11. Interview with random band (continued)

Page 12. Review of my favorite new record

Page 13. Poem

Page 14. Outro (conclusion)

Page 15. Outro (conclusion-continued).

Page 16. Back cover

While you can certainly use some fancy publisher program, you can also use a pen and paper (just make the handwriting neat). The zine *Cometbus* started in 1981 and was mostly handwritten out of necessity because the author, age 14 at the time, believed handwriting was easier. Today, his very neat style of handwriting is well known within the zine community.

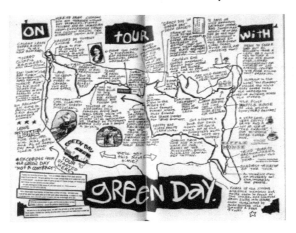

I use a lot of graphics in my zines, but I know other writers who use none. There really are no rules.

That said, as with any piece of writing, few people will pay any attention to a sloppy publication without much thought behind content or writing. Nonetheless, you should still try it. If your first zine isn't great, you'll be in good company. If you keep at it, you'll get better.

The UWF Pace Library has one of the few zine libraries in the United States and is worth perusing for ideas for your own zine. Even if you decide not to create a zine, the genre is worth exploring, and the UWF library is a great place to begin.

Humans of UWF: A Primary Research and Public Writing Project

By Laura Herbek, Jasara Norton, & Bre Garrett

History and Origin of The Assignment

Three UWF Composition faculty members, Laura Herbek, Jasara Norton, and Bre Garrett, originated the idea of teaching a course unit in ENC 1102 called Humans of UWF. We adapted Humans of UWF from Brandon Stanton's Humans of New York (HONY) project. We designed this assignment to teach primary research in the form of interviews and story-collection, and we wanted students to experience a genre of public writing in which publication reached real, live audiences beyond the classroom. Humans of UWF is housed as an active site on Facebook, in which posts reach thousands of viewers. ENC 1102 student Nina Tumminia created the graphic icon used to represent Humans of UWF, and the posts accumulated on the site are all composed by ENC 1102 students.

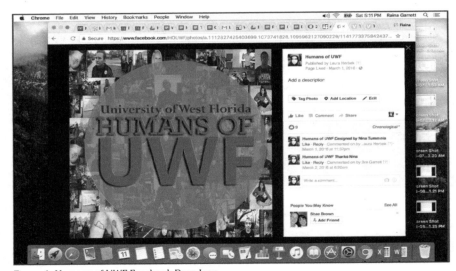

Figure 1. Humans of UWF Facebook Page Icon

When we first thought of adapting HONY to ENC 1102, we were thinking about how important it is to ground public writing in a genre that is most familiar and real-world to students, and social media fits that description best. This generation of students spends more time writing and communicating online than they do any other means. Public writing, as the thematic focus for ENC 1102, needs to reflect that reliance on technology as a foundation for assignments rather than as a supplement. In doing so, we teach students to theorize composing choices around digital spaces and technology platforms.

One thing that's not always present in students' social media communication is a set of clear parameters for quality of writing, something that can only be established through genre analysis, or learning the conventions and expectations of a particular type of communication or writing. Genre analysis is a significant part of public writing, and Brandon Stanton's HONY blog is an ideal tool for genre analysis and, later on, application of writing expectations. By adapting HONY for our public writing purposes, students engage with both the analysis of what makes good writing and circulating that writing to a potentially vast, public audience beyond the classroom.

The first semester we taught the project (Spring 2016), we reflected on the public purpose that the Facebook page might promote—purposes beyond the aims of classroom learning. Students in Bre Garrett's 1102 Honors class came up with the following criteria:

- Highlight UWF/Pensacola activities and lives

- Engage in local community-building—or community engagement

- Conduct research methods that include primary data analysis

- Publish and deliver work on a real public platform

In addition, here are two responses from ENC 1102 students about working on and contributing to Humans of UWF:

"My experience when working on this project was amazing. I have not only grown as a person, but I have also grown in seeing the different views and opinions of others. As students, we aim to become something more during our time in college, and I feel that this project has made me more of what I desire to be." —Ben Lassiter

"Most of us are taking ENC 1102 as college freshmen or sophomores, so we're still getting used to being on our own. Not only is the "Humans of" project the perfect example of public writing, but it also pushes us to go out in public and start a conversation with someone we've never met before. This helps us to become more comfortable out in public...which is essential for relatively new college students like us so that we're more comfortable not only on campus, but also out in town." —Hannah Schwaiger

Why teach Humans of UWF in ENC 1102? What do students learn?

After three semesters of teaching Humans of UWF, we have discovered that the project provides a high-impact learning experience for students. The project teaches academic concepts and public writing principles such as genre analysis, primary research and ethics, story-telling and collection, and rhetorical grammar.

One of the things that makes this project so great is that it helps students to make connections among multiple concepts. For example, analyzing the HONY genre opened up a lot of important conversations about primary research, style, and digital storytelling in the age of social media. In Spring 2016, students across nine sections of ENC 1102 participated in genre analysis on a shared Wiki site. Each student posted a comment to contribute to a larger conversation about genre conventions and audience expectations of HONY. We used the Wiki space to construct our class goals regarding project expectations.

In many instances, students observed that HONY represents a strong element of diversity in the stories told and selected speakers. To follow the HONY tradition, we sought to cover a diverse range of the UWF community, which forced many students to step outside of their comfort zones in terms of daily contact. Topics surfaced on the Wiki such as the ethics of storytelling, the average length of a story and the style choices regarding voice and language, and the relationship between words and images (since all HONY stories include a portrait). Writers must learn how to collect a story on the spot, conversing with an on-the-spot contact, and must place words in dialogue with a portrait.

The Humans of Project series, regardless of location, falls within multiple genres, a photo story mixed with a creative non-fiction interview, characterized by on-the-spot story collection, which requires primary research skills in interviewing and observations. Students must conduct active research through deliberate community engagement. Quinton Fallon, an ENC 1102 student, remarked

> This project was probably one of the most relevant we could have done. This project...challenges students to leave their comfort zone to interact with the greater community as a whole. This is the first non-extracurricular activity to do so, and thus this project is the one most relevant challenge I have undertaken thus far in my academic career.

The project tasks students with capturing stories of the UWF community, on campus community members as well as residents and visitors of Pensacola. All students must follow ethical research practices, including presenting all individuals with a consent to participate form. Participants may pull their stories from the project at any point simply by contacting one of the teacher contacts. All participants are informed that their story and the photo will post on a public Facebook page: Humans of UWF.

This project also allowed us to discuss the function of storytelling in public writing, an integral component often under-recognized. One of the best ways to communicate with each other is by relating information through stories. Using the HONY blog as a template for our project, students analyzed HONY posts for their storytelling impact. From this analysis, students developed a set of project criterion for their own posts that included attention to the story arc in their interviews, such as rising action, climax, and denouement. By treating their interviews, not just as primary source material, but also as opportunities to make a meaningful connection between author and audience, our students understood and felt the real-world impact of public writing.

In-class workshops and peer response sessions offered a valuable opportunity to discuss rhetorical grammar, or a version of grammar instruction based on choices, usage, and contexts (for more on rhetorical grammar, see the section in Chapter 7 "Revising Rhetorically"). Because students collected oral stories, part of the transcription process included making choices about proper documentation of grammar. Student writers had to first identify the possible choices available regarding punctuation, and then, based on the style, tone, and syntax of each sentence, writers had to punctuate both correctly, so as to avoid making any errors, and they had to adhere to a particular style in terms of voice. This grammar exercise very much illuminates the ethics of editing. The project provided a very natural, real way to theorize and practice grammar, something often missing from writing instruction.

Composing Your Own Humans of UWF Project

For this assignment, you will emulate Brandon Stanton's Humans of New York project as you interview fellow inhabitants of the UWF campus. After a careful process of revision and editing, you will have the opportunity to see your work published on the Humans of UWF Facebook page, a public page with hundreds of viewers. This project will test your ability to conduct primary research, analyze and understand genre and audience, compose in an ethically sensitive manner, make rhetorical grammar decisions, and engage with the greater UWF community.

Figure 2. Former UWF President Judy Bense

Genre Analysis

Prior to beginning the project, you'll want to spend some time research-ing this particular genre—a unique intersection of interview, photography, creative nonfiction, and human interest blog. Visit the Humans of New York (HONY) blog and make some observations regarding the format and content of Brandon Stanton's interviews. This blog will be a valuable reference for you throughout the project.

What do Stanton's interviews consist of? Both the photographs and their quotes are equally important, so there should be a clear relationship between the two. You'll notice that most quotations are 100 words or less. Interviews feature the words of the interviewee, but rarely those of the interviewer.

Pay attention to the style of each interview. Interviewees are photographed in a number of ways (headshots, full body shots, close-ups of hands and feet), and photo-editing is kept to a minimum. Quotes highlight an impactful mo-ment in the subject's life, or tell an interesting story that speaks to a common experience many people might share. Creative storytelling is at the heart of HONY, so stories are generally touching, funny, or unusual.

Ask yourself what messages HONY seems to convey. The blog places an em-phasis on diversity by featuring many people who are very different from one another. It's clear that we cannot always judge what story someone will tell by his or her appearance. HONY also promotes the philosophy that human con-nection is a powerful and gratifying experience. A quick scan of the comments section tells us that readers often respond to Stanton's posts with warmth, intimacy, and a sense of community.

It is also helpful to browse the Humans of UWF page for information about how this project has been adapted for our university. UWF campus is very different from New York City in terms of size and culture, and Humans of UWF reflects that reality. Consider the posts in terms of popularity, subject matter, and style. Which posts seem to be most effective, and what do they have in common?

Stanton's audience consists of not only the New York City community, but also a wide array of people, largely social media users, who enjoy human inter-est journalism. Compare this audience to that of the Humans of UWF page. While HOUWF's primary audience consists of the UWF community, the larger Pensacola populace is a secondary group of targeted readers. This audience is much smaller than Stanton's, and may have a different set of values as well.

Figure 3. UWF student on campus

Primary Research: Ethics and Practice

After you have familiarized yourself with the genre, prepare to conduct your own interviews. Think of yourself as both interviewer and a storyteller. Your purpose is to tell your subject's story so that it is compelling while also convey-ing accurately the information your interviewee provides.

Because you are incorporating a live interview into your writing process, plan-ning is an important aspect of this genre. For example, think about how you will approach people. Prepare a pitch and a set of starter questions you might ask. Transparency is also an essential part of this process. When asking for an interview, be clear about the purpose of the interview and the HOUWF project, asking for formal consent.

Approaching strangers might seem daunting at first. Remember that it is a learned skill that gets easier with practice. To find willing participants, observe people's behaviors. Are they relaxed? Do they appear to have time for an interview? Just as importantly, what is your behavior? Are you curious and open-minded? Do you genuinely want to hear others' stories? Finally, you might also plan ahead by considering people and locations that lend themselves to good interviews, such as interviewing a friend of a friend or a professor you admire.

Regardless of your strategy, the more open and genuine you are, the more successful your interview results. Not everyone easily shares personal stories. One of your jobs as the interviewer is to ask follow-up questions that both make your subject comfortable and elicit the kind of human-interest narratives that meet genre conventions.

The technical side of this assignment also requires preparation. To get an accurate transcript of the interview, make a voice or video recording of the conversation, including the subject's consent. You'll also want to think about how you'll take the photo. Will you look for a natural pose? Or pose them yourself? Consider practicing on friends beforehand with your camera.

Even with preparation, you will probably experience rejection. In an NPR interview, HONY's Brandon Stanton describes the hardest part of this process—that some people will reject you no matter how you approach them. Instead of getting discouraged, remember that asking people to share their personal story with a stranger is a kind of unique intimacy that makes the genre difficult but also compelling.

Figure 4. Pensacola Mayor Ashton Hayward

Writing and Publishing

You might be wondering how to "write" an interview if the content is not your own. A good way to think about this process is to think of it as composing a story based on the primary research you generated. Once you have collected that primary material, make a transcript of the interview to see what stories are emerging. All of these steps—asking the questions, transcribing the answers, and seeing the stories—is part of the composing or writing process for this assignment.

At this point, it's helpful to revisit the HONY blog posts and note that most of the longer posts have a story arc to them. Sometimes those stories begin with the rising action. Sometimes they end just after the climax. Other times, Stanton follows the story all the way to the denouement or tells a story across a series of posts, piecing together quotes to create a larger picture. Essentially, each quote is purposefully selected and shaped to tell a story, meaning that every composing choice you make should be rhetorically purposeful as well.

The rhetorical complexity of this assignment stems from the fact that you are working with multiple layers of audience. Your instructor and classmates are your audience, but you also have a real-world audience composed of UWF community members. Negotiating all of these details can be tricky, especially when, for example, your interviewee doesn't use proper grammar. If you include the grammar error, how will that reflect on the interviewee? How will it reflect on you and the project?

Interestingly, your interviewee might not be speaking with as many grammar errors as it first appears. One of the reasons a transcript is so important to this composing process is because it requires you to make rhetorical grammar choices. For instance, what might sound like a run-on sentence could actually be a sentence with a coordinating conjunction or two sentences—one that begins with a discourse connective. Before assuming that your interviewee's oral story is riddled with grammatical errors, revisit the transcript with particular attention to this issue, trying to see the grammar choices you can make that will clearly and smoothly tell your interviewee's story.

Grammar is not the only rhetorical complexity of this genre. Are you concerned that frequent fillers, such as "um" and "like", impede the clarity of the story? Consider omitting some fillers, as long as those omissions don't alter the meaning of the story. Are you wondering if your UWF audience would respond well to graphic language? If possible, select a portion of the interview material that does not contain graphic material. This process of deciding what and where to trim primary research material is what makes this writing assignment challenging but potentially very powerful.

Humans of UWF: A Community Archive

HOUWF's audience has had an overwhelmingly positive response to the project. Students, faculty, administrators, visitors, and even parents have participated in the project via the Facebook page, thus allowing students to understand that their public writing is indeed viewed and appreciated by others. As seen above, we even have portraits from former UWF President Judy Bense and Pensacola Mayor Ashton Hayward.

Several weeks after the project's due date, students still actively post new interview profiles to the site. Humans of UWF is an ongoing, collaborative project with over 600 original posts to date. Currently, the Facebook page has received over 600 likes and maintains a weekly post reach of up to 2,000. A post reach means approximately how many people have been potential audiences. So, the scope and possibility of public audience comes to a real and tangible fruition in this project.

We invite you to check the site to view future contributions. We hope you visit the page regularly, "like" the posts, and share them with your friends and family.

Writing the Right Memoir

by Eman Ogab

Writing a memoir in ENC 1101 and ENC 1102 is not sitting down and writing your autobiography or the first memory you have; it is a creative and inventive process that should take you—and your reader—through an emotional and insightful journey. Your memoir is a reflective glimpse—a snapshot—of something that happened to you within your autobiography that impacted your life in a way that the memory of it makes you want to share it with your audience. You want the reader to remember your memoir by walking away impacted and touched by your experience on a much more meaningful level than before reading it.

When told to write a memoir, your professor is not trying to judge you or snoop on you; your professor wants you to go through the process of theme invention to ground your thesis statement for a bigger project—such as your final research paper. Since your memoir may be substantial to your final paper, you should convey the meaning of a clearly significant moment by starting the invention step of creating a specific theme in your memoir by **narrowing down your focus**. Imagine that your life is an entire book, and your memoir is the chapter where you felt a shift on a specific issue. If you were to give broad details about an entire book, you would lose the importance of that one chapter and distract your reader away from the point you want to make. However, narrowing your focus does not mean less details; it means more details on a specific memory—the important details that made you want to share this specific memory. Give more details on the weather if it is an importance to how you felt. Give more details on the sounds around you during that memory if they impacted you in any way. If the ticking of a clock made you anxious towards a decision you have made, then adding it would make the reader imagine your journey and ride along with you; but if the barking of a dog outside had nothing to do with your memory but noise, then taking that information out would keep your reader engaged and absorbed without confusion.

We have mentioned "**your reader**" or "**audience**," and this does not mean only "your professor." When writing only to a professor, many students might try to bend the truth to impress their professor, and in doing so, their experience might feel forged or exaggerated and become uninteresting. Even though your professor is the primary reader, you should think beyond that. Professors are not looking to be impressed; they are looking for honest, clear, and thoughtful writing while following their instructions. So, when writing your memoir, imagine that you are writing to an audience that can benefit from your experience, and if you are not honest, your writing will come off as artificial, and someone who will want to benefit from your experience will notice this and lose interest. If you write a memoir and it does not have anyone's interest because your reader feels disconnected, then you just wrote words on a paper; however, if you write a memoir that is honest, interesting, and beneficial to many readers by having them connect to it, then you just invented art—and a really interesting thesis topic.

To keep your memoir interesting, write the events of it into a story-like **narrative**. Many readers connect more with a story-like memoir, so instead of writing "here is how I have learned that prejudging a person is unethical," tell a story of how you came to that conclusion through an order of events and details. Let your reader walk in your shoe and feel your experience. A good story always shows, not tells, so by giving your reader a story-like narrative, you let your readers make their own connections in the best way possible by making their own conclusions.

Once you have focused and selected your theme and written your memoir, you are on your way of inventing a theme for your thesis statement. For example, your memoir is written about witnessing the way your friend was discriminated against because of the color of his or her skin, and how that experience changed your way of thinking. Here, we can say that we have the theme of racism. By inventing your thesis theme based on something that you experienced, you will become more interested in the topic. The more you are interested in the topic, the better you will research because for one, you want to convince your audience of your point of view, and second, research will help you realize that you are not alone in this. You will read from experts who speak of the subject that once bothered you in a more cohesive process, which at the end, not only have you invented a thesis topic for your final paper that you are passionate about, but you have also formed a better understanding of your subject.

Another example, your observations of how your relationship with your mother (father, sibling, teacher, coach, or other role model) changed as a result of an event or an experience (their talents, the value of hard work, the fact that they can succeed, that their voice matters, the value of education . . .etc.). Your theme could resolve around the importance of a role model in today's society, or the importance of the relationship between student and teacher as citizens, and you can build upon that theme in order to invent your own thesis statement.

In this chapter "Writing Rhetorically," you learned how to use first person, the pronoun *I*, in your academic writing, and this should help further your understanding of incorporating your experience and turning it into an interesting and well-written research paper. Remember though, whatever you decide to write your memoir on, you need to focus on one theme, so you can keep your memoir interesting and not confusing. Again, this is not a biography, but an exert of your biography. Like a pie, the memoir would be the piece of slice that you think is the tastiest or sourest. The experience can be positive or negative; some of our hardest and finest moments of realization and change come from difficult circumstances or events. The possibilities for finding a theme and inventing a thesis statement are as wide as your experiences. Make certain that you choose to write about something that is important to you and that has played a major role in shaping who you are and how you think.

ENC 1102 Student Memoir

Teacher's Note by Eman Ogab

In his memoir for ENC 1102, "Live Life for You," Malik Ware explores the options of choosing a major and how he came about choosing the one that fits him best. This is usually the first paper assigned to students in the class, so one can say it's a beginning draft for a bigger project. Notice how there is no research or another point-of-view besides the authors. The requirements of a good memoir, whether in ENC 1101 or ENC 1102, is to convey your memory with your own experience in a clear tone, as Ware has done, and then build upon it later in other assignments. Ware explores rather than asserts his decision and experience by asking himself many questions that readers—students—can relate to. He explores the conflicts he endures within himself and within others that many students face when choosing a major: should he choose the major that seems best for him, or should he choose the major everyone else sees best for him. He begins his journey and takes the reader along with him through the disappointments, ups and downs, and indecisive decisions, all while trying to cope with everything around him using good imagery and a story-like narrative to persuade the reader of his struggle in choosing the major that he is passionate about.

Live Life for You

Malik Ware

It was the senior year in high school. The graduating class was in a frantic scramble. The ideal agenda of every senior was the following: get into college, pass all your classes and exams, go to prom and other extracurricular activities, and walk across the stage to graduate. Everyone's agendas varied. Some students were already in college by dual enrollment. Some planned to take up a trade at a technical school. Others would take a year off before heading to school. Some considered their future already planned. *Some* even knew what they would major in. I fell into that bracket of students who were uncertain and wary about their majors. Applying to different colleges and universities and waiting for acceptance letters was daunting enough. Without a clear vision of the next step, my future scared me.

After I received my acceptance letter from the University of West Florida, I began to research the available undergraduate majors actively. With the list of programs and majors, I compared my interests and hobbies to find a compatible major. "Well, AP Psychology was really interesting, not only did I pass, but I've joined the Psi Alpha Psychology Club too. Maybe I could major in that," I thought to myself. Clinical trials, experiments, and case studies—all of which interest me. "Or maybe biology," I considered. "Maybe some sort of politician. A senator or mayor. That seems cool. Heh, maybe a doctor or lawyer." These ideas lit up in my head like flares. A sudden illumination of hope and aspiration. However, like all flares, they burn out into a smoldering pit of the mundane and lackluster drive. There was always one flame that burned brightest: my passion for art. Because of neglect and abandonment for other aspirations, it did not burn out completely. Instead, it grew into a faint ember, burning slowly and emitting an ominous glow. I was always fascinated with art and its implications and effects on the world. Inversely, the world can determine the outcome of art. Different time periods had its own school of thought depending on the events of the times. Baroque period produced dramatic and elaborate artworks and architectural structures to counter the Reformation and reinforce the Catholic Church.

Political unrest and tension were typically reflected in Expressionism. My penchant was Realism. I am awestruck of the photographic painting and realistic sculptures of the past: such skill and careful application. It was the equivalent to the divine power of creating life. Stone would animate and out of it would sprout human forms, and canvas would become an open window into another world. Colors compliment and contrast one another, creating a visual experience that would render the viewers speechless. I wanted to wield that power. Higher education would be the first step to grasping that knowledge.

I declared my Studio Art major and proceeded to fulfill my senior agenda. People would ask about my plans after high school. "I plan to attend the University of West Florida." They were pleased to hear that I was furthering my education. "What are you majoring in," they would ask with eager smiles and wide eyes. "Studio Art." I could never forget the way their expressions melted into disappointment or forget the "oh" or "I see" imbued with a regretful tone. One of my aunts even told me that I need to major in something that will make me money. These obstacles made me uneasy about the future. Was a degree in art a waste of time? What about my career? Would I find a job I'd enjoy? Would I dread coming to work?

I completed my senior agenda and graduated. A small step out of the puddle into the greater ocean. My summer was spent in preparation for college. Despite stockpiling all my needed supplies for my new life in Pensacola, Florida, I still felt unprepared. I thought about switching my major to something more "suitable." Would I end up in a loop of dissatisfaction with a major I chose for others? It was late July, when I visited my aunt. As I was leaving, she asked me when I would return to school. "Sometime in August. I'll let you know before I leave," I replied. "What are you taking up?" I knew she meant what I was majoring. "Studio Art," I replied in a reluctant tone, but what I heard next shocked me. "Well, make sure whatever it is you major in something you're passionate about." I was genuinely shocked. *Something I'm passionate about.*

After that disclosure, my entire outlook shifted. As obvious as it was, I did not think to major in something that is relevant to me. Finding something we enjoy and are exceptionally well at is sometimes rare. We must cherish our gifts and explore our possibilities. It is my life, after all, and I am truly free to do with it whatever I choose. So, I started to claim my goal. When people asked about my major, I proudly declared it. I am no longer worried about the future or finding a career that I will enjoy. If I live my life for me, I will always be happy.

Image credit: "Revision" by Alden David Martinez

To defend what you have written is a sign that ~~your~~ ↳you're alive

chapter 7

Revising Rhetorically

Praxis in Action

How I Revise

Sarah Gray, Ph.D. Candidate and Instructor at Middle Tennessee State University in Nineteenth-Century American and Gothic Literature

I don't think it's possible to overemphasize the importance of revision in the writing process. For me, this process begins with a hard copy of the project on which I'm working. I find that reading my work away from my computer screen allows me to see new angles or incomplete thoughts more clearly than rereading on the computer. By retreating from the computer to a comfortable chair or couch, colorful pen in hand (as long as it's not red!), I allow myself a new perspective that I wouldn't otherwise find.

While changing the mode in which I read my work is important, allowing myself enough time to gain some critical distance from my argument is imperative. Ideally, I allow my paper at least a few days to "rest" while I complete other tasks or work on other projects. This way, the construct I've created for the paper has a chance to fall away, so I don't read my paper already knowing what it's supposed to say. This approach allows me to pay attention to things like organization and clarity; plus, I can see more clearly if my argument is fully supported.

Once I've achieved this critical distance, and I've retreated to an alternate location with my previously mentioned colorful pen, I proceed to annotate my text. I'll ask myself questions in the margins, strike out sentences that no longer seem to fit, draw arrows to rearrange my paragraphs, and rewrite or add information in the margins. I always print these pages one-sided, so I have enough space on the back to do more in-depth revisions, explore new ideas, and take notes for additional research. I often also use this blank space to record questions I may have for my professors.

Allowing enough time for revision also means that I'll have time to reach out to my peers for feedback. I regularly make use of my university's writing center where I've received invaluable advice on everything from brainstorming topics to focusing my argument. Also, a reader who's unfamiliar with my topic or argument is much more likely than me to notice if something isn't explained well enough. After all, an argument is only as good as a writer's ability to make others hear it.

Revision Is Part of the Writing Process

In ancient times, the focus of the rhetor was upon the presentation of oral arguments in the form of speeches, and students trained to perform in pressured situations before a law court or assembly. Though a speaker might spend time in preparation, most speeches were one-time opportunities. If the words were not well-chosen and well-spoken the first time, there was no second chance to influence an audience.

With modern written documents, a composition does not have to be perfect when the words first appear on the page. A document is not truly finished until it is transmitted to an audience, and, even then, important documents are often circulated in draft stages to colleagues for comments before they are presented to an audience.

Many writers claim that revising is the most rewarding step in writing, the time when they have words on a page to work with and can manipulate them to create a composition that communicates effectively. Yet, many students feel that their first drafts should stay exactly the way they've written them because these writings are truest to their feelings and experience. They are sure they have made their point clearly. In reality, a first draft often leaves the reader scratching his or her head and wondering what it was the writer meant to say. To communicate effectively, a writer must learn to interact with readers to ensure he or she communicates a message clearly.

Begin Revision by Rereading

The first step of revising is rereading. This step can be simple, if you are reading something written by someone else. When it is your own writing, it becomes infinitely more difficult. After all, you know what you meant to say—you know the research behind the writing and why you chose certain words or phrases. You even know how every sentence is supposed to read—even though you may have left out a word or two or three—and your mind can trick you into seeing the missing words right where they belong. Unfortunately, the reader does not have your understanding, so communication can break down. You need to learn to read your own work critically, as if it were written by a stranger. One of the first aids in this process is to read your work aloud. You can often hear stumbling blocks quicker than you can see them.

You can also learn to read your own work more objectively by reading and commenting on other writers' work. Look at the structure of essays, at the way the writers use transitions and topic sentences, and at the sentence structure and choice of words. As you learn to see how good writers put ideas and words together, you will begin to think about the readings in a more thorough manner—thinking of alternative, perhaps even better, ways to express the message of each essay. You will also learn to read your own work with a more critical eye.

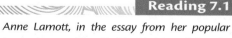

Reading 7.1

Shitty First Drafts

by Anne Lamott

Now, practically even better news than that of short assignments is the idea of shitty first drafts. All good writers write them. This is how they end up with good second drafts and terrific third drafts. People tend to look at suc-

Anne Lamott, in the essay from her popular book about writing, Bird By Bird *(1994), lets the reader in on a secret. Beautiful words do not flow naturally onto the page for even the best-known and most popular writers. Almost all write shitty first drafts. Lamott explains how the process works for her—letting the words pour out without worrying how good they are.*

cessful writers, writers who are getting their books published and maybe even doing well financially, and think that they sit down at their desks every morning feeling like a million dollars, feeling great about who they are and how much talent they have and what a great story they have to tell; that they take in a few deep breaths, push back their sleeves, roll their necks a few times to get all the cricks out, and dive in, typing fully formed passages as fast as a court reporter. But this is just the fantasy of the uninitiated. I know some very great writers, writers you love who write beautifully and have made a great deal of money, and not one of them sits down routinely feeling wildly enthusiastic and confident. Not one of them writes elegant first drafts. All right, one of them does, but we do not like her very much. We do not think that she has a rich inner life or that God likes her or can even stand her. (Although when I mentioned this to my priest friend Tom, he said you can safely assume you've created God in your own image when it turns out that God hates all the same people you do.)

Very few writers really know what they are doing until they've done it. Nor do they go about their business feeling dewy and thrilled. They do not type a few stiff warm-up sentences and then find themselves bounding along like huskies across the snow. One writer I know tells me that he sits down every morning and says to himself nicely, "It's not like you don't have a choice, because you do—you can either type or kill yourself." We all often feel like we are pulling teeth, even those writers whose prose ends up being the most natural and fluid. The right words and sentences just do not come pouring out like ticker tape most of the time. Now, Muriel Spark is said to have felt that she was taking dictation from God every morning—sitting there, one supposes, plugged into a Dictaphone, typing away, humming. But this is a very hostile and aggressive position. One might hope for bad things to rain down on a person like this.

For me and most of the other writers I know, writing is not rapturous. In fact, the only way I can get anything written at all is to write really, really shitty first drafts.

The first draft is the child's draft, where you let it all pour out and then let it romp all over the place, knowing that no one is going to see it and that you can shape it later. You just let this childlike part of you channel whatever voices and visions come through and onto the page. If one of the characters wants to say, "Well, so what, Mr. Poopy Pants?," you let her. No one is going to see it. If the kid wants to get into really sentimental, weepy, emotional territory, you let him. Just get it all down on paper, because there may be something great in those six crazy pages that you would never have gotten to by more rational, grown-up means. There may be something in the very last line of the very last paragraph on page six that you just love, that is so beautiful or wild that you now know what you're supposed to be writing about, more or less, or in what direction you might go—but there was no way to get to this without first getting through the first five and a half pages.

I used to write food reviews for *California Magazine* before it folded. (My writing food reviews had nothing to do with the magazine folding, although every single review did cause a couple of canceled subscriptions. Some readers took umbrage at my comparing mounds of vegetable puree with various ex-presidents' brains.) These reviews always took two days to write. First I'd go to a restaurant several times with a few opinionated, articulate friends in tow. I'd sit there writing down everything anyone said that was at all interesting or funny. Then on the following Monday I'd sit down at my desk with my notes, and try to write the review. Even after I'd been doing this for years, panic would set in. I'd try to write a lead, but instead I'd write a couple of dreadful sentences, xx them out, try again, xx everything out, and then feel despair and worry settle on my chest like an x-ray apron. It's over, I'd think, calmly. I'm not going to be able to get the magic to work this time. I'm ruined. I'm through. I'm toast. Maybe, I'd think, I can get my old job back as a clerk-typist. But probably not. I'd get up and study my teeth in the mirror for a while. Then I'd stop, remember to breathe, make a few phone calls, hit the kitchen and chow down. Eventually I'd go back and sit down at my desk, and sigh for the next ten minutes.

Finally I would pick up my one-inch picture frame, stare into it as if for the answer, and every time the answer would come: all I had to do was to write a really shitty first draft of, say, the opening paragraph. And no one was going to see it. So I'd start writing without reining myself in. It was almost just typing, just making my fingers move. And the writing would be terrible. I'd write a lead paragraph that was a whole page, even though the entire review could only be three pages long, and then I'd start writing up descriptions of the food, one dish at a time, bird by bird, and the critics would be sitting on my shoulders, commenting like cartoon characters. They'd be pretending to snore, or rolling their eyes at my overwrought descriptions, no matter how hard I tried to tone those descriptions down, no matter how conscious I was of what a friend said to me gently in my early days of restaurant reviewing. "Annie," she said, "it is just a piece of chicken. It is just a bit of cake."

But because by then I had been writing for so long, I would eventually let myself trust the process—sort of, more or less. I'd write a first draft that was maybe twice as long as it should be, with a self-indulgent and boring beginning, stupefying descriptions of the meal, lots of quotes from my black-humored friends that made them sound more like the Manson girls than food lovers, and no ending to speak of. The whole thing would be so long and incoherent and hideous that for the rest of the day I'd obsess about getting creamed by a car before I could write a decent second draft. I'd worry that people would read what I'd written and believe that the accident had really been a suicide, that I had panicked because my talent was waning and my mind was shot.

The next day, though, I'd sit down, go through it all with a colored pen, take out everything I possibly could, find a new lead somewhere on the second page, figure out a kicky place to end it, and then write a second draft. It always turned out fine, sometimes even funny and weird and helpful. I'd go over it one more time and mail it in. Then, a month later, when it was time for another review, the whole process would start again, complete with the fears that people would find my first draft before I could rewrite it.

Almost all good writing begins with terrible first efforts. You need to start somewhere. Start by getting something—anything—down on paper. A friend of mine says that the first draft is the down draft—you just get it down. The second draft is the up draft—you fix it up. You try to say what you have to say more accurately. And the third draft is the dental draft, where you check every tooth, to see if it's loose or cramped or decayed, or even, God help us, healthy.

Collaborate

Activity 7.1 • Discussing "Shitty First Drafts"

In your small group, consider these questions in your discussion about "Shitty First Drafts."

1. Anne Lamott says that the image of a writer's process that most people have is "the fantasy of the uninitiated." What does she claim most people think about how professional writer's write?

2. What is the reality of a writer's first draft process, as Lamott describes it? What does she mean by saying that she starts "writing without reining myself in"?

3. Do you agree with Lamott about the process of writing a first draft? Why or why not?

Qualities of Effective Writing

Reading the work of some professional writers, you may have developed the idea that the best writing is writing that is difficult to understand, writing that sends the reader to the dictionary with every sentence, or writing that uses many technical or specialized terms. Often, we think something difficult to read must be well written. Although it is sometimes difficult to read about topics that are new to us because we're learning new vocabulary and struggling with complex ideas, it simply is not true that the best writing is hard to read. Indeed, the most effective writing, the kind of writing you want to produce in your classes, is simple, concise, and direct.

Keep It Simple

Simple means "unadorned" or "not ornate." *Writing simply* means saying something in common, concrete language without too much complication in the sentence structure. Writing simply doesn't mean you have to use only short or easy words. It doesn't mean that all your sentences will be simple sentences. It doesn't mean that you can't use figures of speech or intricate details. Simple writing means that you try to get your point across in a direct and interesting way. You aren't trying to hide your ideas. Instead, you are trying to amplify those ideas and begin an intelligible conversation with your reader.

For example, Greg McKeown, in an article about something Bill Gates and Warren Buffett have in common—focus—uses this analogy about how our eyes focus:

> Imagine if the moment you woke up this morning your eyes focused one time and then never adjusted again. You would be out of focus all day. Our eyes produce clarity through a perpetual process of adjustment.[1]

Using simple sentences, McKeown creates a sophisticated image of how the eyes work.

Simple writing means that you try to get your point across in a direct and interesting way. You aren't trying to hide your ideas. Instead, you are trying to amplify those ideas and begin an intelligible conversation with your reader.

Rely on Everyday Words

When writing about computers or other technical subjects, it's tempting to use **jargon** or specialized words you might use when talking to others with the same knowledge, interest, and background. When writing for a limited audience whose members are familiar with technical terms, a bit of jargon might be acceptable. However, most of the writing you will do in college and later in the workplace will address a larger audience. You will want to avoid the use of highly technical terms, acronyms, and abbreviations.

If it seems that the writers in this text use many big words or technical terms, stop for a minute to consider the original audience for each of the essays. Consider how your vocabulary grows each year as you read, discuss, and consider new ideas. The everyday words of a tenth grade student will probably be fewer in number than the everyday words of a junior in college. Similarly, the everyday words of a college freshman will be different from the everyday words of a computer professional with three years of work experience. Use words that

---

1. McKeown, Greg. "The One-Word Answer to Why Bill Gates and Warren Buffett Have Been So Successful." *LinkedIn Pulse*, LinkedIn, 7 July 2014, www.linkedin.com/pulse/20140707144749-8353952-the-one-word-answer-to-why-bill-gates-and-warren-buffett-have-been-so-successful.

are comfortable and familiar to you and your readers when you write, and you will write clear, effective essays.

Use Precise Words

We sometimes assume that the reader will know what we mean when we use adjectives like "beautiful," "quiet," or "slow." However, the reader has only his or her own ideas of those adjectives. You can make your writing more interesting and effective by adding concrete details to give the reader an image that uses at least two of the five senses.

You can use details from all of the senses to make your writing even more concrete and precise. What are some of the sensual qualities of the experience or thing? Can you compare it to another thing that your readers may be familiar with to help them understand it better? Can you compare it to something totally unlike it? Can you compare it to a different sense to surprise readers and help them understand the image you are trying to create?

A good way to practice your ability to write original concrete images is to expand on a cliché. A **cliché** is an overused saying or expression. Often, clichés begin as similes that help make images more concrete. They become clichéd or overused because they lose their originality, or they don't contain enough detail to give us the entire picture. Choose a cliché and write a sentence that expands the cliché and uses the senses to create a clear picture of the thing described. You might try some of the following clichés:

> She is as pretty as a picture.
>
> It smelled heavenly.
>
> It was as soft as a baby's bottom.
>
> His heart is as hard as stone.
>
> It tastes as sour as a pickle.
>
> We stared at the roaring campfire.
>
> We listened to the babbling brook.

Precise details allow us to experience the world of the writer. We leave our own views and perceptions and learn how someone else sees the world. We learn what "quiet" is like for one writer and what "beautiful" means to another. Fill in the gaps between your words and ideas with vivid images and your writing will become more interesting and more effective.

Be Concise

Rid your writing of excess words and leave only that which makes your meaning clear and concrete. Becoming aware of several common problems can help you make your writing more concise. When you begin a sentence with either "it is" or "there is," you transfer all the meaning of the sentence to the end of the sentence. This is known as a **delayed construction**. You have delayed the meaning. The reader must read on to find out what "it" or "there" refer to. They don't get anything important from the beginning of the sentence.

Examine the following sentences:

It is important to change the oil in older gasoline engines.

There is an apple on the table.

There isn't anything we need to fear except our own fear.

We can rewrite these sentences, making them more concise, by deleting the "there is" or the "it is" and restructuring the sentence.

Changing the oil in older gasoline engines is important.

An apple is on the table.

We have nothing to fear but fear itself.

Notice that the second group of sentences is shorter and the important information is no longer buried in the middle. Revising this type of sentence can make your writing more concise and get information to the reader more effectively.

If you think you may be guilty of using "it is" and "there is" (or "it's" and "there's") too often, you can use most word processing programs to seek these constructions out. Use the "search" or "find and replace" tool that's found in the Edit portion of your pull-down menu. Type "it is" and ask your computer to find every place you use this construction in your document. When you find a sentence that begins with "it is," revise the sentence to make it more concise. Do the same with "there is," "it's," and "there's." After you become more aware of these errors by correcting them, you'll find that you notice the errors before or as you make them. You will begin to write more concisely, and you'll have fewer delayed constructions to revise.

You can also make your writing more concise by avoiding common wordy expressions. Sometimes when we're nervous about writing or insecure about our knowledge of a topic, we try to hide that insecurity behind a wall of meaning-less words, such as in the following sentence:

> At this point in time, you may not have the ability to create a web page due to the fact that you've avoided using computers for any-thing other than playing Solitaire.

This sentence is full of deadwood phrases that add no meaning to the sentence. If we take out the unneeded words, we have this sentence:

> You may not be able to create a web page because you've only used your computer to play Solitaire.

Your computer may have a grammar checker that will identify some commonly used wordy expressions. If your computer doesn't have a grammar checker, or if your instructor has asked you not to use the grammar checker on your computer, you can still learn to revise the wordiness out of your paragraphs. Use the computer to separate a paragraph of your writing into sentences. As you scroll through the paragraph, hit the hard return or "Enter" key on your keyboard twice every time you find a period. Once you have separated the sentences, look at each sentence. What is the important idea in the sentence? What words are used to convey that idea? What words don't add any mean-ing to the sentence? Delete words that don't convey meaning, and revise the sentence to make it more concise.

Use Action Verbs

Action verbs are words that convey the action of a sentence. They carry much of our language's nuance and meaning. Many inexperienced writers use only "to be" verbs: *am, is, are, was, were, be, been,* and *being.* If you use too many of these verbs, you risk losing much of the power of language. If I say someone is coming through the door, I've created a picture of a body and a doorway. If I say someone marches or slinks through the door, I've added information not only about movement but also about the quality of that movement. I've given my subject the attitude of a soldier or a cat. For example, consider this sentence written by Howard Rheingold:

> Thirty thousand years ago, outside a deceptively small hole in a limestone formation in the area now known as southern France, several adolescents shivered in the dark, awaiting initiation into the cult of toolmakers.

By using the verb "shivered," especially when accompanied by the words "in the dark," Rheingold paints a word picture much more vivid than he would have conveyed with the use of a "to be" verb. Using interesting verbs can enliven your writing.

If you want to focus upon using more action verbs, skim through your essay and circle all the "to be" verbs. Read the sentences with circled "to be" verbs more closely, and choose several to rewrite using active verbs in place of the "to be" verbs. You won't be able to do this for every sentence, but replace them where you can and your writing will become more lively, more concise, and more effective.

Fill in the Gaps

When we write, we sometimes forget that we are writing to an audience other than ourselves. We expect that our readers are people just like us, with our experiences, memories, and tastes. Because we have assumed they're so much like us, we expect our readers to be able to read more than what we've written on the page. We expect them to read our minds. We may leave large gaps in our essays, hoping the reader will fill in exactly the information we would have included.

If I'm writing an essay about my childhood in the South, and I say it was always so hot in the summer that I hated to go outside, I might think my reader knows what I mean by hot. However, there are many different ways to be "hot." In east Texas where I grew up, the hot was a sticky hot. Eighty degrees made me long for a big glass of sweetened iced tea with lots of ice. The heat made my clothes cling. Sweating didn't help because the sweat didn't dry. I spent the day feeling as if I'd never dried off after my morning shower. In New Mexico, I never really felt hot unless the temperature got above 110 degrees. At that point, the heat would rush at me, making it difficult to breathe. I would open the door to leave the house, and it felt as if I had opened the oven door to check on a cake. If I say I was hot in the summer without describing how heat felt to me, my reader may not get the message I'm trying to convey. Don't expect your reader to know what you mean by "hot" or by any other general description. Instead, take a minute to add details that will fill in the gaps for the reader.

Speak Directly

To *speak directly* is to say, up front, who is doing what. Sometimes we don't tell the reader who is completing the action or we tell him or her too late. Let's look at a few sentences.

The steak was stolen from the grill.

The decisive battle was fought between the Confederate and the Union armies in Vicksburg, Mississippi.

The red truck has been driven into the side of the green car.

Although we might be able to guess who the actors are in each of the sentences, the first and last sentences don't tell us directly. Even if the reader can guess that it was a dog who stole the steak from the grill or my neighbor who drove the red truck into the side of the green car, the reader has to stop and figure out who is doing what before he or she can read on. This slows the reader down and diminishes the effectiveness of your writing.

Language professionals call this **passive voice**. The action comes before the actor. Note that sometimes, as in the first and last sentences above, the writer doesn't mention the actor at all. To identify passive verbs in your writing, look for verbs coupled with another action word that ends in "-ed" or "-en" such as "was stolen" or "was forgotten."

Find the action and the actor in the sentence to make sure that they are in the most effective order. The most effective sentence order is actor first, then action. If the sentence does not specify the actor but leaves it implied, chances are that it is a passive sentence. For example, read this sentence: "The red truck was driven into the green car." It does not say who the driver was, and thus it is a passive sentence.

Rewriting some of your sentences to eliminate use of the passive voice will make your writing stronger and more interesting.

Strengthen Your Voice

The activities in this book ask you to take positions on controversial issues and make your opinion clear to your audience. You are required to draw upon a range of sources to support your claims in argumentative texts. In effect, your voice joins other voices in a written conversation about your topic, as you use quotes, paraphrases, and summaries from sources combined with your own words.

Beware of over-use of secondary sources, which can cause a paragraph to read like a string of quotations. That may work for a rough draft, but as you revise, include your voice by interpreting what the sources are saying. Table 7.1 is an example of an original, unrevised paragraph on the left that is primarily source material strung together. The column on the right, highlighted in red, shows the student's comments about the source material.

Table 7.1 • Integrating Evidence

Original Paragraph—Poorly integrated evidence	Revised Paragraph—Well integrated evidence
Gabrenya, Latane & Wang (1981) and Albanese & Van Fleet (1985) note that as group sizes increase there is a tendency for the effort put in by the group to be less than the average effort put in by individuals engaged on the same task separately. Albanese & Van Fleet (1985) report on the 'free-rider problem', where the collective nature of the 'contract' obscures the fact of one member failing to honour their part of the contract. Gabrenya, Latane & Wang (1981, p180) discuss the phenomenon of 'social loafing' and typically define it as "one where everyone puts in a little less".	One phenomenon that can greatly impact the effectiveness of groups is that as group sizes increase there is a tendency for the effort put in by the group to be less than the average effort put in by individuals engaged on the same task separately (Gabrenya, Latane & Wang 1981; Albanese & Van Fleet 1985). The phenomenon has been described using various terms. Writers influenced by industrial economics describe it as the 'free-rider problem', where the collective nature of the 'contract' obscures the fact of one member failing to honour their part of the contract (Albanese & Van Fleet 1985, p230). Writers who are organizational psychologists tend to label the phenomenon as 'social loafing' and typically define it as "one where everyone puts in a little less" (Gabrenya, Latane & Wang 1981, p120). Whatever the terminology used to describe this phenomenon, it is one that is problematic for groups.

Source: "Expressing Your Voice in Academic Writing." *UniLearning*, 2000, unilearning.uow.edu.au/academic/4bi.html.

In the highlighted version, the student's voice begins and ends the paragraph. Notice particularly that the last student comment ties together what the sources are saying.

Rhetorical Style

By Laura Herbek

In "Inventing Rhetorically," you learned about the five canons of rhetoric. When revising and editing your work, style is a canon of particular importance. Though the invention and early drafting stages are often focused on *what* you say, it's equally important to contemplate *how* you say it as you refine your writing.

Consider Lewis Carroll's "Jabberwocky," a playful experiment in style and diction. This is one of the most famous nonsense poems in the English language. Try reading it aloud to understand its meaning (don't be afraid to read it more than once):

"Jabberwocky"

'Twas brillig, and the slithy toves
    Did gyre and gimble in the wabe;
All mimsy were the borogoves,
    And the mome raths outgrabe.

"Beware the Jabberwock, my son
    The jaws that bite, the claws that catch!
Beware the Jubjub bird, and shun
    The frumious Bandersnatch!"

He took his vorpal sword in hand;
    Long time the manxome foe he sought—
So rested he by the Tumtum tree,
    And stood awhile in thought.

And, as in uffish thought he stood,
    The Jabberwock, with eyes of flame,
Came whiffling through the tulgey wood,
    And burbled as it came!

One, two! One, two! And through and through
    The vorpal blade went snicker-snack!

He left it dead, and with its head
  He went galumphing back.

"And hast thou slain the Jabberwock?
  Come to my arms, my beamish boy!
O frabjous day! Callooh! Callay!"
  He chortled in his joy.

'Twas brillig, and the slithy toves
  Did gyre and gimble in the wabe;
All mimsy were the borogoves,
  And the mome raths outgrabe.

What story does "Jabberwocky" tell? A close reading of the poem reveals a narrative in which a father warns his young son about several monsters in the forest. The boy takes his sword into the woods and returns with the Jabberwocky's head; celebration ensues.

More importantly, how were you able to understand this story? In other words, how does Carroll manage to convey an intelligible story when so much of the poem is gibberish? Think about the way the poem looks and how it sounds when you read it out loud. "Jabberwocky" may be nonsensical, but it follows a familiar set of rules and organizational strategies. The poem is arranged into traditional stanzas. It utilizes a set meter and rhyme scheme which control the rhythm of the poem. When you read "Jabberwocky," you not only read the words themselves, but also the poem's structure. This suggests that a text's form is equally as important as its content. Though this poem's content is somewhat puzzling, its form helps us to construct meaning. Let's return to the poem and take the "form vs. content" idea a bit further:

1.   Reread "Jabberwocky" to yourself. As you read, cross out all the nonsense words and replace them with standard words of your choosing. Then, spend a few minutes reviewing your version of "Jabberwocky" and analyzing the choices you made. How did you decide which words to include?

      a.   Do any of the nonsense words seem familiar, even if you don't know exactly what they mean? Many English words give hints about their meaning based on the way they look and sound. Take the word "chortled," for example. This a combination of the preexisting words "chuckle" and "snort," a fact that helps us to infer the word's meaning even if we haven't seen that word before. Another example would be "snicker-snack," which sounds like the noise it describes (a sword clattering when it makes contact).

b. When replacing words, how did you decide which parts of speech to use? Take a look at the end of the first line: ". . . the slithy toves." Did you substitute an adjective for "slithy" and a noun for "toves"? A word's position implies something about it's meaning by revealing how that word functions in the sentence. If you replaced both of these words with standard verbs, the sentence would actually make *less* sense than it does in nonsense verse. This is because a sentence is not just a group of words (that's a shopping list!). Rather, a sentence is a series of relationships.

2. A writer's stylistic choices tell the reader about his or her identity and intentions. What does Carroll's "Jabberwocky" suggest about him? Why do you think he utilizes this unusual writing style?

3. "Jabberwocky" reveals much about the ways that language influences meaning. Imagine you are tasked with translating the poem into another language. How might you go about this project? What problems might you face?

Now let's apply some of these ideas to your draft. How can you improve the form of your paper in order to make the most of your content? Determine the strategy you've used to advance your argument. Think of other ways your argument could be organized and assess the pros and cons of each option. Are your topic sentences helping you structure your argument in a coherent and readable way? Have you broken up overlong paragraphs?

Also consider the implications of form at the sentence level. Are the relationships in your sentences clear and intact? How do sentence errors like run-ons, comma splices, and fragments affect these relationships? Are there any words that don't seem to function appropriately in their sentences?

Analyze the style of your paper and ask yourself what messages it sends about you as a writer and your motivation for writing the piece. Is this what you intended to convey? If not, how might you alter things like structure and word choice in order to modify the paper's style?

Activity 7.2 • **Apply Qualities of Effective Writing**

Explore

With a draft of your writing project in front of you, either on a computer screen or in printed form, review the list of Qualities of Effective Writing described in this chapter and listed below. Read the explanation about each quality, and then read your draft, looking for places you can revise to improve your draft.

- Keep it simple.
- Rely on everyday words.
- Use precise words.
- Be concise.
- Use action verbs.
- Fill in the gaps.
- Speak directly.
- Strengthen your voice.

Activity 7.3 • **Share Your Own Grammar Cartoon**

Explore

Find a cartoon that illustrates a point about grammar, print it, and share it with your small group. To locate such cartoons, you could try doing a key-word search in your browser for "grammar cartoons." Have your group choose the cartoons you like best, and share them with the class.

Copyright © 2013 Dan Piraro.

Explore

Activity 7.4 • **When You Reeeaaallly Want to Describe Something**

This activity requires a thesaurus or access to the *Visual Thesaurus* website (www.visualthesaurus.com).

1. Strunk and White's *The Elements of Style*, in an entry on "Misused Words and Expressions," says,

    "*Very*. Use this word sparingly. Where emphasis is necessary, use words strong in themselves."

    With a partner, paraphrase and discuss this Strunk and White writing tip. For example, instead of "very red," you could write "crimson" or "burgundy."

2. To demonstrate Strunk and White's advice in (1) above, revise the following sentence, getting rid of the adverb "very."

    Julie is very pretty.

    No, don't say, "Julie is beautiful." Make a list of more precise and vivid words that could be used instead. Refer to a thesaurus (or the *Visual Thesaurus* website) to find words such as "stunning" and so on.

3. As a class, brainstorm other intensifying adverbs such as "awfully" or "extremely" that you tend to use as words of emphasis (in writing or in everyday speech), and list those words on the board.

4. In pairs again, compose a short paragraph of two or three sentences about a subject or event (e.g., a tornado, a celebrity sighting, a sports event, a news event, a concert, etc.), and intentionally use as many common or trite intensifying words as possible.

5. Exchange the short paragraph you composed in (4) above with another pair of classmates. Revise the other partnership's dialogue with the use of a thesaurus. The revised dialogue should not contain any "intensifiers" or trite words of emphasis. Replace such words and phrases with more powerful and concise language. For example, "I was really happy to see the Hornets win. They totally beat the Giants," could be revised to read (with the help of more concise and powerful words): "I was thrilled to see the Hornets thrash the Giants."

6. Read your "before" and "after" dialogues to the class. Afterward, discuss which words were eliminated and how the words that replaced those intensifiers changed the tone and/or meaning of the dialogue.

Source: Adapted from a lesson plan at "When You Reeeaaallly Want to Say Something." *Lesson Plans*, 3 July 2008. *Thinkmap Visual Thesaurus*, www.visualthesaurus.com/cm/lessons/when-you-reeeaaallly-want-to-say-something/.

Rhetorical Grammar: Introduction & Application

By Michael Mobley, Kara Griffith, Hannah Trevino, Stephanie La Gasse, Alden David Martinez, and Bre Garrett

When we learn about the Aristotelian rhetorical triangle of speaker, audience, and message, we learn to make our writings, our arguments, clearer. The triangle illustrates the relationship among the speaker, audience, message, purpose, and style of an argument. Understanding how these elements work together is vital to understanding how argument works. Unfortunately, the further we become removed from Aristotle's time, the further style becomes divorced from the rhetorical formula. Contemporary composition pedagogies hold precision of word choice and concision of syntactical patterns paramount to effective communication. Upper-level instructors across disciplines and other academic audiences expect first-year composition programs to produce student writers who can generate knowledge in a clear, effective manner. The instruction of grammar is paramount to the accomplishment of such a task, as grammar is an essential element of style. Yet, oddly enough, such instruction is also much maligned among both instructors and students. Why is this?

Most of us, students and instructors included, view grammar as tedious, over-disciplined, and boring. We have come to view grammar prescriptively, meaning as a set of right or wrong rules. The rise of process pedagogies gave birth to a number of popular arguments against the formal instruction of grammar. One argument insists that the integration of grammar instruction into composition courses reduces time spent on more pressing concerns, such as invention and arrangement. Another argument posits that grammatical correctness does little to improve the writing of students who are unable to articulate a cohesive argument or focus. In her article "Making a Case for Rhetorical Grammar," Laura R. Micciche (2004) asserts that if we go beyond the prescriptive methodologies we associate with the instruction of formal grammar, these arguments become faulty. Micciche's article offers insight into what exactly this "going beyond" looks like.

Micciche's central argument is that rhetorical grammar has a place in emancipatory pedagogies, or classroom practices that place active student engagement and student voice and lived experience at the heart of learning. She states that the desire to avoid teaching grammar "does not eclipse the practical reality that nearly every writing teacher struggles with at one time or another: how to teach students to communicate effectively. And effective communication, which entails grammar knowledge, is essential to achieving many of the goals regularly articulated in composition studies" (Micciche 717). Grammar is emancipating in that it allows one to communicate effectively, giving a writer access to participate in discourse and to effect that cultural and social change that liberatory pedagogies hold as pillars of composition instruction. But what exactly is rhetorical grammar?

What is Rhetorical Grammar?

Rhetorical grammar's purpose is to change how writers view grammar, and with this purpose in mind, rhetorical grammar, rather than a formal set of rules, evolves into the writer's use of grammatical elements in order to develop his or her style and affect the audience in an intentional way. When we look at grammar rhetorically, we realize that grammar is more than just punctuation, or marks on a page, more than just part of an editing process that culminates with line-by-line checking of commas, periods, and other tedious squiggles. Rhetorical grammar encompasses style, or the structure, syntax, and voice that makes up sentences. As Micciche asserts, we cannot separate grammar from argument because a particular sentence formation speaks to and persuades audiences in particular ways. When teachers avoid teaching grammar, we disservice students. Further, teaching grammar in a non-contextualized manner is self-defeating. If we can't show a student why grammar is important, then retention and transfer of grammar knowledge simply do not occur at satisfactory rates. This means that writers are not able to put grammar knowledge in practice after learning particular rules or customs. The remedy to this issue of retention and non-contextualization: **provide context**. We raise the stakes. In fact, existing methodologies of contemporary rhetorical grammar pedagogies lend themselves to understanding just how grammar and argument are intertwined. In their placing an emphasis on writing's capacity to effect cultural and societal change, these pedagogies already acknowledge that language is both malleable and transformative.

More often than not, grammar instruction is prescriptive and error-driven. Grammar is taught as a set of rules that, quite often, are given no clear reason for existence. However, grammar instruction that includes contextualizing why grammar is important beyond simply stating "It just is" invites student agency by raising the stakes beyond comprehension of one's argument and into the realm of rhetorical efficacy. According to Micciche (2004), this elevation occurs through students' experimenting with language and then reflecting on the interaction between content and grammatical constructs;

for example, a student may be asked not only to define a dependent clause, but also to construct a sentence with a dependent clause, and going one step further to explain *how* subordinating one idea to another affects his or her argument. What does this concept look like when we expand it into an entire assignment?

Assignments & Application

Rhetorical grammar can be taught through a number of assignments. The following examples each require students to produce an analysis of a text; more advanced assignments require that students analyze their own writing. Regardless of the text selected for analysis, the most vital aspect of any assignment aimed at stoking understanding of rhetorical grammar is a focus on the analysis of style and how style choices effect argument, writer's purpose, and audience.

In the first example, shown in Figure 1 and adapted from an anecdotal version in Micciche's article, students are asked to maintain a commonplace

---

Objectives:

In a journal or notebook, maintain twice weekly entries in which you rhetorically analyze assigned texts. Your analysis should focus on grammatical choices that the author of each piece makes. Their choices may be practical or creative. Consider how the choices work within the context of the rhetorical triangle: speaker, audience, and message. Is the author using grammar to strengthen their argument in some way? (HINT: Chances are that I am assigning you texts that foot this bill.) How are these grammatical moves working with other rhetorical elements? Is the author's word choice affecting the tone or voice of the piece? Why did he or she choose to include a fragment in their piece? What could that possibly accomplish? Even though I am asking you to focus on grammar, by no means should you neglect the other rhetorical elements of the assigned pieces. While you DO NOT have to model your work after our readings, I urge you to consider how the authors of those pieces coupled these elements.

Requirements:

Each entry should be at least 250-500 words.

If you choose to keep a digital commonplace book, our regular formatting rules apply:

12 point font

Times New Roman

DOUBLE-SPACED

Figure 1. An assignment utilized to teach rhetorical grammar. Adapted from "Making a Case for Rhetorical Grammar," by Laura R. Micciche, 2004, *College Composition and Communication*, 55(4), p. 724, copyright 2004 by the National Council of Teachers of English.

book in which they "follow each entry with at least one paragraph of analysis in which they identify the work achieved by specific grammatical techniques in the passage" (p. 724).

This assignment is versatile in that it can be adapted to any text that is already being discussed in class. The instructor need not assign an analysis of the entire text; rather, one can simply assign a selection that is particularly exemplary of grammar's rhetorical significance. Teachers can also modify the assignment to task students with analyzing text they encounter outside of class, including billboards, bulletin boards around campus, Facebook or other social media posts, etc.

The next assignment, shown in Figure 2, asks students to analyze texts that they generate. With this assignment, students get the opportunity to experiment with the rhetorical possibilities of grammar. The invention portion of this assignment recommends a low-stakes discovery and creation opportunity. The pass-fail nature of such an assignment lends itself to invention, removing the fear of a bad grade and fostering experimentation with grammatical and syntactical practices that students may not

---

Objectives:

Write a short creative nonfiction piece or critical analysis of a shorter work that we have read this semester. NOTE: If you choose to write a critical analysis, you must have the primary text approved by me before completing the assignment. Prefered length is 500-1000 words, but if you want to write more, you can. Once you have your piece finished, conduct an analysis of your use of grammar in the piece. Did you always use correct grammar? Did you purposefully choose to include grammar errors in your writing? Why did you make these choices? Your choices may be practical or creative. Consider how the choices work within the context of the rhetorical triangle: speaker, audience, and message. How are your grammatical moves working with other rhetorical elements? Is your word choice affecting the tone or voice of the piece? Did you utilize a fragment or other sentence error? Even though I am asking you to focus on grammar, by no means should you neglect the other rhetorical elements of the assigned pieces. While you DO NOT have to model your work after our readings, I urge you to consider how the authors of those pieces coupled these elements.

Requirements:

Your creative work or critical analysis should be at least 500-1000 words.

Your reflective rhetorical analysis should be 250-500 words.

Our regular formatting guidelines apply:

12 point font

Times New Roman

DOUBLE-SPACED

Figure 2. A creative writing assignment utilized to teach rhetorical grammar.

have used before. By cultivating experimental practices, the assignment also allows the instructor the opportunity to impress upon students, via comments on the returned assignment, the risk involved with such agency of practice while still being able to assign a good grade to the paper. The reflective rhetorical analysis is recommended as a tool for evaluating writers' retention, or extended and learned use, of rhetorical concepts and terminology, including their overall conceptualization of grammar as a rhetorically active tool.

In-Class Lessons and Exercises

Rhetorical grammar classroom activities differ across classes depending on when they enter the writing process. Two activities, described below, can be used in ENC 1101 or 1102 rhetorical grammar instruction.

The first activity, "Grammar Performance," works effectively when paired with a literary or film text, particularly in ENC 1102. For this exercise, divide the class into groups. Assign each group the same section of a screenplay to perform in class on a future date. Texts that can be read in multiple ways, such as the short story "The Hanging Stranger" by Philip K. Dick, work the best. If a text is lengthy, ask students to perform different parts to see how the storyline interpretation changes. Groups are allowed to change only the punctuation and diction of the screenplay. Once groups have performed their versions of the screenplay, the class discusses each group's screenplay changes and how the different choices altered the text's meaning. The purpose of this activity is to emphasize how writers and audiences interpret punctuation in a rhetorical situation; specifically, how punctuation transforms from writing to speaking. Not only does this activity show how we interpret punctuation but also how we interpret characters based on punctuation. When students change the diction of the screenplay, they change the interpretation of their characters as well.

The second activity is a mix of formal and rhetorical grammar instruction, and may be more successful in an ENC 1101 classroom. Begin with a short lecture on the different types of declarative sentences, which are listed below with example sentences. These sentence types have different functions in writing a research paper, and can serve different purposes depending on the author's intention. Instructor provide formal grammar instruction through the explanation and presentation of these sentence types, discussing the rules and defining the grammatical concepts. After the lecture, present the class with a writing sample, asking students to identify a few of these sentences in the sample. Discussing the purpose of the sentence in the sample shifts the activity from formal to rhetorical grammar. Students must identify the audience and argument of the sample in order to situate the sentence types within the sample. Allowing students to decide how these sentence types are used gives students enhanced authority over their writing options. As a subsequent exercise, divide the class into groups and provide them with two more writing samples. Groups can discuss how the same sentence type is used differently or the same; designating a group note-taker might also be beneficial. The groups can then present their discussion points to the class, opening a whole class discussion and debate to the different options. If you want students to reflect further on this topic, assign a post-activity writing on the use or purpose of sentence types in their own writing.

Declarative Sentence Types:

- **Causal sentence**—a sentence in which a cause precedes an effect.

  Ex: <u>Because Johnny was naughty,</u> <u>Santa Claus did not give him a present.</u>
              C   E

- **Effective sentence**—a sentence in which the effect precedes the cause.

  Ex: <u>Santa Claus did not give Johnny a present</u> <u>because he was naughty.</u>
                  E   C

- **Active sentence**—the simplest form of a sentence—subject, verb, complete thought.

  Ex: <u>Santa Claus</u> <u>is</u> <u>coming to town.</u>
        S   V   CT

- **Passive sentence**—a sentence containing a delayed or implied subject.

  Ex: The presents will be delivered **[by Santa]**.
                                   S

- **Transitory sentence**—a sentence that begins with a transitory word.

  Ex: <u>Nevertheless</u>, I hope to get a bike next year.
          TW

- **Gerund sentence**—a sentence that begins with a gerund.

  Ex: <u>Riding</u> in Santa's sleigh is super fun.
        G

- **Conjoined sentence**—a sentence containing two sentences joined by either a comma and a FANBOY, a conjunctive adverb, or a semicolon or colon.

Ex: <u>Mom forgot to buy milk</u>, so <u>Santa will have only cookies.</u>
            Sentence 1   Sentence 2

Collaborative Grammar—Class Activity

Your individual choices regarding where to place a comma or how to organize a sentence depend on your own preference in conjunction with rules of usage. Although you must follow formal grammar rules and guidelines, you still can choose to make your writing your own style. You can identify good (and poor) uses of grammar in advertisements, books, subtitles, and texts. However, your interaction with grammar may be different than others. You can draw on others' grammar knowledge when you work collaboratively to make these rhetorical grammatical choices.

"Grammar Mini-Tests" combine individual grammar skills in a collaborative exercise that extends beyond basic grammar-skill tests and lectures. These mini-tests are not all-encompassing, but they provide a basic understanding of common grammar mistakes. You will not only practice your own grammar skills, but also actively engage in argumentative practices to prove why the answers you choose are correct.

Take a Grammar Mini-Test to test your rhetorical grammar skills. You will take this five-question mini-test individually. Afterwards, you will collaborate with your small group of four or five peers and re-take the test together. Be certain of your answers so that you can articulate and explain why you made the grammatical choices that you did. Argue why you are right and do not forget to use the argumentative techniques that you have been taught during the semester. Grammar is about choices, so work together to make these choices. Your collective knowledge allows you to learn from one another while practicing a more intuitive form of grammar.

Grammar Debates—Class Activity

After getting into groups, you will revise a number of sentences that reflect an error related to a particular grammatical skill. Discuss and revise these sentences with your group, stating and explaining your choices as you develop the revised versions of your sentences with your classmates. Once your group has revised these sentences, discuss your revisions with the rest of the class.

Revise the sentences below if necessary:

Group A:

1. Lee wanted to go to the movies, but he promised Alex he would study with him.
2. After the football game we ordered pizza.

Group B:

1. Next semester Rob will take Comp II, Psychology and Biology.
2. Hitler and Napoleon for example were short people who had a desire to control others.

Re-inventing Grammar with Music—Class Activity

Rhetorical grammar focuses on the grammatical choices you make. Potentially, a text can present multiple functions of grammar and can present a variety of choices regarding those functions. Consider Rick Astley's song "Never Gonna Give You Up." By reading this text in multiple ways, you can change the meaning and context of the song by applying different grammar decisions. You can use this song to learn and employ many grammatical skills, but the choice is up to you as to how you use rhetorical grammar.

Have you ever fangirled over an artist? Maybe you're a fanboy of Rick Astley's! (by the way, FANBOYS is an acronym for the coordinating conjunctions *for, and, nor, but, or, yet,* and *so*). Watch the music video for Rick Astley's famous "Never Gonna Give You Up." Look up the lyrics of the song as well. Let's consider the following line: "Your heart's been aching but you're too shy to say it." In this sentence, there is a punctuation error.

- One comma rule is that we are to use a comma to separate two independent clauses joined by a coordinating conjunction—a fanboy.
  - "Your heart's been aching" is an independent clause—a complete sentence on its own.
  - "you're too shy to say it" is also an independent clause.
  - Since the word *but,* one of the FANBOYS, is joining these two independent clauses, you would place a comma before the word *but.*

- Conversely, a semicolon rule states that you could use a semicolon to separate independent clauses that are not joined by a coordinating conjunction.
  - If we were to remove the word *but* from Astley's previously mentioned line, we would have a run-on:
    - "Your heart's been aching you're too shy to say it."
  - According to the semicolon rule, we would simply place a semicolon between the two independent clauses:
    - "Your heart's been aching; you're too shy to say it."

Rhetorical grammar also gives you choices of quoting a text.

- One comma rule is that we are to use a comma to separate direct quotations from the phrase identifying the speaker.
  - Rick Astley states, "You wouldn't get this from any other guy."
- One colon rule states that we use a colon to separate the introductory words from a quotation only if the introduction is grammatically complete.
  - Rick Astley sang Alden's favorite line: "Never gonna give you up, never gonna let you down / Never gonna run around and desert you."

Rhetorical grammar even gives you the ability to list information several ways.

- The buzzfeed way
  - Here are the eight things Rick Astley will never do: give you up, let you down, run around, desert you, make you cry, say goodbye, tell a lie, and hurt you.
  - a. Another rule states that we are to use commas to separate three or more items in a series. Remember to place the Oxford comma before the conjunction that comes before the last item of the series.
    - i. "[I] Gotta make you understand that [I'm]/ Never gonna give you up, never gonna let you down, never gonna run around, and desert you.
  - b. There are some rules that I could not relate to Astley's song lyrics. For example, one comma rule states that we use a comma to separate the dates in the month-day-year format. If this date is in the middle of a sentence, we are to place a comma after the year.

i. According to Wikipedia, Rick Astley was born on February 6, 1966, in Merseyside, England.

These are just a *few* of the comma rules that you could apply to Rick Astley's song. Now it's your turn. Look at the lyrics of the song and identify other instances in which you can choose a specific grammar choice. Should you use a semicolon between two lines? What if you changed the pronouns in the entire song to third person pronouns? Do all of Rick Astley's subjects and verbs agree? How many rhetorical grammar choices can you make?

Grammar Play with Oral Interviews—Class Activity

This activity can be paired with the Humans of UWF class project (discussed in Chapter 6).

Conduct an oral interview for a research project or, less formally, as just a rhetorical grammar exercise, interview a classmate about her or his writing process—or collect an oral history from a peer. The important part here is that you collect the interview data in an oral manner so you do not have the written text from the interviewee. Interviews are rather difficult methods of primary research (for more on interview techniques, see Chapter 5).

Once you have collected the interview data, either via hand-written account or audio recording, transcribe the words verbatim. Don't worry about punctuation at first; rather, just document the words exactly as the interviewee spoke them. Once you have a transcript of the words, then, go back and examine grammar choices and options. For example, where do you place commas? Where do you provide end punctuation marks? When do you include a semicolon, or when do you select to use a conjunction and a comma to combine sentences? As with the other activities discussed in this rhetorical grammar section, follow up the activity with student presentations about the choices made. Open whole class discussion about how the choices impact the language and speech. This is also a good place to merge formal grammar instruction and discuss whether the choices reflect accurate rules.

Remember to Proofread

It is understandably difficult to find the errors in an essay you have been working on for days. A few tricks used by professional writers might help you see errors in your essay more clearly.

1. With pencil in hand, read the essay aloud, slowly—and preferably to an audience. When you are reading aloud, it is more difficult to add or change words, so you tend to catch errors you would not see reading silently to yourself. Plus the reactions of your audience may point out areas where future readers may become confused or lose interest.

2. Another trick is to read the essay backwards, sentence by sentence. This forces you to look at sentence structure and not at the overall content of the essay. If you are working on a computer, another way to accomplish this is to create a final edit file in which you hit the hard return twice at the end of every question or statement. You might even go so far as to number the sentences so they look more like grammar exercises. Then look at each sentence individually.

Grammar Girl's Top Ten Grammar Myths

by Mignon Fogarty

Reading 7.2

In this blog entry, Mignon Fogarty offers her top-ten list of grammar mistakes and misunderstandings. Notice that Fogarty disagrees with Safire, saying it is okay to split infinitives. Fogarty is writing more recently than Safire and probably has a less formal audience in mind.

10. A run-on sentence is a really long sentence. Wrong! They can actually be quite short. In a run-on sentence, independent clauses are squished together without the help of punctuation or a conjunction. If you write "I am short he is tall," as one sentence without a semicolon, colon, or dash between the two independent clauses, it's a run-on sentence even though it only has six words.

9. You shouldn't start a sentence with the word "however." Wrong! It's fine to start a sentence with "however" so long as you use a comma after it when it means "nevertheless."

8. "Irregardless" is not a word. Wrong! "Irregardless" is a bad word and a word you shouldn't use, but it is a word. "Floogetyflop" isn't a word—I just made it up and you have no idea what it means. "Irregardless," on

the other hand, is in almost every dictionary labeled as nonstandard. You shouldn't use it if you want to be taken seriously, but it has gained wide enough use to qualify as a word.

7.   There is only one way to write the possessive form of a word that ends in "s." Wrong! It's a style choice. For example, in the phrase "Kansas's statute," you can put just an apostrophe at the end of "Kansas" or you can put an apostrophe "s" at the end of "Kansas." Both ways are acceptable.

6.   Passive voice is always wrong. Wrong! Passive voice is when you don't name the person who's responsible for the action. An example is the sentence "Mistakes were made," because it doesn't say who made the mistakes. If you don't know who is responsible for an action, passive voice can be the best choice.

5.   "i.e." and "e.g." mean the same thing. Wrong! "e.g." means "for example," and "i.e." means roughly "in other words." You use "e.g." to provide a list of incomplete examples, and you use "i.e." to provide a complete clarifying list or statement.

4.   You use "a" before words that start with consonants and "an" before words that start with vowels. Wrong! You use "a" before words that start with consonant sounds and "an" before words that start with vowel sounds. So, you'd write that someone has an MBA instead of a MBA, because even though "MBA" starts with "m," which is a consonant, it starts with the sound of the vowel "e"—MBA.

3.   It's incorrect to answer the question "How are you?" with the statement "I'm good." Wrong! "Am" is a linking verb and linking verbs should be modified by adjectives such as "good." Because "well" can also act as an adjective, it's also fine to answer "I'm well," but some grammarians believe "I'm well" should be used to talk about your health and not your general disposition.

2.   You shouldn't split infinitives. Wrong! Nearly all grammarians want to boldly tell you it's OK to split infinitives. An infinitive is a two-word form of a verb. An example is "to tell." In a split infinitive, another word separates the two parts of the verb. "To boldly tell" is a split infinitive because "boldly" separates "to" from "tell."

1.   You shouldn't end a sentence with a preposition. Wrong! You shouldn't end a sentence with a preposition when the sentence would mean

the same thing if you left off the preposition. That means "Where are you at?" is wrong because "Where are you?" means the same thing. But there are many sentences where the final preposition is part of a phrasal verb or is necessary to keep from making stuffy, stilted sentences: "I'm going to throw up," "Let's kiss and make up," and "What are you waiting for" are just a few examples.

© Huffington Post

Stationary means "fixed in place, unable to move;" **stationery** is letterhead or other special writing paper. (Hint: **Stationery** with an *e* comes with an envelope.) Examples: Evan worked out on his **stationary** bike. The duke's initials and crest appeared atop his personal **stationery**.

© Huffington Post

Eminent means "distinguished or superior;" **imminent** means "impending, sure to happen." Also, **eminent** domain is the right of a government to take over private property for public use. Examples: The rain was **imminent**; it would arrive soon, soaking the **eminent** dignitaries on the stage. (Think of **imminent** and **impending**, which both begin with the same letters.)

Reading 7.3

The following list, "Top Ten Distractions for Writers, or Any Job Really," by Sam Scham, was published in the Yahoo Contributor Network.

Top Ten Distractions for Writers, or Any Job Really
by Sam Scham

When you have a set goal in mind, whether it is for personal or work reasons, so many other things can become easy distractions. For writers in particular, life seems to get in the way. There are other pressing matters that we have to worry about.

1. The Internet
The Internet is a very huge distraction these days. For writers who do research online for their great idea, it is easy to stumble upon different links and steer away from the main point in focus. If you find yourself doing this, try to limit the time you do research therefore getting off the Internet earlier and allow more time for writing.

2. The Radio
Music can help a writer generate ideas and feelings. Listening to the radio can be a distraction if you leave it on for too long. If you are like me, you are able to write the best in silence. You need to be able to hear yourself think. If you are listening to the radio and it is hard to turn away from it, listen to it in segments. Listen to some music and when a commercial comes on, mute the radio and start writing. Maybe, before you know it, you will forget that you were ever listening to the radio.

3. The Television
The television and the radio are similar in many ways. For one, it is hard to turn off, especially if you are in the middle of a show that you want to finish. But then, you see a commercial for what is coming up next and you are intrigued to watch it. At the end of the current show, turn off the TV and get writing. Soon, you will not notice the absence of the picture box.

4. Own Procrastination
You want to sit down and write, but at the same time you don't, you have no motivation. The solution is to take a day off, do not think of it at all. Work on any other pressing matters like home chores or calling up an old friend that you've been meaning to catch up with. On the next day, wake up and get writing. Just jump right into it and it will be like you never took a break.

5. Other People

Especially if you live with family or friends other people always being around can be a huge distraction. In order to solve this, find out when everyone will be out and fit in time to write while they are gone. If that just doesn't work with your everyday schedule, find a nice place outside or at the local library where you can work in peace without other people bugging you.

6. Other Responsibilities

Work, chores, walking the dog; these everyday responsibilities are tiring and at the end of the day you just cannot get the energy to write. Try writing in the morning, even if it is just for a few minutes. Get the best out of what you got and do not get discouraged.

7. Telephones

With cell phones these days, you can be getting texts at every minute either from friends or social networks. When you are writing, the best way to refrain from your cell phone is by turning it completely off and leaving it somewhere out of sight so that you are not tempted to check it.

8. Outdoor Activities

Especially on a really nice day, you may want to forget the writing and spend some time outdoors. That is completely fine. Enjoy life to the fullest. If you end up not writing for the day, remember that there is always tomorrow. But be careful not to put it off for too long and too often. If you really want to spend time outside, take the writing with you and kill two birds with one stone.

9. Everyday Needs

You need to eat sometime and when you work and do everything else, cooking can really tire you out and make you not want to write. On those days, try to make simple meals if you absolutely do not want to order out. There is nothing wrong with having a bowl of cereal for dinner.

10. Being Bored

We all get bored sometimes, even of our own writing. Take a break. Do not work on writing your big project, but work on something else. A day or two later go back to that big project and start working on writing it again and if you are still bored, put it to the side again. At least you cannot say that you did not try.

Activity 7.5 • **Write a List of Your Writing Habits**

As you write an essay assigned by your instructor, keep notes about your writing process. What distracts or keeps you from writing? What works well when you write? What kind of prewriting do you do? What are the best (or worst) conditions for you when you write?

Organize your notes about your writing process into a theme such as "Best Places to Write" or "Ways to Avoid Procrastinating." As Sam Scham does, write two or three sentences about each of your writing habits.

Academic Conventions: Style and Grammar

By Justin McCoy

Conformity to style and grammar rules is an important consideration in academic writing because well-written communication establishes and sustains your credibility with readers. Simply put, no one will be interested in reading your ideas if they are not carefully edited.

Perhaps you have never considered how a working knowledge of grammar can be empowering to your identity as a writer. As the "nuts and bolts" of effective communication, grammar functions as a tool for content invention. In other words, if you can visualize variations in sentence structure and understand the relationship of one sentence to another, then you can fill in the blanks with content.

In the context of academic writing, grammar is the prescriptive rules for making sentences. Your composition instructors expect your formal writing projects to reflect Standard Written Edited English (SWEE), which includes grammar, punctuation, and spelling. Use the following rules to make your writing projects reflect SWEE so that you can avoid the dreaded red ink marks from your composition instructors:

- Use commas after introductory elements, which are those elements that precede a complete thought, and between two complete thoughts that are separated by one of the FANBOYS (*for, and, nor, but, or, yet,* and *so*).
- Avoid comma splices, sentence fragments, and run-ons.

- Use a semicolon to separate two complete thoughts that are inter-related.

- Use a colon to separate a complete thought and an elaboration of the complete thought (e.g., *The American flag has three colors: red, white, and blue.*)

- Insert a noun after the following determiner words: *this, that, these,* and *those.*

- Spell the author's name and the title of his or her work correctly.

Outside of composing grammatical sentences in your first-year writing courses, you should also produce papers that reflect manuscript and citation formatting rules prescribed in the most recent edition of *MLA Handbook for Writers of Research Papers.* Among the benefits of MLA style include streamlining how writers engage texts and providing a guide for the ethical use of source materials. For instance, when you quote or paraphrase someone else's ideas in your academic writing project, you cite your sources with in-text, parenthetical citations that correspond with citation entries on your Works Cited page. Additionally, writers know in what tense to write about texts and how to format documents.

Regarding MLA manuscript format, most composition instructors expect you to do the following in formal paper assignments:

- Insert correct MLA heading: your name, instructor's name, class, and date in military style.

- Insert an original title for your paper.

- Double-space your entire document.

- Insert your last name and page number in the top right corner of your paper.

- Set your text to Times New Roman, 12-point font.

- Set your margins to 1 inch on all sides of your paper.

In addition, below are the conventions of MLA style that your composition instructors look for when evaluating MLA style in your formal paper assignments. If you break these rules, the errors are likely to stick out like a sore thumb to your composition instructors.

- Make claims in present tense.

- Write about texts using present-tense verbs.

- Refer to a source's author's full name the first time you mention him or her; thereafter, refer to him or her by using his or her last name only.
- Introduce quoted material.
- If you quote from a source, explain and/or interpret the quotation.
- Italicize titles of large works (e.g., novels, plays, movies, television shows, newspapers, etc.).
- Insert quotation marks around titles of small works (e.g., television episodes, short stories, poems, newspaper articles, academic articles, etc.).
- Include a parenthetical citation after every instance in which you quote or paraphrase someone else's work.

Gain Feedback by Peer Editing

Your instructor may schedule class periods for peer workshops. These workshops are opportunities for you to get responses from your readers. Often, you will be divided into groups of three or four students, and you will be given a list of questions to answer about your peers' essays. Your peers will get copies of your essay, and they will give you comments as well. The first peer workshop can be a difficult experience. It is never easy to take criticism, constructive or not. Taking criticism in a small group is even more difficult. There are several things you can do to make your peer groups more productive.

When Your Essay Is Being Reviewed

1. Write down everything the reviewers say. You think you will remember it later, but often you will forget just that piece of advice you need. More importantly, writing while the reviewers speak is an effective way to keep the channels of communication open. It is hard to come up with a defense for your paper if you are busy writing.

2. Save your comments until all the reviewers are done. If you have specific questions, write them in the margins of your notes. If they ask you questions, make a note to answer them when everyone is done. If you allow yourself to speak, you will be tempted to start defending your essay. Once you start defending your essay, two things happen. First, you stop listening to the comments. Second, you offend your reviewers, making it less likely that they will give you honest criticism in the future.

3. The first comment you should make to your reviewers is "Thank you." The second comment can be anything but a defense. Your readers are

only telling you how they have interpreted your essay. They are giving you their opinions; you do not have to make the changes they suggest.

4. Save all the comments you get on your essay. Set them aside for a day or so. Then make the changes that you think will make your essay better.

When You Are the Reviewer

1. Read an essay through, at least one time, just to browse the content of the essay. Appreciate the essay for what it does well. Try to ignore any problems for now. You will get back to them the second time you read and begin your comments in the margins. Every essay will have at least one thing about it that is good.

2. Always begin your comments with a sincere discussion of what you like about the essay.

3. Be specific in your comments. Your peers will probably understand you better if you say, "The topic sentence in paragraph four really sets the reader up for what the essay accomplishes in paragraph four. But I can't really find a topic sentence for paragraph six, and the topic sentences in paragraphs two and three could be improved." Note how this statement gives a positive response and then identifies specific places where the author can improve the essay. This works much better than a generalized statement like, "Topic sentences need work."

4. Be descriptive in your comments. It is often helpful for students to hear how you are reading their essays. "Paragraph five seems to be telling me . . . " or "I got the feeling the essay's overall message is . . . " are good ways to start descriptive sentences.

5. Realize that you are analyzing a paper and not a person. Directing your comments toward the essay, "Paragraph nine doesn't really have any-thing new to add, does the paper need it?" sounds better to the listener than "You repeat yourself in paragraph nine. Do you really need it?"

Independent Reviewing

If your instructor does not require peer editing, you can ask someone to review your essay. Choose someone you trust to give you an honest opinion. It might not be effective to ask a parent, spouse, or girlfriend/boyfriend to give you a critique if you know they are going to like anything you write, just because you wrote it. It might be better to ask another student who has recently had an English class or one of your current classmates. In exchange, you might offer to look over their work. Remember, you learn to read your own essays better by reading other peoples' essays more critically.

Sample Questions for Peer Review

When you have revised your paper several times, have a peer answer these questions regarding its overall content, paragraph development, and word choice and sentence structure.

Overall Content

1. What is the thesis or main point of the essay? Where does the writer state this main point? If the main point is implied rather than stated, express it in a sentence. Does the main point give a subject and an opinion about the subject? How might the writer improve his/her thesis?

2. What is the purpose of this essay? What are the characteristics of the audience the writer seems to be addressing (formal, fun-loving, serious, cynical, laid-back, etc.)?

Paragraph Development

1. Do each of the paragraphs in the essay work to support the main point of the essay? Which paragraphs seem to wander from that main point? What other information needs to be added to develop the main point?

2. List two places in the essay where the writer uses vivid sensory details. How effective are those details? Are they used to support the thesis of the essay? Identify two places in the essay where the writer needs more effective details. What kind of details might he or she include?

3. What grade would you give the introduction? How does it draw the reader into the essay? What specific things can the writer do to make the introduction more inviting?

4. Which paragraph do you like the best? Why? Which paragraph in the essay do you like the least? Why? What can the writer do to improve his/her paragraphs?

5. What grade would you give the conclusion? How does it provide closure for the essay? What specific things can the writer do to make the conclusion more effective?

Word Choice and Sentence Structure

1. Are adequate transitions used between the paragraphs? Find an effective paragraph transition and identify it. Why does it work? Find two places between paragraphs that need more or better transitions. What can the writer do to improve these transitions?

2. Are a variety of sentences used? Where might the writer vary the sentence structure for better effect? What two sentences in the essay did you find most effective? Why?

3. Are there any words that seem misused or out of place? What positive or negative trigger words are used? Do they enhance the message of the essay or detract from it?

Activity 7.6 • Peer Editing

Compose

As your instructor directs, exchange your paper draft with another student, or work in groups. Then, review the essay you are given, answering the questions about overall content, paragraph development, and word choice and sentence structure that you find in the section "Sample Questions for Peer Review."

Examples of Peer Reviewed Student Essays

Sample Student Essay: Rhetorical Analysis Assignment

Rhetorical Analysis of President Reagan's
"Challenger Speech"

FIVE, FOUR, THREE, TWO, ONE, WE HAVE LIFT OFF! THE SPACE SHUTTLE CHALLENGER HAS CLEARED THE LAUNCH PAD. This was supposed to be a glorious day in American history, a mile stone in the United States Space Program. Instead this day quickly turned into one of the most horrific scenes witnessed live by the American

> This is an effective attention-getting beginning to your essay.

public, which included thousands of school children, who watched from the comfort and safety of their classrooms.

On January 28, 1986, the space shuttle Challenger was scheduled for launch in Florida. It would mark the second flight by the United States Space program and it was the first educational launch program. On this particular flight there was to be a teacher on board, she was the first teacher on a space shuttle as a result of a special program from NASA. Although there were some clear concerns regarding whether the shuttle should launch, NASA officials gave the green light and the mission moved forward. Within seconds of lift off, the space shuttle Challenger burst into flames and disintegrated in mid flight, instantly killing all seven passengers aboard. The nation was shocked, especially thousands of young children who eagerly watched the live coverage on television. Within hours of the explosion President Ronald Reagan went on live television and addressed the nation from the White House. President Reagan was scheduled to address the nation on that particular day to report on the state of the Union, instead he went on television and paid tribute to the Challenger Seven. President Reagan delivered one of the most inspirational, and motivational speeches of his tenure as the President of the United States. It is a speech, like all great speeches, that would out live his presidency, and be regarded as one of the great speeches of our time.

> Background information provides context for the speech.

> The thesis is that Reagan's speech was inspirational.

The nation stood still, not knowing what to make of the days events. In such times of sorrow people tend to need support, guidance, and reassurance. The American people needed someone to follow, a shoulder to lean on, a vision of the future, a leader. President Reagan went on live television and paid tribute to the "Challenger Seven" in a speech from the White House. President Reagan sat alone behind a large desk surrounded in the background by family pictures. President Reagan used his *ethos* as a credible individual; he was the leader of the free Nation. He gave the speech from the White House, which is clearly recognized by the American public as a symbol of power and security. The

> Discusses elements that increased Reagan's *ethos*, such as giving the speech from his desk at the White House, surrounded by family photos. These elements showed him to be a powerful leader who is still a husband and fathe

image of him sitting behind a great desk flanked by pictures of family and loved ones borrowing once again from their *ethos*. This was a not only the President of the United States delivering this speech, this was a husband, a father, and a son too.

The occasion for the speech was obvious: The Nation had just witnessed seven brave individuals perish before their very eyes. These brave souls were, husbands, sons, daughters, fathers, and they had paid the ultimate sacrifice for mankind. President Reagan portrayed all of these different roles played by each of the "Challenger Seven" from behind that desk. As the speech proceeded, President Reagan was careful to not down play the Challenger incident, but he appealed to *logos*, or logic, by saying "But we have never lost an astronaut in flight. We've never had a tragedy like this one." Here he used *pathos* to emphasize the severity of the incident while at the same time letting the nation know that there have been other brave astronauts who have also paid the ultimate price for the visions and progress of mankind. President Reagan throughout his speech used his words very carefully and with great insight. His words and the double meaning or relation to the events of the day made a huge impact on the delivery and acceptance of his speech by the American public. As he stated "Your loved ones were daring and brave, and they had that special grace, that spirit that says, Give me a challenge, and I'll meet it with joy." As one can see, President Reagan is using the word challenge here, this is a direct reference to the space shuttle Challenger.

President Reagan goes on to address the thousands of children who also witnessed the event, addressing the emotion or *pathos* of the occasion. He states, "And I want to say something to the schoolchildren of America who were watching the live coverage of the shuttle's take-off. I know it's hard to understand, but sometimes painful things like this happen. It's all part of the process of exploration and discovery. It is all part of taking a chance and expanding man's horizons. The future doesn't belong to the fainthearted; it belongs to the brave. The Challenger crew was

Identifies the kairos of the situation.

Reagan appeals to logos or logic as he points out that the United States had never before lost an astronaut in flight.

...eal to pathos ...is not as ...g as the ...n the next ...graph.

Significant appeal to pathos, as Reagan addresses school children directly. Millions had been watching the takeoff, as a teacher was aboard.

pulling us into the future, and we'll continue to follow them." Here President Reagan's audience is the children, who in turn are the future of the nation. By saying that the Challenger was taking them towards the future, he is saying what everybody already knows. The children are the future of the nation and he is telling them that they must continue to move forward, for one day they will be the leaders of the country.

President Reagan's message is very clear: This was a tragedy, yet we as a nation must continue to move forward in order to honor the memory of the "Challenger Seven." President Reagan, utilizing *logos*, then mentions the NASA employees in his speech. Here he does not blame or degrade the space program or its employees. Instead he praises there hard work and dedication to the American people and the space program. He does not speculate on the cause of the explosion nor does he address any issues related to who is to blame. He completely omits any negative or accusatory comments in his speech. This was a very tactful and extremely intelligent move by Reagan. He knew the American public had many questions regarding the explosion. He also knew that those questions needed to be answered and that it was his responsibility to provide those answers to the nation. Yet on this day, and in this speech, it was not the right time to do so.

> Your voice comes through as you praise Reagan for not raising questions or making negative remarks during this particular speech.

President Reagan in closing his speech borrows from the *ethos* of the past when he stated "There's a coincidence today. On this day three hundred and ninety years ago, the great explorer Sir Francis Drake died aboard ship off the coast of Panama... a historian later said, He lived by the sea, died on it, and was buried in it. Well, today, we can say of the Challenger crew: their dedication was, like Drake's complete."

President Reagan's speech on the space shuttle Challenger served several purposes. First, it paid tribute to the seven astronauts who lost their lives in the explosion. Second, it provided the nation with a much needed reassurance that everything was going to be all right. And although this was terrible accident

> Discussion of Reagan's purposes makes a good conclusion.

and set back for our country, he also left no doubt that the Nations commitment to NASA and the space program would not only survive, but continue to advance forward into the future.

Sample Student Essay: Short Op-Ed Argument

What Marriage Means to Me

I came out to my parents as a lesbian when I was seventeen years old. My parents cried and I thought I'd never want
to live another day. It seems silly to say, but I met the love of
my life while I was in high school. I had never felt more accepted or loved before in my life till I met her. As a member
of the LGBT community, I was wary of the life ahead of me. I experienced
bullying, denial from my parents, and homophobic comments and ha-
rassment. I believe adamantly in the protests and movements promoting
gay marriage and by extension human rights. From not only a logical
consideration of the facts but also a personal experience of
being a lesbian member in society, I believe the United States
should refute DOMA nationally and allow the LGBT community
to have access to civil marriage to reflect their equality and
discourage otherness in their population.

> Certainly a dramatic opening, which would catch your reader's attention.

> Clear thesis, though you might clarify somewhere in the essay what you mean by "otherness."

Civil marriage is so much more than a recognized partnership. Civil
marriage provides access to many legal benefits in taxes, estate planning,
government, employment, medical, death, family, housing, consumer, and others. Denial of these legal benefits, along with others, reflects multiple human rights violations. Implicitly, a lot of
these benefits reflect at the core of the pursuit of happiness, one
of the most basic human rights in the United States. The inability
to have the rights that come with marriage means that LGBT is a
marginalized population.

> Good that you mention the legal benefits being denied, including taxes, estate planning, medical, etc.

The battle for same sex marriage making national news has happened
in my own hometown, El Paso, Texas. In 2009, our mayor John Cook passed
a law approving benefits for domestic partners, including same sex couples.
A local pastor launched a recall motion and managed to revoke the law in
2012. I remember the movement quite well. John Cook released comments
to the *Huffington Post* that resonated strongly with 16-year-old me and
continue to do so today: "Where do I stop? Do I all of a sudden say ... when

you call 911 when you're divorced, committing adultery, you ain't going to get no ambulance or fire truck? And don't expect me to pick your trash up, because that would be condoning sin?" Where does it stop? At what point is civil marriage recognized as a legal institution, a completely different institution from that of religions?

> Excellent use of a quote. Calls attention to this example from your own hometown.

Civil marriage is not an affront to any religion, but a set of rights and benefits that should be given to everybody. In the separation of church and state, there was a born recognition that in the diversity of religion and opinions, the government was to be held responsible for a certain set of laws that would be extended to everybody. The denial of these rights to the LGBT community reflects negatively on our government's ability to be genuine in its delivery of human rights.

> Yes, many opponents of gay marriage make this claim. Good that you address counterargument, You could say a little more about it.

Nationally recognized civil marriage means more than legal benefits. It is a reflection of the stance the government and American society takes on the LGBT community. This stance as of today is troubling. The LGBT community has had instances of extreme hate crimes that go as far as rape and homicide. The denial of civil marriage only promotes and condones a violation of LGBT members.

> This sentence somewhat repeats what you say in paragraph two.

According to *Time,* 75% of Americans believe there are federal laws prohibiting discrimination based on sexual orientation. They're wrong. There's actually no law stopping this behavior, and this reflects all too much in the reported violence against LGBT members. A 2013 report from the National Coalition of Anti-Violence Programs (NCAVP) revealed a worrying increase in police misconduct against LGBT members. From the survivors of police violence, 48% reported police misconduct and 26.8% reported hostility in police attitudes.

> Interesting statistic.

Violence and discrimination against the LGBT community happens from a very young age. According to the Centers for Disease Control and prevention (CDC), LGBT children are twice as likely as their heterosexual peers to attempt suicide. In a 2009 survey conducted by the CDC, eight of ten students had been verbally harassed at school, four of ten had been physically harassed at school, six of ten felt

> Good that you are using reputable sources such as the CDC.

unsafe at school, and one of five had been the victim of a physical assault at school. Matthew Shepard is only one face of many to experience the horrors of violence against the LGBT community. At the age of 21, he was brutally tortured and left to die in an act of hate crime.

The government has a lot to do with the issue of LGBT individual's safety and legal defenses. Equality in all respects fights against the social stigma held for the LGBT community. A government that provides equal human rights to all, denies discrimination on the basis of sexual orientation and gender identity, and promotes social wellness for all its population is one that makes that population feel undivided and safe. The current social dialogue on civil marriage for same-sex partners reflects a long history of LGBT struggles and a pivotal point in our government's stand in their rights.

The key argument against civil marriage for the LGBT community is driven by the ideal that marriage is a religious institution and threatens the religion along with their idea of family life. This argument is incredibly invalid on multiple levels but ties back to the previously mentioned quote of John Cook. It is unethical on part of the government to deny rights based on religious beliefs or traditions. As a modern country, our government should be able to uphold equality and human rights to all its citizens. Civil marriage is a stepping-stone for equality and human rights for the LGBT community.

> You mention the religion issue earlier. Might be good to edit, so that you do not repeat points.

Wanting to marry and have children is not just a heterosexual American dream. It is mine and it is that of many individuals from the LGBT community. It should not only be a dream, but a right to be able to pursue this dream. I adamantly feel that I shouldn't be discriminated based on my sexual orientation. Speaking as both the sixteen year old feeling hurt and conflicted as the pastor spoke hateful words against the LGBT community and the young woman in love today, I hope that our government is capable of making the right call in my and many other's rights and equalities in the United States. This is an issue that strikes not only in the hearts of adult LGBT individuals but children and generations to come and how they are going to live their lives as equal members or stigmatized populations. Civil marriage for the LGBT community means a step closer to equality.

> Strong conclusion that, like the introduction, connects you personally to the issue.

Sample Student Essay: Short Research Paper in MLA Style

Student last name 1

Name of Student

Name of Professor

Name of Course

Date

Emerging Mobile Phone Technology Empowers

Mobile phone technology is a late 20th century invention, but it is an emerging technology because it continues to evolve and innovate. The earliest phones were huge, affectionately referred to as bricks. They were not cool. Only rich people had them, and they look ridiculous in old photographs with the clunky phones, poised like they think they look cool. As with most technology, when it became more affordable, more people began to use them. Now it is expected that an individual have a mobile phone. In the rare case where someone does not have a mobile phone, it is often seen as a revolutionary choice, a form of protest about the desire to not be connected all of the time. Mobile phones of today are more and more becoming smart phones, essentially handheld computers that do more than computers of the 20th century could do. They are extensions of one's self. They are not just for voice anymore. The newest mobile phones boast about the megapixels of the camera, the quality of the speakers, the processor and the amount of storage it has. Mobile phone technology is revolutionizing the way people use technology, most interestingly in how they are used in developing countries.

Mobile phones are used in restaurants to process credit card transactions. They have apps to process fingerprints at crime scenes. Many of the smartest mobile phones have photo editing and sharing capacity. There are apps to edit music. It is truly a democratization of technology that was previously too expensive for an individual to own. Mobile phones are (usually) less expensive than a

> Your voice comes through as you describe the old, clunky phones that people at the time thought were cool. Also, later in the paragraph when you discuss that not having a mobile phone is a form of protest.

> Your thesis prepares the reader for a discussion of mobile phone technology, including its use in developing countries.

> This paragraph makes good use of your background knowledge.

Student last name 2

computer, but give the same kind of access to information previously only available to those who could afford a computer. Mobile phone technology has revolutionized many industries, including business and even public health. During the Arab Spring and any other form of civic protest around the world, mobile phones were essential for organizing and communication. Mobile phone technology is empowering for women and girls in ways we could not even imagine 10 years ago.

Another advantage to mobile phone technology is that mobile phones, even smart phones with lots of apps, are small and easy to hide. This makes it possible for women and girls to keep the ownership of mobile phones private if they are concerned that their husbands or fathers do not want them to have mobile phones. According to "Connecting to Opportunity: A Survey of Afghan Women's Access to Mobile Technology," conducted by the U.S. Agency for International Development, 48% of the women and girls who report not have a mobile phone cite their husbands or fathers not wanting them to have them as the primary reason they do not have mobile phones. This is an unfortunate cultural issue that needs to be dealt with via education campaigns and may improve as younger generations age ("Connecting to Opportunity"). If Afghan men come to see mobile phones as a way for improving their economic situation, perhaps attitudes toward female online access will shift, and there will be less of this kind of resistance to women and girls having mobile phones.

> Good that you provide a context for the coming paraphrase from a source.

> Here your comment follows up on the point from the USAID article.

Most Americans cannot imagine life without computers and the internet. The two are so ingrained in the culture that it is often expected for high school students to own laptops they are able to bring to school. Children can navigate touch screen tablets before they attend Pre-K school. More than a million people own iPhones, using them for all sorts of things from communication to entertainment to business. Paypal offers a device its customers can use to process credit and debit card payments on an iPhone or iPad. No longer do businesses have to have landlines to process credit cards. Now the farmer who brings her crops to the

> It is a little jarring to have a paragraph about American use of technology in between two paragraphs about mobile phones in developing countries. You might consider reordering your paragraphs.

Student last name 3

farmers' market can accept Visa or Mastercard in addition to cash. Mobile technology has revolutionized the way small business is done in the United States, in addition to developing countries around the world.

Mobile phones used to be too expensive for those in developing nations. "Between 2004 and 2009, approximately 80 percent of new mobile subscribers worldwide came from Africa, the Middle East, Asia and Eastern Europe" ("Connecting to Opportunity"). These countries lack infrastructure resources for landline phones for dialup or DSL and the thought of owning a computer is seen as more of a fantasy. Mobile phones have become less expensive to produce and voice and data plans have come down in price.

According to "Empowering Women through Mobile Technology" a fact sheet published by the United States Department of State, mobile phones and mobile technology are essential to improving the lives of women around the world. Mobile phones create an independence that women have never experienced before. Women farmers are given real time access to information about crops and weather to help handle their crops better. They are able to find out prices for produce and handmade goods in other areas so that they can negotiate a better price in real-time, which improves the economic status of the farmer. Women report feeling safer with a mobile phone. Texting or SMS messaging on mobile phones has lead to literacy campaigns so that women can better communicate using mobile phones. Women also use mobile phones for public action, organizing and civic engagement ("Empowering Women through").

> You might consider occasionally having a quote from one of your sources. A quote would add emphasis.

The Mobil Technology Programme is a response to data published by the GSMA Developing Fund which showed that more than 300 million women in developing countries did not have regular access to mobile technology. The Cherie Blair Foundation for Women, the organization that put together the Mobile Technology Programme, argues that access to mobile technology empowers women by providing access to financial programs and banking that help women to become entrepreneurs ("Mobile Technology Programme").

> Your paper is beginning to focus more on mobile phones empowering women in third world countries. You could have rewritten your thesis to include this aspect.

Afghanistan is a prime example of the power of mobile technology in a developing country. According to Connecting to Opportunity: A Survey of Afghan Women's Access to Mobile Technology, conducted by the U.S. Agency for International Development, Afghanistan was isolated from mobile technology until 2002. Since the first mobile phone contract in 2002, over 20 million people residing in Afghanistan have mobile phones. This is even more impressive when one knows that the total population of Afghanistan is 30 million. Roughly two out of three people have mobile phones in Afghanistan. According to this survey, approximately 80% of Afghan women have access to a mobile phone in some capacity, either owning outright or have the ability to borrow one. Also, according to the survey, young women are one of the largest mobile phone user groups in Afghanistan. In rural areas of Afghanistan, women often engage in mobile phone sharing. Like other developing countries, the use of mobile phones is for banking, farming, and health care. The Afghanistan literacy rate for women is about 18%, according to the survey, which argues that while literacy programs are important, it is also important that mobile phone apps provide a voice option for those whose reading ability is limited. Adding voice commands to mobile phones is an emerging technology that nongovernment organizations are pushing for as a way to empower the population of Afghanistan, especially women and girls ("Connecting to Opportunity").

An amazing statistic.

ExxonMobil Foundation funded an initiative to increase economic opportunity for women. As part of the initiative, ExxonMobil surveyed of mobile phone adoption and use in three developing countries, Egypt, Nigeria, and Indonesia. The results of the survey showed that the "rapid adoption" of mobile technology is a primer for empowering women entrepreneurs. The ExxonMobil report led the Cherie Blair Foundation to develop a pilot program to develop apps tailored for women entrepreneurs in developing countries ("Mobile Technology Can").

The GSMA mWomen Programme is the initiative that was born from ExxonMobil research and Cherie Blair foundation. The focus of the program is to close the gender gap in mobile phone

nteresting that the program addresses reasons why women might not have mobile phones of their own.

Student last name 5

ownership in developing countries. The idea is that if women own mobile phones then they will be empowered in business, healthcare and civic engagement. The program addresses the reasons why women might not own a mobile phone of her own. Barriers to mobile phone ownership is cost, technology literacy and family or cultural reasons such as the husband not wanting the wife to have a mobile phone of her own ("Gsma Mwomen Programme").

In addition to empowering women economically, mobile phone technology can improve the health of women and their families. In May of 2013, PBS reported a story of a first time mother in Africa who received text messages from an organization called Mobile Alliance for Maternal Action, often referred to by MAMA. The mother receives text messages several times a week with medical and health information helpful to her as her baby grows (Cheers).

There have also been technology innovations to improve the sexual health of women with mobile technology. Prototypes of STD testing that can be done with a mobile phone are in development. Testing like this is useful in more than one situation. It makes testing more available for those who are too embarrassed to go to the doctor or have circumstances that prohibit them from accessing a doctor. The technology is also useful for sex workers because the plan is for them to be able to test clients before providing services. It is one more way for women to protect themselves. Thus, mobile phone technology is revolutionizing public health as well (Smith).

> You have cited quite a range of information about mobile technology.

In conclusion, mobile technology can only continue to improve the lives of people in developing countries, particularly empowering women. The more young women who start using mobile technologies, the more open to new technologies they will be. The first step, which is in the process of being accomplished, is to put mobile phones into the hands of as many women and girls in developing countries. Giving them access is revolutionary. The next step is to develop apps tailored to their needs such as farming apps, banking apps, health apps. Making sure these apps work with voice for those who cannot read is imperative and still the revision stage, as they

Student last name 6

do not always work as well as tech developers would like. Literacy programs are needed to teach women and girls how to read, so they can use the apps and communicate via texting or SMS messaging. And, of course, technology like this needs to be subsidized until it is affordable enough for anyone to go in and purchase a mobile phone. Electricity and running water were not considered human rights until the early 20th century. Mobile technology—access to information in real-time—is part of the new frontier of human rights. Women and girls—all people—have a right to technology that can improve their lives. Attitudes need to change. Mobile phones are not a luxury anymore; they are a necessity to participate in the 21st century marketplace.

Well said that mobile technology is a new frontier of human rights.

Student last name 7

Works Cited

Cheers, Imani M. "In South Africa, Using Mobile Technology to Improve Maternal Health Access." *The Rundown: A Blog of News and Insight,* PBS, 5 May 2013, www.pbs.org/newshour/rundown/in-south-africa-using-mobile-technology-to-improve-maternal-health-access/. *PBS Newshour,* PBS, www.pbs.org/newshour.

"Connecting to Opportunity: A Survey of Afghan Women's Access to Mobile Technology." *USAID,* USAID, 21 May 2013, www.usaid.gov/where-we-work/afghanistan-and-pakistan/afghanistan/survey-afghan-women-technology.

"Empowering Women Through Mobile Technology." *U.S. Department of State,* U.S. Department of State, 10 July 2010, www.state.gov/documents/organization/149807.pdf.

"GSMA mWomen Programme." *Katerva,* 23 Apr. 2011, katerva.org/nominees/empowering-women-with-mobile-phones/.

"Mobile Technology Can Help Women Entrepreneurs, Report Finds." *Philanthropy News Digest (PND),* 15 May 2012, philanthropynewsdigest.org/news/mobile-technology-can-help-women-entrepreneurs-report-finds.

"Mobile Technology Programme." *Cherie Blair Foundation for Women RSS,* www.cherieblair-foundation.org/programmes/mobile/.

Smith, Catharine. "Mobile 'App' To Diagnose Sexually Transmitted Diseases." *The Huffington Post,* 9 Nov. 2010, 9:04 a.m., updated 25 May 2011, www.huffingtonpost.com/2010/11/09/mobile-app-to-diagnose-std_n_780847.html.

Sample Student Essay: Research Paper in APA Style

Running Head: OBESITY IN AMERICA   1

Understanding the Negative Impact Food Industry Advertising

Has on Obesity in America

Name of Student

Student's University

OBESITY IN AMERICA   2

Abstract

This paper examines the negative impact food industry advertising has had on the crisis of obesity in America. The articles explored in this paper provide an in depth look at how obesity has multiplied over the years to become an epidemic threatening the lives of millions. These articles also discuss America's public opinion about obesity, as well as the government's role in addressing this challenging national problem. This paper considers the policies that have been implemented to help fight one of the nation's biggest downfalls, as well as what is yet to be done.

Keywords: obesity, food industry, health

Understanding the Negative Impact Food Industry Advertising Has on Obesity in America

In 2004, the U.S. Centers for Disease and Control and Prevention (CDC) ranked obesity as the number one health risk facing America ("Obesity In America"). Ten years later, obesity is not just considered a health risk, but an *epidemic* endangering the lives of millions of Americans. Staggering numbers reveal that the rates of obesity in the United States continue to skyrocket. Countless reports and studies have sought to find answers to the obesity puzzle that plagues America's future, and while useful information has been discovered, we are far from extinguishing the problem. Americans continue on their journey to combat obesity, (which is identified in an individual when their body mass index is 30 or higher), by dieting, exercising, and trying the latest fads in weight loss.

> Good to begin paper with this startling statistic. Then, your next sentence says that the situation is even worse. Very effective.

But despite the efforts to eliminate obesity, studies now suggest that if obesity rates continue to rise, 42% of Americans will be obese by the year 2030 ("Adult Obesity," 2012). Unfortunately there are significant elements working against the millions of people fighting for their lives. The food industry is spending more money than ever before on marketing ads in the United States. Without any strict regulations and policies that limit what these money giants can do, the food industry continues to cater to America's addiction to sugars and fat by marketing unhealthy foods constantly. Policy makers in America must hold the food industry accountable by creating stringent guidelines that create boundaries on the marketing of the food being advertised—not only to children, but to all Americans suffering from this disease; these policies may be what help in lowering the dangerous percentages of obesity threatening the lives of millions.

> Good thesis. This is something you can argue.

Obesity is a major risk factor for non-communicable diseases, such as diabetes, cardiovascular diseases, and cancers (Rodrigo, 2013, pg. 22).

OBESITY IN AMERICA   4

With more than two-thirds of U.S. adults being overweight or obese (Ogden et al., 2014), it is no wonder why obesity is considered America's health crisis. Sadly, obesity in the U.S. is not just affecting adults, but children as well. About 30 percent of low-income preschoolers are also overweight or obese (Centers for Disease Control and Prevention, 2011). Obesity has no specific demographic. It is affecting millions, from the rich to the poor, and the young to the old; the American diet is being equally destructive in terms of the wrath it sheds on its victims. Because obesity is associated with a number of serious physiological ailments, it should be of no surprise that obesity has serious economic consequences, and as a nation, we are paying the price for the extra pounds. "The annual medical costs alone have been estimated as high as $190 billion dollars—21 percent of all medical spending" in the country (Cawley & Meyerhoefer, 2011, pg. 22). Whether you are suffering from obesity or not, we must recognize that obesity is affecting all of us, in one-way or another. There are many factors that contribute to obesity. Some blame obesity on genes, while others think watching too much television and having little physical activity are the main culprits. While these are all valid justifications for America's excess weight, and while many consider obesity to be a simple case of bad personal choices, little has been done to identify the outside sources that might be contributing to this wide spreading disease.

> Your information from sources in this paragraph helps to establish the problem.

> Here you establish that the problem affects everyone, not just the obese.

> This sentence prepares the reader for the next paragraph.

In the 2005 article "Junk-Food Nation" by Gary Ruskin and Juliet Schor, the authors explain the negative influence that the food industry has on the war against obesity in the United States. "Big food's strategy is to deny that the problem (obesity) is caused by the product (junk food). Instead lack of exercise is the culprit" (Ruskin & Schor, 2005, pg.17). In 2001, the Bush administration continuously took sides with the "big food" industry, facilitating their efforts to weaken the World Health Organizations' global anti-obesity strategy. The White House went as far as questioning the scientific basis for the linking of fruit and vegetable consumption to decrease the risk of obesity and diabetes (Ruskin & Schor, 2005 pg.17). More troubling is that these actions happened behind the scenes, where corporate interests took precedents before public health and public opinion. As it turns out, "not a lot of subtlety is required to understand what was driving President Bush's administration policy" (Ruskin & Schor, 2005, pg. 17) in regards to the obesity crisis in America. Many food industry giants such as Coca-Cola, Pepsi, Kraft, were all lead-ing contributors during the 2000 presidential campaign.

> Yes, it is troubling that corporate interests are put before public health.

With the food industry buying its way into everything, including the obesity strategy in America, it is no coincidence that this epi-demic is exploding as rapidly as it is. The food industry spends a whopping $4.2 billion dollars per year on marketing ads in the United States. Energy dense and nutrient poor foods are marketed everywhere, from billboards, to television commercials, and now even social media websites like Facebook. "The food industry spends billions of dollars each year to develop prod-ucts, packaging, advertising and marketing techniques that entice us to buy more food because selling more food means making more prof-its. And businesses exist to make profits" (Cohen 2007). While professional food marketers argue that they are only offering Americans what they want, they dodge the fact that the consumer is largely manipulated by portion size, variety, and cheap prices--all factors strategically created by the marketers themselves.

> Good use of quote to draw attention to this point about the billions spent by the food industry on advertising.

Coca Cola and General Mills make millions of dollars every year by using researched methods of advertising similar to those used by McDonald's and Burger King (Stanish, J.R., 2010). With slogans like "Bet You Can't Eat Just One", the food industry is really giving America a taste of it's lethal feeding. When the primary purpose of food production is profit, and not nutrition, the public really suffers. But catchy slogans and selling points are not the only tools food industry advertising is using to manipulate the public. Food manufacturers are notoriously known for making false or misleading claims about their products, many trying to create a smokescreen that promotes health and nutrition. The truth is that the "Advertising of fruits and veg-etables is almost non-existent," says Frances M. Berg in his book *Underage and Overweight* (as cited in Burg 97). Various studies have shown that out of thousands of ads with regular television advertising exposure, little to

> You made this point in a quote earlier in the paragraph. Better to edit, so you don't repeat yourself.

no advertisements promote fruits and vegetables. With food marketing being a largely self-regulated process, the food industry has been able to take advantage and has not been held accountable for the negative role it plays in America's battle with obesity. If the Federal Trade Commission (FTC) and Federal Communications Commission (FCC) played a larger role in the marketing food process, stronger regulations could be implemented. We must not allow food companies and their billions of dollars to dig deeper graves for Americans fighting obesity.

It is imperative that America understands that the transformation of a nation does not happen with drugs, weight-loss surgery, or other extreme forms of dieting; even all the exercise in the world will not save us. True change stems from a nation's conscious decision to address issues through policy.

> The law has proven an integral part of many major public health victories over the past century. Bans on smoking in public buildings, the removal of lead from paint and gasoline, and the requirement of school vaccinations are all the result of legislation and legal efforts. Today, many experts consider obesity to be the next frontier of public health law ("Law, Nutrition" 2013).

> Interesting point that this strategy worked with bans on smoking and lead paint.

It is unclear whether Americans truly comprehend the severity and the negative role the food advertisement industry has on obesity affecting the nation, but there is a clear understanding that obesity is threatening. In a recent study conducted by the Associated Press-NORC Center for Public Affairs Research, significant findings showed that the American public considers obesity as the most serious health issue, second only to cancer. While the data showed that there is a strong public support for government policies that add more physical activities for children at schools, there is little public support for policies that constrain consumer choices, such as the taxation of unhealthy food and drinks like soda (Associated Press, 2013).

> Yes, effective that you mention resistance to policies that restrict consumer choices.

OBESITY IN AMERICA   7

Clearly there are Americans who oppose obesity in the country, but are also against the government telling them what they can and cannot eat; yet others feel that the government has both the power and the duty to regulate private behavior in order to promote public health (Goston, L.O., 2007). In either case, it is obvious that obesity is making waves in the headlines and is catching many people's attention. The past few years have brought about a decent amount of legislative initiatives to combat obesity in the country, and we are heading in the right direction. First Lady, Michelle Obama has persistently continued to fight against childhood obesity in the United States. Her "Let's Move!" initiative has helped raise awareness about child obesity all throughout the country. "Let's Move!" has been able to promote the implementation of healthier foods in schools and is focused on raising a healthier generation of kids in America. New advertisement regulations have also been enforced to limit the number of ads that target children 18 and younger. Restaurants are now providing calorie counts and nutritional contents in their menus. All steps in the right direction, it is simply not enough.

Good that you mention successful programs.

Additional regulations are needed to regulate the commercial activities of the food industry. Federal responsibility for the regulation of advertising lies mainly with the Federal Trade Commission (FTC). By agreement with the Food and Drug Administration (FDA), the FTC has primary authority over food advertising, whereas the FDA regulates food labeling ("Enforcement policy," 1994). Currently the FTC is taking action only in cases where the agency finds that food advertisement is being deceptive. The agency favors requiring more information over banning information, and avoids broad restrictions limiting both deceptive and non-deceptive speech (FTC, 2002)." The idea that consumers, young and old, should have the freedom to choose what they eat from a broad marketplace continues to be the status quo. Critics have suggested that with food industry lobbyists continuing to buy into the pockets of politicians, no real change will happen any time soon, costing the lives of many. With 150 million Americans that are obese or overweight, Physician Deborah Cohen agrees:

don't find this source in your references.

OBESITY IN AMERICA   8

Too many will die before their time due to heart disease, diabetes and other ailments. While the nation remains focused on waging war on terrorism, which has claimed thousands of lives, millions are dying prematurely because they aren't getting the government protection they need from the Sirens of the food industry (Cohen, 2007).

With more and more research being conducted to identify the correlation between food advertisement and obesity and America, it is possible that if future studies provide compelling evidence, the federal government will be forced to address this issue more firmly. While there are many variables that contribute to a person being overweight and obese, regulations on advertisement and provisions and guidelines to hold the food industry accountable can only help the cause and could very well save the lives of many. We must not allow large food corporations to control the future of America; no amount of profit is worth the lives of millions of people.

This well-writter quote draws attention to you conclusion.

OBESITY IN AMERICA   9

References

Adult obesity rates could exceed 60 percent in 13 states by 2030, according to new study (2012, September 18). Retrieved http://www.rwjf.org/en/library/articles-and-news/2012/09/adult-obesity-rates-could-exceed-60-percent-in-13-states-by-2030.html

Cawley, J., & Meyerhoefer, C. (2012). The medical care costs of obesity: An instrumental variables approach. *Journal of Health Economics, 31*(1), 219-230.

Cohen, D. (2007, February 20). A desired epidemic: Obesity and the food industry. *Washington Post.* Retrieved from http://www.washingtonpost.com/wpdyn/content/article/2007/02/20/AR200702200133

Gostin, L. O. (2007). Theory and definition of public health law. *Journal of Health Care Law & Policy, 10,* 1.

Law, nutrition & obesity. (2013). Retrieved from http://www.yaleruddcenter.org/what_we_do.aspx?id=7

Obesity in America: Understanding obesity. (n.d.). Retrieved from http://obesityinamerica.org/understanding-obesity

Obesity in the United States: Public perceptions. (2014). Retrieved http://www.apnorc.org/projects/Pages/Obesity-in-the-United-States.aspx

Ogden C. L., Carroll, M. D., Kit, B.K., & Flegal K. M. (2014). Prevalence of childhood and adult obesity in the United States, 2011-2012. *Journal of the American Medical Association*, 311(8), 806-814.

Rodrigo, C. P. (2013). *Current mapping of obesity*. Nutricion Hospitalaria, 28, 21-31. Retrieved from http://www.nutricionhospitalaria.com/pdf/6915.pdf

Ruskin, G., & Schor, J. (2005). Junk food nation. *Nation*, 281(6), 15 17. Retrieved from EBSCO.

Stanish, J. (2010, January 1). The Obesity epidemic in America and the responsibility of big food manufacturers. Student Pulse, 2(11). Retrieved from http://www.studentpulse.com/articles/320/the-obesity-epidemic-in-america-and-the-responsibility-of-big-food-manufacturers

United States, Federal Trade Commission. (1994, May 13). Enforcement policy statement on food advertising. Retrieved from http://www.ftc.gov/public- statements/1994/05/enforcement-policy-statement-food-advertising

Additional Sample Student Paper: Research Paper in APA Style

Runnning Head:

CHANGES IN BEHAVIOR CAN AFFECT SPECIES INVASION SUCCESS   1

Changes in Behavior Can Affect Species Invasion Success

Name of Student

Student's University

CHANGES IN BEHAVIOR CAN AFFECT SPECIES INVASION SUCCESS   2

Abstract

This paper explores invader species, including birds, mammals, and insects and the likelihood that a particular species will succeed in a new environment. Once a species has been introduced to a new setting, several factors affect a species' ability to reproduce and adapt. New species must compete with any preexisting species that occupy the same resource niche, so aggressive species are more likely to succeed. Alternatively, if a species can change its behavior or alter the habitat, it increases its chances of survival over time.

Keywords: invader species, species adaptability

Your abstract could briefly mention the research that supports your argument, even mentioning the names of well-known scientists that you cite in your paper.

Changes in Behavior Can Affect Species Invasion Success

Introduction

Invasive species, including birds, mammals, and insects are rapidly changing ecosystems worldwide. Some species make more effective invaders than others. However, the reasons that make some species successful invaders are not clearly understood. Important drivers that affect if a species can invade include ability to move into a new habitat, invadability of the new environment, and niche availability of the new environment. The behavior a species displays can play an important role in the ability to invade. However, some species have behaviors that change, which make them even more likely to be successful invaders.

Some environments are more likely to be invaded than others. Environments are more likely to be invaded if they have resources that can be exploited. In a source-sink environment, organisms will follow increased resources. The amount of biodiversity may also play a role. A large amount of biodiversity and a very small amount of resources do not lend themselves to invasion (Tilman, 1997). Table 1 summarizes some of the factors that may make it possible for invasion to occur. All of these factors are important to consider when analyzing whether a change in behavior will affect susceptibility of an ecosystem to invasive pressure.

In order for an invasion to occur, the species must be propagated to a novel environment. This in itself can be a challenge and many species do not make it. Once introduced into the new environment, the species must colonize. Many species will die off after a few generations. If a species can colonize the new environment and perpetuate itself, then there is a chance that the invasion will be successful and establish itself (Duncan, 2003). Once established, if the species continually moves to new environments, it is an invader.

Interesting th
the reasons a
well understc
I'm glad that
elaborate late
about why th

Your paper is relatively free from jargon, but you might explain the meaning of source-sink, depending upon whether your audience would recognize the term.

Good that you include tables. However, it would be helpful to tell your audience more specifically what the table shows, as many will read the text before looking at tables and graphs.

CHANGES IN BEHAVIOR CAN AFFECT SPECIES INVASION SUCCESS   4

Many of the examples used in this paper are from birds. Birds provide excellent examples for invasion success because they have been frequently introduced into novel ecosystems by humans. The frequency of introduction allows for more successful invasions than in other species. Figure 1 demonstrates the process of a successful invasion when pertaining specifically to birds that have been introduced by humans.

> Excellent that you walk the audience through your argument, explaining any points that the reader might question.

There are many challenges to overcome to move to a new ecosystem. In many cases, there is a preexisting species already occupying the niche the new species could occupy. This may create competition that the invading and native species had not encountered before. A species that is or becomes more aggressive may have a better chance to succeed. As the habitat is different, so are the resources. Species that have the ability to exploit new resources, such as food, have a better chance at thriving in the new environment.

There are two main ways that a species can changes its behavior to become a more successful invader. The first is behavioral flexibility and the ability to adapt to a new environment. This means that the species already has behavioral plasticity in its native range, though it may not necessarily be expressed there. The species will try new behaviors to see if they are successful in the new habitat. If the innovation is successful, then the species fitness is increased. This allows for a species to be more successful in a new environment.

The second way is for a species to adapt to a new environment over time. Through generations, a species will become accustomed to the novel ecosystem. This can happen through changes to the native habitat or other selective pressures. This allows for new behaviors to be expressed and propagate to new environments. The new beneficial behaviors that are successful in the new environment may not have been beneficial in the previous environment. These behaviors could increase fitness and be propagated in the novel habitat. It is also possible for this to occur through a founder's effect. If an invading species is cut off from its previous habitat, it

CHANGES IN BEHAVIOR CAN AFFECT SPECIES INVASION SUCCESS   5

is possible for genetic bottlenecking to occur. This could change the behaviors expressed.

Behavioral Flexibility

Behavioral flexibility in a species is comprised of two main components. First, the species must be able to respond to novel stimuli. This allows for a more rapid response to new conditions, which could potentially aid in colonization. Second, individuals have the ability to identify and consume unfamiliar food and respond to novel stimuli (Martin, 2005). This ability provides a good measure for behavioral flexibility (Sol, 2002). The more a species uses new feeding behaviors, the more flexible they are. The more likely an individual is to consume novel foods the more likely a species will fare better in a new environment. Some species already possess this flexibility in their native range. This may allow these species to be better invaders.

Effective use of topic sentence and transitions in this paragraph.

Another measure of behavioral flexibility is brain size. Larger brain size, relative to body size is directly related to cognitive ability (Sol, 2008). This translates to the ability for innovations or behavioral flexibility. Brain size has also been correlated with feeding innovation (Sol, 2002). Species with larger brain size has been shown to increase success for coping with novel habitats. This has been shown extensively in birds and more recently in mammals.

In birds, feeding innovation and larger brains had a higher probability of introduction success (Sol 2002). This is numerically displayed in Table 1. Sol (2002) controlled for other variables that have been shown to affect successful invasions in birds. There are three other main factors that affect invasion success in birds. Dichromatic birds are more efficacious invaders than monochromatic. Birds that are display human commensalism also have more advantages. Nest location also plays a large role. Ground nesters do better than other nesting sites (Sol, 2002).

Mammals have the largest body size to brain size ratio of any other animals. If brain size does have an impact on the ability to respond well to novel habitats, than mammals should be able to succeed in the new

CHANGES IN BEHAVIOR CAN AFFECT SPECIES INVASION SUCCESS   6

habitats. Sol (2008) compared mammal invasion success and several different factors: habitat generalism, diet, annual fecundity, mating system,
native geographic range, and whether the introduction was on an island
or a mainland. After taking into account all of these factors,
relative brain size was a significant predictor of establish-   Interesting point
                                                                       about brain size.
ment success. The number of individuals originally released
and habitat generalism also increased success.

Some species, such as the house sparrow (Passer domesticus), display more flexibility as an invader than as a resident. This is demonstrated
with, once again, flexibility in feeding. As Figure 3 displays, invaders are
more likely to approach and consume novel foods. This example reveals
that feeding innovation does not necessarily need to be expressed in a
native habitat for a species to possess a capacity for it. This would make
prediction for invasion success based on expressed feeding innovation difficult.

Adaptive Behaviors

Behaviors can change due to selective pressures, causing a species to
diverge a different way. Over time, this could possibly lead to speciation or
just a shift in behavior for the entire species. Selective pressures that could
cause this change could include habitat destruction or climate change. As a
result of these pressures, animals may need to move to new habitats. The
selective pressures could shift the behavior of the species to adapt to the
novel environment.

Western bluebirds (Sialia mexicana) lost much of their natural habitat
in the early 20th century due to logging and agriculture. As nest
Interesting   box programs were implemented, the populations of western blue-
that human
intervention   birds were reestablished. This repopulation brought them closer to
initiates species   the mountain bluebirds (Sialia currucoides) territory. Female west-
invasion.   ern bluebirds usually disperse away from their natal population to
breed and the males would either stay or disperse. More aggressive males
are more likely to disperse away from their natal populations, venturing into

CHANGES IN BEHAVIOR CAN AFFECT SPECIES INVASION SUCCESS   7

novel environments. The more aggressive males are more likely to out compete the less aggressive males for breeding territories of both western and
mountain bluebirds. This aggression is therefore an adaptive trait that makes
these birds a more successful invader (Duckworth, 2007).

The bullfinches in Europe are an example of a species that may lead to
an adaptive behavior that could lead to an invasion. Newton et al. found that
observers in Western Europe heard calls from bullfinches that were previously not heard in that region. After an investigation, it was found that the
northern bullfinch (Pyrrhula p. pyrrhula) was migrating further west than
previously. This example is not a complete invasion, however. This species
had previously migrated to this area but not in the numbers recorded in
2004 (Newton, 2006). This could lead to a changed migratory route over
generations. The possible selective pressures that elicited this change is a
food shortage causing the birds to migrate further is search of more food.

Differentiating between mechanisms of a behavioral change can
sometimes be difficult. There are some examples of invasive species that
have not been studied enough to determine the cause of the change in behavior. For instance, a species of fire ant (Solenopsis invicta) has invaded
southeastern United States from its native range in Argentina.
S. invicta has two social forms polygyne and monogyne. Monogyne means to have only one queen, while polygyne forms
have multiple queens. In Argentina, the queens in the polygyne
social form are closely related while in the invaded ranges the
queens are more distantly related. Another difference in the social make-up of S. invicta is that in the U.S. the colonies are more densely
populated. In the polygyne colonies, the ants have reduced nest mate
recognition allowing for reduced intraspecific aggression. This in turn allow for a reduction in territoriality which leads to a further increase in
colony density. This increase in population density allows the ants to be a
better competitor against the native ants (Holway 1999). After a genetic
study was completed on these ants and a decrease in genetic diversity was
found in comparison to the native populations, it was hypothesized that

Here you discuss
clearly why it is
difficult to identify
the factor that
causes success or
failure for invading
species.

CHANGES IN BEHAVIOR CAN AFFECT SPECIES INVASION SUCCESS   8

the invasion to the United States actually caused a founder effect. This could be the reason that the behavior altered from one location to another (Chapman, 2001). On the other hand, it is possible that without disease or natural predators this type of behavior was more adaptive.

Another Argentine ant (Linepithema humile) is an excellent example of a behavior change that increases its invasion success. In Argentina, L. humile commonly displays intense intraspecific aggression. However, in its introduced ranges in California and Chile these ants show very little intraspecific aggression. This, once again, leads to increased population density, as well as a lack of natural predators. The high densities of L. humile allow it to fight off native ants more easily and collect food more quickly (Holway 1999, Holway 2001).

Conclusion

The affect that behavior changes have on invasion could be studied more. It seems to add another aspect to the invasion issue. However, there are some problems that make this issue difficult to study. Firstly, observation of a species colonizing a novel environment is rare. To catch a species while undergoing the change necessary to invade is not always possible. This can leave questions as to the mechanism of the behavioral change. This is the main reason why birds are so frequently used in this type of study. Birds have been introduced repeatedly by humans providing a large number of successful and unsuccessful invasions to compare. Secondly, it seems that a behavioral change is not always necessary for a species to invade successfully. Many species can invade keeping the same set of behaviors that are displayed in their native habitat. They find niche availability in other habitats without having to adapt.

Behavior change in a species just adds one more dimension to an already complex issue. Although there are trends of what makes a successful invader, it is still difficult to predict whether an individual species will thrive in a new environment. With a better understanding of the mechanisms that cause the change in behavior, a prediction of the type of animal that would take advantage of this type of change could be made. Adding this dimension just gives a fuller understanding of the topic and should be explored further.

You make a good case why species invasion should be studied further.

Table 1. (Lonsdale, 1999) This table describes some of the reasons that habitats are susceptible to invasion.

Term in invasion ecology	Conventional definition
Disturbance	removal of competing vegetation (Hobbs 1991)
Native species resistance to invasion	competitive ability of native species
Resistance to disturbance	ability of native ecosystems or species to recover from disturbance
Ecosystem resistance to invasion	intrinsic resistance of native ecosystem to invasion through community structure (Williamson 1996: 193-196)
Invasibility	overall susceptibility of sites to invasion (Williamson 1996: 55)
Invasion potential	intrinsic ability of species to invade (di Castri 1989)
Propagule pressure	number of propagules arriving at a site (Williamson 1996: 45)

Figure 1. (Duncan, 2002) This figure shows the how birds introduced by humans fail or succeed to become invaders.

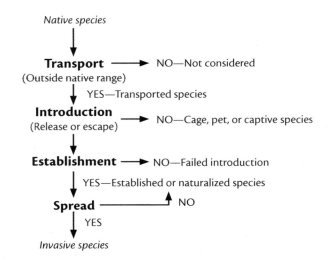

CHANGES IN BEHAVIOR CAN AFFECT SPECIES INVASION SUCCESS   11

Figure 2. (Chapman, 2001) This figure describes the way that unicoloniality can be achieved in eusocial insects.

a.
Introduction ⇒ Ecological release ⇒ Habitat saturation ⇒ Unicoloniality

b.
Introduction ⇒ Loss of genetic variation ⇒ Increase in matched matings and diploid male production ⇒ Reduced success of solitary colony foundation ⇒ Unicoloniality

c.
Introduction ⇒ Evolution of 'green beard' allele ⇒ Unicoloniality

d.
Introduction ⇒ Loss of genetic variation ⇒ Loss of nestmate recognition ⇒ Unicoloniality

CHANGES IN BEHAVIOR CAN AFFECT SPECIES INVASION SUCCESS   12

References

Chapman, Roselle E. & Bourke, Andrew F. G. 2001. The influence of sociality on the conservation biology of social insects. *Ecology Letters,* 4, 650-662.

Duckworth, Renee A. & Badyaev, Alexander V. 2007. Coupling of dispersal and aggression facilitates the rapid range expansion of a passerine bird. *PNAS,* 104, 15017-15022.

Duncan, Richard P., Blackburn, Tim & Sol, Daniel. 2003. The ecology of bird introductions. *Annu. Rev. Ecol. Evol. Syst.,* 34, 71-98.

Holway, David A. & Case, Ted J. 2001. Effects of colony-level variation on competitive ability in the invasive Argentine ant. *Animal Behaviour,* 61, 1181-1192.

Holway, David A. & Suarez, Andrew V. 1999. Animal behavior: an essential component of invasion biology. *Tree,* 14, 328-330.

Ingram, Krista K. 2002. Flexibility in nest density and social structure in invasive populations of the Argentine ant, *Linepithema humile. Oecologia,* 133, 492-500.

Lonsdale, W. M. 1999. Global patterns of plant invasions and the concept of invisibility. *Ecology,* 80, 1522-1536.

CHANGES IN BEHAVIOR CAN AFFECT SPECIES INVASION SUCCESS   13

Mack, Richard N., Simberloff, Daniel, Lonsdale, W. Mark, Evans, Harry, Clout, Michael & Bazzaz, Fakhri. 2000. Biotic invasions: causes, epidemiology, global consequences and control. *Issues in Ecology,* 5, 1-22.

Martin II, Lynn B. & Fitzgerald, Lisa. 2005. A taste for novelty in invading house sparrows, Passer domesticus. *Behavioral Ecology,* 16, 702-707.

Newton, Ian, Hobson, Keith A., Fox, Anthony D. & Marquiss, Mick. 2006. An investigation into the provenance of northern bullfinches Pyrrhula p. pyrrhula found in winter in Scotland and Denmark. *Journal of Avian Biology,* 37, 431- 435.

Sol, Daniel, Bacher, Sven, Reader, Simon M. & Lefebvre, Louis. 2008. Brain size predicts the success of mammal species introduced into novel environments. *The American Naturalist,* 172, 63-71.

Sol, D. & Lefebvre, L. 2000. Behavioral flexibility predicts invasion success in birds introduced to New Zealand. *Oidos,* 90, 599-605.

Sol, Daniel, Timmermans, Sarah & Lefebvre, Louis. 2002. Behavioral flexibility and invasion success in birds. *Animal Behaviour,* 63, 495-502.

Sol, Daniel & Price, Trevor D. 2008. Brain size and the diversification of body size in birds. *The American Naturalist,* 172, 170-177.

Tilman, David. 1997. Community invisibility, recruitment limitation, and grassland biodiversity. *Ecology,* 78, 81-92.

Acknowledgments

Adams, Scott. Dilbert © 2008 Scott Adams. Used by permission of Universal Uclick. All rights reserved.

Ames, Alexander. "Bringing History to Life with Primary Sources." Student essay reprinted with permission.

Cohen, Arna. "Do You Know How Your Mascara is Made?" Reprinted from *All Animals,* Mar/April 2014.

Fogarty, Mignon. *Grammar Girl: Quick and Dirty Tips for Better Writing.* Copyright © 2008 by Mignon Fogarty. Reprinted with permission of St. Martin's Press. All rights reserved.

Hamblin, James. "The Point When Science Becomes Publicity." From *The Atlantic*, Dec. 12, 2014. Reprinted with permission. All rights reserved.

Jayawardhana, Ray. "Alien Life, Coming Slowly into View." From *The New York Times,* March 27, 2011. Reprinted with permission. All rights reserved.

Johnson, Judith. "The Truth About Writer's Block." From *The Huffington Post,* July 25, 2011. Reprinted with permission. All rights reserved.

Kearl, Holly. "Laws Protecting Women From Upskirt Photo Assaults Fall Short." From *The Daily Beast,* Mar. 12, 2014. Reprinted with permission. All rights reserved.

Kilkenny, Katie. "*Guardians of the Galaxy's* Happy Satire of the Sad Origin Story." From *Theatlantic.com*, Aug. 4, 2014. Reprinted with permission. All rights reserved.

King, Jr., Martin Luther. "I Have a Dream" speech given at the Lincoln Memorial, Aug. 28, 1963.

Klocinski, Laura. "Can Social Media Make Us Better Writers?" From mycampus.writingcommons.org, Mar. 12, 2014.

Knowles-Carter, Beyoncé Giselle, Chimamanda Ngozi Adichie, Terius Nash, Chauncey Hollis, Raymond DeAndre Martin. Lyrics from *Flawless*. Produced by Columbia Music Group. Copyright © 2013 by Columbia Music Group.

Lamott, Ann. "Shitty First Drafts." Reprinted from *Bird by Bird*. Copyright © by Ann Lamott. Reprinted with permission of Random House. All rights reserved.

Lewis, Jeff. Photo of the Shout, Color, Throw event at Dodger Stadium. Copyright © 2014 by AP Images. Reprinted with permission. All rights reserved.

Lincoln, Abraham. Gettysburg Address, Soldiers' National Cemetery, Gettysburg, PA, Nov. 19, 1863.

Mayo, Virginia. Photo of flash mob in Brussels, Belgium. Copyright © 2012 by AP Images. Reprinted with permission. All rights reserved.

McArdle, Megan. "Anatomy of a Fake Quotation." From *The Atlantic*, May 2, 2011.

Meyers, Justin. "How to Make a Kindle Cover from a Hollowed Out Hardback Book." Reprinted from *Wonder How To,* March, 2011.

Piraro, Dan. Bizarro Cartoon. Copyright © Dan Piraro. Reprinted with permission. All rights reserved.

Roose, Kevin. "Miscrosoft Just Laid Off Thousands of Employees with a Hilariously Bad Memo." From *New York Magazine*. Reprinted with permission. All rights reserved.

Rosen, Jeffrey. "The Web Means the End of Forgetting." From *The New York Times,* July 25, 2010. Reprinted with permission. All rights reserved.

Salinas, Brenda. "'Columbusing': The Art of Discovering Something that is Not New." From *NPR. org,* July 6, 2014. Reprinted with permission of National Public Radio. All rights reserved.

Schalet, Amy. "The Sleepover Question." From *The New York Times.* Reprinted with Permission. All rights reserved.

Scham, Sam. "Top Ten Distractions for Writers, or Any Job Really." From *Yahoo.com,* Aug. 12, 2008. Reprinted with permission. All rights reserved.

Shemtob, Zachary, and David Lat. "Executions Should Be Televised." From *The New York Times,* July 21, 2011. Reprinted with permission. All rights reserved.

Singh, Rajesh Kumar. Photo of Holi celebration in India. Copyright © 2012 by AP Images. Reprinted with permission. All rights reserved.

Skinner, E. Benjamin. "People for Sale." From *Foreign Policy,* March/April 2008. Reprinted with permission. All rights reserved.

Tham, Jason. "How I Create a Multimedia Presentation." Student essay reprinted with permission.

Wade, Lisa. "Why Has Godzilla Grown?" Reprinted from *Sociological Images*. Copyright © 2014 by Lisa Wade. Reprinted with permission. All rights reserved.

Wynne, Craig. "Take a Leap Into Writing." Reprinted with permission of Craig Wynne.

Index